READING
BITE

GRADE 3

WRITERS

미래엔콘텐츠연구회
No.1 Content를 개발하는 교육 전문 콘텐츠 연구회

PROOFREADER

Sam Woo

COPYRIGHT

인쇄일 2024년 10월 30일(2판 15쇄)
발행일 2020년 9월 14일

펴낸이 신광수
펴낸곳 (주)미래엔
등록번호 제16–67호

교육개발2실장 김용균
개발책임 이보현 **개발** 정규진, 김은송, 김수아, 한고운, 김민지, 정유진, 현수민

디자인실장 손현지
디자인책임 김병석 **디자인** 장병진, 유화연

CS본부장 강윤구
CS지원책임 강승훈

ISBN 979-11-6413-609-4

Don't be afraid to make mistakes.
실수를 두려워하지 말아요.

모국어인 우리말이 이미 익숙한 상태에서
우리말 체계와 전혀 다른 영어를 배운다는 것은 쉽지 않습니다.
영어를 잘하기까지는 꽤 긴 시간이 필요합니다.
특히 독해는 단어도 알아야 하고, 문법 지식도 필요하고, 문장 이해력도 필요합니다.
지문을 읽을 때마다 모르는 단어는 계속 나오고,
어렵고 까다로운 문법으로 인해 문장 해석이 제대로 되지 않을 때도 많습니다.
누구나 다 나와 똑같이 어려움을 느끼고 있다고 생각해 보세요.
자신이 모르는 것을 누가 더 많이, 반복해서 꼼꼼하게 확인하느냐에 따라 영어 실력이 달
라집니다.

이제부터 영어 지문을 읽을 때
알고 있는 단어가 나오면 우선 그 단어를 통해 어떤 문장이 될까 추측해 보세요.
단어만으로 어떤 내용인지를 추측하는 것도 아주 중요한 시작입니다.
내가 추측한 내용을 해석을 보고 확인해 보세요.
틀린 것이 많다고 해서 절대 실망할 필요는 없습니다.
왜 실수했는지 확인하는 과정이 무엇보다 중요합니다.
중등 과정에서는 반복해서 읽는 것이 꼭 필요한 독해 훈련입니다.

독해는 단어, 문법, 문장 이해력을 한꺼번에 올리는 중요한 영역입니다.
문제를 풀고 나서는 지문을 큰 소리로 읽어보세요.
처음에는 쑥스럽기도 하고 자신감이 떨어질 수도 있지만 이를 극복하고 나면
한 단계 업그레이드된 영어 실력을 마주하게 될 것입니다.

한 단계 성장을 고대하는 여러분의 노력을 READING BITE가 응원합니다.

1. 문제 유형별 독해 학습

독해 지문에 따른 문제 유형별 구성으로, 지문의 성격에 따라 글 전체를 파악하는 학습으로 독해 실력을 키울 수 있습니다.

2. 유형 해결 길잡이

문제를 풀기 위해 글을 읽을 때 어떻게 접근해야 하는지 안내해 줍니다.

3. 꼼꼼한 내용 이해

다양한 형태의 문제를 통해 지문의 내용을 잘 이해했는지 꼼꼼히 확인할 수 있습니다.

UNIT 01 주제 파악하기

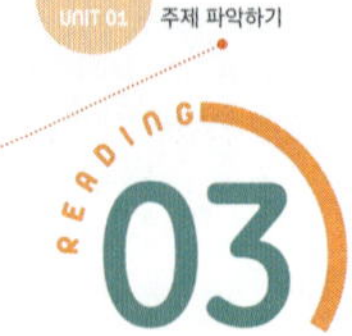

READING 03

READING GUIDE

글을 읽으면서 주제문을 찾아 밑줄을 그어 봅시다.

다음 글의 주제로 가장 적절한 것은? 기출응용

You may wonder whether there is any reason to worry about too much confidence. After all, confidence is often considered a positive thing. In fact, research suggests that students with a lot of confidence in their ability in school tend to do better on exams than those with less confidence. Though that is true, negative results also come from being overconfident in the classroom. Students who are overconfident about their ability in college end up feeling more disconnected than those with lower expectations. Overconfidence can also leave students with mistaken impressions. For example, they think they are fully prepared for tests and no longer need to study. Students who properly assess their progress in learning tend to have more effective study habits. They then do better on tests than those with incorrect views of their knowledge.

① effective ways to change bad study habits
② changing roles of academic tests in school
③ useful strategies for building students' confidence
④ critical factors to consider for choosing a college major
⑤ negative effects of students' overconfidence on school life

UNDERSTAND DEEPLY

1 빈칸에 알맞은 단어를 윗글에서 찾아 쓰시오.

_______________ can make students feel disconnected and get a wrong impression of their progress in learning.

2 윗글의 내용과 일치하면 T, 그렇지 않으면 F를 쓰시오.

(1) Confidence can help students perform better on tests. ______

(2) Students who have incorrect views of their knowledge tend to do better on exams. ______

---

10. UNIT 복습

UNIT별로 구성된 문제를 통해 주요 어휘와 문법 사항을 다시 한번 복습합니다.

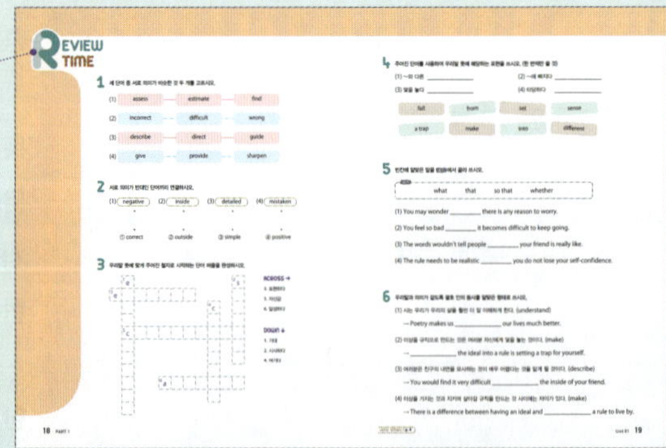

4. 직독직해와 주어-동사 찾기

모든 문장에서 주어와 동사를 찾고, 의미 단위로 끊어 읽고 바로 해석하며 독해 속도를 높이고, 긴 문장에 대한 두려움도 줄일 수 있습니다.

5. 원어민 음성으로 지문 듣기

QR코드를 찍으면 생생한 원어민 발음으로 지문을 들을 수 있습니다.

6. 수능 기출 문제 맛보기

중학교 난이도에 맞게 재구성된 고1~2 전국연합, 평가원 · 수능 기출 문제는 QR코드를 찍으면 기출 원문을 확인할 수 있습니다.

7. 주요 문법 확인

지문에 사용된 문법 중 핵심 문법을 다시 확인하며 구문 이해력을 키우고 내신 대비도 할 수 있습니다.

8. 독해 기술 익히기

독해 지문과 문제 유형별로 적용되는 리딩 스킬은 내용 이해력과 문제 해결력을 높여 줍니다.

9. 어휘 실력 강화

주요 어휘의 의미와 동의어, 반의어, 파생 품사도 함께 확인할 수 있어 어휘력을 탄탄히 다질 수 있습니다.

READ CLOSELY

의미 단위로 끊어 읽고(/), 주어와 동사에 표시해 봅시다.

지문 듣기

기출 원문 보기

❶ Poetry sharpens our senses and makes us understand our lives much better.

❷ Imagine, for a moment, that you are trying to describe one of your friends.

❸ You could say the friend has blue eyes, a mole on the left cheek, or a red nose.

❹ But that would only describe the outside of this person.

❺ It wouldn't tell people what your friend is really like.

❻ It wouldn't show the habits, feelings, and all the little characteristics that make this person different from everyone else.

❼ You would find it very difficult to describe the inside of your friend, even though you know everything about them.

❽ Good poetry tells us about both the outside and the inside of life.

❾ And it helps you know and love the world as much as you know and love a friend.

GRAMMAR TIP

find처럼 목적격 보어를 쓰는 동사의 목적어가 to부정사(구)이면 목적어 자리에 가목적어 it을 대신 쓰고, 진목적어인 to부정사(구)는 뒤로 보내요.
- She found **it** difficult **to breathe.**
- I made **it** a rule **to go to bed early.**

READING TIP

글의 주제문이 먼저 나온 후 For example, For instance, Imagine, Consider 등의 표현과 함께 주제를 구체적으로 설명하기 위한 예시가 이어지기도 해요.

WORDS

poetry (집합적) 시(詩)
cf. poem (한 편의) 시(詩)
sharpen 예리하게[날카롭게] 하다
cf. sharp 날카로운
sense 감각
describe 묘사하다
mole (피부 위의) 점
outside 외면, 외부
characteristic 특징, 특성
different from ~와 다른
find 알게 되다
difficult 어려운
inside 내면, 내부
both A and B A와 B 둘 다
usefulness 유용성
cf. useful 유용한
tip 조언, 비법
difficulty 어려움
misunderstanding 오해
cf. misunderstand 오해하다
express 표현하다

바른답 · 알찬풀이 | p. 2

---

11. 바른답 · 알찬풀이

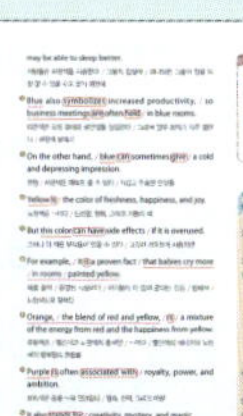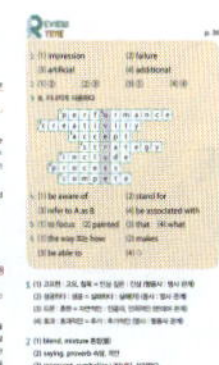

정답 및 해설, 문장의 주어-동사, 직독직해, 지문 해석, 주요 구문 풀이를 확인해 볼 수 있습니다.

Contents
차 례

BITE가 제안하는 독해 방법

독해, 글을 읽고 이해하다!

글을 읽고 이해하는 과정을 "독해"라고 하는데, 영어 독해가 어렵다고 느껴지는 데는 여러 이유가 있습니다. 영어 단어를 많이 알지 못해서, 영어 단어는 알지만 문장을 해석하지 못해서, 문장을 해석할 수 있지만, 무슨 내용을 전달하고 있는지 이해하지 못해서... 등등

중등 과정에서 영어 독해의 과정과 방법을 잘 이해하고 제대로 습득한다면, 글이 점점 길어지고, 복잡한 문장이 나와 어려워지더라도 두려움 없이 글을 이해하고 문제를 풀어 나갈 수 있습니다.

01 글을 읽고 이해(독해)하는 과정

- 이미 알고 있는 단어 확인하기
- 모르는 단어 뜻 문맥 속에서 유추하기
- 다시 읽으면서 모르는 단어 의미 확인하기

- 문법 지식을 활용하여 문장 속 주어, 동사 찾기
- 문장 구조 분석하여 문장 해석하기
- 반복해서 읽을 때 문법 사항 꼼꼼히 확인하기

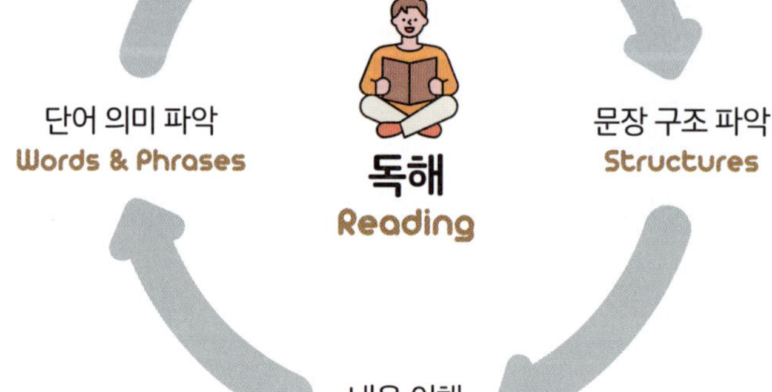

- 글 전체가 어떤 내용을 다루고 있는지 파악하기
- 지문에서 반복되는 어휘, 표현을 통해 주요 정보와 세부 정보를 구분하기

▶▶ 반복해서 읽기
- **첫 번째 읽기**: 모르는 단어가 나오더라도 쉬지 않고 끝까지 한 번에 읽으며 어떤 내용을 다루고 있는지 추측해 봅니다.
- **두 번째 읽기**: 모르는 단어는 밑줄을 치면서 앞뒤 내용을 통해 최대한 단어의 의미를 유추하고, 문제 해결을 위해 글의 전체 내용과 세부 내용을 꼼꼼히 확인합니다.
- **세 번째 읽기**: 문제를 모두 풀었다면, 글을 다시 읽으면서 몰랐던 단어, 이해가 되지 않았던 문장 구조, 문법적인 역할 등을 꼼꼼히 확인하고 정확하게 문장 단위로 해석하면서 정독해 봅시다.

2 글을 읽을 때, 단계별 활동

읽기 전에
before reading

글을 훑어 읽으면서 다음 정보를
확인해 봅시다.
- 글의 제목이나 부제목이 있는가?
- 그림이나 사진 자료는 어떤 것이 있는가?
- 문장 속에 대문자로 시작하는
  이름이나 지명 등은 무엇인가?

읽는 동안
while reading

문제 해결을 위해 글을 집중해서
읽어 봅시다.
- 무슨 내용을 전달하고 있는가?
- 가장 중요한 정보와 덜 중요한 정보를
  구분할 수 있는가?
- 반복되는 단어나 표현, 밑줄을
  칠 수 있는 핵심 문장이 있는가?

읽은 후에
after reading

글을 읽은 후, 제시된 문제를 풀어 봅시다.
- 글의 주제는 무엇인가?
- 등장인물이나 주요 사건을 설명할 수
  있는가?
- 글을 구조적으로 재구성해 볼 수
  있는가?
- 글 전체를 요약할 수 있는가?

3 지문을 이해하는 독해 기법

1 미리보기(Previewing) 글의 제목이나 중간 제목, 이미지 자료 등이 있다면 이를
먼저 확인해 봄으로써 어떤 내용의 글이 나올지 추측할 수 있습니다.

2 훑어읽기(Skimming) 글의 대략적인 주제나 요지를 파악하기 위해
전체 텍스트를 빠르게 눈으로 읽는 것을 말합니다. 전체적으로 훑
어봄으로써 더욱 자세한 읽기를 준비할 수 있습니다. 이 방법은
시간 제한이 있는 시험에서 글의 주제나 요지를 묻는 문제를
해결할 때 유용한 리딩 스킬입니다.

3 꼼꼼히 읽기(Scanning) 주어진 텍스트 안에서 필요한 정보만
빨리 찾아내는 기술을 말합니다. 예를 들어 날짜, 이름, 시간 등
의 특정 정보가 필요한 경우에 효율적으로 활용할 수 있습니다.

4 문맥 속 의미 파악하기(Guessing from the context) 모르는 단어나
해석하기 어려운 문장은 앞뒤의 내용이나 글 전체 내용을 가지고 단어
나 문장의 의미를 추측해 볼 수 있습니다.

5 요약하기(Summarizing) 글 전체를 한 문장이나 짧은 글로 요약해 보는 훈련은
글의 주제나 요지, 제목을 찾을 때, 또는 주요 정보와 세부 정보를 구분할 때 유용한
독해 기법입니다.

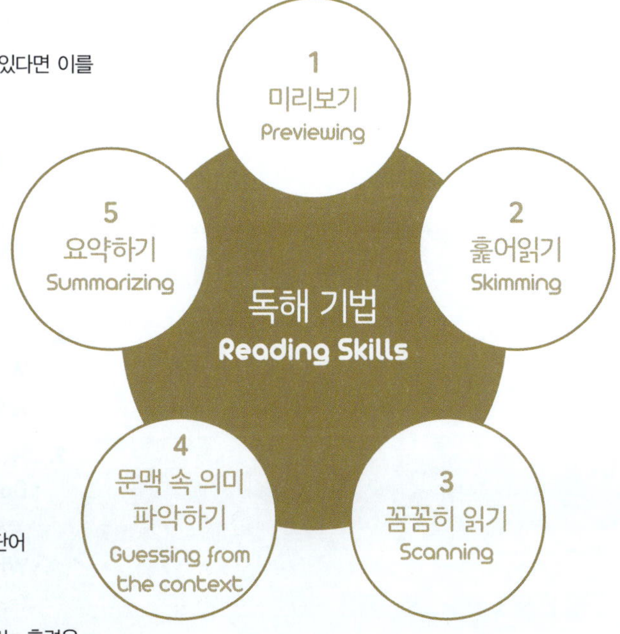

끊어읽기로
영어 독해
실력 쑥쑥!

Why?

의미 단위로 끊어 읽으면 독해가 훨씬 빠르고 쉬워진다

영어 문장을 우리말 어순에 맞춰 해석하는 습관은 독해 실력을 키우는 데 방해가
돼요. 영어는 문장에 나오는 순서대로 의미 단위로 끊어 읽고 직독직해 하는 것이
가장 좋아요. 이런 습관을 들이면 문장이 길고 복잡해지더라도 문장 구조가 쉽게
이해되며, 해석도 빠르고 정확하게 할 수 있어요.

끊 / 어 / 읽 / 는 / 곳

1. 주어가 길면 주어 뒤에서 끊는다.
- **Both mammals and birds** / **are noisy creatures.**
  포유류와 조류 둘 다 / 떠들썩한 동물들이다

2. 보어나 목적어가 길면 동사 뒤에서 끊는다.
- **Blue can sometimes give** / **a cold and depressing impression.**
  파란색은 때때로 줄 수 있다 / 차갑고 우울한 인상을

3. 직접목적어 앞에서 끊는다.
- **His father offered Henry** / **some advice.**
  그의 아버지는 Henry에게 제공했다 / 몇 가지 조언을

4. 목적격 보어 앞에서 끊는다.
- **We encourage you** / **to take advantage of this program.**
  우리는 여러분에게 권합니다 / 이 프로그램을 이용할 것을

5. 주어 앞에 부사(구)가 있으면 주어 앞에서 끊는다.
- **Then** / **they compared** / **the amounts of money** / **in the box.**
  그런 다음 / 그들은 비교했다 / 돈의 총액을 / 상자 안에 있는

6. 〈전치사＋명사〉의 구조가 있다면 전치사 앞에서 끊는다.
- **Winners continue learning** / **throughout life.**
  승자는 배움을 계속한다 / 평생

7. 형용사 및 부사적 용법의 to부정사 앞에서 끊는다.
- **Don't miss** / **this great opportunity** / **to improve your writing.**
  놓치지 마십시오 / 이 좋은 기회를 / 여러분의 글쓰기를 향상시킬
- **What do the eyes do** / **to protect themselves?**
  눈은 무엇을 하는가 / 자신을 보호하기 위해

How?

독해 실력에 따라 끊어 읽는 단위는 달라질 수 있다

처음 끊어 읽기를 시작할 때는 작은 의미 단위로 끊어 읽는 것이 좋아요. 주어, 동사, 목적어, 보어, 수식어 등 주요 문장 성분으로 끊어 읽고 직독직해를 해요. 실력이 쌓이면 더 큰 의미 단위로 끊어 읽을 수 있어요. 예를 들어 주어와 주어를 수식하는 어구를 끊지 않고 한 번에 붙여 읽는다면 독해가 더욱 빨라지겠죠?

8. 부사(구)와 부사절 앞에서 끊는다.
- I began helping / in the kitchen / when I turned three years old.
  나는 돕기 시작했다 / 주방에서 / 내가 세 살이 되었을 때

9. 접속사 앞에서 끊는다. 접속사가 생략된 경우 절 앞에서 끊는다.
- Tests showed / that passengers didn't like his design.
  테스트들이 보여주었다 / 승객들이 그의 디자인을 좋아하지 않았다는 것을
- She thought / cooking was a good learning tool.
  그녀는 생각했다 / 요리가 좋은 학습 도구라고

10. 문장부호가 있는 곳에서 끊는다.
- But as he got bigger, / some of his jokes, / like jumping into fishermen's boats, / became dangerous!
  그러나 그가 더 커짐에 따라 / 그의 몇몇 장난들은 / 어부들의 배 안으로 뛰어들어오는 것과 같은 / 위험해졌다

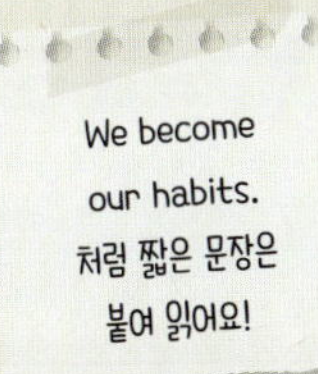

11. 진주어 또는 진목적어는 그 앞에서 끊는다.
- It is clear / that our habits have a powerful effect on us.
  분명하다 / 우리의 습관이 우리에게 강력한 영향을 미친다는 것은
- You would find it / very difficult / to describe the inside of your friend.
  여러분은 알게 될 것이다 / 매우 어렵다는 것을 / 여러분의 친구의 내면을 묘사하는 것이

12. 관계대명사나 관계부사가 있는 문장은 선행사 다음에 끊는다.
- They make correct diagnoses / that are 19 percent faster.
  그들은 정확한 진단을 내린다 / 19퍼센트 더 빠른

달고나 커피

400번 저어 만든다는 달고나 커피.
인기가 있어서 카페에서도 판다.

신메뉴
달고나 커피

하지만 나는 만들어 보기로 한다.

후훗!
잘 만들어서
자랑해야지~

휘적
휘적

까짓것.

휘적
휘적

달고나 커피 한 잔 주세요.

신메뉴

후들
후들

글 / 그림 우쿠쥐

중심 내용 파악하기

중심 내용이란 뭔가요?

필자가 글을 통해 이야기하고자 하는 핵심 내용을 말해요.

어떻게 공부 하나요?

글을 읽으면서 반복 등장하는 핵심어구를 파악하고, 주제문을 찾는 것이 중요해요. 글의 앞부분과 뒷부분, 글의 흐름이 전환되는 곳, 명령문이 쓰인 곳에 특히 주목하여 주제문을 파악하는 연습을 해 보세요.

시험에 어떻게 나오나요?

다음 네 가지 유형으로 출제돼요.

- ✓ **주제 파악하기** — UNIT 01
- ✓ **요지·주장 파악하기** — UNIT 02
- ✓ **제목 추론하기** — UNIT 03
- ✓ **요약하기** — UNIT 04

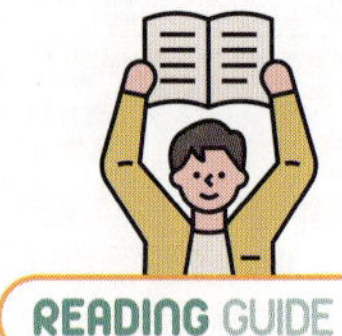

READING GUIDE

글을 읽으면서 주제문을 찾아
밑줄을 그어 봅시다.

다음 글의 주제로 가장 적절한 것은? (기출응용)

[1] There is an important difference between having an ideal and making a rule to live by. [2] The ideal may be a perfect standard that one would be proud to achieve. [3] Such an ideal provides you with a guide, but it should not be a daily standard. [4] Making the ideal into a rule is setting a trap for yourself. [5] If you constantly fall into the trap, you feel so bad about yourself that it becomes increasingly difficult to keep going. [6] The rule needs to direct you toward the ideal. [7] It also needs to be realistic so that you do not lose your self-confidence. [8] That is why it makes more sense to do the best you can — rather than try to be perfect.

① characteristics of perfect standards
② difficulties of setting realistic goals
③ how to make an ideal into a daily rule
④ why rules to live by need to be realistic
⑤ negative effects of detailed goals on our lives

UNDERSTAND DEEPLY

1 윗글의 내용을 다음과 같이 정리할 때, 빈칸에 알맞은 말을 쓰시오.

대조 대상	A(n) (1) ________	A rule to live by
성격	perfect	(2) ________
역할	to (3) ________ you ________ ________ ________	to (4) ________ you ________ ________ ________

2 윗글의 내용과 일치하도록 빈칸에 알맞은 말을 쓰시오.

________은 달성하기 자랑스러운 완벽한 기준일 수 있지만, ______________ ____________________은 덫에 빠뜨려 계속 나아가지 못하게 할 수 있다.

READ CLOSELY

의미 단위로 끊어 읽고(/), 주어와 동사에 표시해 봅시다.

지문 듣기   기출 원문 보기

❶ There **is** an important difference/between having an ideal and making a rule to live by.

중요한 차이가 있다 /

❷ The ideal may be a perfect standard that one would be proud to achieve.

❸ Such an ideal provides you with a guide, **but** it should not be a daily standard.

❹ Making the ideal into a rule is setting a trap for yourself.

❺ If you constantly fall into the trap, you feel **so** bad about yourself **that** it becomes increasingly difficult to keep going.

❻ The rule needs to direct you toward the ideal.

❼ It also needs to be realistic so that you do not lose your self-confidence.

❽ That is why it makes more sense to do the best you can — rather than try to be perfect.

GRAMMAR TIP

「so+형용사/부사+that+주어+동사」 구문은 '너무 ~해서 …하다'라는 의미로 원인과 결과를 나타내요.

- I was **so** tired **that** I didn't know you called.
- He ran **so** quickly **that** I couldn't catch him.

cf. 「so that+주어+동사」 구문은 '~하도록'이라는 의미로 목적을 나타내요.

- I gave her my phone number **so that** she could contact me.

READING TIP

but, however, (even) though 등 글의 흐름을 전환하는 연결어 뒤에 글의 핵심 내용이 제시되는 경우가 많아요.

WORDS

difference 차이
ideal 이상
live by ~에 따라 살다
standard 기준, 수준
achieve 달성하다, 성취하다
provide A with B A에게 B를 제공하다
guide 지침, 안내
make A into B A를 B로 만들다
set a trap 덫[함정]을 놓다
constantly 끊임없이
fall into ~에 빠지다
increasingly 점점 더
cf. increase 증가하다
direct 인도하다, 안내하다
cf. guide 인도하다, 안내하다
realistic 현실적인
self-confidence 자신감
make sense 타당하다, 말이 되다
detailed 상세한

READING 02

READING GUIDE

글을 읽으면서 주제문을 찾아
밑줄을 그어 봅시다.

다음 글의 주제로 가장 적절한 것은? 기출응용

[1] Poetry sharpens our senses and makes us understand our lives much better. [2] Imagine, for a moment, that you are trying to describe one of your friends. [3] You could say the friend has blue eyes, a mole on the left cheek, or a red nose. [4] But that would only describe the outside of this person. [5] It wouldn't tell people what your friend is really like. [6] It wouldn't show the habits, feelings, and all the little characteristics that make this person different from everyone else. [7] You would find it very difficult to describe the inside of your friend, even though you know everything about them. [8] Good poetry tells us about both the outside and the inside of life. [9] And it helps you know and love the world as much as you know and love a friend.

① usefulness of poetry in life
② tips for understanding friends
③ difficulties of describing the inside
④ misunderstanding of reading poetry
⑤ how to express ideas through poetry

UNDERSTAND DEEPLY

1 윗글의 내용과 일치하면 T, 그렇지 않으면 F를 쓰시오.

(1) Describing only the outside of a person doesn't show what they are really like. ______

(2) Poetry can help us see the inside of life and understand the world better. ______

2 윗글에서 the outside와 the inside의 예를 모두 찾아 쓰시오.

(1) the outside	(2) the inside
• ______________	• ______________
• ______________	• ______________
• ______________	• ______________

READ CLOSELY 의미 단위로 끊어 읽고(/), 주어와 동사에 표시해 봅시다.

지문 듣기 기출 원문 보기

❶ Poetry sharpens our senses and makes us understand our lives much better.

❷ Imagine, for a moment, that you are trying to describe one of your friends. (TIP)

❸ You could say the friend has blue eyes, a mole on the left cheek, or a red nose.

❹ But that would only describe the outside of this person.

❺ It wouldn't tell people what your friend is really like.

❻ It wouldn't show the habits, feelings, and all the little characteristics that make this person different from everyone else.

❼ You would find it very difficult to describe the inside of your friend, even though you know everything about them. (TIP)

❽ Good poetry tells us about both the outside and the inside of life.

❾ And it helps you know and love the world as much as you know and love a friend.

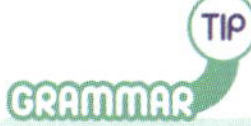

TIP GRAMMAR

find처럼 목적격 보어를 쓰는 동사의 목적어가 to부정사(구)이면 목적어 자리에 가목적어 it을 대신 쓰고, 진목적어인 to부정사(구)는 뒤로 보내요.

- She found **it** difficult **to breathe**.
- I made **it** a rule **to go to bed early**.

READING TIP

글의 주제문이 먼저 나온 후 For example, For instance, Imagine, Consider 등의 표현과 함께 주제를 구체적으로 설명하기 위한 예시가 이어지기도 해요.

WORDS

poetry (집합적) 시(詩)
cf. poem (한 편의) 시(詩)
sharpen 예리하게[날카롭게] 하다
cf. sharp 날카로운
sense 감각
describe 묘사하다
mole (피부 위의) 점
outside 외면, 외부
characteristic 특징, 특성
different from ~와 다른
find 알게 되다
difficult 어려운
inside 내면, 내부
both A and B A와 B 둘 다
usefulness 유용성
cf. useful 유용한
tip 조언, 비법
difficulty 어려움
misunderstanding 오해
cf. misunderstand 오해하다
express 표현하다

바른답·알찬풀이 | p. 2

READING GUIDE

글을 읽으면서 주제문을 찾아
밑줄을 그어 봅시다.

다음 글의 주제로 가장 적절한 것은? (기출응용)

[1]You may wonder whether there is any reason to worry about too much confidence. [2]After all, confidence is often considered a positive thing. [3]In fact, research suggests that students with a lot of confidence in their ability in school tend to do better on exams than those with less confidence. [4]Though that is true, negative results also come from being overconfident in the classroom. [5]Students who are overconfident about their ability in college end up feeling more disconnected than those with lower expectations. [6]Overconfidence can also leave students with mistaken impressions. [7]For example, they think they are fully prepared for tests and no longer need to study. [8]Students who properly assess their progress in learning tend to have more effective study habits. [9]They then do better on tests than those with incorrect views of their knowledge.

① effective ways to change bad study habits
② changing roles of academic tests in school
③ useful strategies for building students' confidence
④ critical factors to consider for choosing a college major
⑤ negative effects of students' overconfidence on school life

UNDERSTAND DEEPLY

1 빈칸에 알맞은 단어를 윗글에서 찾아 쓰시오.

_________________ can make students feel disconnected and get a wrong impression of their progress in learning.

2 윗글의 내용과 일치하면 T, 그렇지 않으면 F를 쓰시오.

(1) Confidence can help students perform better on tests. ______

(2) Students who have incorrect views of their knowledge tend to do better on exams. ______

❶ You may wonder whether there is any reason to worry about too much confidence.

❷ After all, confidence is often considered a positive thing.

❸ In fact, research suggests that students with a lot of confidence in their ability in school tend to do better on exams than those with less confidence.

❹ Though that is true, negative results also come from being overconfident in the classroom.

❺ Students who are overconfident about their ability in college end up feeling more disconnected than those with lower expectations.

❻ Overconfidence can also leave students with mistaken impressions.

❼ For example, they think they are fully prepared for tests and no longer need to study.

❽ Students who properly assess their progress in learning tend to have more effective study habits.

❾ They then do better on tests than those with incorrect views of their knowledge.

GRAMMAR TIP

whether는 '~인지 (아닌지)'라는 의미의 접속사예요. whether가 이끄는 절은 명사처럼 주어, 목적어, 보어 등으로 쓰여요.

- **Whether** it is true or not doesn't matter to me.
- I don't know **whether** they are coming.

WORDS

wonder 궁금하다, 궁금해 하다
confidence 자신감
after all 어쨌든, 결국
consider (~으로) 여기다
positive 긍정적인
suggest 시사하다, 넌지시 나타내다
tend to ~하는 경향이 있다
do well on ~을 잘 보다[하다]
negative 부정적인
result 결과
overconfident 자신감이 지나친
end up -ing 결국 ~하게 되다
disconnected 단절된
expectation 기대
overconfidence 지나친 자신감
leave A with B A에게 B를 남기다
mistaken 잘못된, 틀린
cf. mistake 잘못 생각하다
impression 인상, 느낌
properly 정확하게, 바르게
assess 평가하다
cf. estimate 평가하다
progress 진도, 진전
effective 효과적인
habit 습관
incorrect 부정확한, 틀린
cf. correct 정확한, 옳은
strategy 전략
critical 중대한, 결정적인
factor 요소, 요인

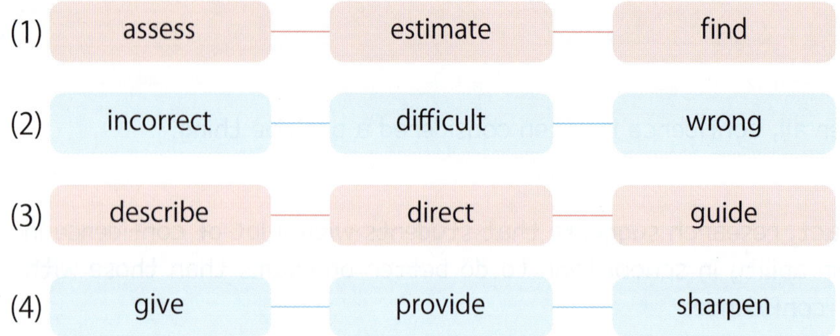

1 세 단어 중 서로 의미가 비슷한 두 개를 고르시오.

(1) assess — estimate — find

(2) incorrect — difficult — wrong

(3) describe — direct — guide

(4) give — provide — sharpen

2 서로 의미가 반대인 단어끼리 연결하시오.

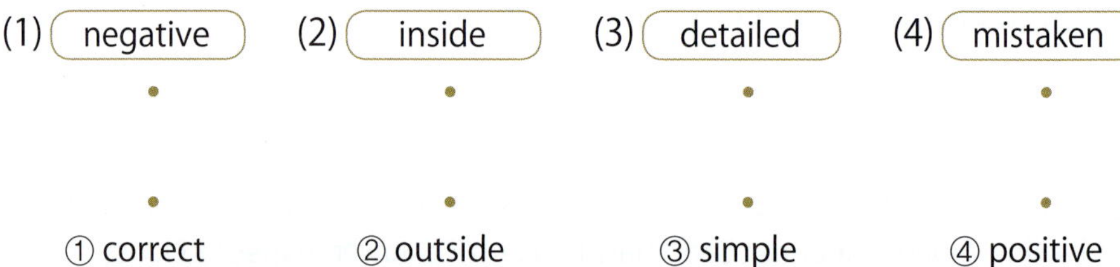

(1) negative (2) inside (3) detailed (4) mistaken

① correct ② outside ③ simple ④ positive

3 우리말 뜻에 맞게 주어진 철자로 시작하는 단어 퍼즐을 완성하시오.

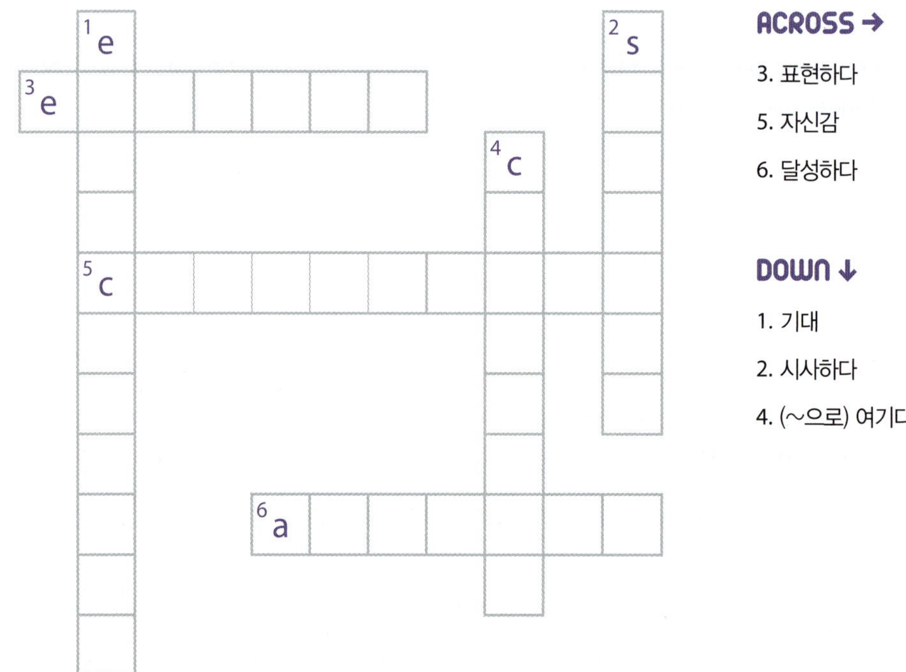

4 주어진 단어를 사용하여 우리말 뜻에 해당하는 표현을 쓰시오. (한 번씩만 쓸 것)

(1) ~와 다른 ＿＿＿＿＿＿＿＿＿＿＿   (2) ~에 빠지다 ＿＿＿＿＿＿＿＿＿＿＿

(3) 덫을 놓다 ＿＿＿＿＿＿＿＿＿＿＿   (4) 타당하다 ＿＿＿＿＿＿＿＿＿＿＿

fall	from	set	sense
a trap	make	into	different

5 빈칸에 알맞은 말을 보기 에서 골라 쓰시오.

> 보기
>
> what   that   so that   whether

(1) You may wonder ＿＿＿＿＿＿ there is any reason to worry.

(2) You feel so bad ＿＿＿＿＿＿ it becomes difficult to keep going.

(3) The words wouldn't tell people ＿＿＿＿＿＿ your friend is really like.

(4) The rule needs to be realistic ＿＿＿＿＿＿ you do not lose your self-confidence.

6 우리말과 의미가 같도록 괄호 안의 동사를 알맞은 형태로 쓰시오.

(1) 시는 우리가 우리의 삶을 훨씬 더 잘 이해하게 한다. (understand)

→ Poetry makes us ＿＿＿＿＿＿＿＿ our lives much better.

(2) 이상을 규칙으로 만드는 것은 여러분 자신에게 덫을 놓는 것이다. (make)

→ ＿＿＿＿＿＿＿＿ the ideal into a rule is setting a trap for yourself.

(3) 여러분은 친구의 내면을 묘사하는 것이 매우 어렵다는 것을 알게 될 것이다. (describe)

→ You would find it very difficult ＿＿＿＿＿＿＿＿ the inside of your friend.

(4) 이상을 가지는 것과 지키며 살아갈 규칙을 만드는 것 사이에는 차이가 있다. (make)

→ There is a difference between having an ideal and ＿＿＿＿＿＿＿＿ a rule to live by.

READING GUIDE

글을 읽으면서 필자의 의견이 드러난 문장에 밑줄을 그어 봅시다.

다음 글의 요지로 가장 적절한 것은? 〔기출응용〕

❶ Recent studies show some interesting findings about habit formation. ❷ In these studies, students who successfully acquired one positive habit reported less stress; less impulsive spending; better dietary habits; decreased caffeine consumption; fewer hours spent watching TV; and even fewer dirty dishes. ❸ Keep working on one habit long enough, and not only does it become easier, but so do other things as well. ❹ It is why those with the right habits seem to do better than others. ❺ They are doing the most important thing regularly and, as a result, everything else is easier.

① 인내심이 많을수록 성공할 가능성이 커진다.
② 한 번 들인 나쁜 습관은 쉽게 고쳐지지 않는다.
③ 나이가 들어갈수록 좋은 습관을 형성하기 힘들다.
④ 무리한 목표를 세우면 달성하지 못할 가능성이 크다.
⑤ 하나의 좋은 습관은 생활 전반에 긍정적 효과를 미친다.

UNDERSTAND DEEPLY

1 다음 중 윗글에서 긍정적인 습관을 형성한 학생들이 보고한 내용이 <u>아닌</u> 것은?
① 스트레스를 덜 받았다.　　　② 충동적 소비가 줄었다.
③ 카페인 섭취가 줄었다.　　　④ TV 시청 시간이 줄었다.
⑤ 식사량이 줄었다.

2 윗글의 내용과 일치하면 T, 그렇지 않으면 F를 쓰시오.
(1) Students who successfully acquired one positive habit consumed less caffeine. ______
(2) Those with the right habits have trouble in doing less important things. ______

READ CLOSELY

의미 단위로 끊어 읽고(/), 주어와 동사에 표시해 봅시다.

지문 듣기　　기출 원문 보기

❶ Recent studies show some interesting findings about habit formation.

❷ In these studies, students who successfully acquired one positive habit reported less stress; less impulsive spending; better dietary habits; decreased caffeine consumption; fewer hours spent watching TV; and even fewer dirty dishes.

❸ Keep working on one habit long enough, and not only does it become easier, but so do other things as well.

❹ It is why those with the right habits seem to do better than others.

❺ They are doing the most important thing regularly and, as a result, everything else is easier.

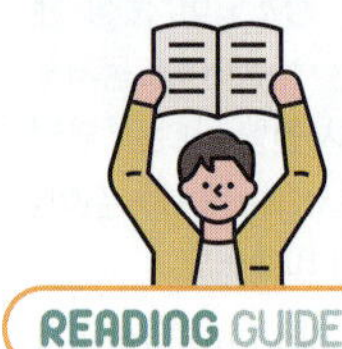

READING GUIDE

글을 읽으면서 핵심어에 모두
동그라미를 쳐 봅시다.

다음 글의 요지로 가장 적절한 것은? (기출응용)

❶ I began helping in the kitchen when I turned three years old. ❷ Everyone told my mom that I would be a hindrance rather than a help. ❸ But my mom let me make a mess in the kitchen because she thought cooking was a good learning tool. ❹ Of course, I didn't care about any of that learning stuff. ❺ I just thought it was fun, and I still do. ❻ I learned to cook through trial and many errors. ❼ I can't remember how many times I have dropped eggs on the floor. ❽ I have often covered the kitchen with flour or boiled things over on the stove. ❾ The point is, I have made many mistakes. ❿ But, as my mom always says, mistakes are the best teachers. ⓫ Through those mistakes I have learned what works and what doesn't.

* hindrance 방해

① 시행착오를 통해서 학습이 이루어질 수 있다.
② 주방에서 요리를 할 때 안전에 유의해야 한다.
③ 요리가 어린아이들의 신체 활동에 도움을 준다.
④ 어릴 때부터 정리하는 습관을 길러 줄 필요가 있다.
⑤ 사소한 실수를 줄이기 위해서는 신중함이 요구된다.

UNDERSTAND DEEPLY

1 윗글의 내용을 다음과 같이 정리할 때, 빈칸에 알맞은 말을 쓰시오.

예시	필자가 어렸을 때 (1) ________ 에서 많은 (2) ________ 를 하면서 (3) ________ 를 배움

↓

주제	(4) ________ 를 통해서 (5) ________ 할 수 있음

2 다음 질문에 알맞은 답을 윗글에서 찾아 문장을 완성하시오.

Q: Why did the writer's mom let her child make a mess in the kitchen?
A: She thought ____.

지문 듣기   기출 원문 보기

❶ I began helping in the kitchen when I turned three years old.

❷ Everyone told my mom that I would be a hindrance rather than a help.

❸ But my mom let me make a mess in the kitchen because she thought cooking was a good learning tool.

❹ Of course, I didn't care about any of that learning stuff.

❺ I just thought it was fun, and I still do.

❻ I learned to cook through trial and many errors.

❼ I can't remember how many times I have dropped eggs on the floor. →TIP

❽ I have often covered the kitchen with flour or boiled things over on the stove.

❾ The point is, I have made many mistakes.

❿ But, as my mom always says, mistakes are the best teachers.

⓫ Through those mistakes I have learned what works and what doesn't. →TIP →TIP

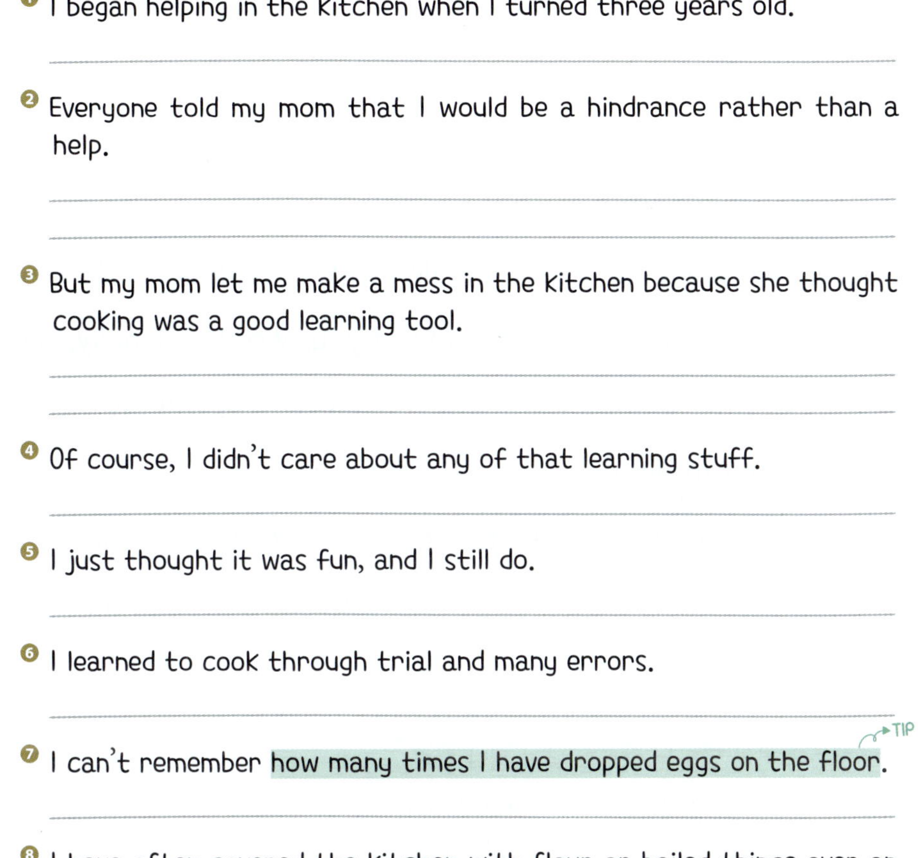

WORDS

turn ～이 되다
rather than ～보다는
make a mess 어지르다, 엉망으로 만들다
cf. mess 엉망진창, 혼란
tool 도구
care about ～에 관심을 가지다, ～에 신경 쓰다
stuff ～ 것, 물건
trial and error 시행착오
drop 떨어뜨리다
cover A with B A를 B로 뒤덮다
flour 밀가루
boil over 끓어 넘치게 하다
cf. boil 끓이다, 끓다
stove (요리용) 레인지, 스토브
point 요점, 핵심
make a mistake 실수하다
work 잘되다, 작용하다

READING GUIDE

글을 읽으면서 주제문을 찾아
밑줄을 그어 봅시다.

다음 글에서 필자가 주장하는 바로 가장 적절한 것은?

[1] Do you often give presentations in front of people? [2] When you are giving a presentation, do you tend to speak faster than usual? [3] I have given a lot of presentations, and what I have come to realize is if I think I am speaking at a normal speed, then I am speaking too fast. [4] It is unlikely that we will ever speak too slowly when we give presentations, because our nerves automatically speed us up. [5] So, focus on your words, think carefully, and try to relax a little. [6] Also, focus on the stress and intonation of your words. [7] Finally, pause before saying an important word, because this will give it more impact. [8] A presentation is not about the number of things that we say, but rather it's about the number of things that are understood. [9] Good presenters master what is simple but powerful: they speak more slowly.

① 청중에 따라 말하는 속도를 달리 해야 한다.
② 경청은 의사소통에서 가장 중요한 기술이다.
③ 발표에 앞서 준비 시간을 충분히 가져야 한다.
④ 말하는 내용에 따라 전달 방식이 달라져야 한다.
⑤ 발표 속도를 늦추고 청중의 이해도를 높여야 한다.

UNDERSTAND DEEPLY

1 다음 중 윗글에서 필자가 제안한 내용이 <u>아닌</u> 것은?

① 자신의 말에 집중하라.　　　② 신중하게 생각하라.
③ 긴장감을 유지하라.　　　④ 강세와 억양에 집중하라.
⑤ 중요한 단어를 말하기 전에 잠시 멈춰라.

2 윗글의 내용을 다음과 같이 요약할 때, 빈칸에 알맞은 단어를 쓰시오.

When you give a ___________, your words should be ___________ by the audience. So, try to speak more ___________.

READ CLOSELY

의미 단위로 끊어 읽고(/), 주어와 동사에 표시해 봅시다.

지문 듣기

❶ Do you often give presentations in front of people?

❷ When you are giving a presentation, do you tend to speak faster than usual?

❸ I have given a lot of presentations, and what I have come to realize is if I think I am speaking at a normal speed, then I am speaking too fast.

❹ It is unlikely that we will ever speak too slowly when we give presentations, because our nerves automatically speed us up.

❺ So, focus on your words, think carefully, and try to relax a little.

❻ Also, focus on the stress and intonation of your words.

❼ Finally, pause before saying an important word, because this will give it more impact.

❽ A presentation is not about the number of things that we say, but rather it's about the number of things that are understood.

❾ Good presenters master what is simple but powerful: they speak more slowly.

GRAMMAR TIP

what은 선행사를 포함하는 관계대명사로, '~하는 것'을 의미하는 명사절을 이끌어요. 관계대명사 what이 이끄는 절은 주어, 목적어, 보어 역할을 해요.

- **What** you have to do now is to take a rest.
- We couldn't understand **what** you said.
- This is **what** I want to buy.

WORDS

give a presentation 발표[프레젠테이션]를 하다
cf. presentation 발표, 프레젠테이션
in front of ~ 앞에서
tend to ~하는 경향이 있다
than usual 평소보다
come to ~하게 되다
realize 깨닫다
normal 보통의
unlikely ~할 것 같지 않은
cf. likely ~할 것 같은
nerve 신경
cf. nervous 불안해하는
automatically 자동으로
speed up 속도를 높이다
focus on ~에 집중하다
cf. concentrate on ~에 집중하다
relax 긴장을 풀다
stress 강세
intonation 억양, 어조
pause 잠시 멈추다
impact 효과, 영향
cf. effect 효과, 영향
rather 오히려
presenter 발표자
master 숙달하다, 터득하다
powerful 강력한

READING GUIDE

글을 읽으면서 필자의 주장이 드러난 문장에 밑줄을 그어 봅시다.

다음 글에서 필자가 주장하는 바로 가장 적절한 것은? (기출응용)

[1] Too many people suffer from destination disease. [2] In other words, once they reach a certain point in life, earn their degrees, buy their dream homes, and so on, then they just stop working hard. [3] Studies tell us that 50 percent of people, after they graduate from high school, will never read an entire book for the rest of their life. [4] One reason may be that they see learning as something you do only in school instead of as a way of life. [5] We all learned when we were in school. [6] Our teachers, coaches, and parents taught us. [7] We were expected to learn when we were of school age. [8] But some tend to think, "I'm out of school forever. I've got my job," once they finish a certain level of education. [9] Winners continue learning throughout life. [10] Whether you're nine or ninety years old, you should constantly be learning, improving your skills, and getting better at what you do.

① 연령에 맞는 학습 방법을 활용해야 한다.
② 깊이 생각하며 책을 읽는 습관을 들여야 한다.
③ 삶의 단계별 목표를 구체적으로 설정해야 한다.
④ 학창 시절 이후에도 배움을 멈추지 말아야 한다.
⑤ 학교는 평생 교육 프로그램 개발에 힘써야 한다.

UNDERSTAND DEEPLY

1 빈칸에 알맞은 단어를 윗글에서 찾아 쓰시오.

__________ __________ is the belief that once we achieve a certain goal, we no longer have to learn or grow.

2 윗글의 내용과 일치하도록 괄호 안에서 알맞은 말을 고르시오.

(1) According to studies, [most / half] of people won't read even one book after high school graduation.

(2) Successful people never stop learning at any [age / place].

READ CLOSELY

의미 단위로 끊어 읽고(/), 주어와 동사에 표시해 봅시다.

① Too many people suffer from destination disease.

② In other words, once they reach a certain point in life, earn their ►TIP degrees, buy their dream homes, and so on, then they just stop working hard.

③ Studies tell us that 50 percent of people, after they graduate from high school, will never read an entire book for the rest of their life.

④ One reason may be that they see learning as something you do only in school instead of as a way of life.

⑤ We all learned when we were in school.

⑥ Our teachers, coaches, and parents taught us.

⑦ We were expected to learn when we were of school age.

⑧ But some tend to think, "I'm out of school forever. I've got my job," once they finish a certain level of education.

⑨ Winners continue learning throughout life.

⑩ Whether you're nine or ninety years old, you should constantly be learning, improving your skills, and getting better at what you do.

WORDS

suffer from ~을 앓다[겪다]

destination 종착지, 목적지

disease 질병, 병

in other words 다시 말해서, 즉

reach ~에 이르다

certain 일정한, 어떤

point 시점, 요점

earn 받다, 얻다

degree 학위

and so on 기타 등등

graduate from ~을 졸업하다

cf. graduation 졸업

entire 전체의, 모든

cf. whole 전체의, 모든

rest 나머지

instead of ~ 대신에

expect 기대하다, 예상하다

be out of school 학교를 떠나다[졸업하다]

level 수준

education 교육

continue 계속하다

throughout ~ 동안 내내

constantly 끊임없이

improve 향상시키다

cf. develop 개발하다

REVIEW TIME

1 우리말 뜻에 해당하는 단어가 되도록 주어진 철자를 바르게 배열하시오.

(1) 습득하다   r a i q e u c   → _______________

(2) 억양   t n i o n t a n i o   → _______________

(3) 시점, 요점   t o p n i   → _______________

(4) 계속하다   n o c t e n i u   → _______________

2 서로 의미가 비슷한 단어끼리 연결하시오.

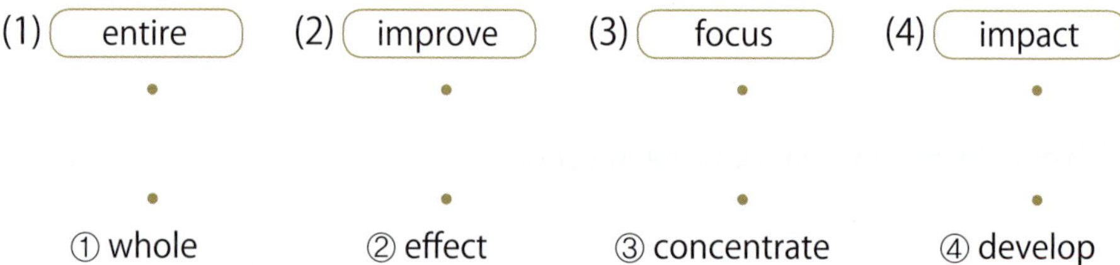

(1) entire   (2) improve   (3) focus   (4) impact

① whole   ② effect   ③ concentrate   ④ develop

3 우리말 뜻에 해당하는 단어를 찾아 동그라미 하고 빈칸에 쓰시오.

M	A	S	T	E	R	B	U	N	F	W
B	I	Y	N	Q	X	Y	J	K	X	B
D	V	R	W	D	F	I	T	U	T	Z
H	R	E	P	I	U	R	B	O	Z	H
Z	U	C	N	E	B	P	S	H	O	C
X	B	E	H	T	H	M	D	T	H	L
M	U	N	E	A	O	A	V	Z	Y	J
L	C	T	T	R	C	O	B	X	J	M
T	J	O	N	Y	Y	W	L	I	O	F
E	M	L	I	S	D	V	K	S	T	K
S	T	U	F	F	K	O	E	G	S	Q
N	L	H	A	Y	W	C	T	Y	C	H

(1) 식사의 _______________

(2) 습관 _______________

(3) 숙달하다 _______________

(4) 최근의 _______________

(5) ~ 것, 물건 _______________

(6) 도구 _______________

4 주어진 단어를 사용하여 우리말 뜻에 해당하는 표현을 쓰시오. (한 번씩만 쓸 것)

(1) ~에 집중하다 _________________   (2) ~보다는 _________________

(3) ~을 앓다 _________________   (4) ~ 대신에 _________________

instead	than	on	of
from	focus	suffer	rather

5 네모 안에서 어법에 맞는 것을 고르시오.

(1) My mom let me make / to make a mess in the kitchen.

(2) Good presenters master that / what is simple but powerful.

(3) You should constantly be getting better at that / what you do.

(4) I can't remember how many times I have / have I dropped eggs on the floor.

6 우리말과 의미가 같도록 괄호 안의 말을 이용하여 문장을 완성하시오.

(1) 학생들은 TV를 시청하는 데 보낸 더 적은 시간을 보고했다. (spend, watch)

    → Students reported fewer hours _________________ TV.

(2) 한 가지 습관을 들이고자 계속 노력해라, 그러면 다른 모든 것이 쉬워질 것이다. (keep, work)

    → _________________ on one habit, and everything else will be easier.

(3) 그것이 더 쉬워질 뿐만 아니라 다른 일들 또한 그렇게 된다. (it, do, become)

    → Not only _________________ easier, but so do other things as well.

(4) 사람들은 일단 삶의 어느 시점에 도달하면, 열심히 노력하는 것을 멈춘다. (stop, work)

    → Once people reach a certain point in life, they _________________ hard.

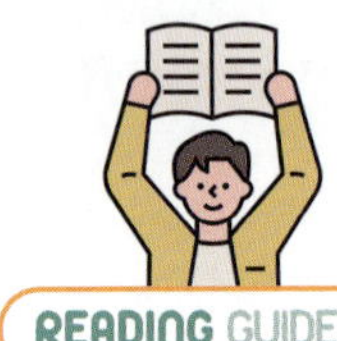

READING GUIDE

첫 문장에서 글의 중심 소재를
찾아 밑줄을 그어 봅시다.

다음 글의 제목으로 가장 적절한 것은? 기출응용

❶ Anne Mangen at the University of Oslo compared the performance of readers using a computer screen to that of readers using paper. ❷ Her study showed that reading on a computer screen includes various strategies — from quick reading to simple word finding. ❸ Applying those different strategies on screen makes reading comprehension poorer than when you are reading the same texts on paper. ❹ Also, screens have an additional feature: hypertext. ❺ Someone else makes hypertext, and it may not always be connected with the way you think. ❻ Therefore, it may not help you understand what you are reading, and it may even make it hard to focus.

* hypertext 하이퍼텍스트(텍스트와 결합된 링크)

① Importance of Teaching Reading Skills
② Strategies for Increasing Reading Speed
③ Why Reading on Screen Is Not That Effective
④ Children's Reading Habits and Technology Use
⑤ E-books: An Excellent Alternative to Paper Books

UNDERSTAND DEEPLY

1 다음 중 컴퓨터 화면으로 읽는 것에 관한 윗글의 내용과 일치하는 것은?
　① 업무 수행 시 종이를 이용해 읽는 것보다 선호된다.
　② 빠르게 읽기, 단순한 단어 찾기 등의 독해 전략을 포함한다.
　③ 하이퍼텍스트로 글의 내용을 쉽게 이해할 수 있다.
　④ 종이로 읽을 때보다 집중하기 쉽다.

2 빈칸에 알맞은 단어를 윗글에서 찾아 쓰시오.
　(1) Readers show better comprehension of texts on ___________ rather than on ___________.
　(2) ___________ can make it difficult to understand what you are reading.

READ CLOSELY

의미 단위로 끊어 읽고(/), 주어와 동사에 표시해 봅시다.

지문 듣기　　기출 원문 보기

❶ Anne Mangen at the University of Oslo compared the performance of readers using a computer screen to that of readers using paper.

❷ Her study showed **that** reading on a computer screen includes various strategies — from quick reading to simple word finding.

❸ Applying those different strategies on screen makes reading comprehension poorer than when you are reading the same texts on paper.

❹ Also, screens have an additional feature: hypertext.

❺ Someone else makes hypertext, and it may not always be connected with the way you think.

❻ **Therefore**, it may not help you understand what you are reading, and it may even make it hard to focus.

WORDS

compare A to B A를 B와 비교하다
performance 수행 (능력), 성과
cf. perform 수행하다, 실행하다
include 포함하다
various 다양한
strategy 전략
apply 적용하다
cf. apply for ~에 지원하다, ~을 신청하다
different 다양한
comprehension 이해(력)
additional 추가적인
cf. addition 추가, 부가물
feature 특징, 특색
be connected with ~와 관계가 있다
importance 중요성
effective 효과적인
cf. effect 효과
alternative 대안

READING GUIDE

글을 읽으면서 주제문을 찾아 밑줄을 그어 봅시다.

다음 글의 제목으로 가장 적절한 것은? 기출응용

[1] There is a saying in sports culture: "Winning is everything." [2] However, I'm not aware of anyone who ever won every game, or every event, or every championship he or she competed in. [3] Roger Federer, the tennis player whom people refer to as the greatest of all time, has won a record seventeen Grand Slam titles. [4] Yet, he has competed in more than sixty Grand Slam events. [5] This means that even the greatest tennis player has failed more than two-thirds of the time. [6] Yet, we don't think of him as a failure, but rather as a champion. [7] The fact is that he failed much more than he succeeded, and that's generally the way things are for everyone. [8] Failure comes before success. [9] Simply accept that failure is part of the process to succeed.

① Success Doesn't Come Without Failure
② You Create Your Own Opportunities
③ A Goal with No Plan Is Just a Wish
④ Don't Compare Yourself with Others
⑤ The Saddest Thing in Life Is Wasted Talent

UNDERSTAND DEEPLY

1 윗글의 내용을 다음과 같이 정리할 때, 빈칸에 알맞은 말을 쓰시오.

도입	늘 우승만 하는 사람은 없음
예시	최고의 테니스 선수 Roger Federer도 (1) ________ 보다 (2) ________ 를 훨씬 더 많이 했지만 (3) ________ 가 아니라 (4) ________ 으로 여겨짐
결론	(5) ________ 는 (6) ________ 하기 위한 과정의 일부임

2 윗글의 내용과 일치하면 T, 그렇지 않으면 F를 쓰시오.

(1) Roger Federer won every game he competed in. ______

(2) Failure is necessary for success. ______

READ CLOSELY

의미 단위로 끊어 읽고(/), 주어와 동사에 표시해 봅시다.

GRAMMAR TIP

방법, 방식을 나타내는 선행사 the way와 관계부사 how는 함께 쓰지 않아요. the way나 how 중 하나만 쓸 수 있음을 유의하세요.

- I like **the way** they dress.
  = I like **how** they dress.
- That's **the way** I want to live my life.
  = That's **how** I want to live my life.

❶ There is a saying in sports culture: "Winning is everything."

❷ However, I'm not aware of anyone who ever won every game, or every event, or every championship he or she competed in.

❸ Roger Federer, the tennis player whom people refer to as the greatest of all time, has won a record seventeen Grand Slam titles.

❹ Yet, he has competed in more than sixty Grand Slam events.

❺ This means that even the greatest tennis player has failed more than two-thirds of the time.

❻ Yet, we don't think of him as a failure, but rather as a champion.

❼ The fact is that he failed much more than he succeeded, and that's generally the way things are for everyone.
 TIP

❽ Failure comes before success.

❾ Simply accept that failure is part of the process to succeed.

WORDS

saying 속담, 격언
cf. proverb 속담, 격언
be aware of ~을 알다
event 경기, 시합
championship 선수권 대회
compete in ~에 출전하다
cf. competition 경쟁, 시합
refer to A as B A를 B라고 부르다
of all time 역대
record 기록적인
Grand Slam 그랜드 슬램(특정 스포츠 종목의 모든 주요 대회에서 우승하는 것)
fail 실패하다
think of A as B A를 B로 생각하다
failure 실패자, 실패
fact 사실
succeed 성공하다
generally 일반적으로
success 성공
accept 받아들이다
process 과정

READING GUIDE

첫 문장에서 글의 중심 소재를
찾아 밑줄을 그어 봅시다.

다음 글의 제목으로 가장 적절한 것은?

❶The meanings of certain colors have changed throughout the course of history, but some facts remain true. ❷Blue means silence and peace. ❸People use blue in their bedrooms because they may be able to sleep better. ❹Blue also symbolizes increased productivity, so business meetings are often held in blue rooms. ❺On the other hand, blue can sometimes give a cold and depressing impression. ❻Yellow is the color of freshness, happiness, and joy. ❼But this color can have side effects if it is overused. ❽For example, it is a proven fact that babies cry more in rooms painted yellow. ❾Orange, the blend of red and yellow, is a mixture of the energy from red and the happiness from yellow. ❿Purple is often associated with royalty, power, and ambition. ⓫It also stands for creativity, mystery, and magic. ⓬However, because it is rare in nature, purple is sometimes thought to be artificial.

① What Is Color Therapy?
② How Do We See Color?
③ What Do Colors Represent?
④ How Color Affects Our Lives?
⑤ Which Colors Match Well Together?

UNDERSTAND DEEPLY

1 윗글의 내용을 바탕으로 다음 빈칸에 알맞은 색상 이름을 쓰시오.

(1) 민호: 잠을 잘 자기 위해 침실을 ___________으로 꾸몄다.

(2) 재희: 방을 ___________으로 칠했더니 아이가 더 많이 운다.

2 다음 질문에 알맞은 답을 윗글에서 찾아 문장을 완성하시오.

Q: Why is purple sometimes thought to be artificial?

A: That's because it is ___________________________.

지문 듣기

① GRAMMAR TIP

수동의 의미를 나타내는 과거분사는 주로 명사의 앞에서 명사를 수식해요.
- Look at the **broken** windows over there.
  깨진 창문
- There are many **fallen** leaves on the street.
  떨어진 잎
과거분사가 구를 이루면 명사의 앞이 아닌 뒤에서 명사를 수식해요.
- The store sells bags **made** in Italy.
  과거분사구

❶ The meanings of certain colors have changed throughout the course of history, but some facts remain true.

❷ Blue means silence and peace.

❸ People use blue in their bedrooms because they may be able to sleep better.

❹ Blue also symbolizes increased productivity, so business meetings are often held in blue rooms. →TIP

❺ On the other hand, blue can sometimes give a cold and depressing impression.

❻ Yellow is the color of freshness, happiness, and joy.

❼ But this color can have side effects if it is overused.

❽ For example, it is a proven fact that babies cry more in rooms painted yellow. →TIP

❾ Orange, the blend of red and yellow, is a mixture of the energy from red and the happiness from yellow.

❿ Purple is often associated with royalty, power, and ambition.

⓫ It also stands for creativity, mystery, and magic.

⓬ However, because it is rare in nature, purple is sometimes thought to be artificial.

WORDS

certain 어떤, 특정한
remain ~한 상태로 있다
silence 고요, 침묵
cf. silent 고요한
symbolize 상징하다
increase 증가하다
productivity 생산성
be held 열리다, 개최되다
on the other hand 한편, 반면에
depressing 우울하게 하는, 우울한
impression 인상
cf. impressive 인상 깊은
side effect 부작용
overuse 지나치게 사용하다
blend 혼색, 혼합(물)
mixture 혼합(물)
be associated with ~와 연관되다
royalty 왕족, 왕위
ambition 야망, 야심
stand for ~을 의미하다[상징하다]
creativity 창의성
rare 드문
cf. common 흔한, 일반적인
artificial 인공의, 인위적인
cf. natural 자연적인
therapy 요법, 치료
represent 나타내다, 상징하다
affect ~에 영향을 미치다

1 짝지어진 단어들이 같은 관계가 되도록 빈칸에 알맞은 단어를 쓰시오.

(1) silent : silence = impressive : _______________

(2) succeed : success = fail : _______________

(3) rare : common = natural : _______________

(4) effect : effective = addition : _______________

2 서로 의미가 비슷한 단어끼리 연결하시오.

(1) blend　　(2) saying　　(3) represent　　(4) various

① symbolize　　② mixture　　③ proverb　　④ different

3 우리말 뜻에 맞게 퍼즐을 완성한 후, 8번 단어의 우리말 뜻을 쓰시오.

ACROSS →

1. 수행 (능력)　　2. 창의성

3. 받아들이다　　4. 전략

5. 포함하다　　6. 과정

7. 출전하다

DOWN ↓

8. _______________

4 주어진 단어를 사용하여 우리말 뜻에 해당하는 표현을 쓰시오. (중복 사용 가능)

(1) ~을 알아차리다 _______________________ (2) ~을 상징하다 _______________________

(3) A를 B라고 부르다 _______________________ (4) ~와 연관되다 _______________________

| stand | with | associated | for | be |
| as | refer | of | aware | to |

5 네모 안에서 어법에 맞는 것을 고르시오.

(1) Hypertext may even make it hard focus / to focus .

(2) Babies cry more in rooms painting / painted yellow.

(3) Accept that / what failure is part of the process to succeed.

(4) Hypertext may not help you understand that / what you're reading.

6 밑줄 친 부분이 어법에 맞으면 ○표 하고, 그렇지 않으면 바르게 고치시오.

(1) That's generally <u>the way how</u> things are for everyone.

(2) Applying those strategies <u>make</u> reading comprehension poor.

(3) People use blue in their bedrooms because they may <u>can</u> sleep better.

(4) Her study showed <u>that</u> reading on a computer screen includes various strategies.

READING 11

READING GUIDE

요약문을 먼저 읽고, 글을 읽으면서 요약문의 각 빈칸에 들어갈 내용과 관련 있는 문장에 밑줄을 그어 봅시다.

다음 글의 내용을 한 문장으로 요약하고자 한다. 빈칸 (A)와 (B)에 들어갈 말로 가장 적절한 것은? (기출응용)

❶ When I was in eighth grade, we were studying longitude and latitude in geography class. ❷ Every day for a week, we had a quiz, and I kept confusing longitude and latitude. ❸ I went home and almost cried because I got so frustrated and embarrassed by the fact that I couldn't properly understand them. ❹ I stared and stared at those words until suddenly I figured out what to do. ❺ I told myself, 'When you see that *n* in longitude, it will remind you of the word *north*. So it will be easy to remember that longitude lines go from north to south.' ❻ It worked; I got them all right on all the quizzes and also on the final test.

> → The story above suggests that _____(A)_____ what you are learning with what you already know helps you _____(B)_____ the learning material.

	(A)		(B)		(A)		(B)
①	connecting	……	memorize	②	connecting	……	publish
③	presenting	……	publish	④	replacing	……	evaluate
⑤	replacing	……	memorize				

UNDERSTAND DEEPLY

1 다음 중 윗글에서 추론할 수 있는 필자의 심경 변화로 가장 적절한 것은?

① confused → upset
② surprised → sad
③ satisfied → nervous
④ lonely → frightened
⑤ depressed → delighted

2 윗글에서 필자가 겪은 문제와 이를 해결한 방법을 우리말로 간단히 쓰시오.

(1) 문제: ________________________________

(2) 해결법: ________________________________

의미 단위로 끊어 읽고(/), 주어와 동사에 표시해 봅시다.

지문 듣기　　기출 원문 보기

① When I was in eighth grade, we were studying longitude and latitude in geography class.

② Every day for a week, we had a quiz, and I kept confusing longitude and latitude.

③ I went home and almost cried because I got so frustrated and embarrassed by the fact that I couldn't properly understand them.
→ TIP

④ I stared and stared at those words until suddenly I figured out what to do.

⑤ I told myself, 'When you see that *n* in longitude, it will remind you of the word *north*. So it will be easy to remember that longitude lines go from north to south.'

⑥ It worked; I got them all right on all the quizzes and also on the final test.

GRAMMAR TIP

접속사 that이 이끄는 절은 fact, news, idea, truth, belief, thought 등의 명사 뒤에서 동격을 이루어 명사의 내용을 구체적으로 설명해 주기도 해요.

• **The news that** Tom lost the game made me sad.

• I agree with **the idea that** money isn't everything.

READING TIP

요약문을 먼저 읽고 지문이 무엇에 관한 내용인지 힌트를 얻어 보세요.

WORDS

longitude 경도

latitude 위도

geography 지리

quiz 쪽지 시험, 퀴즈

confuse (A와 B를) 혼동하다

cf. confusing 혼란스럽게 하는

frustrated 좌절감을 느끼는

cf. frustrate 좌절감을 주다

embarrassed 창피한, 당황한

cf. embarrass 부끄럽게 하다, 당황하게 하다

properly 제대로, 바르게

stare at ~을 쳐다보다

figure out 알아내다

remind A of B A에게 B를 생각나게 하다

work 효과가 있다

suggest 시사하다, 넌지시 나타내다

connect A with B A와 B를 연결하다[관련지어 생각하다]

memorize 암기하다, 기억하다

publish 출판하다

present 제시하다, 보여 주다

replace 대체하다, 교체하다

evaluate 평가하다

READING 12

READING GUIDE

요약문을 먼저 읽고, 글을 읽으면서 요약문의 각 빈칸에 들어갈 내용과 관련 있는 문장에 밑줄을 그어 봅시다.

다음 글의 내용을 한 문장으로 요약하고자 한다. 빈칸 (A)와 (B)에 들어갈 말로 가장 적절한 것은? 기출응용

❶ Participants in a laboratory study were asked to listen to a pair of very loud, unpleasant noises played through headphones. ❷ One noise lasted for eight seconds. ❸ The other lasted for sixteen. ❹ The first eight seconds of the second noise were identical to the first noise. ❺ The second eight seconds, while still unpleasant, were not as loud as the first eight seconds. ❻ Later, the participants were told that they would have to listen to one of the noises again, but that they could choose which one to listen to. ❼ Clearly, the second noise is worse — the unpleasantness lasted twice as long. ❽ Nevertheless, most people chose the second noise. Why? ❾ Although both noises were unpleasant, the second one had a less unpleasant ending. ❿ So, people remembered the second one as less annoying than the first one.

> → According to an experiment, what influences the decisions about which noise they should listen to again is not the ＿＿(A)＿＿ of the noise, but how they felt at the ＿＿(B)＿＿.

	(A)	(B)		(A)	(B)
①	length	...... last moment	②	length	...... peak
③	loudness	...... start	④	loudness	...... last moment
⑤	pleasantness	...... peak			

UNDERSTAND DEEPLY

1 윗글의 내용과 일치하면 T, 그렇지 않으면 F를 쓰시오.

(1) 참가자들은 길이가 다른 두 가지 소음을 들었다. ＿＿＿＿

(2) 두 번째 소음의 뒷부분 절반은 앞부분 절반보다 소리가 컸다. ＿＿＿＿

2 윗글의 내용과 일치하도록 괄호 안에서 알맞은 말을 고르시오.

(1) The second noise was [longer / louder] than the first one.

(2) More people decided to listen to the [first / second] noise again.

READ CLOSELY

의미 단위로 끊어 읽고(/), 주어와 동사에 표시해 봅시다.

GRAMMAR **TIP**

「as+형용사/부사의 원급+as」는 '~만큼 …한/하게'라는 뜻으로 동등 비교를 할 때 쓰여요.

- Julia is **as young as** my sister.
- Please give me a call **as soon as** you can.

앞에 not이 오면 '~만큼 …하지 않은/않게'로 해석해요.

- This book is **not as interesting as** that one.
- I can't run **as fast as** you.

❶ Participants in a laboratory study were asked to listen to a pair of very loud, unpleasant noises played through headphones.

❷ One noise lasted for eight seconds.

❸ The other lasted for sixteen.

❹ The first eight seconds of the second noise were identical to the first noise.

❺ The second eight seconds, while still unpleasant, were not  as loud as the first eight seconds.

❻ Later, the participants were told that they would have to listen to one of the noises again, but that they could choose which one to listen to.

❼ Clearly, the second noise is worse — the unpleasantness lasted twice as long.

❽ Nevertheless, most people chose the second noise. Why?

❾ Although both noises were unpleasant, the second one had a less unpleasant ending.

❿ So, people remembered the second one as less annoying than the first one.

WORDS

participant 참가자
cf. participate 참가하다
laboratory 실험실
a pair of 2개의, 한 쌍의
unpleasant 불쾌한
cf. pleasant 기분 좋은, 유쾌한
last 지속되다
be identical to ~와 동일하다
be told 듣다, 들어서 알다
clearly 분명히, 확실히
unpleasantness 불쾌함
annoying 짜증 나게 하는
cf. annoyed 짜증이 난
according to ~에 따르면
experiment 실험
influence ~에 영향을 주다
decision 결정
cf. decide 결정하다, 결심하다
length 길이
peak 절정, 최고조
pleasantness 유쾌함

READING GUIDE

요약문을 먼저 읽고, 글을 읽
으면서 요약문의 각 빈칸에
들어갈 내용과 관련 있는 문장
에 밑줄을 그어 봅시다.

READING 13

다음 글의 내용을 한 문장으로 요약하고자 한다. 빈칸 (A)와 (B)에 들어갈 말로 가장 적절한 것은? 기출응용

❶ An experiment proved the importance of reputation in increasing cooperation. ❷ Bateson and colleagues analyzed the amounts of money put into an 'honesty box' for drinks in a coffee room. ❸ Images (always posted above the recommended price list) of a pair of eyes were swapped every week with images of flowers. ❹ Then they compared the amounts of money in the box. ❺ The amount of drinks consumed each week was almost the same. ❻ Surprisingly, almost three times more money was paid in weeks when eyes were shown, compared to when flowers were shown. ❼ Of course this experiment was only conducted in one location, but the effect size was impressive. ❽ It seems to show that people don't want others to see them cheating the system.

* effect size 효과 크기

> → The amount of money people put into an 'honesty box'
> _____(A)_____ when an image made them feel that they were
> being ____(B)____ .

	(A)		(B)			(A)		(B)
①	decreased	⋯⋯	cheated		②	decreased	⋯⋯	watched
③	changed	⋯⋯	supported		④	increased	⋯⋯	watched
⑤	increased	⋯⋯	supported					

UNDERSTAND DEEPLY

1 윗글의 실험 내용을 다음과 같이 정리할 때, 빈칸에 알맞은 말을 쓰시오.

방법	한 쌍의 (1)__________ 이미지와 (2)__________ 이미지를 매주 바꿔 게시함
결과	(3)__________ 이미지가 게시되었을 때 거의 (4)__________ 배 더 많은 돈이 지불됨
결론	사람들은 자신이 (5)__________ 때 더 정직하게 행동하는 경향이 있음

2 윗글에서 눈(eyes) 이미지의 역할을 찾아 빈칸에 알맞은 말을 쓰시오.

to see people _______________________________

READ CLOSELY

의미 단위로 끊어 읽고(/), 주어와 동사에 표시해 봅시다.

지문 듣기   기출 원문 보기

① An experiment proved the importance of reputation in increasing cooperation.

② Bateson and colleagues analyzed the amounts of money put into an 'honesty box' for drinks in a coffee room.

③ Images (always posted above the recommended price list) of a pair of eyes were swapped every week with images of flowers.

④ Then they compared the amounts of money in the box.

⑤ The amount of drinks consumed each week was almost the same.

⑥ Surprisingly, almost three times more money was paid in weeks when eyes were shown, compared to when flowers were shown.

➤TIP

⑦ Of course this experiment was only conducted in one location, but the effect size was impressive.

⑧ It seems to show that people don't want others to see them cheating the system.

➤TIP

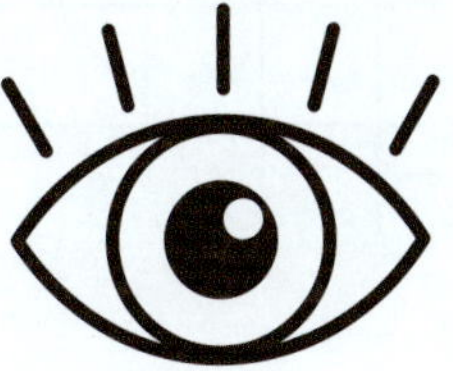

GRAMMAR TIP

관계부사 when이 이끄는 절은 시간을 나타내는 선행사를 수식해요.

- Christmas is *a holiday* **when** people celebrate the birth of Jesus Christ.
- Sunday is *the only day* **when** I can relax.

READING TIP

실험이나 연구를 소재로 하는 글에서는 show, prove, turn out, find (out) 등의 동사(구) 뒤에 실험이나 연구의 결과 또는 시사점이 언급되기도 해요.

WORDS

prove 증명하다
reputation 평판
increase 증진시키다, 늘리다
cooperation 협력, 협동
colleague 동료
analyze 분석하다
cf. analysis 분석
amount 총액, 액수, 양
post 게시하다
recommend 권장하다
swap 바꾸다, 교환하다
consume 소비하다
cf. consumption 소비
surprisingly 놀랍게도
compared to ~와 비교하여
conduct 실시하다, 수행하다
location 장소
impressive 인상적인
cheat 속이다
decrease 감소하다
support 지지하다

REVIEW TIME

1 우리말 뜻에 해당하는 단어가 되도록 주어진 철자를 바르게 배열하시오.

(1) 실시하다   c u n o c d t   → _______________

(2) 실험   i x r e n e m t p e   → _______________

(3) 동료   e u o l c g e a l   → _______________

(4) 출판하다   s u l i h p b   → _______________

2 우리말 뜻에 해당하는 단어가 되도록 빈칸에 알맞은 철자를 쓰시오.

(1) 평판   ▢ e ▢ u ▢ ation

(2) 불쾌한   un ▢ le ▢ s ▢ nt

(3) 암기하다   ▢ e ▢ o ▢ ize

(4) 결정   d ▢ c ▢ s ▢ on

3 우리말 뜻에 맞게 주어진 철자로 시작하는 단어 퍼즐을 완성하시오.

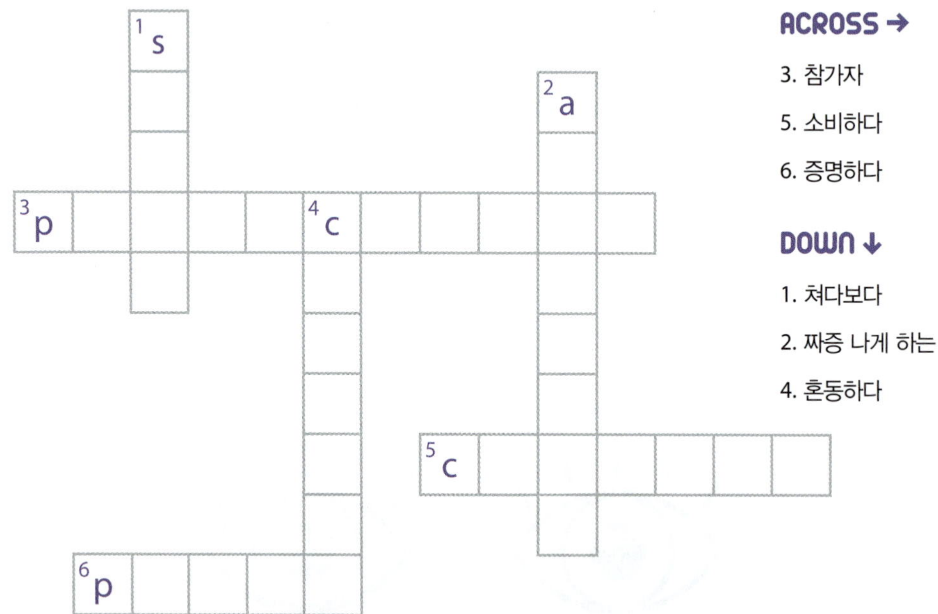

ACROSS →

3. 참가자

5. 소비하다

6. 증명하다

DOWN ↓

1. 쳐다보다

2. 짜증 나게 하는

4. 혼동하다

4 주어진 단어를 사용하여 우리말 뜻에 해당하는 표현을 쓰시오. (중복 사용 가능)

(1) ~와 비교하여 _________________

(2) ~을 알아내다 _________________

(3) ~에 따르면 _________________

(4) ~와 동일하다 _________________

figure	be	compared	out

to	according	identical

5 네모 안에서 어법에 맞는 것을 고르시오.

(1) I kept confusing / to confuse longitude and latitude.

(2) The second noise lasted twice as long / longer as the first one.

(3) People don't want others to see them cheating / to cheat the system.

(4) The second eight seconds were not as loud / loudly as the first eight seconds.

6 빈칸에 알맞은 말을 보기 에서 골라 쓰시오. (중복 사용 가능)

보기

what   that   when

(1) More money was paid in weeks _________ eyes were shown.

(2) I stared and stared at those words until I figured out _________ to do.

(3) Connect _________ you are learning with _________ you already know.

(4) I got so frustrated by the fact _________ I couldn't properly understand them.

Play Time

Find the top view for each paper plane.

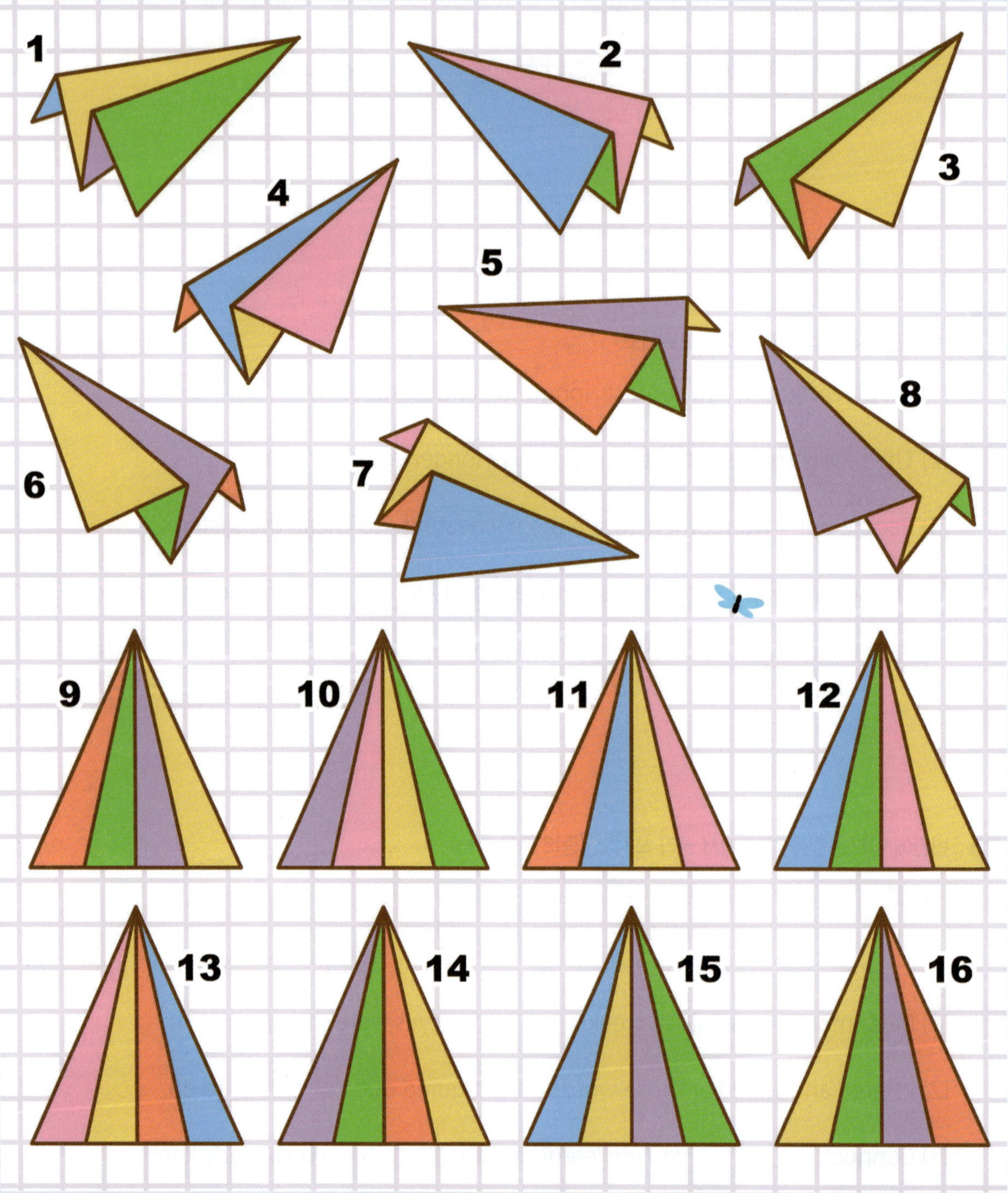

PART 2

세부 내용 파악하기

세부 내용이란 뭔가요?

하나의 글을 이루는 다양한 정보를 말해요.

어떻게 공부 하나요?

먼저 지시문과 선택지를 읽고 무엇에 관한 글인지 파악하는 습관을 들여요. 선택지를 읽은 후에는 선택지 순으로 관련 내용을 글에서 하나씩 확인해요.

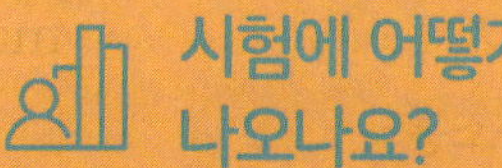

시험에 어떻게 나오나요?

다음 두 가지 유형으로 출제돼요.

- ✅ **내용 일치 파악하기** `UNIT 05`
- ✅ **안내문·도표 파악하기** `UNIT 06`

READING GUIDE

선택지를 먼저 읽고, 글을 읽으면서 ①~⑤의 내용과 관련된 문장에 밑줄을 그어 봅시다.

marsupial에 관한 다음 글의 내용과 일치하지 <u>않는</u> 것은?

① In many species, the young are carried on their mother's back. **②** However, this is not the case for all animals. **③** A marsupial is an animal that has a pouch to carry and raise its young. **④** Wallabies, kangaroos, and koalas are all examples of marsupials. **⑤** Its baby is born at a very early stage of development when it is about the size of a jelly bean. **⑥** At birth, it takes a long journey to reach the pouch by holding the mother's fur. **⑦** There, it continues to grow. **⑧** At first, the baby has no power to suck milk with its mouth, so the mother's milk goes into the baby's mouth directly. **⑨** Even after the young no longer need the mother's milk, they return at times to the pouch for protection.

* **wallaby** 왈라비(작은 캥거루같이 생긴 동물)

① 새끼는 어미의 주머니 속에서 자란다.
② 왈라비, 캥거루, 코알라 등이 포함된다.
③ 새끼는 젤리빈 정도의 크기로 태어난다.
④ 새끼는 태어나서 어미의 주머니를 찾아 들어간다.
⑤ 새끼는 젖을 뗀 뒤 어미의 주머니에 들어가지 않는다.

UNDERSTAND DEEPLY

1 다음 중 윗글의 중심 소재로 가장 적절한 것은?

① marsupial의 성장
② marsupial의 대표 동물
③ marsupial의 서식지
④ marsupial의 취약점
⑤ marsupial의 의사소통

2 다음 질문에 알맞은 답을 윗글에서 찾아 문장을 완성하시오.

(1) **Q:** What kind of an animal is a marsupial?
　　A: It is an animal ____.

(2) **Q:** Why does the mother's milk go into the baby's mouth directly at first?
　　A: It is because the baby ____.

READ CLOSELY

의미 단위로 끊어 읽고(/), 주어와 동사에 표시해 봅시다.

❶ In many species, the young are carried on their mother's back.

❷ However, this is not the case for all animals.

❸ A marsupial is an animal that has a pouch to carry and raise its young.

❹ Wallabies, kangaroos, and koalas are all examples of marsupials.

❺ Its baby is born at a very early stage of development when it is about the size of a jelly bean.

❻ At birth, it takes a long journey to reach the pouch by holding the mother's fur.

❼ There, it continues to grow.

❽ At first, the baby has no power to suck milk with its mouth, so the mother's milk goes into the baby's mouth directly.

❾ Even after the young no longer need the mother's milk, they return at times to the pouch for protection.

GRAMMAR TIP

형용사적 용법의 to부정사는 '~할', '~하는' 등의 의미로 명사를 뒤에서 수식해 줘요.

- I have a lot of <u>work</u> **to do**.
- Their <u>efforts</u> **to reduce** crime payed off.

cf. to부정사가 수식하는 명사가 전치사의 목적어일 때는 to부정사 뒤에 전치사를 꼭 써야 해요.

- Give me <u>a pencil</u> **to write** *with*.

READING TIP

내용 일치 파악 유형은 선택지의 순서와 각 선택지 관련 내용이 글에 제시되는 순서가 같으므로 하나씩 차례대로 확인하도록 해요.

WORDS

species 종(種)
the young 새끼들, 젊은이들
carry 운반하다, 가지고 다니다
marsupial 유대류 (동물)
pouch 주머니
raise 키우다, 기르다
development 발달
jelly bean 젤리빈(콩 모양 과자)
journey 여행, 여정
fur (일부 동물의) 털
grow 성장하다, 자라다
cf. growth 성장
at first 처음에는
suck 빨아들이다, 빨아 먹다
directly 직접적으로
no longer 더 이상 ~ 아닌
return 돌아가다
at times 가끔
protection 보호
cf. protect 보호하다

READING **15**

READING GUIDE

선택지를 먼저 읽고, 글을 읽으면서 ①~⑤의 내용과 관련된 문장에 밑줄을 그어 봅시다.

Dorothy West에 관한 다음 글의 내용과 일치하지 <u>않는</u> 것은? 기출응용

❶ Dorothy West, born on June 2, 1907, is remembered as one of the Harlem Renaissance writers. ❷ West mainly wrote about the life of rich African Americans. ❸ Her first novel, *The Living Is Easy*, published in 1948, received positive responses from critics, but failed to draw many readers. ❹ She wrote her second novel, *The Wedding*, in 1950, but did not complete it because she was not able to find a publisher. ❺ Jacqueline Onassis noticed the short stories that West submitted to the local newspaper at Martha's Vineyard. ❻ Onassis encouraged West to complete her novel and later served as her editor. ❼ Her second novel was published in 1995 and was made into a television movie produced by Oprah Winfrey. ❽ It was aired in 1998. ❾ West died on August 16, 1998.

① 할렘 르네상스 작가 중 한 명으로 기억된다.
② 주로 부유한 아프리카계 미국인의 삶을 글의 소재로 삼았다.
③ 첫 소설이 평론가들로부터 긍정적인 반응을 얻지 못했다.
④ Martha's Vineyard의 지역 신문에 단편 소설을 기고했다.
⑤ 두 번째 소설이 텔레비전 영화로 제작되어 방영되었다.

UNDERSTAND DEEPLY

1 윗글에 언급된 West의 작품을 다음과 같이 정리할 때, 빈칸에 알맞은 말을 쓰시오.

	첫 번째 소설	두 번째 소설
제목	(1) ____________	(3) ____________
출판 연도	(2) ____________	(4) ____________

2 윗글의 내용과 일치하면 T, 그렇지 않으면 F를 쓰시오.

(1) Dorothy West's first novel attracted a lot of readers. ______

(2) Jacqueline Onassis helped West submit her short stories to the local newspaper at Martha's Vineyard. ______

지문 듣기   기출 원문 보기

GRAMMAR TIP

because(~하기 때문에)는 이유의 부사절을 이끄는 접속사로, 뒤에 주어와 동사를 포함하는 절이 와요.

• I stayed home **because** it was raining heavily.
절(주어+동사 ~)

cf. because of(~ 때문에) 역시 이유를 나타내지만 접속사가 아닌 전치사이므로 뒤에 절이 아닌 명사(구)가 와요.

• I stayed home **because of** the heavy rain.
명사구

❶ Dorothy West, born on June 2, 1907, is remembered as one of the Harlem Renaissance writers.

❷ West mainly wrote about the life of rich African Americans.

❸ Her first novel, *The Living Is Easy*, published in 1948, received positive responses from critics, but failed to draw many readers.

❹ She wrote her second novel, *The Wedding*, in 1950, but did not complete it because she was not able to find a publisher.
↳ TIP

❺ Jacqueline Onassis noticed the short stories that West submitted to the local newspaper at Martha's Vineyard.

❻ Onassis encouraged West to complete her novel and later served as her editor.

❼ Her second novel was published in 1995 and was made into a television movie produced by Oprah Winfrey.

❽ It was aired in 1998.

❾ West died on August 16, 1998.

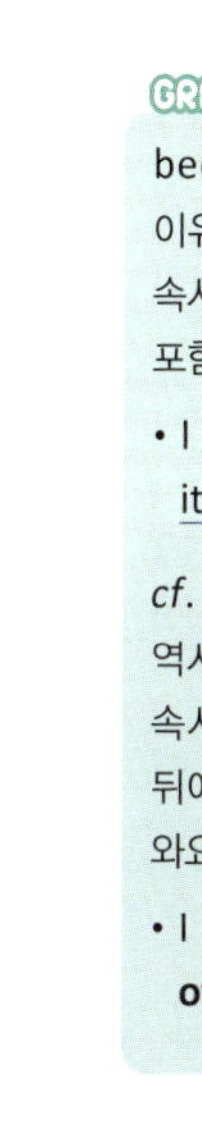

WORDS

Harlem Renaissance 할렘 르네상스(1920년대 뉴욕 시 할렘에서의 아프리카계 미국인의 문학 및 음악 문화 부흥)

mainly 주로
cf. main 주된, 주요한

novel (장편) 소설

publish 출판하다

response 반응
cf. respond 반응하다, 대답하다

critic 비평가
cf. criticize 비평하다, 비판하다

draw 끌다, 잡아끌다
cf. attract 끌어당기다, 매혹하다

complete 완성하다, 끝내다

publisher 출판업자, 출판사

notice ~에 주목하다

submit 제출하다

local (특정) 지역의

encourage 격려하다, 용기를 북돋우다

serve as ~의 역할을 하다, ~으로 일하다

editor 편집자
cf. edit 편집하다

be made into ~으로 만들어지다

produce 제작하다

air 방송하다

READING **16**

READING GUIDE

선택지를 먼저 읽고, 글을 읽으면서 ①~⑤의 내용과 관련된 문장에 밑줄을 그어 봅시다.

Paul Klee에 관한 다음 글의 내용과 일치하지 않는 것은? 기출응용

❶ Paul Klee was born in Bern, Switzerland, on December 18, 1879. ❷ His father was a music teacher and his mother was a singer and an amateur painter. ❸ As a child, Paul drew constantly. ❹ His favorite subject was cats. ❺ Then at the age of seven, he learned how to play the violin, and he continued to play as an adult, too. ❻ In fact, he even played with the Berlin Municipal Orchestra for a while. ❼ Although music was important to Paul, he decided to pursue visual art and became an artist. ❽ In 1898, he began his art career by studying at the Munich Academy. ❾ Afterwards, he taught painting at the Bauhaus from January 1921 to April 1931. ❿ Paul also kept a notebook filled with his artistic beliefs and ideas, and published a number of books about art. ⓫ By his death in 1940, he had created an impressive amount of work: over ten thousand drawings and nearly five thousand paintings.

* municipal 시[읍/군]의

① 어머니가 가수이자 아마추어 화가였다.
② 어렸을 때 고양이를 그리는 것을 좋아했다.
③ Berlin Municipal Orchestra와 함께 연주한 적이 있다.
④ 1898년에 Munich Academy에서 회화를 가르쳤다.
⑤ 미술에 관한 많은 책을 출판했다.

UNDERSTAND DEEPLY

1 Paul Klee에 관한 윗글의 내용을 다음과 같이 정리할 때, 빈칸에 알맞은 말을 쓰시오.

주요 경력	• (1) __________ 년: (2) __________ 에서 공부함
	• (3) __________ 년~1931년: (4) __________ 에서 회화를 가르침
업적	• (5) __________ 점이 넘는 소묘, (6) __________ 점에 가까운 회화를 그림

2 다음 중 윗글을 읽고 Paul Klee에 대해 알 수 없는 것은?

① 출생지   ② 부모의 직업   ③ 바이올린을 배운 나이
④ 대표 작품의 제목   ⑤ 미술 경력을 시작한 해

지문 듣기 　　기출 원문 보기

① GRAMMAR TIP

continue, like, love, begin, start 등의 동사는 to부정사와 동명사를 모두 목적어로 쓸 수 있어요.

- He **continued to play** [**playing**] the violin.
- They **began to learn** [**learning**] English last year.

cf. remember나 forget 등의 동사도 to부정사와 동명사를 모두 목적어로 쓸 수 있지만, 각 경우에 의미가 달라져요.

- He **forgot to buy** the T-shirt. (미래에) 살 것을 잊었다
- He **forgot buying** the T-shirt. (과거에) 산 것을 잊었다

❶ Paul Klee was born in Bern, Switzerland, on December 18, 1879.

❷ His father was a music teacher and his mother was a singer and an amateur painter.

❸ As a child, Paul drew constantly.

❹ His favorite subject was cats.

❺ Then at the age of seven, he learned how to play the violin, and he continued to play as an adult, too. → TIP

❻ In fact, he even played with the Berlin Municipal Orchestra for a while.

❼ Although music was important to Paul, he decided to pursue visual art and became an artist.

❽ In 1898, he began his art career by studying at the Munich Academy.

❾ Afterwards, he taught painting at the Bauhaus from January 1921 to April 1931.

❿ Paul also kept a notebook filled with his artistic beliefs and ideas, and published a number of books about art.

⓫ By his death in 1940, he had created an impressive amount of work: over ten thousand drawings and nearly five thousand paintings.

WORDS

amateur 아마추어의, 비전문적인
cf. **professional** 직업적인, 전문적인
constantly 끊임없이
subject (그림 등의) 대상[주제]
continue 계속하다
for a while 한동안, 잠시 동안
decide 결심하다
pursue 추구하다, 쫓다
visual 시각의, 눈에 보이는
career 경력, (일생의) 직업
painting 회화, 그림
keep (일기 등을) 적다, 기록하다 (keep - kept - kept)
filled with ~으로 가득 차 있는
artistic 예술적인
belief 믿음, 신념
a number of 많은
cf. **the number of** ~의 수
impressive 인상적인
drawing 소묘, 데생
nearly 거의
cf. **near** 가까운

REVIEW TIME

1 짝지어진 단어들이 같은 관계가 되도록 빈칸에 알맞은 단어를 쓰시오.

(1) edit : editor = criticize : ________________

(2) near : nearly = main : ________________

(3) respond : response = grow : ________________

(4) easy : difficult = professional : ________________

2 우리말 뜻에 해당하는 단어가 되도록 빈칸에 알맞은 철자를 쓰시오.

(1) 보호   p ⬜ o ⬜ e ⬜ tion

(2) 발달   de ⬜ e ⬜ o ⬜ ment

(3) 완성하다   c ⬜ m ⬜ le ⬜ e

(4) 격려하다   e ⬜ c ⬜ u ⬜ a ⬜ e

(5) 계속하다   c ⬜ n ⬜ i ⬜ u ⬜

(6) 인상적인   i ⬜ p ⬜ e ⬜ si ⬜ e

3 우리말 뜻에 해당하는 단어를 찾아 동그라미 하고 빈칸에 쓰시오.

A	Q	B	X	V	N	B	L	B	F	P
K	R	W	J	I	T	O	B	C	Q	D
J	L	V	K	O	P	N	V	X	C	L
L	C	N	O	J	U	A	T	E	B	P
C	A	R	E	E	R	R	S	S	L	Z
K	U	Q	Z	P	S	T	N	X	P	S
V	T	Z	Y	B	U	I	Z	E	U	W
S	Y	G	Y	O	E	S	S	A	Y	R
C	E	P	G	L	K	T	I	A	B	L
O	W	S	P	E	C	I	E	S	D	C
K	T	G	E	Z	M	C	H	R	G	H

(1) 종(種) ________________

(2) 예술적인 ________________

(3) 추구하다 ________________

(4) 소설 ________________

(5) 여행, 여정 ________________

(6) 경력 ________________

4 주어진 단어를 사용하여 우리말 뜻에 해당하는 표현을 쓰시오. (한 번씩만 쓸 것)

(1) ~으로 가득 찬 _________________

(2) ~으로 만들어지다 _________________

(3) 한동안, 잠시 동안 _________________

(4) 가끔 _________________

times	made	at	with	be
while	filled	into	for	a

5 네모 안에서 어법에 맞는 것을 고르시오.

(1) He continued play / to play the violin as an adult, too.

(2) Onassis encouraged West to complete / completing her novel.

(3) In many species, the young is / are carried on their mother's back.

(4) She didn't complete her novel because / because of she wasn't able to find a publisher.

6 우리말과 의미가 같도록 괄호 안의 동사를 알맞은 형태로 쓰시오.

(1) 새끼 유대류는 어미의 주머니 안에서 계속 성장한다. (grow)

→ A baby marsupial continues _________________ in the mother's pouch.

(2) 처음에 새끼는 제 입으로 젖을 빨아들일 힘이 전혀 없다. (suck)

→ At first, the baby has no power _________________ milk with its mouth.

(3) Paul은 그의 예술적 신념과 아이디어로 가득 찬 노트를 기록했다. (fill)

→ Paul kept a notebook _________________ with his artistic beliefs and ideas.

(4) 1948년에 출간된 그녀의 첫 번째 소설 *The Living Is Easy*는 많은 독자를 끄는 데 실패했다. (publish)

→ Her first novel, *The Living Is Easy*, _________________ in 1948, failed to draw many readers.

READING **17**

READING GUIDE

선택지를 먼저 읽고, 안내문을 읽으면서 ①~⑤의 내용과 관련된 문장에 밑줄을 그어 봅시다.

Acting Course Audition에 관한 다음 안내문의 내용과 일치하는 것은? (기출응용)

Acting Course Audition

❶ Hello, applicants!

❷ You will be given a chance to demonstrate your talent and potential. ❸ You must attend the audition in person. ❹ It is not possible to audition by sending in a video clip of your presentation.

- ❺ Your monologue must be no longer than two minutes.
- ❻ You should memorize your monologue completely.
- ❼ Bring two copies of your monologue with you on audition day.
- ❽ Choose your monologue from plays. ❾ DO NOT select it from films, TV dramas, or poems.

---

① 동영상 제출로 오디션 참가를 대신할 수 있다.
② 독백 발표 시간은 적어도 2분이 넘어야 한다.
③ 독백 대본을 완전히 암기해야 한다.
④ 오디션 날 독백 대본을 가져올 수 없다.
⑤ 영화나 TV 드라마의 대본을 활용할 수 있다.

UNDERSTAND DEEPLY

1 다음 중 위 안내문의 중심 내용으로 가장 적절한 것은?

① how to improve acting skills
② how to choose an acting school
③ how to participate in an audition
④ how to film a video for an audition

2 빈칸에 알맞은 단어를 윗글에서 찾아 쓰시오.

(1) On audition day, applicants should bring two copies of their ___________ with them.

(2) Applicants should choose their monologue from ___________.

지문 듣기   기출 원문 보기

GRAMMAR TIP

주어가 to부정사(구)일 때는 보통 주어 자리에 아무 뜻이 없는 가주어 it을 대신 쓰고 진주어 to부정사(구)는 뒤로 보내요.

- **To break a habit** is difficult.
  → **It** is difficult **to break a habit**.
- **It** takes long **to go there by bus**.

READING TIP

안내문을 읽을 때는 장소, 날짜, 시간, 비용 등의 주요 항목에 주목하여 관련 정보를 파악해 보세요.

❶ Hello, applicants!

❷ You will be given a chance to demonstrate your talent and potential.

❸ You must attend the audition in person.

❹ It is not possible to audition by sending in a video clip of your presentation.  TIP

❺ Your monologue must be no longer than two minutes.

❻ You should memorize your monologue completely.

❼ Bring two copies of your monologue with you on audition day.

❽ Choose your monologue from plays.

❾ DO NOT select it from films, TV dramas, or poems.

WORDS

applicant 지원자
cf. apply 지원하다, 신청하다
demonstrate 보여 주다, 증명하다
talent 재능
potential 잠재력, 가능성
attend 참석하다
audition 오디션; 오디션을 받다
in person 직접, 몸소
send in 제출하다, 내다
cf. submit, hand in 제출하다, 내다
presentation 발표
cf. present 제시하다, 보여 주다
monologue 독백
memorize 암기하다
completely 완전히
cf. complete 완전한; 완료하다
choose 선택하다, 선정하다
select 선택하다, 선정하다
poem (한 편의) 시(詩)
cf. poetry (문학 양식으로서의) 시(詩)

READING GUIDE

선택지를 먼저 읽고, 안내문을 읽으면서 ①~⑤의 내용과 관련된 부분에 밑줄을 그어 봅시다.

The Great Green Bike Ride에 관한 다음 안내문의 내용과 일치하지 <u>않는</u> 것은? 기출응용

The Great Green Bike Ride

❶The Great Green Bike Ride is an annual two-wheeled weekend adventure event to raise funds for local environmental conservation. ❷Join the event, and you can help save the environment.

- ❸**Date:** Saturday 26 – Sunday 27, September 2020
- ❹**Route:** Day 1 – City Hall to the Central Forest: 85 miles
  ❺Day 2 – Explore the Central Forest: 35 miles
- ❻**Event Fee:** $50 and FREE for children under 12
- ❼**Bike Reservation:** Reserve your free bikes before the event day at www.greatgreenbike.org. ❽You have to make a reservation if you want to use our bikes.
- ❾**Overnight Stay:** We offer a delicious BBQ dinner and a place to stay.

---

① 지역 환경 보존 기금을 마련하기 위한 행사이다.
② 둘째 날의 자전거 주행 거리는 35마일이다.
③ 12세 미만의 어린이는 무료로 참가할 수 있다.
④ 행사 당일에 자전거 대여가 가능하다.
⑤ 저녁 식사와 숙소를 제공한다.

UNDERSTAND DEEPLY

1 다음 중 위 안내문을 읽고 The Great Green Bike Ride 행사에 대해 알 수 <u>없는</u> 것은?

① 개최 목적 ② 개최 기간 ③ 주행 경로
④ 자전거 예약 방법 ⑤ 숙박 장소

2 위 안내문의 내용을 바탕으로 다음 질문에 알맞은 답을 완성하시오.

Q: Two adults and one 10-year-old boy want to join the event. How much should they pay for it?
A: They should pay ________ dollars.

지문 듣기   기출 원문 보기

① The Great Green Bike Ride is an annual two-wheeled weekend adventure event to raise funds for local environmental conservation.

② Join the event, and you can help save the environment.

③ Date: Saturday 26 – Sunday 27, September 2020

④ Route: Day 1 – City Hall to the Central Forest: 85 miles

⑤ Day 2 – Explore the Central Forest: 35 miles

⑥ Event Fee: $50 and FREE for children under 12

⑦ Bike Reservation: Reserve your free bikes before the event day at www.greatgreenbike.org.

⑧ You have to make a reservation if you want to use our bikes.

⑨ Overnight Stay: We offer a delicious BBQ dinner and a place to stay.

GRAMMAR TIP

「명령문, and …」 구문은 '~해라, 그러면 …'을 의미해요.
- **Leave** early, **and** you will catch the bus.
- **Go** straight, **and** you will see the building.

cf. 「명령문, or …」 구문은 '~해라, 그렇지 않으면 …'을 의미해요.
- Please **be** careful, **or** you will break the glass.
- **Wear** a coat, **or** you will catch a cold.

WORDS

annual 연례의, 1년에 한 번의
cf. anniversary 기념일
two-wheeled 바퀴가 두 개인
adventure 모험
raise 모금하다
cf. rise 일어나다, 오르다
fund 기금, 자금
local (특정) 지역의
environmental 환경의
conservation 보존, 보호
cf. preservation 보존, 보호
join 참가하다, 가입하다
save 구하다, 지키다
environment 환경
route 길, 경로
explore 탐험하다
fee 요금
cf. charge 요금
free 무료의
reservation 예약
reserve 예약하다
cf. book 예약하다
overnight 일박의
stay 머무름, 체류; 숙박하다
offer 제공하다
delicious 맛있는

READING GUIDE

글을 읽기 전에 도표의 제목과 범례를 확인해 봅시다.

READING 19

다음 도표의 내용과 일치하지 <u>않는</u> 것은? 기출응용

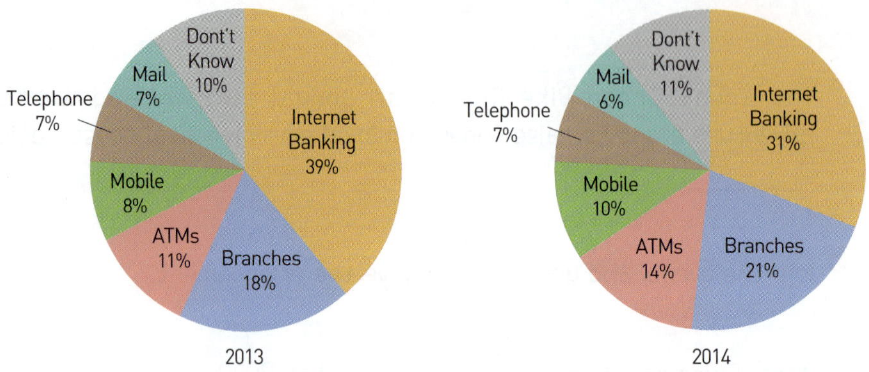

❶ The charts above show preferred banking methods based on a survey of 1,000 Americans in 2013 and 2014. ❷ ① The sum of the percentages of people preferring Internet Banking and Branches was over 50 percent in both years. ❸ ② In 2013, 39 percent of people said Internet Banking was their favorite way of banking, while the preference dropped 8 percentage points in 2014. ❹ ③ The preference of Branches increased 3 percentage points in 2014 compared to 2013. ❺ ④ Mail, Mobile, and ATMs increased slightly from 2013 to 2014. ❻ ⑤ Telephone remained the same at 7 percent in both years.

* percentage point 퍼센트포인트(퍼센트 수치가 증가하거나 감소한 양)

UNDERSTAND DEEPLY

1 위 도표의 내용과 일치하면 T, 그렇지 않으면 F를 쓰시오.

(1) Internet Banking was less preferred than Branches in both years. ______

(2) In 2014, the sum of the percentages of people preferring Telephone and Mail was 13 percent. ______

2 윗글의 내용과 일치하도록 괄호 안에서 알맞은 말을 고르시오.

(1) The preference of Mail [increased / decreased] in 2014 compared to 2013.

(2) Internet Banking was the [most / least] preferred banking method in both years.

READ CLOSELY

의미 단위로 끊어 읽고(/), 주어와 동사에 표시해 봅시다.

❶ The charts above show preferred banking methods based on a survey of 1,000 Americans in 2013 and 2014.

❷ The sum of the percentages of people preferring Internet Banking and Branches was over 50 percent in both years.

❸ In 2013, 39 percent of people said Internet Banking was their favorite way of banking, while the preference dropped 8 percentage points in 2014.

❹ The preference of Branches increased 3 percentage points in 2014 compared to 2013.

❺ Mail, Mobile, and ATMs increased slightly from 2013 to 2014.

❻ Telephone remained the same at 7 percent in both years.

GRAMMAR TIP

접속사 while은 '~하는 동안에'라는 의미 외에도 '~하는 반면에'라는 의미로 쓰여 두 가지 사실을 대조하는 역할을 해요.

- Some have blue eyes **while** others have brown ones.
- **While** I am good at English, I am not good at math.

READING TIP

변화 정도를 나타내는 부사

slightly(약간), dramatically(극적으로), steeply(가파르게), gradually(서서히), steadily(꾸준히), continuously(계속해서)

증감을 나타내는 동사

increase/rise(증가하다/오르다), decrease/decline/drop(감소하다/떨어지다)

WORDS

prefer 선호하다
banking 은행 업무
method 방법, 방식
cf. **way** 방법, 방식
chart 도표, 그래프
based on ~에 기초한
survey 설문 조사
sum 합계
branch 지점, 지사
preference 선호(도)
drop 떨어지다
cf. **fall** 떨어지다
increase 증가하다
compared to ~와 비교하여
slightly 약간, 조금
cf. **significantly** 상당히
remain 여전히 ~하다, (~한 상태로) 남다

글을 읽기 전에 도표의 제목
과 범례를 확인해 봅시다.

다음 도표의 내용과 일치하지 <u>않는</u> 것은? (기출응용)

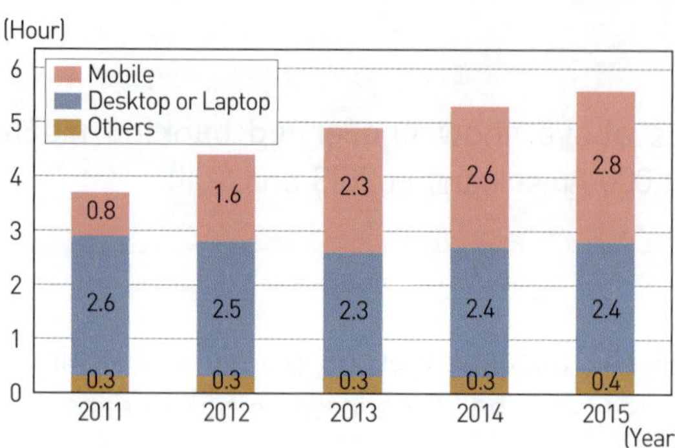

❶ The graph above shows Americans' average daily Internet usage time by device from 2011 to 2015. ❷ ① Overall, the total Internet usage time increased steadily from 2011 to 2015. ❸ ② In 2011, Internet usage time via mobile was shorter than that via desktop or laptop. ❹ ③ In 2012, however, Americans spent the same hours on mobile devices as they did on desktops or laptops. ❺ ④ In 2014, Internet usage time from mobile devices was longer than that from desktops or laptops. ❻ ⑤ In 2015, Americans spent an average of 5.6 hours a day on the Internet.

UNDERSTAND DEEPLY

1 위 도표의 내용과 일치하면 T, 그렇지 않으면 F를 쓰시오.

(1) In 2011, Internet usage time via desktop or laptop was longer than that via mobile. ______

(2) In 2012, the average daily Internet usage time from mobile devices was 2.5 hours. ______

2 위 도표의 내용과 일치하도록 빈칸에 알맞은 단어를 쓰시오.

(1) In 2013, Americans spent the __________ average hours on desktops or laptops as they did on mobile devices.

(2) In 2014, Internet usage time via mobile was __________ than that via desktop or laptop.

READ CLOSELY

의미 단위로 끊어 읽고(/), 주어와 동사에 표시해 봅시다.

❶ The graph above shows Americans' average daily Internet usage time by device from 2011 to 2015.

❷ Overall, the total Internet usage time increased steadily from 2011 to 2015.

❸ In 2011, Internet usage time via mobile was **shorter than** that via desktop or laptop. →TIP

❹ In 2012, however, Americans spent **the same** hours on mobile devices **as** they did on desktops or laptops. →TIP

❺ In 2014, Internet usage time from mobile devices was **longer than** that from desktops or laptops. →TIP

❻ In 2015, Americans spent an average of 5.6 hours a day on the Internet.

REVIEW TIME

1 우리말 뜻에 해당하는 단어가 되도록 주어진 철자를 바르게 배열하시오.

(1) 선호(도) rfepeerecn → _________________

(2) 지원자 paitnlcpa → _________________

(3) 독백 ougomnloe → _________________

(4) 꾸준히 dsateyil → _________________

(5) 모험 duvranete → _________________

(6) 환경 nerivteonmn → _________________

2 서로 의미가 비슷한 단어끼리 연결하시오.

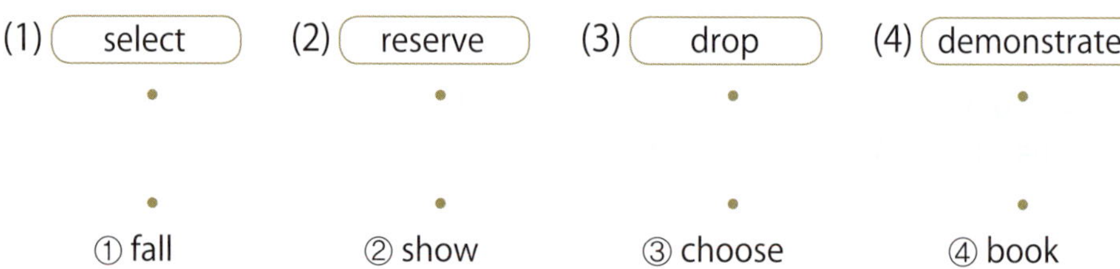

3 우리말 뜻에 맞게 주어진 철자로 시작하는 단어 퍼즐을 완성하시오.

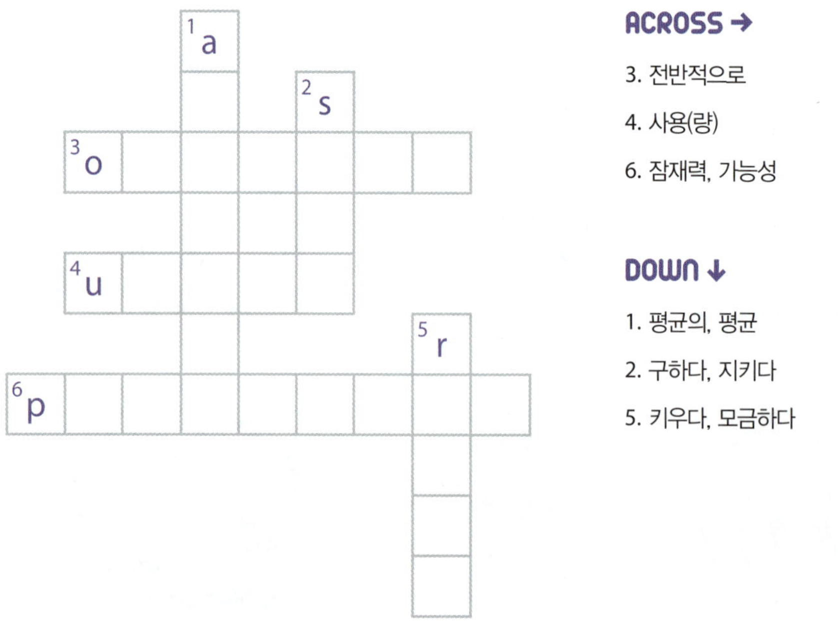

ACROSS →

3. 전반적으로

4. 사용(량)

6. 잠재력, 가능성

DOWN ↓

1. 평균의, 평균

2. 구하다, 지키다

5. 키우다, 모금하다

READ CLOSELY

의미 단위로 끊어 읽고(/), 주어와 동사에 표시해 봅시다.

지문 듣기   기출 원문 보기

① Dear Ms. Jones,

② Thank you for raising your concerns.

③ I know it can be hard to ask these kinds of questions as a parent.

④ I understand your concern about the degree of work involved in this class project, as well as your request for a deadline extension.

⑤ We've been working hard over the course of the last month in order to finish the work in time.

⑥ In case you didn't see it, I'm enclosing a copy of our class calendar.

⑦ As we've been working hard to keep this schedule, I'm afraid I can't extend the deadline.

⑧ I'm sure that this is a fair timeline.

⑨ I believe we can understand each other.

⑩ Thank you.

⑪ Sincerely, Bryan Roberts

WORDS

raise (문제 등을) 제기하다
concern 걱정, 관심
cf. concerned 걱정스러운
degree 정도
involved in ~에 관련된
cf. involve 포함하다, 관련시키다
B as well as A A뿐만 아니라 B도
cf. not only A but also B A뿐만 아니라 B도
request 요청
deadline 마감일, 최종 기한
extension 연장
over the course of ~ 동안[내내]
in order to ~하기 위해서
in time 제시간에
in case ~할 경우에 대비해서
enclose 동봉하다
extend 연장하다
fair 타당한, 공정한
cf. reasonable 타당한, 합리적인
timeline 일정

READING **22**

READING GUIDE

글을 읽으면서 글의 목적이
드러나 있는 문장에 밑줄을
그어 봅시다.

다음 글의 목적으로 가장 적절한 것은? (기출응용)

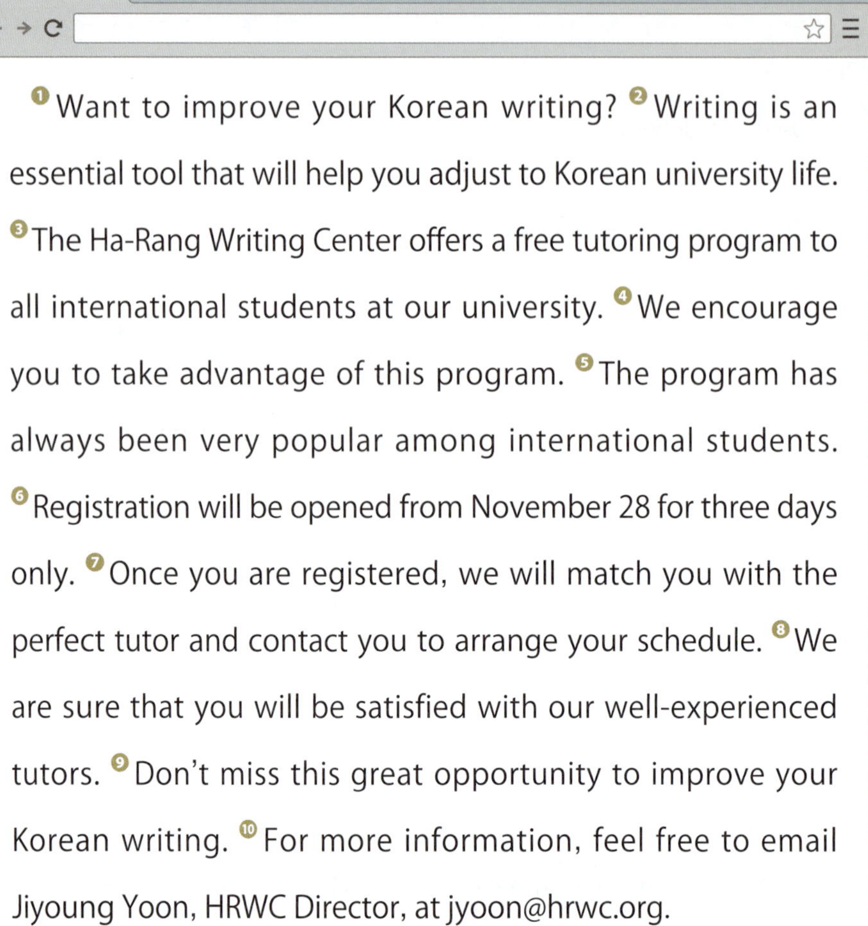

① 한국의 대학 생활과 관련한 유의 사항을 알리려고
② 유학생을 위한 글쓰기 센터 설립을 건의하려고
③ 한국어 글쓰기 지도를 받을 유학생을 모집하려고
④ 한국어 글쓰기 강좌의 변경된 등록 절차를 공지하려고
⑤ 한국어 글쓰기 지도 강사의 자격 요건을 안내하려고

UNDERSTAND DEEPLY

1 다음 중 윗글의 내용과 일치하는 것은?

① 대학 내 유학생들에게 유료 글쓰기 프로그램이 제공된다.
② 프로그램 등록은 11월 중 3일 동안만 가능하다.
③ 프로그램에 등록할 때 원하는 지도 강사를 선택해야 한다.

2 다음 문장에서 윗글의 내용과 다른 부분을 찾아 바르게 고쳐 쓰시오.

If you want to get more information, you can call HRWC Director.

_______________ → _______________

의미 단위로 끊어 읽고(/), 주어와 동사에 표시해 봅시다.

지문 듣기　　기출 원문 보기

❶ Want to improve your Korean writing?

❷ Writing is an essential tool that will help you adjust to Korean university life.

❸ The Ha-Rang Writing Center offers a free tutoring program to all international students at our university.

❹ We encourage you to take advantage of this program.

❺ The program has always been very popular among international students.

❻ Registration will be opened from November 28 for three days only.

❼ Once you are registered, we will match you with the perfect tutor and contact you to arrange your schedule.

❽ We are sure that you will be satisfied with our well-experienced tutors.

❾ Don't miss this great opportunity to improve your Korean writing.

❿ For more information, feel free to email Jiyoung Yoon, HRWC Director, at jyoon@hrwc.org.

GRAMMAR TIP

encourage, want, ask, tell, expect, allow, order, advise, force 등의 동사는 목적격 보어로 to부정사를 써요.

- She **asked** me **to close** the door.
- I **told** you **to come** home early.

cf. 사역동사처럼 '~하게 하다'를 뜻하는 동사 get도 목적격 보어로 to부정사를 써요.

- Dad **got** me **to eat** vegetables.

READING TIP

We[I] encourage you to ~나 명령문과 같이 필자의 권유 또는 주장이 드러나 있는 곳에 주목해 보세요.

WORDS

improve 향상시키다
cf. develop 개발하다
essential 필수의
cf. necessary 필수의, 필요한
adjust to ~에 적응하다
offer 제공하다
tutor 개인 교습을 하다; 개인 지도 교사
encourage 권장하다, 장려하다
take advantage of ~을 이용하다[활용하다]
cf. advantage 이점, 장점
registration 등록
register 등록하다
contact ~에게 연락을 취하다
arrange 조정하다
be satisfied with ~에 만족하다
cf. satisfy 만족시키다
well-experienced 경험 많은
opportunity 기회
cf. chance 기회

READING 23

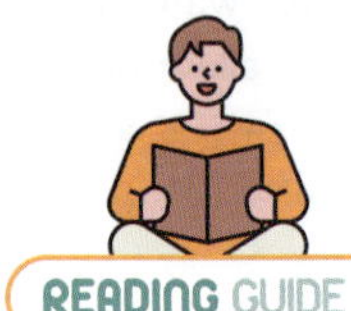

READING GUIDE

글을 읽으면서 인물의 심경이 드러나 있는 문장에 모두 밑줄을 그어 봅시다.

다음 글에 드러난 Amy의 심경으로 가장 적절한 것은? (기출응용)

❶When Amy heard someone call her name, she stood up from her seat and went up on the stage. ❷Dr. Wilkinson was giving a gold medal to each of the top five medical graduates. ❸He shook Amy's hand and congratulated her on her performance. ❹Amy felt really thrilled to be recognized as one of the top five medical graduates of her school. ❺Amy walked back to her seat, satisfied with her academic performance and pleased with her success. ❻She just received a special honor. ❼This special recognition would help her to continue realizing her life-long dream of becoming a passionate doctor.

① proud and happy   ② calm and relieved
③ irritated and nervous   ④ fearful and desperate
⑤ disappointed and furious

UNDERSTAND DEEPLY

1 윗글의 내용과 일치하면 T, 그렇지 않으면 F를 쓰시오.

(1) Top ten medical graduates received gold medals. ______

(2) Dr. Wilkinson congratulated Amy on her performance. ______

2 다음 질문에 알맞은 답을 윗글에서 찾아 문장을 완성하시오.

Q: What is Amy's life-long dream?
A: It is to become ________________________.

3 Amy가 다음 각 상황에서 느낀 감정을 윗글에서 찾아 쓰시오.

단상 위에 서서	자리에 돌아오면서
• 인정받아서 정말로 (1) ______	• 학업 성과에 대한 (2) ______ • 성공에 대한 (3) ______

READ CLOSELY

의미 단위로 끊어 읽고(/), 주어와 동사에 표시해 봅시다.

지문 듣기   기출 원문 보기

1 When Amy heard someone call her name, she stood up from her seat and went up on the stage.

2 Dr. Wilkinson was giving a gold medal to each of the top five medical graduates.

3 He shook Amy's hand and congratulated her on her performance.

4 Amy felt really thrilled to be recognized as one of the top five medical graduates of her school.

5 Amy walked back to her seat, satisfied with her academic performance and pleased with her success.

6 She just received a special honor.

7 This special recognition would help her to continue realizing her life-long dream of becoming a passionate doctor.

GRAMMAR TIP

지각동사(hear, listen to, see, watch, look at, smell, feel 등)는 목적격 보어로 동사원형을 써서 '~이 …하는 것을 듣다[보다, 냄새 맡다, 느끼다]'라는 뜻을 나타내요. 진행의 의미를 강조할 때는 목적격 보어로 현재분사를 쓸 수 있어요.

- I **saw** him **dance** on the stage.
- I **felt** my heart **beating** fast.

READING TIP

인물이 처한 상황을 파악하며 글을 읽고, 인물의 심경을 나타내는 표현에 주목하여 관련 선택지를 찾아보세요.

WORDS

medical 의학의

graduate 졸업생

shake one's hand ~와 악수하다 (shake-shook-shaken)

congratulate A on B A의 B를 축하하다

cf. congratulation 축하

performance 성과, 성취

cf. perform 수행하다

thrilled (아주) 신이 난

recognize 인정하다, 표창하다

academic 학업의, 학문의

pleased 기뻐하는

cf. pleasure 기쁨, 즐거움

honor 우등(상), 명예

recognition 인정, 표창

realize 실현하다

life-long 평생의

passionate 열정적인

relieved 안도하는

irritated 짜증이 난

fearful 무서워하는

desperate 필사적인

furious 분노한

READING **24**

READING GUIDE

글을 읽으면서 글의 분위기를
추론할 수 있는 단어에 모두
표시해 봅시다.

다음 글의 분위기로 가장 적절한 것은? 기출응용

❶ Six holes were drilled into different areas of the mine. ❷ They sent oxygen sensors, cameras, and microphones down through plastic pipes to search for the six missing miners. ❸ During the search, the oxygen levels were misread and determined to be dangerously low. ❹ Three rescue team members, trying to dig the trapped miners out, were killed when a wall of the mine exploded. ❺ Rescuers never saw or heard any sign of the miners, and all six men were considered missing and dead. ❻ All rescue efforts were eventually stopped. ❼ They simply switched off the drills and unplugged all the other equipment.

* misread 잘못 해석하다, 잘못 읽다

① weird and strange
② calm and peaceful
③ scary and mysterious
④ tragic and discouraging
⑤ monotonous and boring

UNDERSTAND DEEPLY

1 윗글의 내용과 일치하도록 빈칸에 알맞은 말을 쓰시오.

(1) Rescuers sent different equipment into the mine in order to __________ __________ __________ __________ __________ __________.

(2) Rescuers thought all the six miners were __________ __________ __________.

2 윗글의 내용을 바탕으로 다음 질문에 알맞은 답을 숫자로 쓰시오.

(1) How many holes were drilled into the mine? ______

(2) How many miners were trapped in the mine? ______

(3) How many rescue team members died during the search? ______

(4) How many signs of the missing miners were found? ______

READ CLOSELY

의미 단위로 끊어 읽고(/), 주어와 동사에 표시해 봅시다.

❶ Six holes were drilled into different areas of the mine.

❷ They sent oxygen sensors, cameras, and microphones down through plastic pipes to search for the six missing miners.

❸ During the search, the oxygen levels were misread and determined to be dangerously low.

❹ Three rescue team members, trying to dig the trapped miners out, were killed when a wall of the mine exploded.

❺ Rescuers never saw or heard any sign of the miners, and all six men were considered missing and dead. ↳ TIP

❻ All rescue efforts were eventually stopped.

❼ They simply switched off the drills and unplugged all the other equipment.

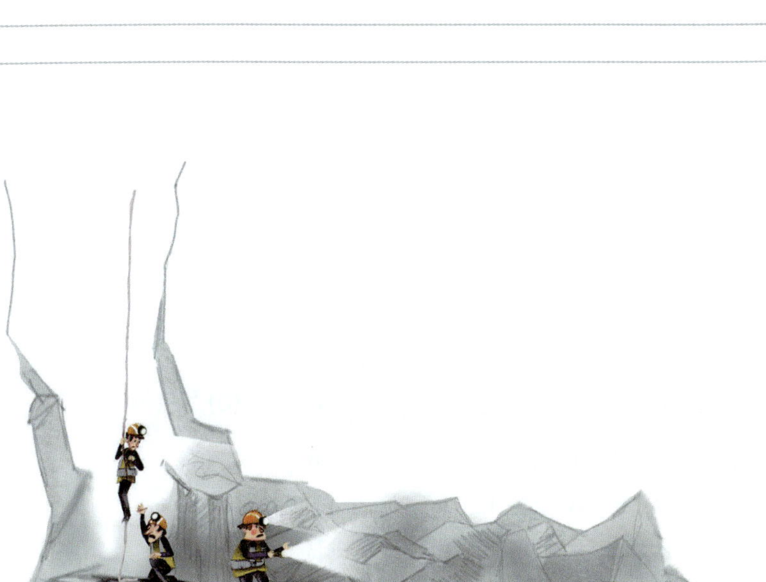

GRAMMAR TIP

형용사 목적격 보어가 쓰인 문장이 수동태 문장이 될 때, 형용사 목적격 보어는 「be + 과거분사」 뒤에 와요.

- They **considered** the miners **missing**.
- → The miners **were considered missing** (by them).

cf. 형용사 목적격 보어를 쓰는 동사에는 consider 외에도 make, keep, find, think, leave 등이 있어요.

- The chefs **keep** the kitchen **clean**.
- → The kitchen **is kept clean** (by the chefs).

WORDS

drill 드릴로 뚫다; 드릴
mine 광산
oxygen 산소
sensor 감지기, 센서
search for ～을 수색하다
missing 실종된
miner 광부
search 수색
determine 결정하다
rescue 구조
dig out ～을 파내다[구조하다]
trap 가두다
explode 폭발하다
rescuer 구출자[구조대원]
sign 자취, 기색
consider (～으로) 여기다
eventually 결국, 마침내
switch off 스위치를 끄다
unplug 플러그를 뽑다
equipment 장비, 기기
tragic 비극적인
discouraging 낙담하게 하는
cf. encouraging 용기를 북돋우는
monotonous 단조로운

1 세 단어가 서로 관련 있도록 빈칸에 알맞은 단어를 보기 에서 골라 쓰시오.

보기

| academic | drill | timeline | pleased |

(1) ____________ — schedule — calendar

(2) proud — nervous — ____________

(3) microphone — ____________ — sensor

(4) ____________ — honor — graduate

2 다음 단어를 괄호 안의 지시대로 바꿔 쓰시오.

(1) extend → ________________ (명사형)

(2) encouraging → ________________ (반의어)

(3) recognize → ________________ (명사형)

(4) registration → ________________ (동사형)

3 우리말 뜻에 해당하는 단어를 찾아 동그라미 하고 빈칸에 쓰시오.

G	I	S	Q	O	V	C	O	P	F	C	M
M	Y	V	A	H	R	I	W	E	L	D	I
F	P	A	S	S	I	O	N	A	T	E	N
T	K	Q	R	E	B	R	W	M	U	R	E
A	A	K	B	R	N	V	B	K	R	A	R
W	Y	F	W	T	A	C	G	U	Z	D	H
Z	K	Y	E	X	V	N	L	C	I	U	S
Y	L	D	T	Q	M	B	G	O	X	A	D
B	Z	N	R	D	I	L	I	E	S	T	R
I	F	T	D	E	A	D	L	I	N	E	P
C	W	H	B	O	P	D	B	C	P	D	H
A	Y	P	E	Q	U	I	P	M	E	N	T

(1) 조정하다 ________________

(2) 마감일 ________________

(3) 장비 ________________

(4) 광부 ________________

(5) 열정적인 ________________

(6) 동봉하다 ________________

4 주어진 단어를 사용하여 우리말 뜻에 해당하는 표현을 쓰시오. (중복 사용 가능)

(1) A뿐만 아니라 B도 _________________ (2) ~을 수색하다 _________________

(3) ~에 적응하다 _________________ (4) 제시간에 _________________

for	adjust	well	time
in	search	to	as

5 밑줄 친 부분이 어법에 맞으면 ○표 하고, 그렇지 않으면 바르게 고치시오.

(1) All six men were considered <u>missing and dead</u>.

(2) Dr. Wilkinson was <u>given</u> a gold medal to each of us.

(3) <u>We've been working</u> hard to keep this schedule for a month.

(4) Don't miss this great opportunity <u>improves</u> your writing.

6 우리말과 의미가 같도록 괄호 안의 동사를 알맞은 형태로 쓰시오.

(1) Amy는 누군가가 자신의 이름을 부르는 것을 들었다. (call)

→ Amy heard someone _________________ her name.

(2) 저는 이러한 종류의 질문을 하는 것이 어려울 수 있다는 것을 압니다. (ask)

→ I know it can be hard _________________ these kinds of questions.

(3) 우리는 여러분에게 이 프로그램을 이용할 것을 권합니다. (take)

→ We encourage you _________________ advantage of this program.

(4) 저는 이 프로젝트에 관련된 작업에 대한 당신의 우려를 이해합니다. (involve)

→ I understand your concern about the work _________________ in this project.

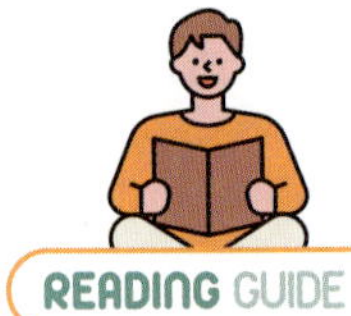

READING GUIDE

글을 읽으면서 반복 등장하는 명사 중 it이 가리킬 수 있는 것을 모두 찾아봅시다.

밑줄 친 부분이 가리키는 대상이 나머지 넷과 <u>다른</u> 것은?

❶ Some scientists succeeded in growing hamburger meat in their lab. **❷** They didn't grow ① a cow in the lab but just grew muscle tissue taken from a cow. **❸** They raised the tissue until there was enough to make ② a patty. **❹** Costing $325,000 to make, ③ it won't be showing up at a grocery store around you any time soon. **❺** So what does this mean for humans? **❻** If we grow meat in a lab, we won't have to kill animals anymore. **❼** In addition, ④ it could help us solve hunger problems around the world. **❽** If we grow as much meat as we want, we will be able to feed as many people as needed. **❾** Raising cows requires a lot of resources. **❿** Growing ⑤ meat could help the environment by saving time, energy, and space.

* tissue (세포들로 이루어진) 조직

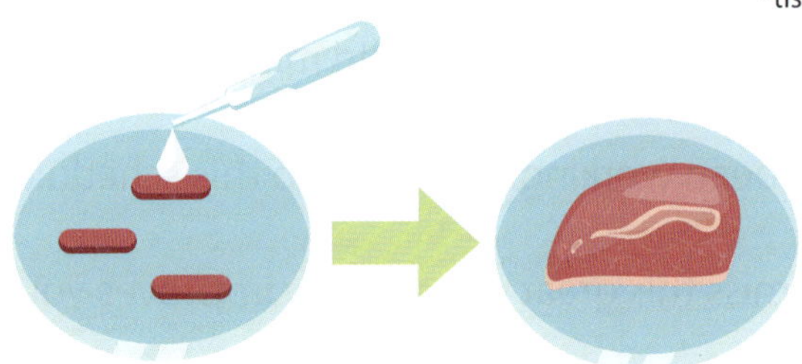

UNDERSTAND DEEPLY

1 윗글에 언급된 고기 배양의 기대 효과를 다음과 같이 정리할 때, 빈칸에 알맞은 말을 쓰시오.

- (1) __________ 을 죽일 필요가 없을 것이다.
- 전 세계의 (2) __________ 를 해결하는 데 도움을 줄 수 있다.
- (3) __________ 을 절약해서 (4) __________ 에 도움이 될 수 있다.

2 다음 질문에 알맞은 답을 윗글에서 찾아 문장을 완성하시오.

(1) Q: What did the scientists grow to make hamburger meat?
   A: They grew ________________________________.

(2) Q: How much does it cost to make meat?
   A: It costs __________ dollars.

READ CLOSELY

의미 단위로 끊어 읽고(/), 주어와 동사에 표시해 봅시다.

지문 듣기

❶ Some scientists succeeded in growing hamburger meat in their lab.

❷ They didn't grow a cow in the lab but just grew muscle tissue taken from a cow.

❸ They raised the tissue until there was enough to make a patty.

❹ Costing $325,000 to make, it won't be showing up at a grocery store around you any time soon.

❺ So what does this mean for humans?

❻ If we grow meat in a lab, we won't have to kill animals anymore.

❼ In addition, it could help us solve hunger problems around the world.

❽ If we grow as much meat as we want, we will be able to feed as many people as needed.

❾ Raising cows requires a lot of resources.

❿ Growing meat could help the environment by saving time, energy, and space.

TIP GRAMMAR

「help+목적어+목적격 보어」는 '~이 …하는 것을 돕다', '~이 …하도록 돕다'의 의미를 나타내요. 이때 동사 help의 목적격 보어로 동사 원형과 to부정사를 모두 쓸 수 있어요.

- She will **help** him (**to**) **get** a job.
- Fred **helped** us (**to**) **clean** the house.

WORDS

scientist 과학자
cf. science 과학
succeed in ~에 성공하다
grow 기르다[배양하다], 사육하다
(grow - grew - grown)
cf. growth 성장
meat 고기
lab 실험실 (laboratory)
muscle 근육
raise 기르다[배양하다], 사육하다
patty (고기) 패티
cost 비용이 (얼마가) 들다
show up 등장하다, 나타나다
grocery store 식료품점
cf. grocery 식료품
in addition 게다가
hunger 기아, 굶주림
cf. hungry 배고픈
feed ~에게 먹을 것을 주다
require ~을 필요로 하다
resource 자원
environment 환경
save 절약하다
space 공간

글을 읽으면서 반복 등장하는 두 대상을 찾고 간단히 설명해 봅시다.

밑줄 친 부분이 가리키는 대상이 나머지 넷과 <u>다른</u> 것은?

❶Conan was just a baby seal when Harry found ①<u>him</u> along the coast of New England. ❷Harry raised him in the harbor, but Conan lived freely. ❸②<u>He</u> went up and down the coast, and always came back to Harry. ❹Conan liked to play, and learned a lot of tricks. ❺But as ③<u>he</u> got bigger, some of his jokes, like jumping into fishermen's boats, became dangerous! ❻Harry didn't know what to do. ❼One day, Harry was made an offer by the New England Aquarium. ❽They offered to take Conan in the winter and return ④<u>him</u> in the spring. ❾Harry agreed. Then spring came. ❿The aquarium took the seal to the beach and let him go. ⓫But Harry couldn't see Conan anywhere. ⑤<u>He</u> got uneasy. ⓬Then two days later, a fisherman saw a seal on one side of his boat. ⓭Conan was back home again!

1 다음 (A)~(D)를 윗글의 흐름에 맞게 배열하시오.

> (A) Harry decided to send him to an Aquarium in the winter.
> (B) When spring came, Conan finally came back.
> (C) Harry raised Conan, a baby seal, in the harbor.
> (D) As Conan grew up, his jokes became dangerous.

_____ - _____ - _____ - _____

2 다음 중 윗글의 마지막 부분에서 Harry가 느꼈을 심경 변화로 가장 적절한 것은?

① uneasy → sad　　　　② uneasy → scared
③ uneasy → relieved　　④ uneasy → disappointed
⑤ uneasy → embarrassed

지문 듣기

1. Conan was just a baby seal when Harry found him along the coast of New England.

2. Harry raised him in the harbor, but Conan lived freely.

3. He went up and down the coast, and always came back to Harry.

4. Conan liked to play, and learned a lot of tricks.

5. But as he got bigger, some of his jokes, like jumping into fishermen's boats, became dangerous!

6. Harry didn't know **what to do**. →TIP

7. One day, Harry was made an offer by the New England Aquarium.

8. They offered to take Conan in the winter and return him in the spring.

9. Harry agreed. Then spring came.

10. The aquarium took the seal to the beach and let him go.

11. But Harry couldn't see Conan anywhere. He got uneasy.

12. Then two days later, a fisherman saw a seal on one side of his boat.

13. Conan was back home again!

GRAMMAR TIP

「의문사(what/which/where/when/who(m)/how)+to부정사」는 명사처럼 쓰이며 '무엇을/어느 것을/어디서/언제/누구를/어떻게 ~(해야)할지'라는 뜻을 나타내요. 「의문사+주어+should+동사원형」과 같은 의미예요.

• I'll show you **how to play** this game.
  어떻게 하는지

• We planned **where to go** and **what to do**.
  어디에 갈지 / 무엇을 할지

READING TIP

글에 등장하는 주요 대상들의 성별과 단수/복수를 확인하고, 각 선택지의 인칭대명사가 이 중 어느 대상을 가리키는지 앞뒤 문맥을 통해 파악해 보세요.

WORDS

seal 바다표범
along ~을 따라
coast 해안(가)
harbor 항구
go up and down 이리저리 다니다
trick 재주, 장난
fisherman 어부 (*pl.* fishermen)
make an offer 제안하다
cf. suggest 제안하다
aquarium 수족관
offer 제안하다; 제안
return 돌려주다
agree 동의하다
cf. disagree 동의하지 않다
uneasy 불안한, 걱정되는
cf. anxious 불안한, 걱정되는

READING **27**

READING GUIDE

글을 읽으면서 새로 등장하는 인물에 모두 동그라미를 쳐 봅시다.

밑줄 친 부분이 가리키는 대상이 나머지 넷과 다른 것은? (기출응용)

❶Two brothers were punished for stealing sheep. ❷They each were branded on the forehead with the letters ST for "sheep thief." ❸One brother was so embarrassed by this branding that he ran away; he was never heard from again. ❹①The other brother chose to stay in the village and tried to make up for his offenses. ❺Whenever there was any work to be done, ②the sheep thief came to help. ❻He never accepted pay for his good deeds, and ③he lived his life for others. ❼Many years later, a traveler came through the village. ❽Sitting at a sidewalk cafe, the traveler saw an old man with a strange brand on his forehead seated nearby. ❾He noticed that all the villagers who passed ④the man stopped to pay their respects. ❿The stranger asked one villager what the letters stood for. ⓫⑤The villager replied, "I don't know. It happened so long ago... but I think it stands for 'saint.'"

* **brand** 낙인을 찍다; 낙인

UNDERSTAND DEEPLY

1 괄호 안의 말을 바르게 배열하여 윗글의 요지를 완성하고, 우리말로 해석하시오.

A sheep thief ____.

(a saint / by / to change / making an effort / can be)

→ ____

2 다음 중 윗글의 **an old man**에 관한 내용과 일치하지 <u>않는</u> 것은?

① 양을 훔친 적이 있다.
② 이마에 ST라는 낙인이 찍혔다.
③ 낙인찍힌 것이 부끄러워 다른 마을로 도망쳤다.
④ 자신의 선행에 대한 대가를 받지 않았다.
⑤ 마을 사람들에게 존경받게 되었다.

READ CLOSELY

의미 단위로 끊어 읽고(/), 주어와 동사에 표시해 봅시다.

지문 듣기　　기출 원문 보기

❶ Two brothers were punished for stealing sheep.

❷ They each were branded on the forehead with the letters ST for "sheep thief."

❸ One brother was so embarrassed by this branding that he ran away; he was never heard from again.

❹ The other brother chose to stay in the village and tried to make up for his offenses.

❺ Whenever there was any work to be done, the sheep thief came to help.

❻ He never accepted pay for his good deeds, and he lived his life for others.

❼ Many years later, a traveler came through the village.

❽ Sitting at a sidewalk cafe, the traveler saw an old man with a strange brand on his forehead seated nearby.

❾ He noticed that all the villagers who passed the man stopped to pay their respects.

❿ The stranger asked one villager what the letters stood for.

⓫ The villager replied, "I don't know. It happened so long ago... but I think it stands for 'saint.'"

GRAMMAR TIP

to부정사를 목적어로 하는 동사에는 choose 외에도 want, hope, plan, wait, expect, prepare, decide, agree, manage, learn, offer, attempt 등이 있어요.

- We **decided to go** there by subway.
- I **am planning to travel** Europe.

cf. 동명사를 목적어로 하는 동사에는 enjoy, finish, mind, stop, give up, keep, avoid, quit 등이 있어요.

- Somi **enjoys dancing**.
- My uncle **quit smoking**.

WORDS

be punished for ~에 대해 벌을 받다

cf. punishment 벌

steal 훔치다

forehead 이마

be embarrassed by ~에 부끄러워하다[당황하다]

hear from ~에게서 소식을 듣다

make up for ~을 만회하다, ~에 대해 보상하다

offense 죄, 범죄

accept 받다, 받아들이다

deed 행위, 행동

cf. act 행위, 행동

sidewalk 보도, 인도

nearby 근처에

notice 알아차리다

villager 마을 사람

pay one's respect 존경을 표하다

cf. respect 존경(심); 존경하다

stranger 이방인

stand for ~을 의미하다[상징하다]

cf. symbolize 상징하다

saint 성인(聖人)

1 세 단어 중 서로 의미가 비슷한 두 개를 고르시오.

(1) uneasy —— anxious —— nearby

(2) raise —— require —— grow

(3) accept —— deed —— act

(4) suggest —— offer —— notice

2 우리말 뜻에 해당하는 단어가 되도록 주어진 철자를 바르게 배열하시오.

(1) 식료품   c r e r y g o   → ________________

(2) 존경   e p e t r c s   → ________________

(3) 자원   c r s e u o r e   → ________________

(4) 보도, 인도   i d l k e s w a   → ________________

3 우리말 뜻에 맞게 퍼즐을 완성한 후, 7번 단어의 우리말 뜻을 쓰시오.

ACROSS →

1. 어부   2. 근육

3. 환경   4. 이방인

5. 죄, 범죄   6. 이마

DOWN ↓

7. ________________

4 주어진 단어를 사용하여 우리말 뜻에 해당하는 표현을 쓰시오. (중복 사용 가능)

(1) ~을 의미하다 ___________________   (2) ~을 만회하다 ___________________

(3) ~에 성공하다 ___________________   (4) 등장하다 ___________________

show	in	for

make	stand	up	succeed

5 괄호 안의 동사를 알맞은 형태로 써서 문장을 완성하시오.

(1) The other brother chose _______________ (stay) in the village.

(2) _______________ (sit) at a sidewalk cafe, the traveler saw an old man.

(3) Growing meat could help us _______________ (solve) hunger problems.

(4) Some scientists grew muscle tissue _______________ (take) from a cow.

6 우리말과 의미가 같도록 괄호 안의 말을 이용하여 문장을 완성하시오.

(1) Harry는 무엇을 해야 할지를 몰랐다. (what, do)

→ Harry didn't know ______________________________.

(2) Harry는 뉴잉글랜드 수족관으로부터 제안을 받았다. (make, an offer)

→ Harry ______________________________ by the New England Aquarium.

(3) 그 남자를 지나가던 모든 마을 사람들이 존경을 표하기 위해 멈췄다. (stop, pay)

→ All the villagers who passed the man ______________________________ their respects.

(4) 고기를 배양하는 것은 자원을 절약함으로써 환경에 도움이 될 수 있다. (by, save)

→ Growing meat could help the environment ______________________________ resources.

READING 28

글을 읽으면서 빈칸에 들어갈 말의 직접적인 단서가 되는 문장을 찾아 밑줄을 그어 봅시다.

다음 빈칸에 들어갈 말로 가장 적절한 것은? (기출응용)

❶ We are more successful when we ___________________.
❷ For example, doctors who make a diagnosis while in a positive mood show almost three times more intelligence than doctors in a neutral state. ❸ Also, they make correct diagnoses that are 19 percent faster. ❹ Salespeople who are positive sell more than those who are negative. ❺ Students who are made to feel happy before taking math exams do much better than their neutral peers. ❻ It has been proven that our brains are programmed to perform best not when we are feeling negative or neutral, but when we are feeling positive.

* diagnosis 진단 (*pl.* diagnoses)

① focus on a specific goal
② get along well with others
③ are the best at what we do
④ are happier and more positive
⑤ feel more inspired and creative

1 윗글에서 예로 제시된 사람들을 모두 찾아 쓰시오.

____

2 다음 중 윗글의 내용과 일치하는 것은?
① 중립적인 기분 상태에서 성과를 가장 잘 낼 수 있다.
② 기분이 좋은 상태에서는 정확한 판단을 내리는 것이 어렵다.
③ 기분 상태가 뇌의 수행 능력에 영향을 줄 수 있다.

3 윗글의 내용을 다음과 같이 요약할 때, 빈칸에 알맞은 말을 쓰시오.
People who are in a _________ mood tend to be more _________ in their job than those who are in a _________ or _________ mood.

지문 듣기   기출 원문 보기

❶ We are more successful when we ________________________.

❷ For example, doctors who make a diagnosis while in a positive mood show almost three times more intelligence than doctors in a neutral state.

❸ Also, they make correct diagnoses that are 19 percent faster.

❹ Salespeople who are positive sell more than those who are negative.

❺ Students who are made to feel happy before taking math exams do much better than their neutral peers.

❻ It has been proven that our brains are programmed to perform best not when we are feeling negative or neutral, but when we are feeling positive.

GRAMMAR TIP

사역동사 make가 쓰인 문장이 수동태 문장으로 바뀔 때, 목적격 보어인 동사원형은 to부정사 형태로 바뀌어요.

- Dad **made** me **clean** the desk.
  - → I **was made to clean** the desk by Dad.
- She **made** us **stay** awake all night.
  - → We **were made to stay** awake all night by her.

READING TIP

빈칸이 있는 문장은 주로 글의 주제에 해당하며, 빈칸에 들어갈 내용은 글 전반에 같거나 유사한 표현으로 반복해 등장하는 경우가 많아요.

WORDS

successful 성공적인, 성공한
make a diagnosis 진단하다
cf. diagnose 진단하다
positive 긍정적인
cf. optimistic 낙천적인
mood 기분
intelligence 지능
neutral 중립적인
state 상태
salesperson 영업사원, 판매원
(*pl.* salespeople)
negative 부정적인
peer 또래 친구, 동료
prove 증명하다
cf. proof 증거
perform 수행하다
cf. performance 수행, 성과
focus on ~에 집중하다
specific 특정한, 구체적인
get along with ~와 잘 지내다
inspired 영감을 받은

READING 29

READING GUIDE

빈칸이 있는 문장의 내용에
유의하며 글의 중심 소재를
파악해 봅시다.

다음 빈칸에 들어갈 말로 가장 적절한 것은? (기출응용)

❶A study suggests a way to make negotiations easier. ❷In this study, students negotiated the purchase of a motorcycle over an online messenger. ❸It was shown that negotiations went smoother when students believed they were far apart from the seller. ❹They were more agreeable than those who believed they were only a few feet away. ❺The researchers explained that when people are farther apart, they consider factors in a different way. ❻They focus more on the main issues rather than other less important points. ❼So, the researchers recommend that next time you have to achieve a difficult deal, it may be helpful to ________________________.

① set a clear time limit
② begin from a distance
③ be close to each other
④ pay attention to details
⑤ deal with smaller problems first

UNDERSTAND DEEPLY

1 윗글의 첫 문장에서 글의 소재를 찾아 우리말로 쓰시오.

____

2 윗글의 연구 결과와 일치하면 T, 그렇지 않으면 F를 쓰시오.

(1) Students who thought they were close to the seller were more agreeable. ______

(2) People give less attention to main factors in negotiating when they are farther apart. ______

3 윗글의 내용을 다음과 같이 요약할 때, 빈칸에 알맞은 말을 쓰시오.

When you negotiate, you can achieve a deal easier with people who are ________ ________ from you.

지문 듣기   기출 원문 보기

❶ A study suggests a way to make negotiations easier.

❷ In this study, students negotiated the purchase of a motorcycle over an online messenger.

❸ It was shown that negotiations went smoother when students believed they were far apart from the seller. → TIP

❹ They were more agreeable than those who believed they were only a few feet away.

❺ The researchers explained that when people are farther apart, they consider factors in a different way.

❻ They focus more on the main issues rather than other less important points.

❼ So, the researchers recommend that next time you have to achieve a difficult deal, it may be helpful to ________________________.

GRAMMAR (TIP)

문장의 주어로 that절이 쓰여 주어가 너무 길어지면, 주어 자리에 가주어 it을 대신 쓰고 진주어인 that절은 뒤로 보내요.

- **That** Kevin will win the game tomorrow is certain.
  → **It** is certain **that** Kevin will win the game tomorrow.
- **It** is no wonder **that** Kevin won the game yesterday.

WORDS

suggest 시사하다, 넌지시 나타내다
negotiation 협상
negotiate 협상하다
purchase 구매
smooth 순조로운, 매끄러운
far apart 멀리 떨어져
agreeable 흔쾌히 응하는
cf. agree 동의하다, 응하다
farther 더 멀리
consider 고려하다
factor 요인, 요소
main 주요한
rather than ~보다는 (오히려)
recommend 권하다, 추천하다
achieve 성취하다, 이루다
deal 거래
limit 제한, 한계
from a distance 멀리서
cf. distance 거리
pay attention to ~에 주의를 기울이다
cf. attention 주의, 주목
deal with ~을 처리하다

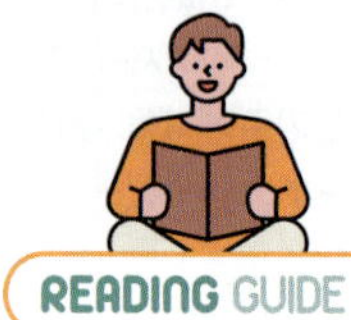

READING GUIDE

빈칸이 있는 문장의 내용에 유의하며 글의 중심 소재를 파악해 봅시다.

다음 빈칸에 들어갈 말로 가장 적절한 것은? (기출응용)

❶Judgments about flavor are often affected by predictions based on the ______________ of the food. ❷For example, strawberry-flavored foods are expected to be red. ❸However, if that food is colored green, it would be difficult to identify the flavor as strawberry. ❹That's because green foods are usually related to flavors such as lime or melon. ❺The degree of the color also affects the way we identify flavor. ❻A stronger color may give an impression of a stronger flavor in a product, even if the stronger color results from adding more food coloring. ❼Texture can also lead to misunderstandings. ❽A thicker product may be considered richer tasting or stronger even though it was simply made thicker with thickening substances.

* coloring 색소

① origin   ② recipe   ③ ingredients
④ appearance   ⑤ size

UNDERSTAND DEEPLY

1 윗글의 내용을 네 부분으로 나눌 때, 각 부분의 첫 두 단어를 쓰시오.

첫 번째 부분	Judgments about
두 번째 부분	(1) ______________
세 번째 부분	(2) ______________
네 번째 부분	(3) ______________

2 윗글의 내용과 일치하도록 괄호 안에서 알맞은 말을 고르시오.

The way food [looks / smells] can affect how people judge its [texture / taste].

3 다음 중 윗글에서 맛을 판단하는 데 영향을 미치는 요소로 언급되지 <u>않은</u> 것을 <u>모두</u> 고르면?

① color   ② smell   ③ texture   ④ price

READ CLOSELY

의미 단위로 끊어 읽고(/), 주어와 동사에 표시해 봅시다.

지문 듣기　기출 원문 보기

양보의 접속사에는 '〜에도 불구하고', '〜이긴 하지만'(사실)을 의미하는 although, though, even though 등과 '〜이라 할지라도'(가정)라는 뜻의 even if가 있어요.

- **Even though** there are problems, she won't be serious.
- I will buy his new book **even if** it is expensive.

cf. in spite of와 despite도 '〜에도 불구하고'를 의미하지만 전치사이므로 뒤에 명사(구)가 와요.

- **In spite of** rain, they arrived on time.

❶ Judgments about flavor are often affected by predictions based on the _______________ of the food.

❷ For example, strawberry-flavored foods are expected to be red.

❸ However, if that food is colored green, it would be difficult to identify the flavor as strawberry.

❹ That's because green foods are usually related to flavors such as lime or melon.

❺ The degree of the color also affects the way we identify flavor.

❻ A stronger color may give an impression of a stronger flavor in a product, even if the stronger color results from adding more food coloring. → TIP

❼ Texture can also lead to misunderstandings.

❽ A thicker product may be considered richer tasting or stronger even though it was simply made thicker with thickening substances. → TIP

WORDS

judgment 판단
cf. judge 판단하다; 판사
flavor 맛; 맛을 내다
affect 영향을 미치다
cf. influence 영향을 미치다
prediction 예측
cf. predict 예측하다
based on 〜에 근거한
expect 예상하다, 기대하다
color 색을 입히다; 색깔
identify 식별하다, 확인하다
be related to 〜와 관계가 있다
degree 정도
impression 인상, 느낌
result from 〜에서 비롯되다
cf. result in 〜을 초래하다
texture 질감
lead to 〜으로 이어지다
thick 걸쭉한, 진한
consider (〜으로) 여기다
taste 맛이 나다; 맛
thicken 걸쭉하게 만들다
substance 물질
appearance 겉모습, 외관

REVIEW TIME

1 다음 동사의 우리말 뜻을 <보기>에서 골라 번호를 쓰고, 명사형으로 바꿔 쓰시오.

<보기>

① 협상하다   ② 예측하다   ③ 판단하다   ④ 증명하다

(1) predict ◯ → _____________   (2) prove ◯ → _____________

(3) judge ◯ → _____________   (4) negotiate ◯ → _____________

2 서로 의미가 비슷한 단어끼리 연결하시오.

(1) taste   (2) affect   (3) positive   (4) consider

① optimistic   ② influence   ③ believe   ④ flavor

3 우리말 뜻에 맞게 주어진 철자로 시작하는 단어 퍼즐을 완성하시오.

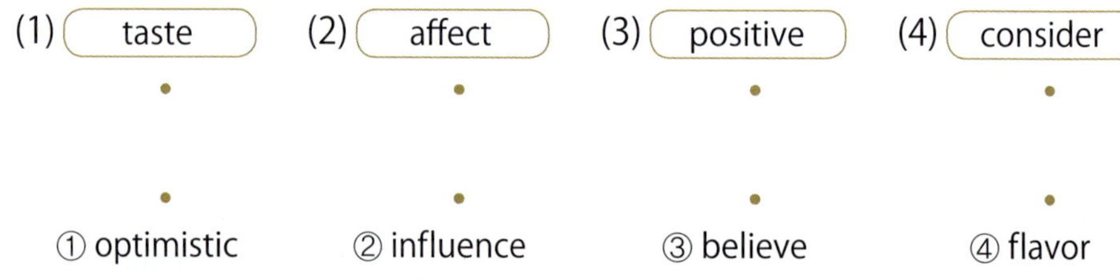

ACROSS →

1. 걸쭉한, 진한

4. 겉모습, 외관

6. 중립적인

DOWN ↓

2. 식별하다, 확인하다

3. 질감

5. 예상하다, 기대하다

4 주어진 단어를 사용하여 우리말 뜻에 해당하는 표현을 쓰시오. (중복 사용 가능)

(1) ~에 집중하다 _________________

(2) ~에 기초한 _________________

(3) 멀리서 _________________

(4) ~와 관계가 있다 _________________

| to | be | from | based |
| on | a distance | related | focus |

5 네모 안에서 어법에 맞는 것을 고르시오.

(1) Students who are made feel / to feel happy do much better.

(2) Judgments about flavor is / are often affected by the appearance of the food.

(3) A thicker product is considered richer tasting even though / in spite of it was simply made thicker with substances.

6 어법상 <u>틀린</u> 부분을 찾아 바르게 고치시오.

(1) Studies suggest a way makes negotiations easier.

(2) It would be difficult identify the flavor as strawberry.

(3) The degree of the color affects the way how we identify flavor.

(4) It has been proven what our brains perform best when we are feeling positive.

Play Time

Find the side views A, B, and C for object 5.

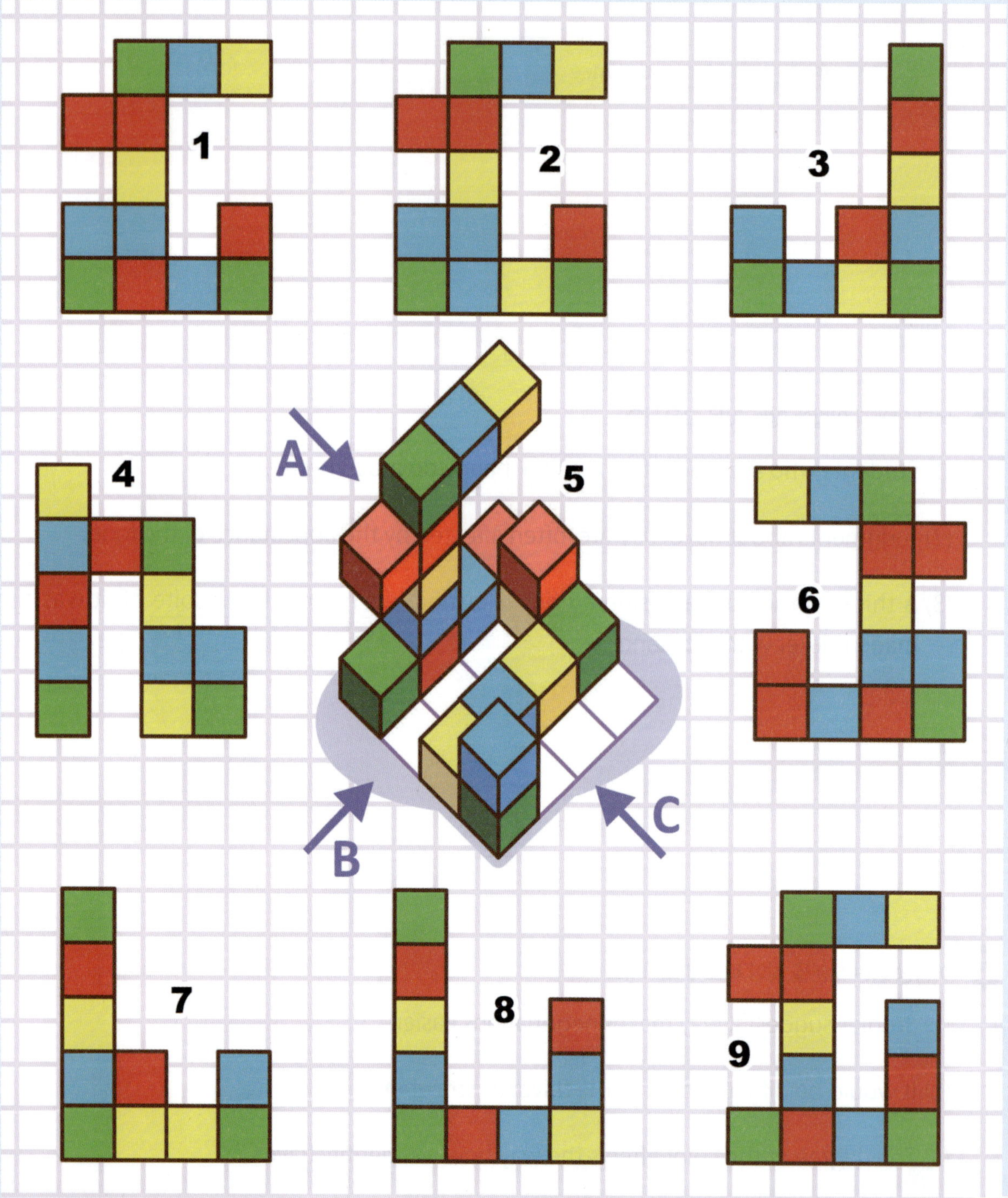

PART 4

흐름 파악하기

 **글의 흐름이란 뭔가요?**

글이 논리적으로 자연스럽게 이어지는 것을 말해요.

 **어떻게 공부 하나요?**

글의 주제와 구조, 문장 간의 논리적 관계를 파악하여 글의 전체적인 흐름이 자연스러운지 판단하는 연습을 해요. 연결어, 대명사, 지시어 등의 연결고리도 주의 깊게 살펴보세요.

 **시험에 어떻게 나오나요?**

다음 네 가지 유형으로 출제돼요.

- ✓ **연결어 넣기** — UNIT 10
- ✓ **무관한 문장 찾기** — UNIT 11
- ✓ **글의 순서 찾기** — UNIT 12
- ✓ **주어진 문장 넣기** — UNIT 13

READING 31

READING GUIDE

도입부에서 글의 중심 소재를 파악하고, 문맥을 살피며 글을 읽어 봅시다.

다음 글의 빈칸 (A), (B)에 들어갈 말로 가장 적절한 것은? 기출응용

[1] Many news stories report that breakfast is the most important meal of the day. [2] According to those stories, we should have the biggest meal for breakfast and eat less as the day passes by. [3] This is because breakfast provides the main energy for both your body and brain all day long. [4] _______(A)_______, this idea can reduce the worth of lunch and dinner. [5] Having a big breakfast is not a good rule for everyone. [6] People's lifestyle and health condition differ from one another. [7] Lunch and dinner can also give quality energy to people. [8] _______(B)_______, it is the kind of food people eat for each meal — rather than just increasing the amount of food for breakfast — that plays an important role in improving one's health.

	(A)		(B)
①	However	······	Similarly
②	However	······	Therefore
③	In contrast	······	Nevertheless
④	For example	······	Similarly
⑤	For example	······	Therefore

UNDERSTAND DEEPLY

1 윗글의 내용과 일치하면 T, 그렇지 않으면 F를 쓰시오.

(1) News stories report we should have the same amount of food for each meal. ______

(2) Lunch and dinner provide the main energy for our body all day. ______

2 윗글의 마지막 문장에서 뉴스 기사들과 필자가 중요하다고 강조하는 요소를 각각 찾아 쓰시오.

(1) 뉴스 기사들: ____

(2) 필자: ____

READ CLOSELY

의미 단위로 끊어 읽고(/), 주어와 동사에 표시해 봅시다.

❶ Many news stories report that breakfast is the most important meal of the day.

❷ According to those stories, we should have the biggest meal for breakfast and eat less as the day passes by.

❸ This is because breakfast provides the main energy for both your body and brain all day long.

❹ ________________, this idea can reduce the worth of lunch and dinner.

❺ Having a big breakfast is not a good rule for everyone. → TIP

❻ People's lifestyle and health condition differ from one another.

❼ Lunch and dinner can also give quality energy to people.

❽ ________________, it is the kind of food people eat for each meal — rather than just increasing the amount of food for breakfast — that plays an important role in improving one's health.

GRAMMAR TIP

동명사(구) 주어는 단수 취급하므로 동사를 단수형으로 써야 해요.

- **Washing** hands *helps* you to stay healthy.
- **Keeping** a diary *is* a good habit.
- **Exercising** every day *was* on my to-do list.

READING TIP

자주 나오는 연결어

- 역접: However, Nevertheless, Nonetheless
- 대조: In contrast, On the other hand
- 결론: Therefore, Thus, As a result

WORDS

report 보도하다

meal 식사, 끼니

according to ~에 따르면

pass by (시간이) 지나가다

provide A for B A를 B에게 제공하다

cf. provide B with A A를 B에게 제공하다

all day long 하루 종일

reduce 감소시키다, 줄이다

cf. decrease 감소시키다, 줄이다

worth 가치

cf. worthwhile 가치 있는

condition 상태

differ from ~와 다르다

quality 양질의

increase 증가시키다, 늘리다

amount 양

play a role 역할을 하다

improve 증진하다, 개선하다

32

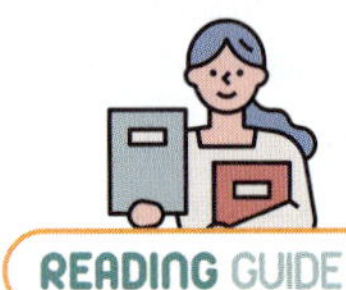

READING GUIDE

도입부에서 글의 중심 소재를
파악하고, 문맥을 살피며 글을
읽어 봅시다.

다음 글의 빈칸 (A), (B)에 들어갈 말로 가장 적절한 것은? (기출응용)

❶You can do a number of things to keep the air in your home clean. ❷Most of them don't require much effort. ❸House plants are by far the best way to filter indoor air. ❹_______(A)_______, spider plants love to absorb carbon dioxide, and they are easy to grow. ❺In fact, they grow so thick that before long you'll have a huge number of little baby spider plants. ❻Other house plants also absorb different kinds of air pollutants. ❼They can reduce air pollution by changing carbon dioxide back into oxygen. ❽_______(B)_______, remember that, if you don't take good care of the plants, they can be excellent breeding grounds for harmful bugs. ❾If you want plants in your house, you should be prepared to take care of them.

* spider plant 자주달개비 ** carbon dioxide 이산화 탄소 *** pollutant 오염 물질

	(A)		(B)
①	Similarly	……	Moreover
②	As a result	……	However
③	As a result	……	Moreover
④	For example	……	In other words
⑤	For example	……	However

UNDERSTAND DEEPLY

1 윗글의 내용을 다음과 같이 정리할 때, 빈칸에 알맞은 말을 쓰시오.

소재	실내 식물은 (1)__________를 정화하는 가장 좋은 방법임
예시	자주달개비는 (2)__________를 잘 흡수하고 기르기 쉬움
부연	실내 식물은 (3)__________를 (4)__________로 바꿈으로써 (5)__________을 감소시킴
유의점	식물은 (6)__________의 번식지가 될 수 있으므로 잘 돌볼 준비가 되어 있어야 함

2 윗글의 내용을 다음과 같이 요약할 때, 빈칸에 알맞은 단어를 쓰시오.
Growing __________ __________ is the best way to keep __________ __________ clean.

READ CLOSELY

의미 단위로 끊어 읽고(/), 주어와 동사에 표시해 봅시다.

지문 듣기　　기출 원문 보기

① You can do a number of things to keep the air in your home clean.

② Most of them don't require much effort.

③ House plants are by far the best way to filter indoor air.

④ _______________, spider plants love to absorb carbon dioxide, and they are easy to grow.

⑤ In fact, they grow so thick that before long you'll have a huge number of little baby spider plants.

⑥ Other house plants also absorb different kinds of air pollutants.

⑦ They can reduce air pollution by changing carbon dioxide back into oxygen.

⑧ _______________, remember that, if you don't take good care of the plants, they can be excellent breeding grounds for harmful bugs.

⑨ If you want plants in your house, you should be prepared to take care of them.

WORDS

require ~을 필요로 하다
effort 노력, 수고
house plant 실내 식물
by far 단연(코)
filter 거르다, 여과하다
indoor 실내의
cf. outdoor 실외의
absorb 흡수하다
grow 기르다, 자라다
thick 무성하게, 빽빽하게
before long 머지않아, 곧
different 다양한
pollution 오염
cf. pollute 오염시키다
oxygen 산소
take care of ~을 돌보다
breeding ground 번식지
cf. breed 번식하다
harmful 해로운
cf. harmless 무해한
bug 벌레

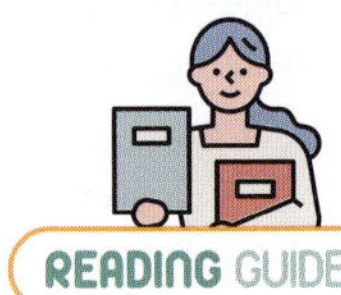

READING GUIDE

도입부에서 글의 중심 소재를 파악하고, 문맥을 살피며 글을 읽어 봅시다.

다음 글의 빈칸 (A), (B)에 들어갈 말로 가장 적절한 것은?

❶ Most people would agree that if you planned a big project for your company but failed in a big way, you could lose your job. ❷ That's no longer always the case. ❸ _______(A)_______, take Virgin Airlines. ❹ The airline wanted to design a new kind of seat for business class that would allow passengers to lean back so that they could sleep comfortably. ❺ The man who led the project was Joe Ferry. ❻ _______(B)_______, tests showed that passengers didn't like his design. ❼ To make matters worse, British Airways developed much better seats that could actually lie flat, and Virgin lost out. ❽ But Virgin Airlines was smart enough to keep Joe Ferry. ❾ A few years later, he came up with a great design that worked nicely for the company, and it increased Virgin's sales. ❿ If the company had fired him, it would have resulted in a big loss.

	(A)		(B)
①	That is	⋯⋯	Therefore
②	That is	⋯⋯	In addition
③	For instance	⋯⋯	In addition
④	For instance	⋯⋯	However
⑤	In other words	⋯⋯	However

UNDERSTAND DEEPLY

1 괄호 안의 말을 바르게 배열하여 윗글의 요지를 완성하고, 우리말로 해석하시오.

Give ____.

(to people / failed / another chance / who / a loss / caused / and)

→ ____

2 윗글의 내용과 일치하면 T, 그렇지 않으면 F를 쓰시오.

(1) Joe Ferry designed a seat that could actually lie flat. ______

(2) Virgin Airlines didn't fire Joe although he failed a project. ______

READ CLOSELY

의미 단위로 끊어 읽고(/), 주어와 동사에 표시해 봅시다.

➊ Most people would agree that if you planned a big project for your company but failed in a big way, you could lose your job.

➋ That's no longer always the case.

➌ _______________, take Virgin Airlines.

➍ The airline wanted to design a new kind of seat for business class that would allow passengers to lean back so that they could sleep comfortably.

➎ The man who led the project was Joe Ferry.

➏ _______________, tests showed that passengers didn't like his design.

➐ To make matters worse, British Airways developed much better seats that could actually lie flat, and Virgin lost out.

➑ But Virgin Airlines was smart enough to keep Joe Ferry.

➒ A few years later, he came up with a great design that worked nicely for the company, and it increased Virgin's sales.

➓ If the company had fired him, it would have resulted in a big loss.

GRAMMAR TIP

가정법 과거는 현재 사실과 반대되는 가정을 하는 것으로, '만약 ~한다면 …할 텐데'를 의미해요. 「if+주어+동사의 과거형, 주어+조동사의 과거형+동사원형」 형태로 표현해요.

- **If** he **lived** near my house, we **could meet** more often.

이때 if절의 동사가 be동사이면 수와 인칭에 관계없이 were로 써요.

- **If** I _were_ you, I **wouldn't go** there.

READING TIP

자주 나오는 연결어

- 예시: For example, For instance
- 부연: Similarly, Moreover, In addition, That is, In other words

---

WORDS

in a big way 크게, 굉장히

no longer 더 이상 ~ 아닌

allow (~하도록) 허락하다

passenger 승객

lean back 뒤로 젖히다

comfortably 편안하게

lead 이끌다 (lead-led-led)

to make matters worse 설상가상으로

develop 개발하다

flat 평평하게

lose out 손해를 보다

come up with ~을 생각해 내다

sale 매출, 판매

fire 해고하다

cf. hire 고용하다

result in ~을 초래하다

loss 손실

1 우리말 뜻에 해당하는 단어가 되도록 주어진 철자를 바르게 배열하시오.

(1) 흡수하다   b a s r b o   → ________________

(2) 필요로 하다   q i e u r e r   → ________________

(3) 승객   e a s p s n e g r   → ________________

(4) 산소   x o e y n g   → ________________

2 서로 의미가 반대인 단어끼리 연결하시오.

(1) fire   (2) harmful   (3) indoor   (4) reduce

① outdoor   ② hire   ③ increase   ④ harmless

3 우리말 뜻에 해당하는 단어를 찾아 동그라미 하고 빈칸에 쓰시오.

Y	C	B	Z	P	D	U	B	C	E	O	L
E	S	O	J	T	A	O	N	W	O	L	Y
T	W	N	M	K	R	F	R	Y	X	M	H
S	O	G	P	F	P	S	T	O	I	N	O
B	R	T	N	O	O	I	I	H	P	Y	N
L	T	S	V	T	L	R	Q	R	D	K	D
S	H	X	K	A	L	L	T	U	P	F	H
F	U	Z	U	E	S	E	U	A	Q	R	Y
L	O	Q	D	B	N	V	C	T	B	H	N
A	E	T	Z	E	I	P	I	D	I	L	L
T	B	E	J	H	K	W	X	A	L	O	Y
X	A	G	L	U	H	R	G	B	U	G	N

(1) 편안하게 ________________

(2) 평평하게 ________________

(3) 가치 ________________

(4) 오염 ________________

(5) 벌레 ________________

(6) 양질의 ________________

4 주어진 단어를 사용하여 우리말 뜻에 해당하는 표현을 쓰시오. (한 번씩만 쓸 것)

(1) ~을 초래하다 ________________   (2) ~을 생각해 내다 ________________

(3) ~을 돌보다 ________________   (4) ~와 다르다 ________________

| come | differ | with | of | in |
| care | up | result | from | take |

5 네모 안에서 어법에 맞는 것을 고르시오.

(1) Having a big breakfast is / are not a good rule for everyone.

(2) House plants are by far the good / the best way to filter indoor air.

(3) It is the kind of food that play / plays an important role in improving one's health.

(4) You can do a number of / the number of things to keep the air in your home clean.

6 우리말과 의미가 같도록 괄호 안의 동사 또는 조동사를 알맞은 형태로 쓰시오.

(1) Virgin 항공사는 Joe Ferry를 계속 데리고 있을 만큼 충분히 현명했다. (keep)

→ Virgin Airlines was smart enough ________________ Joe Ferry.

(2) 만약 회사를 위한 큰 프로젝트에 실패하면 여러분은 일자리를 잃을 수도 있다. (can)

→ If you failed a big project for your company, you ________________ lose your job.

(3) 그 항공사는 승객들이 뒤로 젖힐 수 있게 할 좌석을 디자인하기를 원했다. (lean)

→ The airline wanted to design a seat that would allow passengers ________________ back.

(4) 실내 식물들은 이산화 탄소를 다시 산소로 바꿈으로써 공기 오염을 줄일 수 있다. (change)

→ House plants can reduce air pollution by ________________ carbon dioxide back into oxygen.

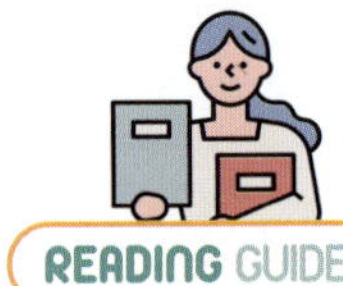

READING GUIDE

글의 핵심어를 모두 찾고, 앞뒤 문맥에 유의하여 글을 읽어 봅시다.

다음 글에서 전체 흐름과 관계 없는 문장은? (기출응용)

❶Have you ever thrown the peeled potato into the bin and the peelings into the pot? ❷How about sending an email without attaching a file? ❸① Mistakes like these always happen. ❹② That's because our brains have to respond to thousands of different stimuli all the time when we're awake. ❺③ Even though a second earlier we wrote that we were attaching a file to the email, the very next second our brain orders our fingers to send the email without the file. ❻④ It's dangerous to open some files from an unknown source. ❼⑤ Sometimes we don't even realize our mistake until we get an email from the receiver pointing it out.

* stimulus 자극 (*pl.* stimuli)

UNDERSTAND DEEPLY

1 다음 중 윗글의 중심 소재로 가장 적절한 것은?
① 끊임없이 다양한 자극에 반응하는 뇌
② 실수를 줄이고 주의력을 높이는 방법
③ 이메일 전송 전 첨부 파일 확인의 필요성

2 윗글의 내용을 다음과 같이 요약할 때, 빈칸에 알맞은 단어를 쓰시오.
The reason we often make ___________ is because our brains must ___________ to a variety of stimuli every moment.

3 윗글에 예로 제시된 실수들을 찾아 우리말로 쓰시오.
- ______________________________________
- ______________________________________

READ CLOSELY

의미 단위로 끊어 읽고(/), 주어와 동사에 표시해 봅시다.

지문 듣기　기출 원문 보기

❶ **Have** you ever **thrown** the peeled potato into the bin and the peelings into the pot?

❷ How about sending an email without attaching a file?

❸ Mistakes like these always happen.

❹ That's because our brains have to respond to thousands of different stimuli all the time when we're awake.

❺ Even though a second earlier we wrote that we were attaching a file to the email, the very next second our brain orders our fingers to send the email without the file.

❻ It's dangerous to open some files from an unknown source.

❼ Sometimes we don't even realize our mistake until we get an email from the receiver pointing it out.

READING GUIDE

도입부에서 글의 중심 소재를 파악하고, 앞뒤 문맥에 유의하여 글을 읽어 봅시다.

다음 글에서 전체 흐름과 관계 없는 문장은? (기출응용)

❶Both mammals and birds are noisy creatures. ❷They commonly use sounds for announcing their presence and for communicating with each other. ❸But birds are far better at it. ❹Birds also make sounds to warn other birds that a predator is nearby. ❺① Many mammals produce different sounds for different reasons, but few mammals can make as many different kinds of sounds as birds. ❻② With the exception of human beings, mammals in general are not musical and there is little evidence that they try to be. ❼③ Mammals differ depending on where they live, how they move around, and what they eat. ❽④ Some mammals make loud sounds, but few mammals sing, apart from human beings and perhaps whales. ❾⑤ Yet many birds are famous for their songs, and some of the most wonderful songsters are the ones we encounter most often.

(UNDERSTAND DEEPLY)

1 빈칸에 알맞은 단어를 윗글에서 찾아 쓰시오.

Both birds and mammals communicate with each other by using __________, but __________ are much more musical than __________.

2 윗글의 내용과 일치하면 T, 그렇지 않으면 F를 쓰시오.

(1) Many mammals can make as many different kinds of sounds as birds. ______

(2) Not all mammals make loud sounds or sing. ______

3 윗글의 세 번째 문장에서 it이 가리키는 바를 우리말로 쓰시오.

____

지문 듣기　　기출 원문 보기

❶ Both mammals and birds are noisy creatures.

❷ They commonly use sounds for announcing their presence and for communicating with each other.

❸ But birds are far better at it.

❹ Birds also make sounds to warn other birds that a predator is nearby.

❺ Many mammals produce different sounds for different reasons, but few mammals can make as many different kinds of sounds as birds.
　↳ TIP

❻ With the exception of human beings, mammals in general are not musical and there is little evidence that they try to be.
　↳ TIP

❼ Mammals differ depending on where they live, how they move around, and what they eat.

❽ Some mammals make loud sounds, but few mammals sing, apart from human beings and perhaps whales.
　↗ TIP

❾ Yet many birds are famous for their songs, and some of the most wonderful songsters are the ones we encounter most often.

GRAMMAR TIP

few는 셀 수 있는 명사 앞에서 '(수가) 거의 없는'이라는 부정의 의미를 나타내요.
• I have **few** books to read.

little은 셀 수 없는 명사 앞에서 '(양이) 거의 없는'이라는 부정의 의미를 나타내요.
• I have **little** money left.

WORDS

mammal 포유류
noisy 시끄러운, 떠들썩한
cf. quiet 조용한
creature 동물, 생물
cf. create 창조하다
commonly 흔히
cf. common 흔히 있는, 일반적인
announce 알리다
presence 존재
cf. present 존재하는, 참석한
communicate 의사소통하다
be good at ~에 능숙하다
warn 경고하다
predator 포식자
nearby 근처에
with the exception of ~을 제외하고
in general 일반적으로, 보통
evidence 증거
differ 다르다
cf. different (서로) 다른
depending on ~에 따라
loud 소리가 큰
apart from ~을 제외하고
be famous for ~으로 유명하다
songster 명금(고운 소리로 우는 새)
encounter 마주치다

READING **36**

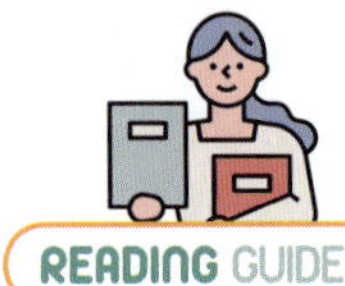

READING GUIDE

첫 문장에서 글의 핵심어를
찾고, 앞뒤 문맥에 유의하여
글을 읽어 봅시다.

다음 글에서 전체 흐름과 관계 없는 문장은? (기출응용)

❶It is impossible to imagine a modern city without glass. ❷① We expect our buildings to protect us from the weather; this is what they are for, after all. ❸② And yet, when it comes to a new home or workplace, one of the first questions people ask is, "How much natural light is there?" ❹③ Modern glass buildings satisfy these different desires: the desire to be protected from bad weather, such as the wind, the cold, and the rain; the desire to be secure from the invasion of thieves; and, at the same time, the desire not to live in darkness. ❺④ Although glass is a reasonable building material, glass engineering is expensive and it causes the glass building market to be exclusive. ❻⑤ Glass makes our lives, which are spent mostly indoors, much brighter and more delightful.

UNDERSTAND
DEEPLY

1 다음 질문에 알맞은 답을 윗글에서 찾아 문장을 완성하시오.

Q: What is one of the first questions people ask when they want a new home?

A: It is "______________________________?"

2 윗글의 내용과 일치하도록 괄호 안에서 알맞은 말을 고르시오.

(1) It is [dangerous / reasonable] to use glass for building houses.

(2) Modern glass buildings let us live [brighter / darker] lives indoors.

3 윗글의 내용을 다음과 같이 요약할 때, 빈칸에 알맞은 단어를 쓰시오.

__________ is an important building material in a modern city because it not only __________ us from __________ __________ and invasion but also provides enough __________ __________.

READ CLOSELY

의미 단위로 끊어 읽고(/), 주어와 동사에 표시해 봅시다.

지문 듣기　기출 원문 보기

❶ It is impossible to imagine a modern city without glass.

❷ We expect our buildings to protect us from the weather; this is what they are for, after all.

❸ And yet, when it comes to a new home or workplace, one of the first questions people ask is, "How much natural light is there?"

❹ Modern glass buildings satisfy these different desires: the desire to be protected from bad weather, such as the wind, the cold, and the rain; the desire to be secure from the invasion of the thieves; and, at the same time, the desire not to live in darkness.

❺ Although glass is a reasonable building material, glass engineering is expensive and it causes the glass building market to be exclusive.

❻ Glass makes our lives, which are spent mostly indoors, much brighter and more delightful.

GRAMMAR TIP

목적격 관계대명사는 명사구 선행사를 수식하는 절을 이끌 때 자주 생략돼요. 이 글에서는 people ask 앞에 목적격 관계대명사 that이 생략되어 있어요.

- *The bread* (**which[that]**) I like sold out today.
- Fred knew *the man* (**who[whom]**) I met yesterday.

WORDS

imagine 상상하다
cf. imagination 상상
modern 현대의
expect 기대하다, 예상하다
protect 보호하다
cf. protection 보호
after all 결국, 어쨌든
when it comes to ～에 관해서라면, ～에 관한 한
workplace 직장, 일터
natural light 자연광
satisfy 충족시키다, 만족시키다
desire 욕구, 욕망
secure 안전한
cf. security 안전, 안보
invasion 침입, 침범
cf. invade 침입하다, 침범하다
at the same time 동시에
darkness 어둠, 암흑
cf. brightness 밝음, 채광
reasonable (가격이나 의견이) 합리적인
material 자재, 재료
engineering 공학
cause (～이) …하게 하다
exclusive 독점적인
indoors 실내에서
cf. outdoors 실외에서
delightful 즐거운, 기쁜

REVIEW TIME

1 다음 단어를 괄호 안의 지시대로 바꿔 쓰시오.

(1) invade   → _________________ (명사형)

(2) response   → _________________ (동사형)

(3) presence   → _________________ (형용사형)

(4) attach   → _________________ (명사형)

2 서로 의미가 반대인 단어끼리 연결하시오.

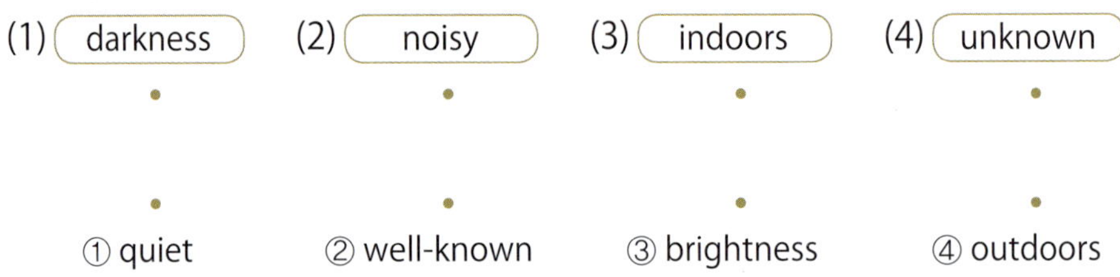

(1) darkness   (2) noisy   (3) indoors   (4) unknown

① quiet   ② well-known   ③ brightness   ④ outdoors

3 우리말 뜻에 맞게 주어진 철자로 시작하는 단어 퍼즐을 완성하시오.

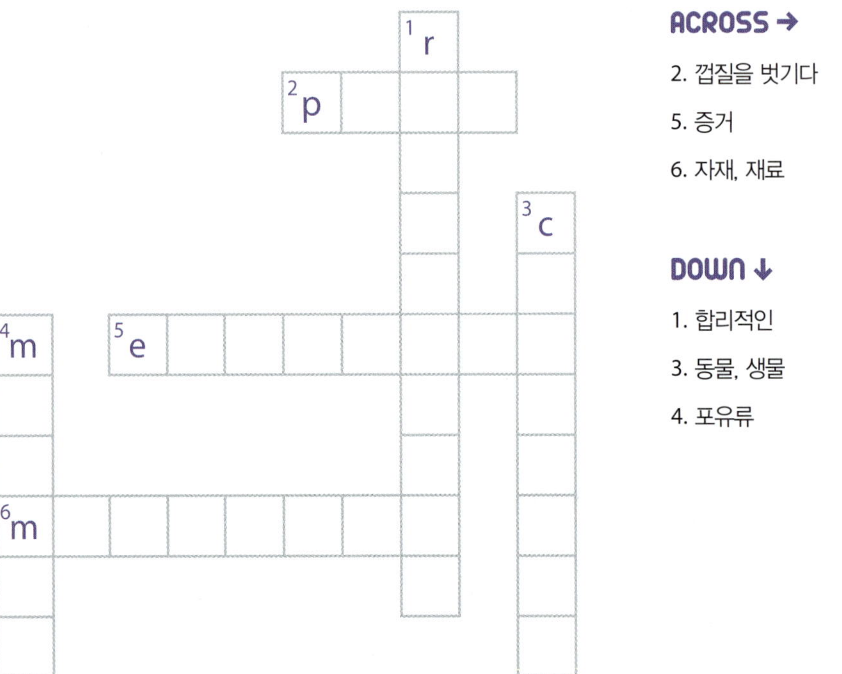

ACROSS →

2. 껍질을 벗기다

5. 증거

6. 자재, 재료

DOWN ↓

1. 합리적인

3. 동물, 생물

4. 포유류

4 주어진 단어를 사용하여 우리말 뜻에 해당하는 표현을 쓰시오. (한 번씩만 쓸 것)

(1) ~에 따라 ________________   (2) ~에 관해서라면 ________________

(3) 지적하다 ________________   (4) 결국, 어쨌든 ________________

after	out	when	on	to
comes	depending	all	point	it

5 우리말과 의미가 같도록 괄호 안의 동사를 알맞은 형태로 쓰시오.

(1) 우리는 우리의 건물이 날씨로부터 우리를 보호해 주기를 기대한다. (protect)

  → We expect our buildings ________________ us from the weather.

(2) 알려지지 않은 출처로부터 온 어떤 파일들을 여는 것은 위험하다. (open)

  → It's dangerous ________________ some files from an unknown source.

(3) 현대 유리 건물들은 어둠 속에서 살지 않고자 하는 욕구를 충족시킨다. (live)

  → Modern glass buildings satisfy the desire not ________________ in darkness.

(4) 여러분은 껍질을 벗긴 감자를 쓰레기통에 던져 넣은 적이 있는가? (throw)

  → ________________ you ever ________________ the peeled potato into the bin?

6 빈칸에 알맞은 말을 보기 에서 골라 쓰시오.

보기

little	until	few	that

(1) There is ________________ evidence that mammals try to be musical.

(2) ________________ mammals can make as many different kinds of sounds as birds.

(3) We don't even realize our mistake ________________ we get an email pointing it out.

(4) The first question ________________ people ask is, "How much natural light is there?"

37

READING

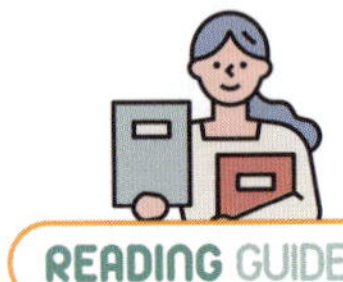

READING GUIDE

각 단락의 첫 문장에서 글의 순서를 알려 주는 단서를 찾아 표시해 봅시다.

주어진 글 다음에 이어질 글의 순서로 가장 적절한 것은? (기출응용)

> [1] Blinking is an action that protects the eyes. [2] When the eyes are open, one-tenth of the total eye surface area is exposed to the air.

(A) [3] That is the physiological reason behind blinking, but we blink for mental reasons as well. [4] For instance, worries, fear, stress, and tension have an effect on the number of times we blink.

(B) [5] They blink. [6] Blinking makes the eyes wet and keeps the front part of the eyes clear for good vision. [7] When we blink, a layer of tears covers the eyes and washes away all the tiny bits of dust on them.

(C) [8] This means the eye, the weakest and most sensitive part of the body, has to resist the dust present in the air. [9] So, what do the eyes do to protect themselves?

* **physiological** 생리적인(신체의 조직이나 기능에 관련된)

① (A) – (C) – (B)   ② (B) – (A) – (C)   ③ (B) – (C) – (A)
④ (C) – (A) – (B)   ⑤ (C) – (B) – (A)

UNDERSTAND DEEPLY

1 빈칸에 알맞은 단어를 윗글에서 찾아 쓰시오.

The physiological reason why we blink is to __________ eyes from __________ in the air. We blink for mental reasons as well, such as __________, __________, __________, and __________.

2 다음 질문에 알맞은 답을 윗글에서 찾아 쓰시오.

Q: What happens when we blink?

A: __________________________________

READ CLOSELY

의미 단위로 끊어 읽고(/), 주어와 동사에 표시해 봅시다.

지문 듣기　기출 원문 보기

❶ Blinking is an action that protects the eyes.

❷ When the eyes are open, one-tenth of the total eye surface area is exposed to the air.

❸ That is the physiological reason behind blinking, but we blink for mental reasons as well.

❹ For instance, worries, fear, stress, and tension have an effect on the number of times we blink.

❺ They blink.

❻ Blinking makes the eyes wet and keeps the front part of the eyes clear for good vision.
TIP
TIP

❼ When we blink, a layer of tears covers the eyes and washes away all the tiny bits of dust on them.

❽ This means the eye, the weakest and most sensitive part of the body, has to resist the dust present in the air.

❾ So, what do the eyes do to protect themselves?

WORDS

blink (눈을) 깜빡이다
protect 보호하다
cf. protection 보호
total 전체의
surface 표면
area 범위, 영역
be exposed to ~에 노출되다
mental 정신적인
as well ~도, ~ 역시
fear 두려움
tension 긴장
have an effect on ~에 영향을 미치다
cf. affect ~에 영향을 미치다
wet (물기로) 촉촉한, 젖은
front 앞의
vision 시야, 시력
cf. visible (눈에) 보이는
layer 막
cover 덮다, 가리다
wash away 씻어내다
tiny 아주 작은
dust 먼지
sensitive 민감한
cf. sense 감각; 감지하다
resist 저항하다, 견디다
present 존재하는
cf. absent 부재하는

"

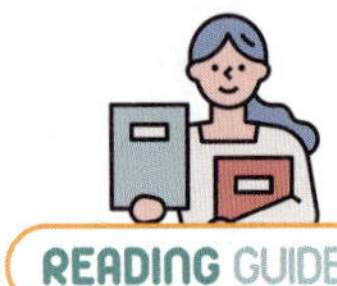

READING GUIDE

각 단락에서 글의 순서를 알려 주는 단서를 모두 찾아 표시 해 봅시다.

주어진 글 다음에 이어질 글의 순서로 가장 적절한 것은?

> ❶Monkeys are similar to humans in many ways. ❷For example, the relationships in a monkey family, such as between brothers and sisters, are often very close.

(A) ❸However, his sister Panbanisha could not make a knife. ❹The researchers did not let Kanzi give his knife to her. ❺So, Kanzi secretly put his knife where his sister could easily find it, and she finally got her banana.

(B) ❻A team of researchers studied a pair of bonobo monkeys named Kanzi and Panbanisha. ❼The brother and sister learned how to make knives from stones. ❽The researchers decided to record how good they were at making knives.

(C) ❾The researchers got two boxes and put a banana in each box. ❿Then they gave the bonobos whatever they needed to make a knife. ⓫Kanzi made a very good knife. ⓬With the knife, he cut open his box and succeeded in getting the banana.

① (A) – (B) – (C)　　② (A) – (C) – (B)　　③ (B) – (A) – (C)
④ (B) – (C) – (A)　　⑤ (C) – (A) – (B)

UNDERSTAND DEEPLY

1 윗글의 연구 결과와 결론을 다음과 같이 정리할 때, 빈칸에 알맞은 말을 쓰시오.

결과	Kanzi는 (1) ________ 을 잘 만들어 (2) ________ 를 얻었고, 그의 (3) ________ 인 Panbanisha를 도와줌
결론	(4) ________ 도 인간처럼 가족 간의 관계가 매우 (5) ________

2 윗글의 내용과 일치하면 T, 그렇지 않으면 F를 쓰시오.

(1) Both bonobo monkeys learned how to make a knife. ______

(2) One of the bonobo monkeys couldn't get a banana. ______

지문 듣기

❶ Monkeys are similar to humans in many ways.

❷ For example, the relationships in a monkey family, such as between brothers and sisters, are often very close.

❸ However, his sister Panbanisha could not make a knife.

❹ The researchers did not let Kanzi give his knife to her.

❺ So, Kanzi secretly put his knife where his sister could easily find it, and she finally got her banana.

❻ A team of researchers studied a pair of bonobo monkeys named Kanzi and Panbanisha.

❼ The brother and sister learned how to make knives from stones.

❽ The researchers decided to record how good they were at making knives.

❾ The researchers got two boxes and put a banana in each box.

❿ Then they gave the bonobos **whatever** they needed to make a knife.

⓫ Kanzi made a very good knife.

⓬ With the knife, he cut open his box and succeeded in getting the banana.

GRAMMAR TIP

이 글에 쓰인 복합관계대명사 whatever는 '~하는 것은 무엇이든지'라는 의미로 명사절을 이끌어요. 「선행사 anything + 관계대명사 that」과 같은 의미예요.

- Let me know **whatever you need**. = anything that you need
- Tell me **whatever** you want to have for dinner.

cf. whatever는 '무엇을 ~ 하든지'라는 의미로 부사절을 이끌기도 해요.

- **Whatever** you do, you should do your best.

READING TIP

주어진 글을 먼저 읽은 후, 각 단락의 첫 문장에서 연결어, 대명사, 관사, 지시어 등 글의 흐름을 알려주는 단서들을 찾아보세요.

WORDS

be similar to ~와 유사하다
in many ways 여러 면에서
relationship 관계
such as ~와 같은
close 가까운, 친밀한
researcher 연구원
secretly 몰래, 비밀스럽게
finally 마침내, 결국
study 연구하다
a pair of 한 쌍의, 두 개[마리]의
decide 결정하다, 결심하다
record 녹화하다, 기록하다
be good at ~에 능숙하다
cut open 절개하다, 잘라서 열다
succeed in ~에 성공하다
cf. success 성공

READING 39

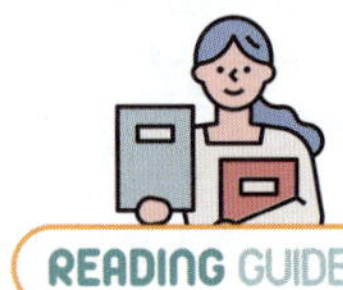

READING GUIDE

각 단락에서 글의 순서를 알려 주는 단서를 모두 찾아 표시 해 봅시다.

주어진 글 다음에 이어질 글의 순서로 가장 적절한 것은? (기출응용)

> ❶ We're creatures of habit, and I've never seen anyone argue against that old expression. ❷ It's probably because there's so much truth to it.

(A) ❸ While someone might disagree with that particular number, it is clear that our habits have a powerful effect on us. ❹ Most of them start innocently and unintentionally. ❺ At the beginning, they form a kind of invisible thread.

(B) ❻ In fact, we're even more the result of habit than most people realize. ❼ Some psychologists believe that up to ninety-five percent of our behavior is formed through habit.

(C) ❽ But through repetition, that thread becomes twisted into a cord and later into a rope. ❾ Each time we repeat an act, we add to it and strengthen it. ❿ The rope becomes a chain and then a cable. ⓫ Eventually, we become our habits. ⓬ As English poet John Dryden said, we first make our habits, and then our habits make us.

① (A) – (C) – (B)　　② (B) – (A) – (C)　　③ (B) – (C) – (A)
④ (C) – (A) – (B)　　⑤ (C) – (B) – (A)

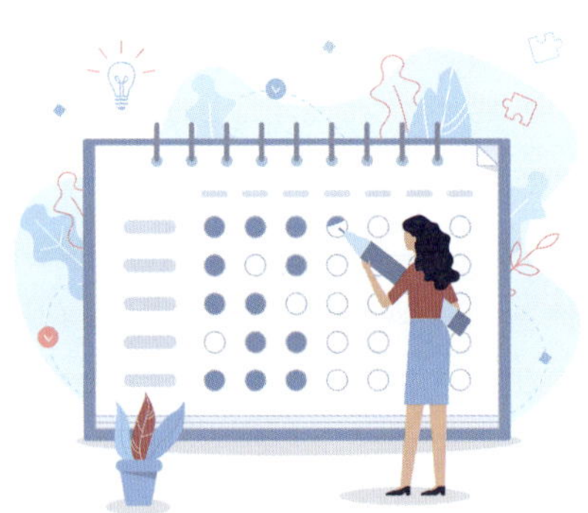

UNDERSTAND DEEPLY

1 빈칸에 알맞은 단어를 윗글에서 찾아 쓰시오.

Humans are creatures of ___________ and much of human behavior is formed through ___________.

2 다음 질문에 알맞은 답을 윗글에서 찾아 문장을 완성하시오.

Q: How do we make an act into our habit?
A: We do it through ___________ of the act.

READ CLOSELY

의미 단위로 끊어 읽고(/), 주어와 동사에 표시해 봅시다.

지문 듣기 　 기출 원문 보기

❶ We're creatures of habit, and I've never seen anyone argue against that old expression.

❷ It's probably because there's so much truth to it.

❸ While someone might disagree with that particular number, it is clear that our habits have a powerful effect on us.

❹ Most of them start innocently and unintentionally.

❺ At the beginning, they form a kind of invisible thread.

❻ In fact, we're even more the result of habit than most people realize.

❼ Some psychologists believe that up to ninety-five percent of our behavior is formed through habit.

❽ But through repetition, that thread becomes twisted into a cord and later into a rope.

❾ Each time we repeat an act, we add to it and strengthen it.

❿ The rope becomes a chain and then a cable.

⓫ Eventually, we become our habits.

⓬ As English poet John Dryden said, we first make our habits, and then our habits make us.

주어가 「all/most/some/half/percent/분수+of+명사」 형태일 경우, of 뒤의 명사가 단수이면 단수 동사가 오고, 복수이면 복수 동사가 와요.

- **Half of the show** *was* successful.
- **Most of the students** *like* the class.

WORDS

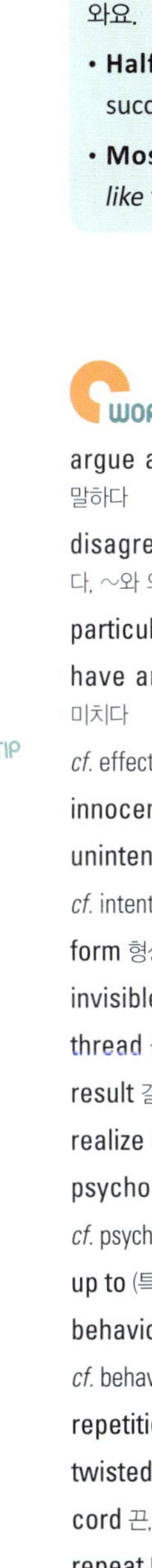

argue against ~에 반대 의견을 말하다

disagree with ~에 동의하지 않다, ~와 의견이 다르다

particular 특정한

have an effect on ~에 영향을 미치다

cf. **effect** 영향(력), 효과

innocently 순수하게

unintentionally 무심코

cf. **intentionally** 고의로

form 형성하다

invisible 보이지 않는

thread 실

result 결과

realize 깨닫다, 자각하다

psychologist 심리학자

cf. **psychology** 심리학

up to (특정한 수)까지

behavior 행동

cf. **behave** 행동하다

repetition 반복

twisted 꼬인

cord 끈, 줄

repeat 반복하다

add to ~에 더하다

strengthen 강화하다

cf. **strength** 힘

cable 굵은 철제 밧줄

eventually 결국, 마침내

REVIEW TIME

1 다음 단어를 명사형으로 바꿔 쓰시오.

(1) protect → ______________   (2) succeed → ______________

(3) repeat → ______________   (4) strengthen → ______________

2 우리말 뜻에 해당하는 단어가 되도록 빈칸에 알맞은 철자를 쓰시오.

(1) 보이지 않는　　n　i　le

(2) 결국, 마침내　e　e　t　a　ly

(3) 순수하게　　n oc n ly

(4) 관계　　r l t o s ip

(5) 존재하는　　re e t

(6) 민감한　　s n i i e

3 우리말 뜻에 해당하는 단어를 찾아 동그라미 하고 빈칸에 쓰시오.

P	Q	B	Z	P	D	H	P	C	E	V	L
S	L	O	J	T	A	M	N	W	O	L	Y
J	P	N	M	B	E	H	A	V	I	O	R
S	A	G	P	L	P	S	T	O	Y	W	O
B	R	E	S	I	S	T	I	H	R	P	T
A	T	S	V	N	L	E	C	R	D	J	D
E	I	X	K	K	V	L	L	U	M	F	H
F	C	Z	U	C	S	I	O	A	Q	R	Y
L	U	Q	D	B	N	V	S	T	U	D	Y
H	L	T	X	E	I	P	E	I	I	B	L
C	A	E	J	Z	K	W	X	A	O	S	Y
X	R	G	L	U	H	R	G	B	U	N	N

(1) 특정한　______________

(2) 시야　______________

(3) 연구하다　______________

(4) 저항하다　______________

(5) 행동　______________

(6) 가까운　______________

4 주어진 단어를 사용하여 우리말 뜻에 해당하는 표현을 쓰시오. (중복 사용 가능)

(1) ~와 유사하다 ___________________

(2) ~에 영향을 미치다 ___________________

(3) ~에 능숙하다 ___________________

(4) ~에 성공하다 ___________________

have	similar	succeed	good	be
to	at	an effect	in	on

5 네모 안에서 어법에 맞는 것을 고르시오.

(1) Most of the habits [starts / start] innocently and unintentionally.

(2) We're [very / even] more the result of habit than most people realize.

(3) Blinking keeps the front part of the eyes [clear / clearly] for good vision.

(4) This means the eye, the weakest part of the body, [has / have] to resist the dust.

6 밑줄 친 부분이 어법에 맞으면 ○표 하고, 그렇지 않으면 바르게 고치시오.

(1) Blinking makes the eyes <u>wetly</u>.

(2) The researchers did not let Kanzi <u>to give</u> his knife to his sister.

(3) Ninety-five percent of our behavior <u>are</u> formed through habit.

(4) The researchers gave the bonobos <u>whatever</u> they needed to make a knife.

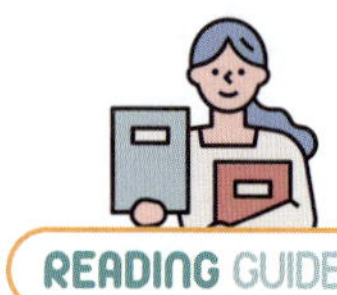

주어진 문장에서 연결어와 핵심어에 밑줄을 긋고, 이에 유의하여 글을 읽어봅시다.

글의 흐름으로 보아, 주어진 문장이 들어가기에 가장 적절한 곳은? 〈기출응용〉

> **①** However, the actual chance of a shark attack is very small.

② Fear of sharks has kept many pool swimmers from testing the ocean water. (①) **③** The 1975 movie *Jaws* provided images of a series of shark attacks in a small beach town. **④** These images made many people believe that ocean swimming is only for these big fish. (②) **⑤** In reality, you are at greater risk while driving to and from the beach. (③) **⑥** According to the International Shark Attack File, there is a low number of shark attacks and these big fish do not feed on humans by nature. (④) **⑦** Most shark attacks simply happen because of sharks mistaking humans for fish. (⑤) **⑧** In 2007, there were 71 reported shark attacks worldwide and only one death. **⑨** It is much lower than the 2007 death rate for bee stings and snake bites.

1 윗글에서 세 번째 문장의 These images가 가리키는 바를 우리말로 쓰시오.

____

2 윗글의 내용과 일치하면 T, 그렇지 않으면 F를 쓰시오.

(1) The 1975 movie *Jaws* encouraged many people to try ocean swimming. ______

(2) There was no death by a shark attack in 2007. ______

(3) In 2007, the death rate for bee stings and snake bites was higher than that for shark attacks. ______

READ CLOSELY 의미 단위로 끊어 읽고(/), 주어와 동사에 표시해 봅시다.

지문 듣기 기출 원문 보기

❶ However, the actual chance of a shark attack is very small.

❷ Fear of sharks has kept many pool swimmers from testing the ocean water.

❸ The 1975 movie *Jaws* provided images of a series of shark attacks in a small beach town.

❹ These images made many people believe that ocean swimming is only for these big fish.

❺ In reality, you are at greater risk while driving to and from the beach.

❻ According to the International Shark Attack File, there is a low number of shark attacks and these big fish do not feed on humans by nature.

❼ Most shark attacks simply happen because of sharks mistaking humans for fish.

❽ In 2007, there were 71 reported shark attacks worldwide and only one death.

❾ It is much lower than the 2007 death rate for bee stings and snake bites.

TIP GRAMMAR

사역동사 make는 주어가 목적어에게 어떤 행동을 하게 하는 것을 의미해요. 「make+목적어+목적격 보어(동사원형)」 형태로 쓰여요.

- Don't **make** me **wait** too long.
- The sad movie **made** him **cry** a lot.

READING TIP

주어진 문장에는 글의 흐름을 전환하는 연결어(but, however, on the other hand, instead 등)가 자주 등장해요. 이 경우, 글을 읽으면서 흐름이 갑자기 바뀌는 곳을 잘 찾아보세요.

WORDS

actual 실제의
cf. actually 실제로, 사실은
chance 가능성
cf. possibility 가능성
attack 공격
fear 두려움, 공포
provide 제공하다, 주다
a series of 일련의
in reality 실제로, 사실은
be at risk 위험에 처하다
according to ~에 따르면
international 국제적인
a low number of 적은 수의
feed on ~을 먹이로 하다
by nature 본래, 천성은
mistake A for B A를 B로 착각하다
report 보고하다, 전하다
worldwide 전 세계적으로
bee sting 벌에 쏘임
snake bite 뱀에 물림

바른답·알찬풀이 | p. 46

READING **41**

READING GUIDE

주어진 문장에서 핵심어에 밑줄을 긋고, 글을 읽으면서 이와 관련된 부분을 찾아봅시다.

글의 흐름으로 보아, 주어진 문장이 들어가기에 가장 적절한 곳은? 기출응용

[1] Instead of putting more police on the street, they chose to play classical music.

[2] A very interesting experiment took place in a small Australian village. (①) [3] At that time, the number of street crimes in the village was much higher than two years earlier, and it was still rapidly increasing. (②) [4] Local people, scared by the increase in street crime, got together and decided on the best way to deal with the problem. [5] The idea was to remove the dangerous characters from the main street after dark. (③) [6] Loud speakers began playing the music of Mozart, Bach, and Beethoven. (④) [7] In less than a week, the village reported a rapid decrease in crime. (⑤) [8] The experiment was so successful that the main train station in Copenhagen, Denmark adopted the same solution — with similar results, too. [9] It seems that classical music is very effective for reducing crime.

UNDERSTAND DEEPLY

1 다음 중 윗글의 주제로 가장 적절한 것은?
① reasons of the rapid increase in street crime
② effect of classical music on decreasing crime
③ importance of math in solving social problems
④ decline in popularity of classical music in Australia

2 윗글의 내용을 다음과 같이 정리할 때, 빈칸에 알맞은 말을 쓰시오.

문제	한 호주 마을에서 (1) __________ 수가 빠르게 증가함
대책	거리에서 (2) __________ 을 재생함으로써 (3) __________ 들을 제거하고자 함
결과	마을에서 범죄가 빠르게 감소했고, 덴마크 코펜하겐의 주요 (4) __________ 에서도 같은 해결책이 적용됨
결론	범죄를 줄이는 데 (5) __________ 이 매우 효과적인 것으로 보임

READ CLOSELY

의미 단위로 끊어 읽고(/), 주어와 동사에 표시해 봅시다.

지문 듣기   기출 원문 보기

❶ Instead of putting more police on the street, they chose to play classical music.

❷ A very interesting experiment took place in a small Australian village.

❸ At that time, the number of street crimes in the village was much higher than two years earlier, and it was still rapidly increasing.

❹ Local people, scared by the increase in street crime, got together and decided on the best way to deal with the problem.

❺ The idea was to remove the dangerous characters from the main street after dark.

❻ Loud speakers began playing the music of Mozart, Bach, and Beethoven.

❼ In less than a week, the village reported a rapid decrease in crime.

❽ The experiment was so successful that the main train station in Copenhagen, Denmark adopted the same solution—with similar results, too.

❾ It seems that classical music is very effective for reducing crime.

GRAMMAR TIP

현재분사 형태의 형용사는 능동의 의미로 명사를 수식해요.

- I heard some **surprising** news. (놀라운 소식)
- I saw a **flying** object last night. (날아다니는 물체)

현재분사구는 명사의 뒤에서 명사를 수식해요.

- *The boy* **wearing a blue cap** is my brother.

WORDS

instead of ~ 대신에
classical music 클래식 음악
interesting 흥미로운
cf. interested 흥미 있어 하는
experiment 실험
take place 실시되다, 발생하다
crime 범죄
earlier ~ 전에
rapidly 빠르게, 급속히
increase 증가하다; 증가
get together 한데 모이다
decide on ~을 결정하다
deal with ~을 처리하다
remove 제거하다
report 보고하다, 전하다
rapid 빠른, 급속한
decrease 감소
successful 성공적인, 성공한
adopt 채택하다
solution 해결책
cf. solve 해결하다, 풀다
similar 유사한
result 결과
effective 효과적인
cf. effect 효과
reduce 줄이다, 감소시키다

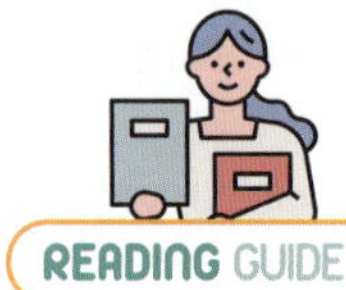

READING GUIDE

주어진 문장에서 연결어에 밑줄을 긋고, 이에 유의하여 글을 읽어봅시다.

글의 흐름으로 보아, 주어진 문장이 들어가기에 가장 적절한 곳은? 기출응용

> As time passes, however, people get used to what they have and, just like the smell of bread, these wonderful things disappear from their consciousness.

When walking into a room that smells of freshly baked bread, you quickly sense the pleasant aroma. (①) However, if you stay there for a few minutes, the smell will seem to disappear. (②) You won't even be able to remember the good feeling you got when you stepped into the room. In fact, the only way to feel it again is to walk out of the room and come back in again. (③) Exactly the same concept applies to many areas of our lives, including happiness. (④) Everyone has something to be happy about: a lovely spouse, good health, or a satisfying job. (⑤) As the old saying goes, you don't know what you've got till it's gone.

* consciousness 의식, 자각

UNDERSTAND DEEPLY

1　윗글에서 글의 요지에 해당하는 문장을 찾아 우리말로 해석하시오.

____

2　윗글의 내용과 일치하도록 각 괄호 안에서 알맞은 말을 고르시오.

As the smell of fresh bread [appears / disappears] from our consciousness, we get used to the [pleasant / unpleasant] things that we have and [remember / forget] them.

3　윗글의 내용을 다음과 같이 나눌 때, 본론 부분의 첫 세 단어를 쓰시오.

비유	When walking into
본론	_______________

READ CLOSELY

의미 단위로 끊어 읽고(/), 주어와 동사에 표시해 봅시다.

지문 듣기   기출 원문 보기

❶ As time passes, however, people get used to what they have and, just like the smell of bread, these wonderful things disappear from their consciousness.

❷ When walking into a room that smells of freshly baked bread, you quickly sense the pleasant aroma.

❸ However, if you stay there for a few minutes, the smell will seem to disappear.

❹ You won't even be able to remember the good feeling you got when you stepped into the room.

❺ In fact, the only way to feel it again is to walk out of the room and come back in again.

❻ Exactly the same concept applies to many areas of our lives, including happiness.

❼ Everyone has something to be happy about: a lovely spouse, good health, or a satisfying job.

❽ As the old saying goes, you don't know what you've got till it's gone.

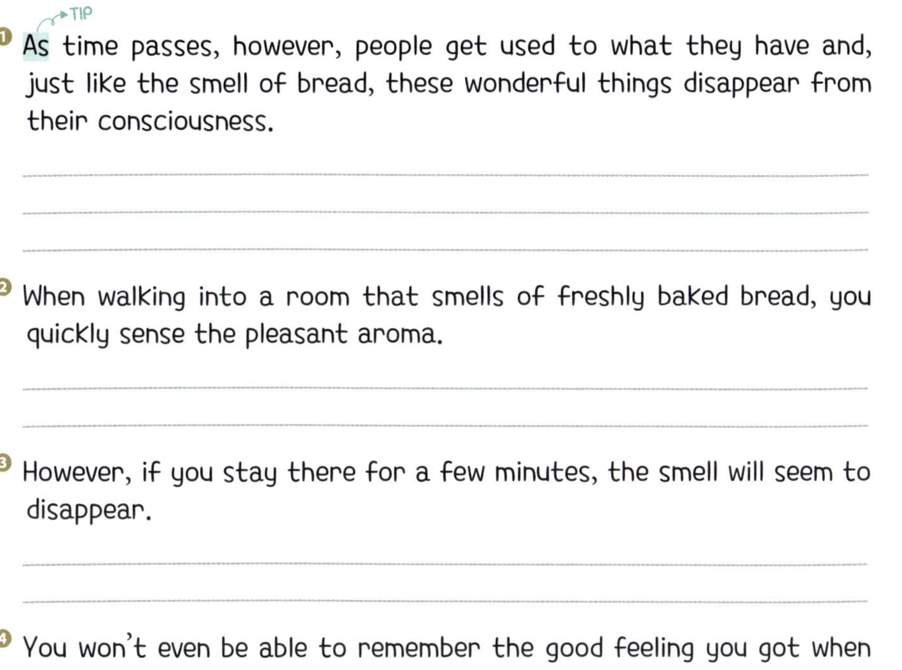

WORDS

get used to 〜에 익숙해지다
cf. get accustomed to 〜에 익숙해지다
disappear from 〜에서 사라지다
cf. appear 나타나다
smell of 〜의 냄새가 나다
quickly 빨리, 곧
sense 감지하다
pleasant 기분 좋은
cf. unpleasant 불쾌한
aroma 향기, (좋은) 냄새
step into 〜으로 (걸어) 들어가다
concept 개념
apply to 〜에 적용되다
cf. apply for 〜에 지원하다, 〜을 신청하다
area 영역, 분야
including 〜을 포함하여
spouse 배우자
satisfying 만족스러운
cf. satisfy 만족시키다
old saying 옛말, 속담
cf. proverb 속담, 격언

1 세 단어 중 서로 의미가 비슷한 두 개를 고르시오.

(1) result — chance — possibility

(2) give — provide — choose

(3) smell — aroma — area

(4) rapidly — quickly — actually

2 다음 단어를 괄호 안의 지시대로 바꿔 쓰시오.

(1) solve → _________________ (명사형)

(2) effect → _________________ (형용사형)

(3) satisfy → _________________ (현재분사형)

(4) disappear → _________________ (반의어)

3 우리말 뜻에 맞게 퍼즐을 완성한 후, 8번 단어의 우리말 뜻을 쓰시오.

ACROSS →

1. 공격 2. 제거하다

3. 기분 좋은 4. 줄이다

5. 보고하다 6. 배우자

7. 채택하다

DOWN ↓

8. _________________

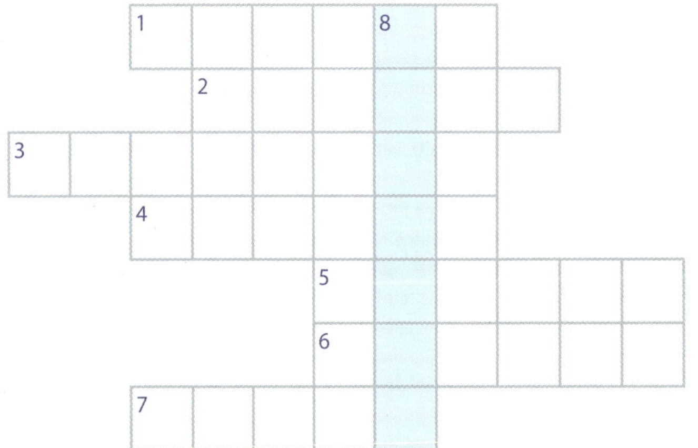

4 주어진 단어를 사용하여 우리말 뜻에 해당하는 표현을 쓰시오. (한 번씩만 쓸 것)

(1) ~을 처리하다 _______________________ (2) ~을 먹이로 하다 _______________________

(3) ~에 익숙해지다 _______________________ (4) 실시되다, 발생하다 _______________________

with	used	on	place

feed	deal	take	get	to

5 네모 안에서 어법에 맞는 것을 고르시오.

(1) A very interesting / interested experiment took place in a small village.

(2) These images made people believe / to believe that ocean swimming is dangerous.

(3) Most shark attacks happen because of sharks mistaking / mistaken humans for fish.

(4) Local people, scaring / scared by the increase in street crime, decided on the way to deal with the problem.

6 우리말과 의미가 같도록 빈칸에 알맞은 말을 A 와 B 에서 하나씩 골라 쓰시오. (중복 사용 가능)

A
so   even   as   while

B
what   how   that   when

(1) 시간이 지남에 따라 사람들은 자신이 가지고 있는 것에 익숙해진다.

→ _________ time passes, people get accustomed to _________ they have.

(2) 옛말에서 그러하듯이, 여러분은 그것이 사라질 때까지 여러분이 무엇을 가지고 있는지 알지 못한다.

→ _________ the old saying goes, you don't know _________ you've got till it's gone.

(3) 그 실험이 매우 성공적이어서 코펜하겐이 동일한 해결책을 채택했다.

→ The experiment was _________ successful _________ Copenhagen adopted the same solution.

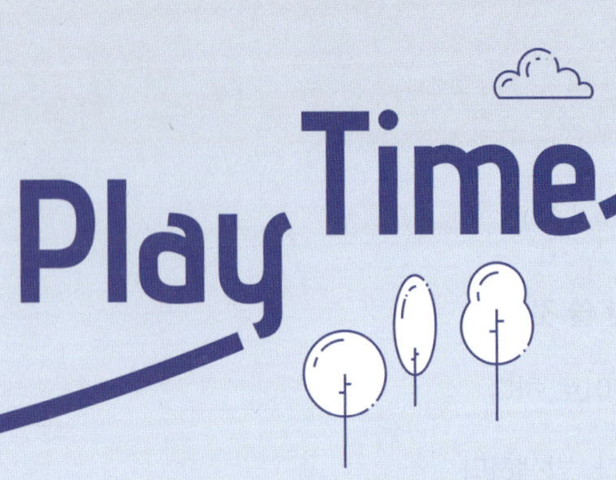

Play Time

바른답·알찬풀이 | p. 49

In each task, move one matchstick to make the equation correct.

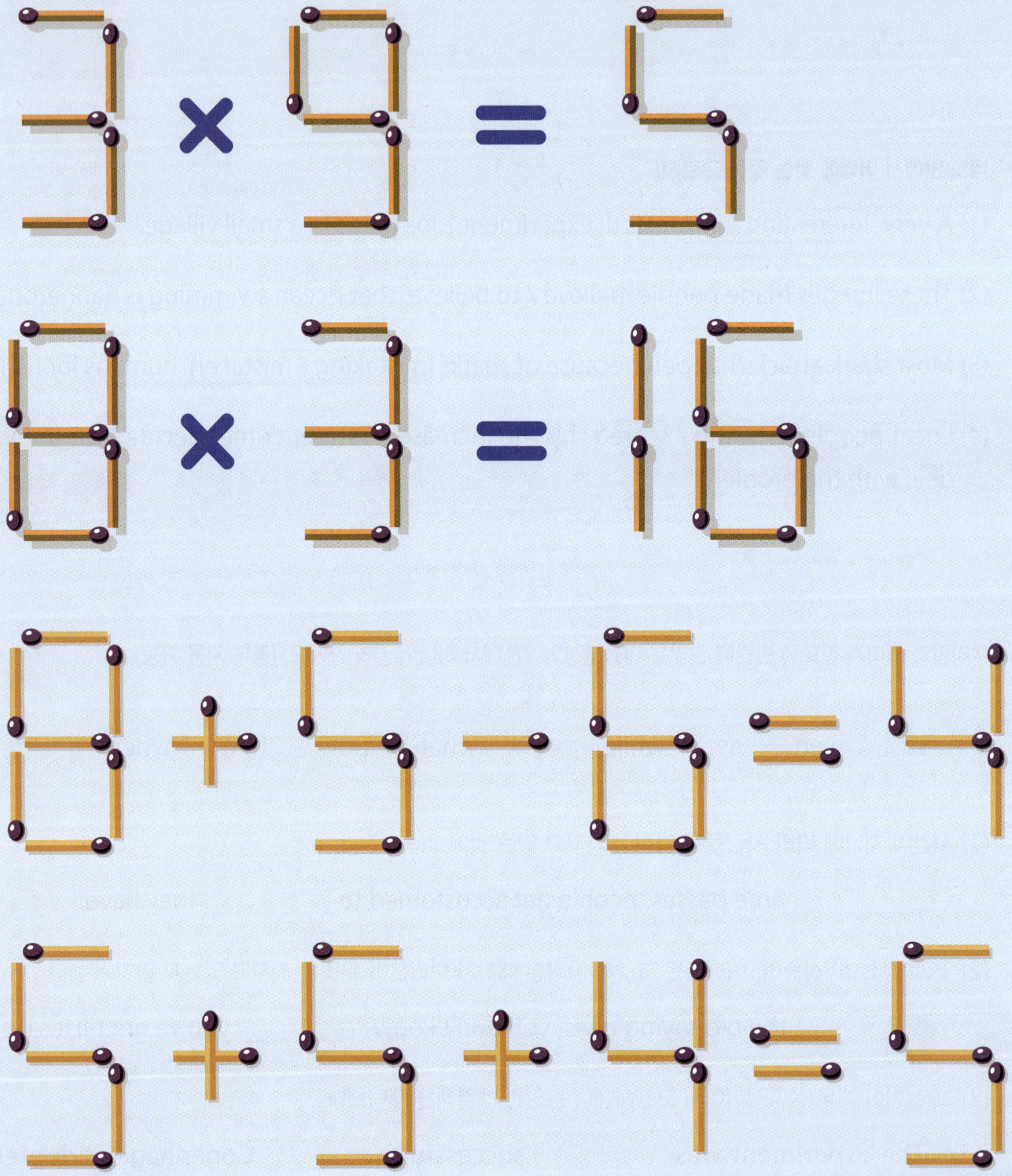

3 × 9 = 5
8 × 3 = 16
8 + 5 − 6 = 4
5 + 5 + 4 = 5

PART 5

긴 글 이해하기

긴 글이란 뭔가요?

다른 유형의 지문보다 길이가 긴 지문을 말해요. 장문은 긴 한 단락으로, 복합문단은 짤막한 네 단락으로 이루어져 있어요. 길이가 긴 만큼 한 지문을 읽고 여러 개의 문제를 풀어야 해요.

어떻게 공부하나요?

장문은 중심 내용을 정리하면서 글을 읽고, 복합문단은 각 단락의 내용과 연결고리를 바탕으로 글의 순서를 바로잡는 연습을 해 보세요.

시험에 어떻게 나오나요?

다음 두 가지 유형으로 출제돼요.
- ✓ 장문 이해하기　　　UNIT 14
- ✓ 복합문단 이해하기　　UNIT 15

GET READY

1~2의 지시문을 먼저 읽고, 무엇에 중점을 두어 글을 읽어야 할지 파악해 봅시다.

READING 43

다음 글을 읽고, 물음에 답하시오. (기출응용)

❶ We can help our babies learn to love healthy foods even before they're born. ❷ The latest science shows interesting connections between what moms eat while pregnant and what foods their babies enjoy after birth. ❸ Hard to believe, but it's true. ❹ Babies taste, remember, and form preferences for what Mom has eaten. ❺ Consider an interesting study about carrot juice. ❻ As part of the study, one group of pregnant women drank carrot juice four times a week for three weeks. ❼ Another group of women in the study drank water. ❽ When their babies were old enough to start eating cereal, it was time to look for a difference between the groups. ❾ A researcher who didn't know which group each baby belonged to studied the babies as they ate cereal mixed with carrot juice. ❿ The babies who _______________ the earlier experience of tasting carrot juice refused and made unhappy faces about the taste. ⓫ On the other hand, the other group of babies easily accepted and enjoyed the carrot juice in the cereal. ⓬ There was a big difference between babies who experienced carrot juice before they were born and babies who didn't.

도입부에서 글의 중심 소재를 찾아 밑줄을 그어 봅시다.

1 윗글의 제목으로 가장 적절한 것은?

① Change Your Diet for Your Health
② Learn about the Recipes Using Carrots
③ The Important Time for a Baby's Growth
④ What Mom Eats Influences the Baby's Taste
⑤ Various Ways to Encourage Eating Healthy Foods

글을 읽으면서 빈칸에 들어갈 말의 단서가 되는 문장을 찾아 밑줄을 그어 봅시다.

2 윗글의 빈칸에 들어갈 말로 가장 적절한 것은?

① used　　　② forgot　　　③ lacked
④ recalled　　　⑤ overcame

1 다음 질문에 알맞은 답을 윗글에서 찾아 문장을 완성하시오.

Q: How can mothers help their babies love healthy foods?
A: They can help by eating ________________ while __________.

2 윗글의 연구 내용을 다음과 같이 정리할 때, 빈칸에 알맞은 말을 쓰시오.

방법	• 두 임신한 여성 집단이 각각 (1) __________ 와 (2) ______ 을 (3) ________ 동안 섭취함 • 각 집단의 출생한 아기들에게 (4) __________ 와 섞인 (5) ________ 을 먹임
결과	임신 중 (6) __________ 를 마셨던 집단의 아기들은 그 맛을 좋아했고, (7) ______ 을 마셨던 집단의 아기들은 거부 반응을 보임

3 빈칸에 알맞은 단어를 윗글에서 찾아 쓰시오.

Babies' __________ for foods are related to their __________ of tasting them before birth.

의미 단위로 끊어 읽고(/), 주어와 동사에 표시해 봅시다.

지문 듣기　기출 원문 보기

TIP

「형용사/부사＋enough＋to 부정사」는 '~할 만큼 충분히 …한/하게'를 의미해요. 이는 「so＋형용사/부사＋that＋주어＋can＋동사원형」('너무 ~해서 …할 수 있다')으로 바꿔 쓸 수 있어요.

- He is **smart enough to solve** all the math problems.
  (= He is **so smart that** he **can solve** all the math problems.)
- Jamie ran **fast enough to beat** all the other runners.
  (= Jamie ran **so fast that** he **could beat** all the other runners.)

❶ We can help our babies learn to love healthy foods even before they're born.

❷ The latest science shows interesting connections between what moms eat while pregnant and what foods their babies enjoy after birth.

❸ Hard to believe, but it's true.

❹ Babies taste, remember, and form preferences for what Mom has eaten.

❺ Consider an interesting study about carrot juice.

❻ As part of the study, one group of pregnant women drank carrot juice four times a week for three weeks.

❼ Another group of women in the study drank water.

❽ When their babies were old enough to start eating cereal, it was time to look for a difference between the groups.

9 A researcher who didn't know which group each baby belonged to studied the babies as they ate cereal mixed with carrot juice.

10 The babies who ___________ the earlier experience of tasting carrot juice refused and made unhappy faces about the taste.

11 On the other hand, the other group of babies easily accepted and enjoyed the carrot juice in the cereal.

12 There was a big difference between babies who experienced carrot juice before they were born and babies who didn't.

READING 44

1~2의 지시문을 먼저 읽고, 무엇에 중점을 두어 글을 읽어야 할지 파악해 봅시다.

다음 글을 읽고, 물음에 답하시오. (기출응용)

[1] *Harry Potter and the Deathly Hallows*, the seventh and final book of J. K. Rowling's fantasy series, was released in the United States in 2007. [2] It sold 8.3 million copies in its first 24 hours on sale. [3] Is the last *Harry Potter* book that good? [4] Perhaps it and the earlier six books of the series are truly excellent, although eight publishers refused to publish the first one. [5] Success is at least partly decided by quality. [6] In today's world, however, it is also possible that what people come to like depends very much on what they believe others like. [7] The explanation for why a particular book becomes a hit may be as simple as this publisher's opinion: "It sold well because lots of people bought it." [8] ________________________ is now shared much more widely than in the past. [9] Cultural artifacts such as books and movies can have 'a snowball effect' in popularity in ways they could not a century ago. [10] It turns the cultural industries into difficult-to-predict, winner-take-all markets. [11] Tiny differences in performance can make great differences in making money.

* artifact 가공품, 인공물

글을 읽으면서 본론이 시작되는 문장에 밑줄을 그어 봅시다.

1 윗글의 제목으로 가장 적절한 것은?

① Book vs. Movie: An Endless Debate
② What You Read Shows Who You Are
③ Creativity: A Basic Quality of a Writer
④ Popularity Greatly Affects Product Success
⑤ How Popular Movies Influence Children

빈칸 앞에서 빈칸에 들어갈 말의 단서가 되는 어구를 모두 찾아 네모 표시를 해 봅시다.

2 윗글의 빈칸에 들어갈 말로 가장 적절한 것은?

① Traditional knowledge
② Social information
③ Moral philosophy
④ Physical similarity
⑤ Artistic freedom

1 다음 중 윗글의 내용과 일치하지 <u>않는</u> 것을 2개 고르면?

① *Harry Potter* 시리즈의 마지막 책은 미국에서 2007년에 출간되었다.
② *Harry Potter and the Deathly Hallows*는 여러 차례 출간 거절된 적 있다.
③ 오늘날 문화 상품의 성공은 전적으로 작품성과 완성도에 달려 있다.
④ 문화 상품은 많이 팔릴수록 더 큰 인기를 얻게 되기도 한다.
⑤ 문화 상품 인기의 '눈덩이 효과'는 문화 산업 시장을 예측할 수 없게 만든다.

2 빈칸에 알맞은 단어를 윗글에서 찾아 쓰시오.

A(n) ＿＿＿＿＿ ＿＿＿＿＿ is a situation where something increases in size or importance faster and faster.

3 윗글의 내용을 다음과 같이 요약할 때, 빈칸에 알맞은 단어를 쓰시오.

＿＿＿＿＿ of a cultural product can be influenced not only by its ＿＿＿＿＿ but also very much by its ＿＿＿＿＿.

지문 듣기   기출 원문 보기

GRAMMAR (TIP)

'훨씬'이라는 의미로 비교급을 강조하여 수식하는 부사에는 much, still, even, far, a lot 등이 있어요.

• The product arrived **much** earlier than expected.

• The soup tastes **a lot** better than it looks.

cf. 부사 very는 주로 '매우'라는 의미로 원급을 수식하고, '단연코'라는 의미로 최상급도 수식해요. 비교급은 수식할 수 없음을 유의하세요.

• His explanation was **very** clear.

• It is the **very** best movie of the year.

❶ *Harry Potter and the Deathly Hallows*, the seventh and final book of J. K. Rowling's fantasy series, was released in the United States in 2007.

❷ It sold 8.3 million copies in its first 24 hours on sale.

❸ Is the last *Harry Potter* book that good?

❹ Perhaps it and the earlier six books of the series are truly excellent, although eight publishers refused to publish the first one.

❺ Success is at least partly decided by quality.

❻ In today's world, however, it is also possible that what people come to like depends very much on what they believe others like.

❼ The explanation for why a particular book becomes a hit may be as simple as this publisher's opinion: "It sold well because lots of people bought it."

❽ ______________ is now shared much `TIP` more widely than in the past.

❾ Cultural artifacts such as books and movies can have 'a snowball effect' in popularity in ways they could not a century ago.

❿ It turns the cultural industries into difficult-to-predict, winner-take-all markets.

⓫ Tiny differences in performance can make great differences in making money.

WORDS

release 발매하다[출간하다]

on sale 판매되는

truly 정말로

publisher 출판업자, 출판사

publish 출판하다, 출간하다

at least 적어도

partly 부분적으로

decide 결정하다

quality 품질, 자질

depend on ~에 달려 있다, ~에 의해 결정되다

explanation 설명

cf. explain 설명하다

particular 특정한

hit 인기작

cultural 문화의, 문화적인

cf. culture 문화

popularity 인기

cf. popular 인기 있는

turn A into B A를 B로 바꿔 놓다

industry 산업

predict 예측하다

winner-take-all 승자독식의

tiny 아주 작은

performance 성과, 흥행

endless 끝없는

debate 논쟁

traditional 전통적인

social 사회적인

moral 도덕상의

philosophy 철학

physical 신체의

similarity 유사점

artistic 예술적인

READING

45

GET READY

1~2의 지시문을 먼저 읽고, 무엇에 중점을 두어 글을 읽어야 할지 파악해 봅시다.

다음 글을 읽고, 물음에 답하시오. (기출응용)

① Imagine *Jaws* without a hungry white shark, *Superman* without Kryptonite, or the tale of *Little Red Riding Hood* without a scary wolf. ② The teenagers in *Jaws* would have had a great summer at the beach, Superman would not have had a worry in the world, and Little Red Riding Hood would visit her grandmother and then go home. ③ Words like "boring" and "predictable" have just come across your mind. Right? ④ Movie director Nils Malmros once said, "Paradise on a Sunday afternoon sounds great, but it would be a boring scene in film." ⑤ In other words, too much harmony and not enough conflict in movies doesn't appeal to audiences. ⑥ Conflict is one of the great sources of making a good story. ⑦ No conflict, no story. ⑧ But why is this the case? ⑨ The answer lies in human nature. ⑩ As humans, we naturally look for balance and harmony in our lives. ⑪ We simply don't like to break the balance between our surroundings and ourselves. ⑫ So, as soon as harmony is interrupted, we do whatever we can to restore it. ⑬ We avoid unpleasant situations, feelings of stress, or anxiety. ⑭ If we have an unresolved problem with our friends, family, or our colleagues, it bothers us until we take care of it and return to a peaceful state. ⑮ When faced with a problem — a conflict — we automatically start to look for a solution. ⑯ Conflict forces us to act. ⑰ Thus, a story becomes more lively and energetic from changes that _______________ this sense of harmony.

글을 읽으면서 주제문을 찾아 밑줄을 그어 봅시다.

1 윗글의 제목으로 가장 적절한 것은?

① How to Be a Good Actor
② Conflict: A Key to a Good Story
③ What Causes Conflicts among People?
④ Everyone Can Be Someone's Superhero
⑤ Make a Difference by Changing Yourself

글을 읽으면서 빈칸에 들어갈 말의 단서가 되는 글의 핵심어를 찾아봅시다.

2 윗글의 빈칸에 들어갈 말로 가장 적절한 것은?

① disturb　　② simplify　　③ restore
④ promote　　⑤ represent

1 다음 중 윗글의 내용과 일치하지 <u>않는</u> 것은?

① 갈등이 부족한 영화는 관객의 흥미를 끌지 못한다.
② 평화는 좋은 이야기를 만드는 훌륭한 원천 중 하나이다.
③ 인간은 자연스럽게 삶 속에서 균형과 조화를 찾는다.
④ 인간은 불쾌한 상황, 스트레스의 감정 또는 불안감을 피한다.
⑤ 인간은 문제에 직면하면 자동적으로 해결책을 찾기 시작한다.

2 다음 각 작품 속 갈등 요소를 윗글에서 찾아 쓰시오.

(1) *Jaws*　　　　　　　→ ______________________________

(2) *Superman*　　　　　→ ______________________________

(3) *Little Red Riding Hood*　→ ______________________________

3 윗글의 내용을 다음과 같이 요약할 때, 빈칸에 알맞은 단어를 쓰시오.

____________ is an important source of a good story because it makes a story more ____________ ____________ ____________.

지문 듣기   기출 원문 보기

GRAMMAR TIP

가정법 과거완료는 과거 사실과 반대로 가정하여 '~했다면 …했을 텐데'를 의미하는 것으로, 「If+주어+had+과거분사, 주어+조동사의 과거형+have+과거분사」 형태로 표현해요. if절이 '~이 없었다면'을 의미하는 경우에는 if절 대신 without을 써서 나타낼 수 있어요.

- If I **had slept** early last night, I **would have woken up** early this morning.
- **Without** your help, I **could not have finished** this work.
  (= If there **had not been** your help, I **could not have finished** this work.)

❶ Imagine *Jaws* without a hungry white shark, *Superman* without Kryptonite, or the tale of *Little Red Riding Hood* without a scary wolf.

❷ The teenagers in *Jaws* would have had a great summer at the beach, Superman would not have had a worry in the world, and Little Red Riding Hood would visit her grandmother and then go home.

❸ Words like "boring" and "predictable" have just come across your mind. Right?

❹ Movie director Nils Malmros once said, "Paradise on a Sunday afternoon sounds great, but it would be a boring scene in film."

❺ In other words, too much harmony and not enough conflict in movies doesn't appeal to audiences.

❻ Conflict is one of the great sources of making a good story.

❼ No conflict, no story.

❽ But why is this the case?

⑨ The answer lies in human nature.

⑩ As humans, we naturally look for balance and harmony in our lives.

⑪ We simply don't like to break the balance between our surroundings and ourselves.

⑫ So, as soon as harmony is interrupted, we do whatever we can to restore it.

⑬ We avoid unpleasant situations, feelings of stress, or anxiety.

⑭ If we have an unresolved problem with our friends, family, or our colleagues, it bothers us until we take care of it and return to a peaceful state.

⑮ When faced with a problem—a conflict—we automatically start to look for a solution.

⑯ Conflict forces us to act.

⑰ Thus, a story becomes more lively and energetic from changes that ____________ this sense of harmony.

1 세 단어 중 서로 의미가 비슷한 두 개를 고르시오.

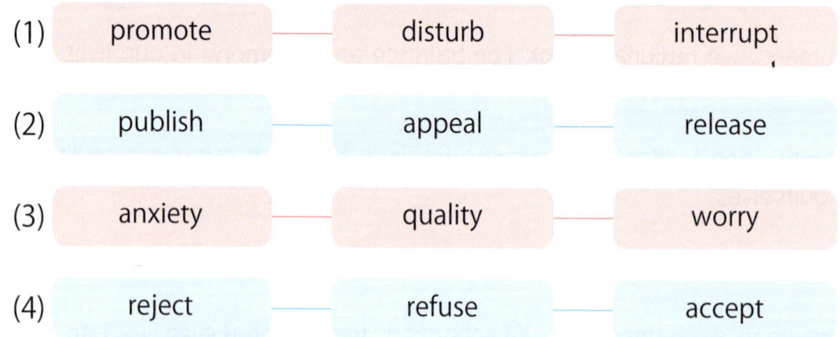

2 단어와 우리말 뜻을 바르게 연결하시오.

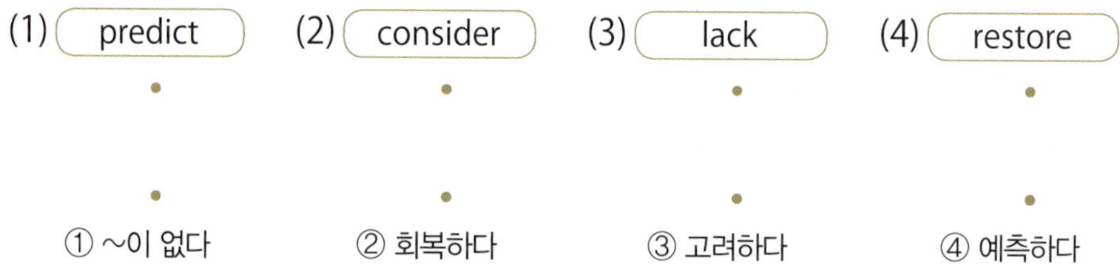

① ~이 없다   ② 회복하다   ③ 고려하다   ④ 예측하다

3 우리말 뜻에 해당하는 단어를 찾아 동그라미 하고 빈칸에 쓰시오.

D	C	B	Z	P	D	U	B	S	E	O	H
E	S	S	J	T	A	O	N	O	I	L	Y
T	H	N	O	K	R	F	R	U	C	M	P
S	K	B	P	C	P	S	T	R	O	N	O
B	O	T	N	O	I	I	I	C	N	S	A
L	T	N	D	E	B	A	T	E	F	P	D
D	L	X	R	O	G	Z	L	U	L	B	R
C	I	N	J	A	Y	C	F	A	I	N	Y
O	O	Q	D	Y	N	V	O	T	C	G	K
N	P	O	P	U	L	A	R	I	T	Y	L
F	B	E	N	J	K	W	M	A	L	H	B
L	C	G	L	U	H	R	G	B	U	R	A

(1) 사회적인 _______________

(2) 논쟁 _______________

(3) 원천 _______________

(4) 인기 _______________

(5) 형성하다 _______________

(6) 갈등 _______________

4 주어진 단어를 사용하여 우리말 뜻에 해당하는 표현을 쓰시오. (한 번씩만 쓸 것)

(1) ~에 직면하다 ___________________

(2) ~에 달려 있다 ___________________

(3) ~에 속하다 ___________________

(4) A를 B로 바꿔 놓다 ___________________

be   to   on   with

belong   depend   turn   faced   into

5 네모 안에서 어법에 맞는 것을 고르시오.

(1) Their babies were enough old / old enough to start eating cereal.

(2) Conflict is one of the great source / sources of making a good story.

(3) Social information is now shared much / very more widely than in the past.

(4) If there had not been a hungry white shark in *Jaws*, the teenagers would have / have had a great summer at the beach.

6 우리말과 의미가 같도록 괄호 안의 동사를 알맞은 형태로 쓰시오.

(1) 우리는 조화를 회복하기 위해 우리가 할 수 있는 것은 무엇이든지 한다. (restore)

→ We do whatever we can ___________________ harmony.

(2) 이제 그 집단 간의 차이점을 찾아볼 때였다. (look)

→ It was time ___________________ for a difference between the groups.

(3) 사람들이 좋아하게 되는 것은 그들이 다른 사람들이 좋아한다고 믿는 것에 달려 있다. (depend)

→ What people come to like ___________________ on what they believe others like.

(4) 크립토나이트가 없었다면 슈퍼맨은 세상에 걱정거리가 없었을 것이다. (have)

→ Without Kryptonite, Superman would not ___________________ a worry in the world.

GET READY

1~3의 지시문을 먼저 읽고, 무엇에 중점을 두어 글을 읽어야 할지 파악해 봅시다.

다음 글을 읽고, 물음에 답하시오. (기출응용)

(A) ❶ Captain Charlie Plumb was a U.S. Navy jet pilot. ❷ He flew many successful fighting missions. ❸ However, on his 75th mission, his fighter plane was shot down. ❹ He escaped and reached the ground safely using a parachute. ❺ Unfortunately, (a) he was captured and spent six years in a Vietnamese prison. ❻ He survived the terrible situation and in 1973 returned to his hometown. ❼ He was awarded the Silver Star Medal. ❽ After that, he gave lectures about the lessons he learned from his war experiences.

(B) ❾ After that experience, Plumb would ask the audiences in his lectures, "Who's packing your parachute?" ❿ (b) He would continue to explain that we all have someone who has performed services for us. ⓫ He inspired thousands of people through his lectures and was even selected as one of the top ten speakers in a survey of U.S. meeting planners.

(C) ⓬ One day, while he was traveling to a lecture, he went into a restaurant to eat. ⓭ A man came up to his table and said, "You're Plumb! You flew jet fighters in Vietnam from the aircraft carrier Kitty Hawk. You were shot down." ⓮ Plumb looked at the man and asked, "How did you know that?" ⓯ (c) He replied, "I was a sailor on the Kitty Hawk. I packed your parachute that day." ⓰ Plumb shook hands with the man and thanked him.

(D) ⓱ Plumb couldn't sleep that night, thinking about the sailor. ⓲ He felt sorry because he neither recognized him nor remembered his name. ⓳ When he was a fighter pilot, (d) he never thought about who packed his parachute before every mission. ⓴ The sailor and others used to spend long hours carefully folding and packing parachutes for (e) his personal safety during his service in the Navy.

글을 읽으면서 각 단락의 중심 내용을 요약해 봅시다.

1 주어진 글 (A)에 이어질 내용을 순서에 맞게 배열한 것으로 가장 적절한 것은?

① (B) − (D) − (C)　　　② (C) − (B) − (D)　　　③ (C) − (D) − (B)

④ (D) − (B) − (C)　　　⑤ (D) − (C) − (B)

글에 등장하는 주요 인물 2명을 찾고 간단히 설명해 봅시다.

2 밑줄 친 (a)～(e) 중에서 가리키는 대상이 나머지 넷과 <u>다른</u> 것은?

① (a)　　　② (b)　　　③ (c)　　　④ (d)　　　⑤ (e)

글을 읽으면서 ①～⑤의 내용과 관련된 문장에 밑줄을 그어 봅시다.

3 윗글의 Plumb에 관한 내용과 일치하지 <u>않는</u> 것은?

① 전투 임무 중 조종하던 전투기가 격추되었다.

② 고향으로 돌아와 은성훈장을 받았다.

③ 한 조사에서 10인의 명연설가 중 한 명으로 선정되었다.

④ 식당에서 자신을 알아본 남자를 만났다.

⑤ 낙하산을 포장해 준 선원의 이름을 기억하고 있었다.

1 다음 질문에 알맞은 답을 윗글에서 찾아 문장을 완성하시오.

(1) **Q:** When did Plumb return to his hometown?

　A: He returned to his hometown in ___________.

(2) **Q:** How did the man at the restaurant know about Plumb?

　A: He had been _______________ on the Kitty Hawk.

2 윗글에서 Plumb 대령을 위해 선원들이 했던 일을 찾아 우리말로 쓰시오.

____

지문 듣기   기출 원문 보기

GRAMMAR TIP

「neither A nor B」는 'A도 B도 아닌'을 의미해요. 여기서 A와 B에는 문법적으로 같은 성격의 문장 성분이 와야 해요.

- My hobby is **neither** listening to music **nor** watching movies.
  동명사구 / 동명사구
- Sarah **neither** called me **nor** sent me a message.
  과거동사구 / 과거동사구

「neither A nor B」가 주어로 쓰일 때는 B에 동사의 수와 인칭을 일치시켜요.

- **Neither** you **nor** he *is* good at sports.

❶ Captain Charlie Plumb was a U.S. Navy jet pilot.

❷ He flew many successful fighting missions.

❸ However, on his 75th mission, his fighter plane was shot down.

❹ He escaped and reached the ground safely using a parachute.

❺ Unfortunately, he was captured and spent six years in a Vietnamese prison.

❻ He survived the terrible situation and in 1973 returned to his hometown.

❼ He was awarded the Silver Star Medal.

❽ After that, he gave lectures about the lessons he learned from his war experiences.

❾ After that experience, Plumb would ask the audiences in his lectures, "Who's packing your parachute?"

❿ He would continue to explain that we all have someone who has performed services for us.

⓫ He inspired thousands of people through his lectures and was even selected as one of the top ten speakers in a survey of U.S. meeting planners.

⑫ One day, while he was traveling to a lecture, he went into a restaurant to eat.

⑬ A man came up to his table and said, "You're Plumb! You flew jet fighters in Vietnam from the aircraft carrier Kitty Hawk. You were shot down."

⑭ Plumb looked at the man and asked, "How did you know that?"

⑮ He replied, "I was a sailor on the Kitty Hawk. I packed your parachute that day."

⑯ Plumb shook hands with the man and thanked him.

⑰ Plumb couldn't sleep that night, thinking about the sailor.

⑱ He felt sorry because he neither recognized him nor remembered his name.

⑲ When he was a fighter pilot, he never thought about who packed his parachute before every mission.

⑳ The sailor and others used to spend long hours carefully folding and packing parachutes for his personal safety during his service in the Navy.

WORDS

pilot 조종사
successful 성공적인, 성공한
mission (비행) 임무
shoot down 격추하다
escape 탈출하다
parachute 낙하산
unfortunately 불행하게도
capture 붙잡다
cf. catch 붙잡다
survive ~에서 살아남다
cf. survival 생존
award (상 등을) 수여하다
give a lecture 강연하다
experience 경험
audience 청중
pack 포장하다, 싸다
continue 계속하다
explain 설명하다
perform 수행하다
cf. performance 수행, 성취
service 일, 봉사, 군무
inspire 영감을 주다
select 선정하다, 선발하다
travel 이동하다, 여행하다
come up to ~에게 다가가다
cf. approach 다가가다
aircraft carrier 항공모함
sailor 선원
neither A nor B A도 B도 아닌
recognize 알아보다
personal 개인의, 개인적인
safety 안전
cf. safe 안전한

GET READY

1~3의 지시문을 먼저 읽고, 무엇에 중점을 두어 글을 읽어야 할지 파악해 봅시다.

다음 글을 읽고, 물음에 답하시오. 기출응용

(A) ❶ Henry's father was a house painter. ❷ In his lifetime, he must have painted hundreds of houses, inside and out. ❸ He was a happy, outgoing man who made friends easily. ❹ It wasn't hard to tell that he loved his work as well as his life. ❺ He was also an excellent painter. ❻ No one could paint a wall like him, which is why (a) his service was always popular with people.

(B) ❼ Finally, his father offered Henry some advice. ❽ "Don't worry about spills and messes. ❾ They can always be cleaned up. ❿ Treat a wall the way you treat people—be generous and have fun. ⓫ Always put enough paint on the brush." ⓬ Then, (b) he turned around and applied a thick coat of paint to the wall, and continued his conversation with the homeowner. ⓭ Henry's father did spill a few drops, but he made a better-looking wall while having fun.

(C) ⓮ Once, while in college, Henry went to help his father paint a house. ⓯ Henry was working inside and noticed how skilled his father was. ⓰ He was quickly applying a quality coat of paint to a wall. ⓱ He was actually laughing and talking with the homeowner while applying a good amount of paint to the wall. ⓲ (c) He painted three walls compared to Henry's one.

(D) ⓳ At one point, Henry's father stopped working and watched him. ⓴ (d) He noticed how Henry took his time dipping the brush in the paint bucket and how carefully he wiped off both sides of the brush when he pulled it out trying not to waste any paint. ㉑ Henry then spread a thin coat of paint on the wall without spilling a drop. ㉒ It was a slow, boring process. ㉓ (e) He didn't laugh or "joke around" because he was afraid that he might make a mess and embarrass his father.

1 주어진 글 (A)에 이어질 내용을 순서에 맞게 배열한 것으로 가장 적절한 것은?

① (B) − (D) − (C)   ② (C) − (B) − (D)   ③ (C) − (D) − (B)
④ (D) − (B) − (C)   ⑤ (D) − (C) − (B)

2 밑줄 친 (a)~(e) 중에서 가리키는 대상이 나머지 넷과 다른 것은?

① (a)   ② (b)   ③ (c)   ④ (d)   ⑤ (e)

3 윗글의 Henry의 아버지에 관한 내용과 일치하지 <u>않는</u> 것은?

① 친구를 쉽게 사귀는 외향적인 사람이었다.
② Henry에게 붓에 페인트를 충분히 묻히라고 조언했다.
③ 페인트를 벽에 칠할 때 한 방울도 흘리지 않았다.
④ 집주인과 대화를 나누면서 페인트칠을 했다.
⑤ 하던 일을 멈추고 Henry를 지켜보았다.

1 윗글에서 Henry의 아버지가 Henry에게 한 조언 세 가지를 우리말로 쓰시오.

- ____
- ____
- ____

2 다음 질문에 알맞은 답을 윗글에서 찾아 문장을 완성하시오.

Q: Why didn't Henry laugh or joke around while painting?
A: He didn't want to ____.

지문 듣기   기출 원문 보기

GRAMMAR TIP

「must have+과거분사」는 '~했음에 틀림없다'라고 과거에 대한 강한 추측을 나타내는 표현이에요.

• He didn't call me. He **must have forgotten** my number.

• The ground is wet. It **must have rained** last night.

cf. 「should have+과거분사」는 '~했어야 했다'라고 과거에 대한 후회나 유감을 나타내는 표현이에요.

• I got a poor grade. I **should have studied** harder.

❶ Henry's father was a house painter.

❷ In his lifetime, he must have painted hundreds of houses, inside and out.

❸ He was a happy, outgoing man who made friends easily.

❹ It wasn't hard to tell that he loved his work as well as his life.

❺ He was also an excellent painter.

❻ No one could paint a wall like him, which is why his service was always popular with people.

❼ Finally, his father offered Henry some advice.

❽ "Don't worry about spills and messes.

❾ They can always be cleaned up.

❿ Treat a wall the way you treat people — be generous and have fun.

⓫ Always put enough paint on the brush."

⓬ Then, he turned around and applied a thick coat of paint to the wall, and continued his conversation with the homeowner.

⓭ Henry's father did spill a few drops, but he made a better-looking wall while having fun.

⑭ Once, while in college, Henry went to help his father paint a house.

⑮ Henry was working inside and noticed how skilled his father was.

⑯ He was quickly applying a quality coat of paint to a wall.

⑰ He was actually laughing and talking with the homeowner while applying a good amount of paint to the wall.

⑱ He painted three walls compared to Henry's one.

⑲ At one point, Henry's father stopped working and watched him.

⑳ He noticed how Henry took his time dipping the brush in the paint bucket and how carefully he wiped off both sides of the brush when he pulled it out trying not to waste any paint.

㉑ Henry then spread a thin coat of paint on the wall without spilling a drop.

㉒ It was a slow, boring process.

㉓ He didn't laugh or "joke around" because he was afraid that he might make a mess and embarrass his father.

READING **48**

GET READY

1~3의 지시문을 먼저 읽고, 무엇에 중점을 두어 글을 읽어야 할지 파악해 봅시다.

다음 글을 읽고, 물음에 답하시오. (기출응용)

(A) ❶ I was running late. ❷ My wife, Eleanor, and I had agreed to meet at the restaurant at seven o'clock, and it was already half past. ❸ I had a good excuse: a client meeting lasted longer than expected, and I'd wasted no time getting to the dinner as quickly as possible. ❹ When I arrived at the restaurant, I apologized and told my wife I didn't mean to be late. ❺ She answered, "You never mean to be late." ❻ Uh oh, she was mad. ❼ "Sorry," I replied. "It was unavoidable." ❽ I told her about the client meeting. ❾ My explanation seemed to make things worse. ❿ And that started to make (a) me angry.

(B) ⓫ In other words, he meant, I was focused on my intention, while Eleanor was focused on the outcome. ⓬ She and I were having two different conversations. ⓭ In the end, we both felt misunderstood and angry. ⓮ The more I thought about what my friend had said, the more (b) I recognized that this battle was about the misunderstanding between us.

(C) ⓯ As it turns out, the important thing is neither the thought nor the action. ⓰ That's because Eleanor doesn't experience (c) my thoughts or actions. ⓱ She experiences the outcome of my actions. ⓲ From this battle, I came to realize that when I upset her or someone else — no matter who's right — I should always start the conversation by noticing how my actions have affected the other person. ⓳ After all, my intentions don't matter much.

(D) ⓴ Several weeks later, when I described the situation to my friend who is a professor of family therapy, he smiled. ㉑ "You made a classic mistake, as (d) I have done before," he told me. ㉒ "You only think about yourself," he said. ㉓ "You didn't mean to be late but that's not the point. ㉔ What's important in your communication is how (e) your lateness affected Eleanor."

1 주어진 글 (A)에 이어질 내용을 순서에 맞게 배열한 것으로 가장 적절한 것은?

① (B) – (D) – (C)　　　② (C) – (B) – (D)　　　③ (C) – (D) – (B)

④ (D) – (B) – (C)　　　⑤ (D) – (C) – (B)

2 밑줄 친 (a)~(e) 중에서 가리키는 대상이 나머지 넷과 <u>다른</u> 것은?

① (a)　　　② (b)　　　③ (c)　　　④ (d)　　　⑤ (e)

3 윗글의 필자에 관한 내용과 일치하지 <u>않는</u> 것은?

① 아내에게 고객과의 만남 때문에 약속에 늦었다고 말했다.
② 약속에 늦은 것을 이해해 주지 않는 아내에게 화가 났다.
③ 행동의 결과에만 집중해서 다툼이 일어났음을 깨달았다.
④ 다툼을 계기로 아내와의 생각 차이를 이해하게 되었다.
⑤ 가족 치료 교수인 친구에게 자신의 문제를 털어놓았다.

UNDERSTAND DEEPLY

1 다음 질문 중 윗글을 읽고 대답할 수 <u>없는</u> 것은?

① Where did the writer and his wife meet?
② What made the writer angry?
③ Where does the writer's friend teach students?
④ What caused the battle between the writer and his wife?
⑤ What did the writer realize from the battle?

2 다음 중 윗글에 나타난 필자의 심경 변화로 가장 적절한 것은?

① upset → misunderstood　　　② anxious → jealous
③ delighted → nervous　　　④ uncomfortable → indifferent
⑤ angry → understanding

지문 듣기   기출 원문 보기

GRAMMAR TIP

「the 비교급＋주어＋동사,
the 비교급＋주어＋동사」는
'〜할수록 더 …하다'를 의미
해요.

• **The more** I walked, **the
  thirstier** I got.

• **The higher** you go up,
  the colder it gets.

cf. 「비교급＋and＋비교급」은
'점점 더 〜한'이라는 의미로,
동사 get, be, become 등과
함께 자주 쓰여요. 비교급이
「more＋원급」형태이면
「more and more＋원급」으
로 써요.

• It was getting **darker
  and darker**.

• The actor became **more
  and more popular**.

❶ I was running late.

❷ My wife, Eleanor, and I had agreed to meet at the restaurant at seven o'clock, and it was already half past.

❸ I had a good excuse: a client meeting lasted longer than expected, and I'd wasted no time getting to the dinner as quickly as possible.

❹ When I arrived at the restaurant, I apologized and told my wife I didn't mean to be late.

❺ She answered, "You never mean to be late."

❻ Uh oh, she was mad.

❼ "Sorry," I replied. "It was unavoidable."

❽ I told her about the client meeting.

❾ My explanation seemed to make things worse.

❿ And that started to make me angry.

⓫ In other words, he meant, I was focused on my intention, while Eleanor was focused on the outcome.

⓬ She and I were having two different conversations.

⓭ In the end, we both felt misunderstood and angry.

⑭ **The more** I thought about what my friend had said, **the more** I recognized that this battle was about the misunderstanding between us.

⑮ As it turns out, the important thing is neither the thought nor the action.

⑯ That's because Eleanor doesn't experience my thoughts or actions.

⑰ She experiences the outcome of my actions.

⑱ From this battle, I came to realize that when I upset her or someone else — no matter who's right — I should always start the conversation by noticing how my actions have affected the other person.

⑲ After all, my intentions don't matter much.

⑳ Several weeks later, when I described the situation to my friend who is a professor of family therapy, he smiled.

㉑ "You made a classic mistake, as I have done before," he told me.

㉒ "You only think about yourself," he said.

㉓ "You didn't mean to be late but that's not the point.

㉔ What's important in your communication is how your lateness affected Eleanor."

REVIEW TIME

1 짝지어진 단어들이 같은 관계가 되도록 빈칸에 알맞은 단어를 쓰시오.

(1) safe : safety = late : ________________

(2) refuse : accept = thin : ________________

(3) explain : describe = result : ________________

(4) performance : perform = apology : ________________

2 서로 의미가 비슷한 단어끼리 연결하시오.

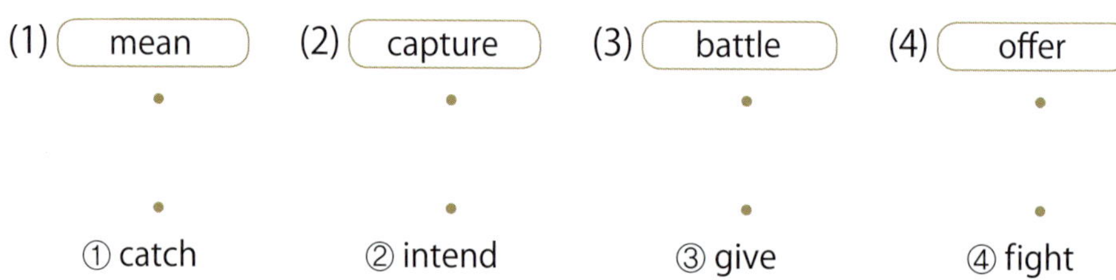

3 우리말 뜻에 맞게 주어진 철자로 시작하는 단어 퍼즐을 완성하시오.

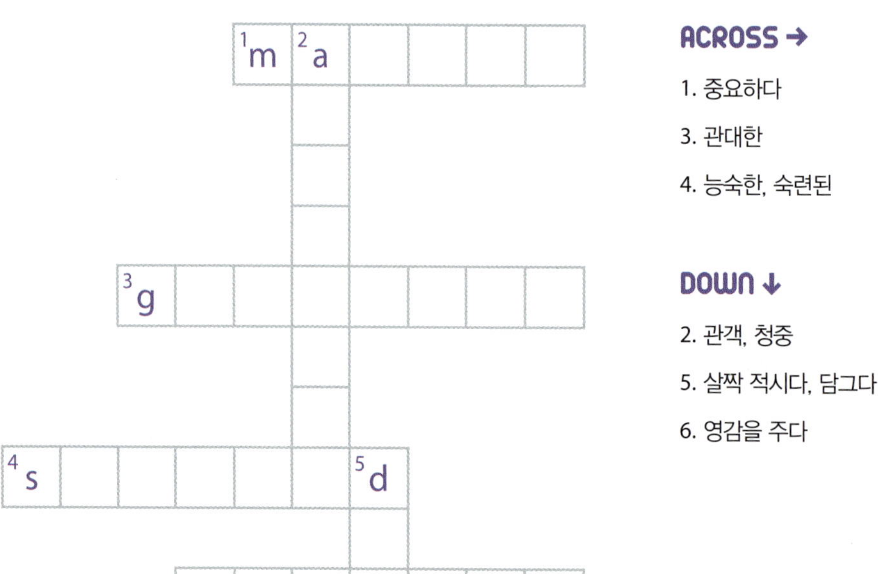

4 주어진 단어를 사용하여 우리말 뜻에 해당하는 표현을 쓰시오. (한 번씩만 쓸 것)

(1) 밝혀지다 ________________   (2) 격추하다 ________________

(3) ~에게 인기가 있다 ________________   (4) 닦아 내다 ________________

with	off	out	down

popular	shoot	turn	wipe	be

5 네모 안에서 어법에 맞는 것을 고르시오.

(1) Plumb neither recognized him or / nor remembered his name.

(2) The sailor used to spend long hours packing / to pack parachutes for Plumb.

(3) What / That is important in your communication is how your lateness affected Eleanor.

(4) The much / more I thought about his words, the much / more I recognized that the battle was about the misunderstanding.

6 우리말과 의미가 같도록 괄호 안의 동사를 알맞은 형태로 쓰시오.

(1) Plumb은 그 선원에 대해 생각하면서 그날 밤 잠을 이룰 수 없었다. (think)

→ Plumb couldn't sleep that night, ________________ about the sailor.

(2) 그가 자신의 삶뿐만 아니라 자신의 일을 사랑한다는 것을 아는 것은 어렵지 않았다. (tell)

→ It wasn't hard ________________ that he loved his work as well as his life.

(3) 일생 동안 그는 집 수백 채의 안과 밖을 칠했음에 틀림없다. (paint)

→ In his lifetime, he ________ ________ hundreds of houses, inside and out.

Play Time

바른답·알찬풀이 | p. 61

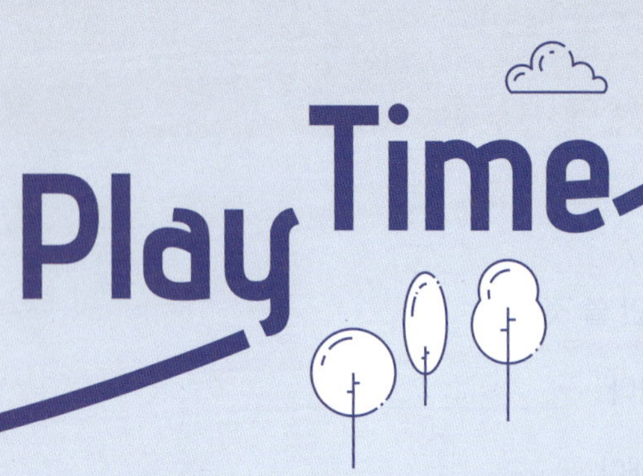

Draw dots in the empty squares so that the template matches all the dices.

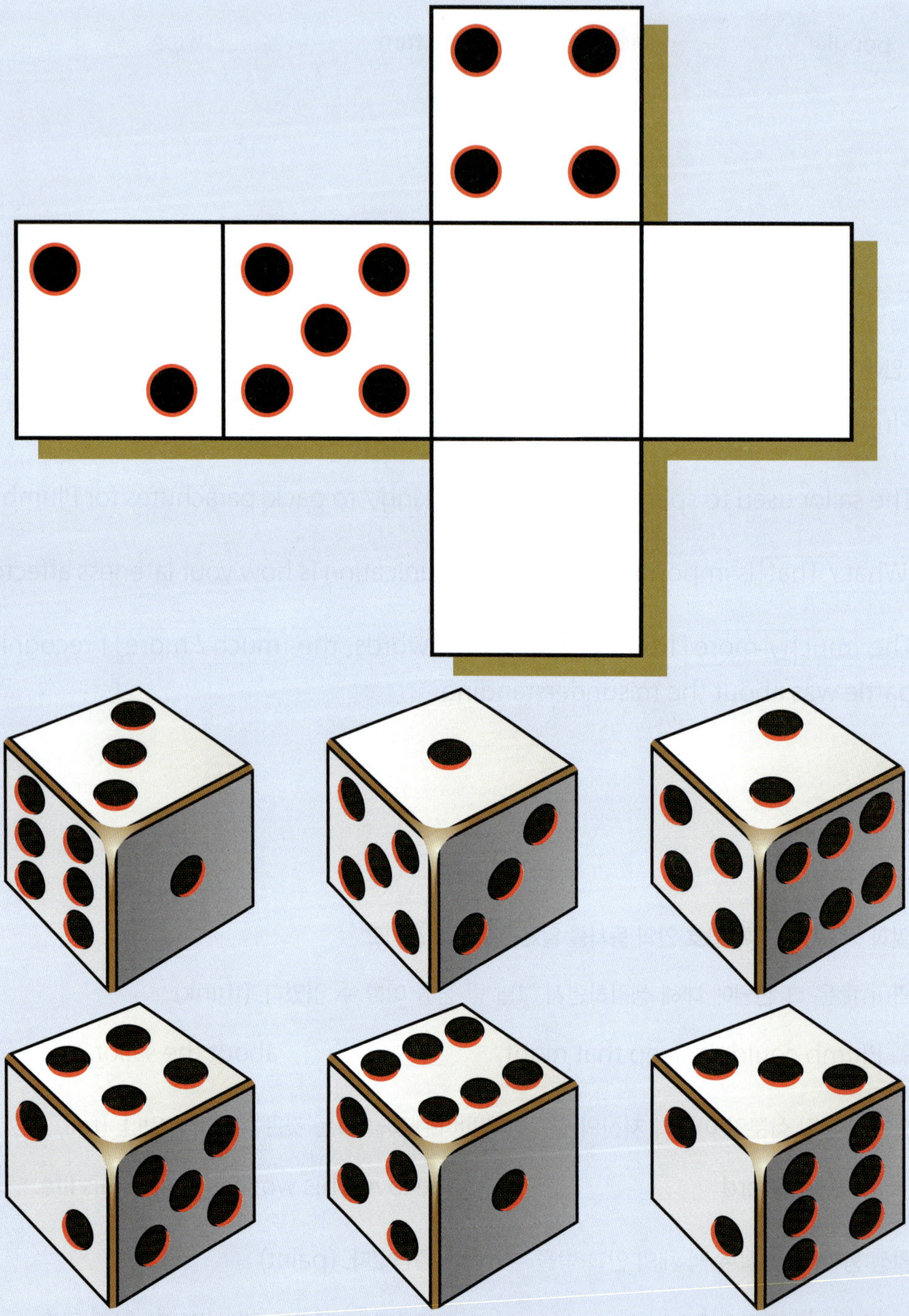

말 없는 위로

아무에게도 들키고 싶지 않은 기분일 때
말없이 위로해 주는 너에게 고마워.

그래서..
왜 울었어?
ㅋㅋㅋㅋ
야...
흑역사는 놀려야 제 맛!

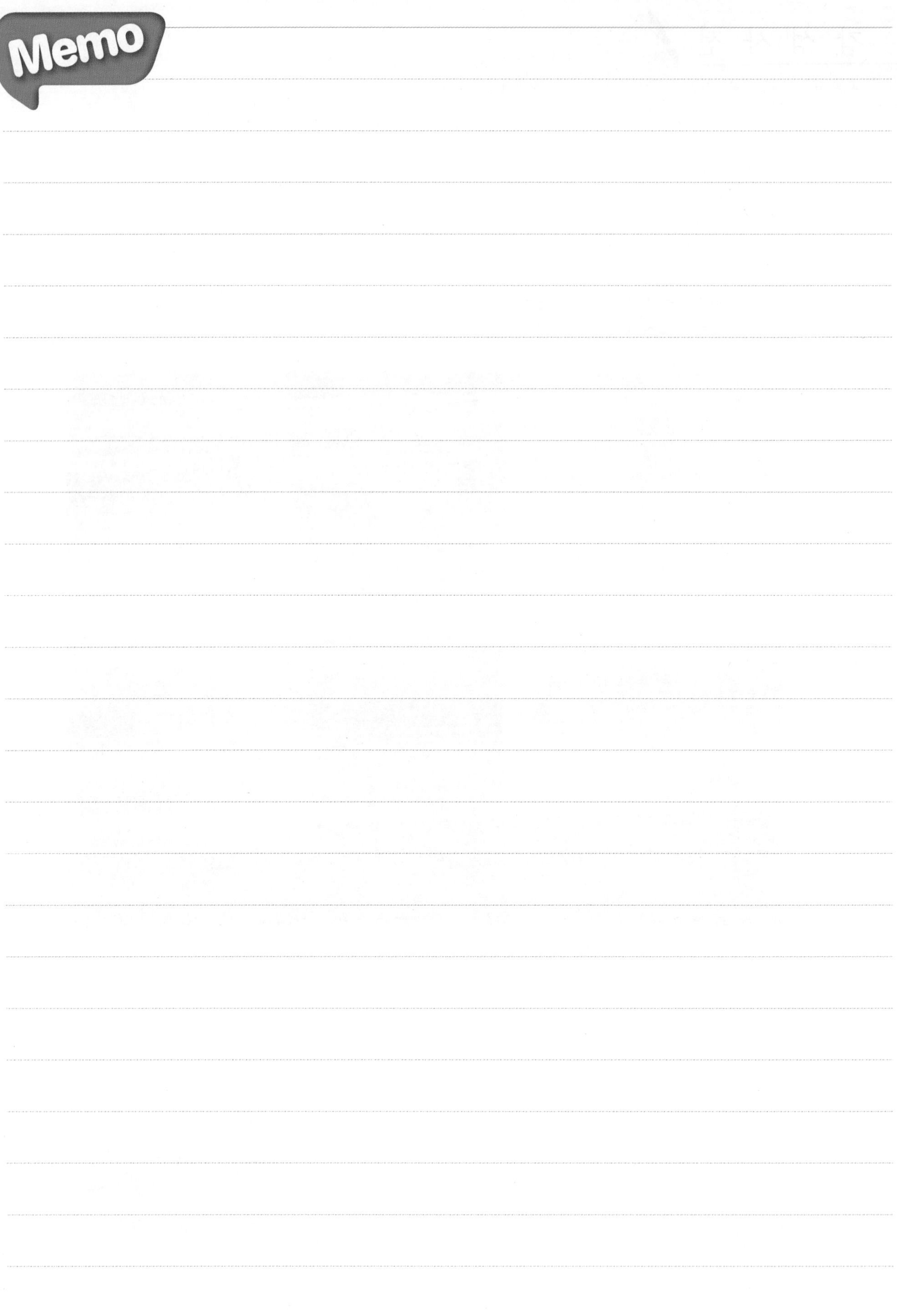

Memo

수학 개념을 쉽게 이해하는 방법?
개념수다로 시작하자!

수학의 진짜 실력자가 되는 비결 –
나에게 딱 맞는 개념서를 술술 읽으며 시작하자!

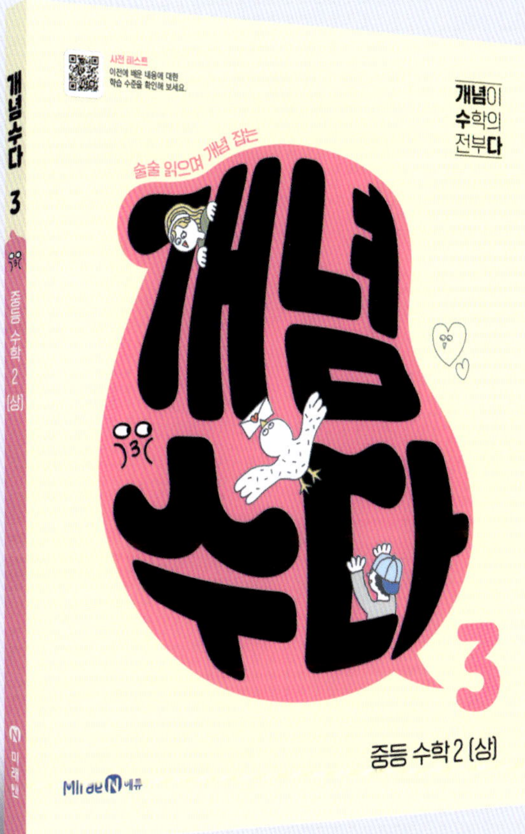

개념 이해
친구와 수다 떨듯 쉽고 재미있게,
베테랑 선생님의 동영상 강의로 완벽하게

개념 확인·정리
깔끔하게 구조화된 문제로 개념을 확인하고,
개념 전체의 흐름을 한 번에 정리

개념 끝장
온라인을 통해 개개인별 성취도 분석과
틀린 문항에 대한 맞춤 클리닉 제공

| 추천 대상 |
- 중등 수학 과정을 예습하고 싶은 초등 5~6학년
- 중등 수학을 어려워하는 중학생

수학은 순서를 따라 학습해야 효과적이므로,
초등 수학부터 꼼꼼하게 공부해 보자.

개념이 수학의 전부다
수학 개념을 제대로 공부하는 EASY 개념서
개념수다 시리즈

0_초등 핵심 개념
3_중등 수학 2(상), 4_중등 수학 2(하)
5_중등 수학 3(상), 6_중등 수학 3(하)

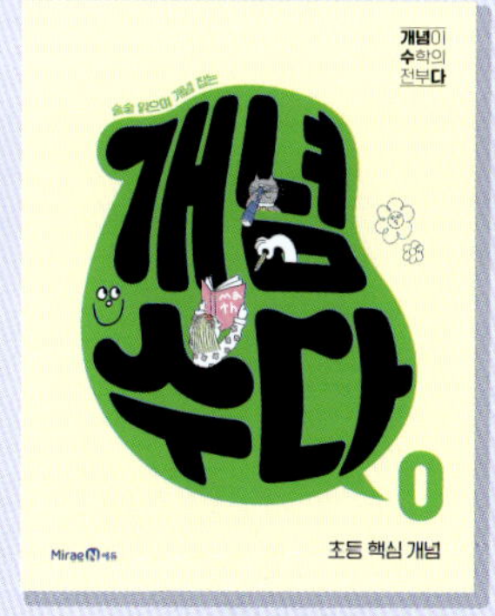

초등 핵심 개념
한 권으로 빠르게 정리!

중등 도서 안내

국어 독해·문법·어휘 훈련서

수능 국어의 자신감을 깨우는 단계별 실력 완성 훈련서

깨독

독해   0.준비편, 1.기본편, 2.실력편, 3.수능편
어휘   1.종합편, 2.수능편
문법   1.기본편, 2.수능편

영어 문법·독해 훈련서

중학교 영어의 핵심 문법과 독해 스킬 공략으로
내신·서술형·수능까지 단계별 완성 훈련서

GRAMMAR BITE

문법   PREP
문법   Grade 1, Grade 2, Grade 3
문법   PLUS 수능

READING BITE

독해   PREP
독해   Grade 1, Grade 2, Grade 3
독해   SUM

내신 필수 기본서

자세하고 쉬운 설명으로 개념을 이해하고, 특별한 비법으로 자신 있게
시험을 대비하는 필수 기본서

엔픽

[2022 개정]
사회   ①-1, ①-2*
역사   ①-1, ①-2*
과학   1-1, 1-2*
　　　*2025년 상반기 출간 예정

올리드

[2022 개정]
국어   (신유식) 1-1, 1-2*
　　　(민병곤) 1-1, 1-2*
영어   1-1, 1-2*
　　　*2025년 상반기 출간 예정

[2015 개정]
국어   2-1, 2-2, 3-1, 3-2
영어   2-1, 2-2, 3-1, 3-2
수학   2(상), 2(하), 3(상), 3(하)
사회   ①-1, ①-2, ②-1, ②-2
역사   ①-1, ①-2, ②-1, ②-2
과학   2-1, 2-2, 3-1, 3-2
*국어, 영어는 미래엔 교과서 연계 도서입니다.

수학 개념·유형 훈련서

빠르게 반복하며 수학 실력을 제대로 완성하는
단계별 내신 완성 훈련서

리피트

[2022 개정]
수학   1(상), 1(하), 2(상), 2(하), 3(상)*, 3(하)*
　　　*2025년 상반기 출간 예정

 **개념수다**

[2015 개정]
수학   2(상), 2(하), 3(상), 3(하)

 올리드 **유형완성**

[2015 개정]
수학   2(상), 2(하), 3(상), 3(하)

READING
BITE | 바른답·알찬풀이

바른답·알찬풀이

바른답·알찬풀이

Answers

UNIT 01　주제 파악하기

01　정답 ④　　　p. 12

이상과 삶의 규칙은 서로 다른 것이므로 이 둘을 구별해서 삶의 규칙을 이상적이기보다는 현실적으로 만들어야 한다는 내용의 글이다. 따라서 글의 주제로 ④ '지키며 살아갈 규칙이 현실적일 필요가 있는 이유'가 가장 적절하다.

오답풀이 ① 완벽한 기준의 특징　② 현실적인 목표를 세우는 것의 어려움　③ 이상을 일상적인 규칙으로 만드는 방법　⑤ 상세한 목표가 우리 삶에 미치는 부정적인 영향

READING GUIDE ❶

UNDERSTAND DEEPLY

1 (1) ideal　(2) realistic　(3) provide, with a guide　(4) direct, toward the ideal

2 이상, 이상을 규칙으로 만드는 것

1 첫 문장에서 알 수 있듯이 이 글은 이상과 지키며 살아갈 규칙을 대조하고 있다.

해석 [대조 대상] 이상 – 지키며 살아갈 규칙 [성격] 완벽한 – 현실적인 [역할] 지침을 제공하는 것 – 이상으로 인도하는 것

2 이상은 달성하기 자랑스러워할 완벽한 기준일 수 있으며, 이상을 규칙으로 만드는 것은 자기 자신에게 실망하여 계속 나아가는 것을 점점 더 어렵게 만든다고 했다.

READ CLOSELY　　　p. 13

❶ There ⟨is⟩ an important difference / between having an ideal and making a rule to live by.

중요한 차이가 있다 / 이상을 가지는 것과 지키며 살아갈 규칙을 만드는 것 사이에

❷ The ideal ⟨may be⟩ a perfect standard / that one would be proud to achieve.

이상은 완벽한 기준일 수 있다 / 달성하기 자랑스러워할

❸ Such an ideal / ⟨provides⟩ you with a guide, / but it ⟨should not be⟩ a daily standard.

그러한 이상은 / 여러분에게 지침을 제공한다 / 그러나 그것은 일상적인 기준이어서는 안 된다

❹ Making the ideal into a rule / ⟨is⟩ setting a trap / for yourself.

이상을 규칙으로 만드는 것은 / 덫을 놓는 것이다 / 여러분 자신에게

❺ If you constantly fall into the trap, / you ⟨feel⟩ so bad about yourself / that it becomes increasingly difficult / to keep going.

만약 여러분이 끊임없이 그 덫에 빠지면 / 여러분은 여러분 자신에게 너무 실망한다 / 그래서 점점 더 어려워진다 / 계속 나아가는 것이

❻ The rule ⟨needs⟩ to direct you / toward the ideal.

규칙은 여러분을 인도할 필요가 있다 / 이상을 향하여

❼ It also ⟨needs⟩ to be realistic / so that you do not lose your self-confidence.

그것은 또한 현실적일 필요가 있다 / 여러분이 자신감을 잃지 않도록

❽ That ⟨is⟩ why it makes more sense / to do the best / you can / — rather than try to be perfect.

그것이 더 타당한 이유이다 / 최선을 다하는 것이 / 여러분이 할 수 있는 / 완벽해지려고 노력하기보다는

지문해석 이상을 가지는 것과 지키며 살아갈 규칙을 만드는 것 사이에는 중요한 차이가 있다. 이상은 달성하기 자랑스러워할 완벽한 기준일 수 있다. 그러한 이상은 여러분에게 지침을 제공하지만 그것이 일상적인 기준이어서는 안 된다. 이상을 규칙으로 만드는 것은 여러분 자신에게 덫을 놓는 것이다. 만약 여러분이 끊임없이 그 덫에 빠지면 여러분은 여러분 자신에게 너무 실망하여 계속 나아가는 것이 점점 더 어려워진다. 규칙은 여러분을 이상으로 인도할 필요가 있다. 그것은 또한 여러분이 자신감을 잃지 않도록 현실적일 필요가 있다. 그것이 완벽해지려고 노력하기보다는 여러분이 할 수 있는 최선을 다하는 게 더 타당한 이유이다.

문장 돋보기

❷ The ideal may be a perfect standard [that one would be proud to achieve].
주어 / 목적격 관계대명사절 / to부정사의 부사적 용법(형용사 수식)

❹ Making the ideal into a rule is setting a trap for yourself.
동명사구 주어(단수 취급) / 단수 동사

❽ That is why it makes more sense to do the best you can — rather than try to be perfect.
그것이 ~한 이유이다 / 가주어 / 진주어(to부정사구) / ~보다는

02　정답 ①　　　p. 14

시를 통해 삶의 외면뿐만 아니라 내면까지도 들여다볼 수 있어 삶을 더 잘 이해하게 된다는 내용의 글로, 시가 우리 삶에 가져다주는 이점을 설명하고 있다. 따라서 글의 주제로 ① '삶에서의 시의 유용성'이 가장 알맞다.

오답풀이 ② 친구들을 이해하기 위한 조언들　③ 내면을 묘사하는 것의 어려움　④ 시를 읽는 것에 대한 오해　⑤ 시를 통해서 생각을 표현하는 방법

READING GUIDE ❶

UNDERSTAND DEEPLY

1 (1) T　(2) T　**2** (1) blue eyes / a mole on the left cheek / a red nose　(2) the habits / feelings / all the little characteristics (that ~ else)

1 (1) 친구의 외면만을 묘사하는 것은 그들이 정말 어떤 사람인지를 말해

주지 않을 것이라고 했으므로 일치한다. (2) 좋은 시는 삶의 외면뿐만 아니라 내면에 대해서도 말해 주며 세상을 친구만큼 잘 알게 해 준다고 했으므로 일치한다.

해석 (1) 사람의 외면만을 묘사하는 것은 그들이 실제로 어떤 사람들인지를 보여 주지 않는다. (2) 시는 우리가 삶의 내면을 들여다보고 세상을 더 잘 이해하도록 도울 수 있다.

2 친구로 비유를 든 내용 중 푸른 눈, 왼쪽 뺨에 있는 점, 빨간 코는 묘사하기 쉬운 '외면(the outside)'에 해당하고, 습관, 감정, 모든 사소한 특징들은 묘사하기 매우 어려운 '내면(the inside)'에 해당한다.

READ CLOSELY
p. 15

❶ Poetry sharpens our senses / and makes us / understand our lives / much better.

시는 우리의 감각을 예리하게 한다 / 그리고 우리를 만든다 / 우리의 삶을 이해하게 / 훨씬 더 잘

❷ Imagine, / for a moment, / that you are trying to describe / one of your friends.

상상해 보아라 / 잠시 동안 / 여러분이 묘사하려고 하고 있다고 / 여러분의 친구들 중 한 명을

❸ You could say / the friend has / blue eyes, / a mole on the left cheek, / or a red nose.

여러분은 말할 수도 있을 것이다 / 그 친구가 가지고 있다고 / 푸른 눈을 / 왼쪽 뺨에 점 하나를 / 또는 빨간 코를

❹ But that would only describe / the outside of this person.

하지만 그것은 단지 묘사할 것이다 / 이 사람의 외면을

❺ It wouldn't tell people / what your friend is really like.

그것은 사람들에게 말해 주지 않을 것이다 / 여러분의 친구가 실제로 어떠한지

❻ It wouldn't show / the habits, / feelings, / and all the little characteristics / that make this person / different from everyone else.

그것은 보여 주지 않을 것이다 / 습관을 / 감정을 / 그리고 모든 사소한 특징들을 / 이 사람을 만드는 / 다른 모든 사람들과 다르게

❼ You would find it / very difficult / to describe the inside of your friend, / even though you know everything / about them.

여러분은 알게 될 것이다 / 매우 어렵다는 것을 / 여러분의 친구의 내면을 묘사하는 것이 / 여러분이 모든 것을 알고 있음에도 불구하고 / 그들에 대해

❽ Good poetry tells us / about both the outside and the inside of life.

좋은 시는 우리에게 말해 준다 / 삶의 외면과 내면 둘 다에 관해서

❾ And it helps you / know and love the world / as much as you know and love a friend.

그리고 그것은 여러분을 도와준다 / 세상을 알고 사랑하도록 / 여러분이 한 친구를 알고 사랑하는 만큼

지문해석 시는 우리의 감각을 예리하게 하고 우리가 우리의 삶을 훨씬 더 잘 이해하게 해 준다. 잠시 동안 여러분이 여러분의 친구들 중 한 명을 묘사하려고 하고 있다고 상상해 보아라. 여러분은 그 친구가 푸른 눈, 왼쪽 뺨에 점 하나, 또는 빨간 코를 가지고 있다고 말할 수도 있을 것이다. 하지만 그것은 단지 이 사람의 외면만을 묘사할 것이다. 그것은 여러분의 친구가 실제로 어떤 사람인지는 사람들에게 말해 주지 않을 것이다. 그것은 습관, 감정 그리고 이 사람을 다른 모든 사람들과 다르게 만드는 모든 사소한 특징들을 보여 주지 않을 것이다. 여러분은 그들에 대한 모든 것을 알고 있음에도 불구하고 여러분 친구의 내면을 묘사하는 것이 매우 어렵다는 것을 알게 될 것이다. 좋은 시는 우리에게 삶의 외면과 내면 둘 다에 관해서 말해 준다. 그리고 그것은 여러분이 한 친구를 알고 사랑하는 만큼 세상을 알고 사랑하도록 도와준다.

문장 돋보기

❷ Imagine, for a moment, [that you are trying to
　　　동사　　　　　　　　　목적어(that절)
describe one of your friends].
　　　　　one of+복수 명사: ~ 중 하나

❺ It wouldn't tell people [what your friend is really
　　　　수여동사　간접목적어　직접목적어(간접의문문: 의문사+주어+동사)
like].

❻ It wouldn't show the habits, feelings, and all the
　　　　　　　　　　　　　　　　　주격 관계대명사절
little characteristics [that make this person different
　　　　　　　　　　↑　　　make+목적어+목적격 보어(형용사):
from everyone else].　　　~을 …하게 만들다

READING 03 정답 ⑤
p. 16

자신감은 흔히 긍정적인 것으로 여겨지지만 지나친 자신감은 학업에 부정적인 영향을 줄 수 있다는 내용의 글이므로, 글의 주제로 ⑤ '학생들의 지나친 자신감이 학교생활에 미치는 부정적인 영향들'이 가장 적절하다.

오답풀이 ① 나쁜 공부 습관을 바꾸는 효과적인 방법들 ② 학교 학업 시험의 변화하는 역할들 ③ 학생들의 자신감을 키우기 위한 유용한 전략들 ④ 대학 전공 선택 시 고려해야 할 중대한 요소들

READING GUIDE ❹

UNDERSTAND DEEPLY **1** Overconfidence **2** (1) T (2) F

1 지나친 자신감은 학생들에게 더 단절됨을 느끼게 하고, 자신이 더 이상 공부할 필요가 없다고 생각하게 하는 등 자신의 학습 진도에 대한 잘못된 인상을 줄 수 있다고 했다.

해석 지나친 자신감은 학생들이 단절되었다고 느끼게 하고 자신의 학습 진도에 대한 잘못된 인상을 가지게 할 수 있다.

2 (1) 연구에 따르면 자신감이 많은 학생들은 자신감이 덜한 학생들보다 시험을 더 잘 보는 경향이 있다고 했으므로 일치한다. (2) 자신의 지식에 대

해 잘못된 견해를 가지고 있는 학생들보다 자신의 학습 진도를 정확히 평가하는 학생들이 시험을 더 잘 본다고 했으므로 일치하지 않는다.

해석 (1) 자신감은 학생들이 시험을 더 잘 보도록 도움을 줄 수 있다. (2) 자신의 지식에 대해 잘못된 견해를 가지고 있는 학생들은 시험을 더 잘 보는 경향이 있다.

READ CLOSELY

p. 17

① You may wonder / whether there is any reason / to worry about too much confidence.

여러분은 궁금할 수도 있다 / 어떤 이유라도 있는지 / 너무 많은 자신감에 대해 걱정할

② After all, / confidence is often considered / a positive thing.

어쨌든 / 자신감은 자주 여겨진다 / 긍정적인 것으로

③ In fact, / research suggests / that students with a lot of confidence / in their ability / in school / tend to do better on exams / than those with less confidence.

실제로 / 연구는 시사한다 / 많은 자신감을 가진 학생들이 / 자신의 능력에 / 학교에서 / 시험을 더 잘 보는 경향이 있다 / 자신감이 덜한 학생들보다

④ Though that is true, / negative results also come from / being overconfident / in the classroom.

그것이 사실이긴 하지만 / 부정적인 결과 또한 ~으로부터 나온다 / 자신감이 지나친 것 / 교실에서

⑤ Students / who are overconfident about their ability / in college / end up feeling more disconnected / than those with lower expectations.

학생들은 / 자신의 능력에 대해 자신감이 지나친 / 대학에서 / 결국 더 단절됨을 느끼게 된다 / 더 낮은 기대를 가진 학생들보다

⑥ Overconfidence can also leave students / with mistaken impressions.

지나친 자신감은 또한 학생들에게 남길 수 있다 / 잘못된 인상을

⑦ For example, / they think / they are fully prepared for tests / and no longer need to study.

예를 들어 / 그들은 생각한다 / 자신이 시험에 충분히 준비가 되어 있다고 / 그리고 더 이상 공부할 필요가 없다고

⑧ Students / who properly assess / their progress in learning / tend to have / more effective study habits.

학생들은 / 정확하게 평가하는 / 학습에서의 자신의 진도를 / 가지고 있는 경향이 있다 / 더 효과적인 학습 습관들을

⑨ They then do better on tests / than those with incorrect views / of their knowledge.

그들은 따라서 시험을 더 잘 본다 / 잘못된 견해를 가진 학생들보다 / 자신의 지식에 대해

지문해석 여러분은 너무 많은 자신감에 대해 걱정할 어떤 이유라도 있는지 궁금할 수도 있다. 어쨌든 자신감은 흔히 긍정적인 것으로 여겨진다. 실제로, 연구는 학교에서 자신의 능력에 많은 자신감을 가진 학생들이 자신감이 덜한 학생들보다 시험을 더 잘 보는 경향이 있음을 시사한다. 그것이 사실이긴 하지만 교실에서 자신감이 지나친 것으로부터는 부정적인 결과 또한 생긴다. 대학에서 자신의 능력에 대해 자신감이 지나친 학생들은 더 낮은 기대를 가진 학생들보다 결국 더 단절된 느낌을 가지게 된다. 지나친 자신감은 또한 학생들에게 잘못된 인상을 남길 수 있다. 예를 들어, 그들은 자신이 시험에 충분히 준비가 되었고 더 이상 공부할 필요가 없다고 생각한다. 자신의 학습 진도를 정확하게 평가하는 학생들은 더 효과적인 학습 습관들을 가지고 있는 경향이 있다. 그들은 따라서 자신의 지식에 대해 잘못된 견해를 가진 학생들보다 시험을 더 잘 본다.

문장 돋보기

① You may wonder [whether there is any reason {to worry about too much confidence}].
동사 / 목적어(whether절) / ~인지 (아닌지) / to부정사의 형용사적 용법

③ In fact, research suggests [that students with a lot of confidence in their ability in school tend to do better on exams than those with less confidence].
실제로 / 동사 / 목적어(that절) / that절의 주어 / that절의 동사 / = students

⑤ Students [who are overconfident about their ability in college] end up feeling more disconnected than those with lower expectations.
주격 관계대명사절 / end up+동명사: 결국 ~하게 되다 / = students

REVIEW TIME

1 (1) assess, estimate   (2) incorrect, wrong
 (3) direct, guide   (4) give, provide

2 (1) ④   (2) ②   (3) ③   (4) ①

3

		¹e				²s	
³e	x	p	r	e	s	s	
		p		⁴c		u	
		e		o		g	
⁵c	o	n	f	i	d	e	n	c	e
		t		s		s	
		a		i		t	
		t		d			
		i	⁶a	c	h	i	e	v	e
		o		r			
		n					

4 (1) different from   (2) fall into
 (3) set a trap   (4) make sense

5 (1) whether   (2) that   (3) what   (4) so that

6 (1) understand   (2) Making
 (3) to describe   (4) making

1 (1) assess, estimate 평가하다 / find 알게 되다
 (2) incorrect, wrong 부정확한, 틀린 / difficult 어려운
 (3) direct, guide 인도하다, 안내하다 / describe 묘사하다
 (4) give, provide 주다, 제공하다 / sharpen 예리하게 하다

2 (1) negative 부정적인 ↔ ④ positive 긍정적인
 (2) inside 내면, 내부 ↔ ② outside 외면, 외부
 (3) detailed 상세한 ↔ ③ simple 간단한, 단순한
 (4) mistaken 잘못된, 틀린 ↔ ① correct 정확한, 옳은

5 (1) '~인지 (아닌지)'를 뜻하는 접속사 whether가 알맞다.
 해석 여러분은 걱정할 어떤 이유라도 있는지 궁금할 수도 있다.
 (2) '너무 ~해서 …하다'라는 의미는 「so+형용사/부사+that+주어+동사」 형태로 표현하므로 that이 알맞다.
 해석 여러분은 너무 실망하여 계속 나아가는 것이 어려워진다.
 (3) tell의 직접목적어로 쓰인 간접의문문을 이끄는 것으로 의문사 what이 알맞다.
 해석 그 말들은 여러분의 친구가 실제로 어떤 사람인지 사람들에게 말해 주지 않을 것이다.
 (4) '~하도록'이라는 뜻으로 목적을 나타내는 접속사 so that이 알맞다.
 해석 그 규칙은 여러분이 자신감을 잃지 않도록 현실적일 필요가 있다.

6 (1) 「사역동사 make+목적어+목적격 보어(동사원형)」 형태가 되어야 하므로 동사원형 understand가 알맞다.
 (2) 문장의 동사가 is이므로 주어 역할을 하는 동명사 Making이 알맞다.

---

(3) 「주어+동사+가목적어(it)+목적격 보어+진목적어(to부정사)」 구문이므로 to부정사 to describe가 알맞다.
(4) between A and B에서 A와 B는 문법적으로 같은 형태가 되어야 하므로 동명사 making이 알맞다.

PART 1   중심 내용 파악하기
UNIT 02

요지·주장 파악하기

04   정답 ⑤

하나의 긍정적인 습관 형성이 생활 전반에 미치는 좋은 영향을 연구 사례를 들어 설명하는 글이다. 한 가지 긍정적인 습관을 들인 학생들이 생활 전반의 긍정적인 변화를 보고했으며, 가장 중요한 일을 규칙적으로 하면 다른 모든 일도 쉬워진다고 했으므로 글의 요지로 가장 적절한 것은 ⑤이다.

오답풀이 ② 긍정적인 습관 형성에 관해서만 언급되었다. ③ 나이가 습관 형성에 미치는 영향은 언급되지 않았다.

READING GUIDE ❸

UNDERSTAND DEEPLY   1 ⑤   2 (1) T   (2) F

1 지저분한 접시는 훨씬 줄었다고 했지만 식사량이 줄었다는 내용은 언급되지 않았다.

2 (1) 긍정적인 습관을 형성한 학생들이 감소한 카페인 섭취량을 보고했다고 했으므로 일치한다. (2) 올바른 습관을 지닌 사람들은 가장 중요한 일을 규칙적으로 하여 다른 모든 일도 쉽게 한다고 했으므로, 덜 중요한 일에는 어려움을 겪는다는 내용은 글의 내용과 일치하지 않는다.

해석 (1) 하나의 긍정적인 습관을 성공적으로 익힌 학생들은 카페인을 덜 섭취했다. (2) 올바른 습관을 가진 사람들은 덜 중요한 일들을 하는 데 어려움을 겪는다.

READ CLOSELY

❶ Recent studies show / some interesting findings / about habit formation.

최근 연구들은 보여 준다 / 몇 가지 흥미로운 결과를 / 습관 형성에 관한

❷ In these studies, / students / who successfully acquired one positive habit / reported / less stress; / less impulsive spending; / better dietary habits; / decreased caffeine consumption; / fewer hours / spent watching TV; / and even fewer dirty dishes.

이 연구들에서 / 학생들은 / 하나의 긍정적인 습관을 성공적으로 익힌 / 보고했다 / 더 적은 스트레스와 / 더 적은 충동적 소비와 / 더 나은 식습관과 / 줄어든 카페인 섭취량과 / 더 적은 시간 / TV를 시청하는 데 보낸 / 그리고 훨씬 더 적은 지저분한 접시를

❸ Keep working on one habit / long enough, / and not only does it become easier, / but so do other things as well.

한 가지 습관에 대해 계속해서 노력해라 / 충분히 오랫동안 / 그러면 그것이 더 쉬워질 뿐만 아니라 / 다른 일들도 그렇게 된다

❹ It is why those with the right habits / seem to do better / than others.

이것이 올바른 습관을 지닌 사람들이 ~한 이유이다 / 더 잘하는 것처럼 보이는 / 다른 사람들보다

❺ They are doing / the most important thing / regularly / and, as a result, / everything else is easier.

그들은 하고 있다 / 가장 중요한 일을 / 규칙적으로 / 그리고 그 결과 / 다른 모든 일이 더 쉽다

지문해석 최근 연구들은 습관 형성에 관한 몇 가지 흥미로운 결과를 보여 준다. 이 연구들에서 하나의 긍정적인 습관을 성공적으로 익힌 학생들은 더 적은 스트레스, 더 적은 충동적 소비, 더 나은 식습관, 줄어든 카페인 섭취량, 더 적은 TV 시청 시간, 그리고 훨씬 더 적은 (음식을 남겨) 지저분한 접시를 보고했다. 충분히 오랫동안 한 가지 습관을 들이고자 계속 노력해라, 그러면 그 습관이 더 쉬워질 뿐만 아니라 다른 일들 또한 더 쉬워진다. 이것이 올바른 습관을 지닌 사람들이 다른 사람들보다 일을 더 잘하는 것처럼 보이는 이유이다. 그들은 가장 중요한 일을 규칙적으로 하고 있고, 그 결과 다른 모든 일이 더 쉬운 것이다.

문장 돋보기

❷ In these studies, students [who successfully
　　　　　　　　　　　주어　　　주격 관계대명사절
acquired one positive habit] reported less stress;
　　　　　　　　　　　　　　　동사　　목적어1
less impulsive spending; better dietary habits;
　　목적어2　　　　　　　　목적어3
decreased caffeine consumption; fewer hours
　　과거분사구　　　　　목적어4　　　　　목적어5
[spent watching TV]; and even fewer dirty dishes.
원형: spend+시간+동명사　　　　　목적어6
❸ Keep working on one habit long enough, and not
명령문, and …: ~해라, 그러면 … (keep+동명사: 계속 ~하다)
only [does it become easier], but [so do other
not only A but B as well: A뿐만 아니라 B도　　= become easier
things] as well.　(= not only A but also B)

05 정답 ① p. 22

필자가 어렸을 때 많은 실수를 하면서 요리를 배운 경험을 예로 들어 시행착오를 통해서 학습할 수 있음을 이야기하는 글이다. 글 전반에 학습이나 실수와 관련된 핵심어가 반복하여 등장하고, 마지막 두 문장에서 실수를 통한 학습 가능성을 직접적으로 이야기하고 있으므로, 글의 요지로 ①이 가장 적절하다.
오답풀이 주방에서 요리하는 것은 시행착오를 통해 배울 수 있음을 설명하기 위해 제시된 소재에 불과하므로 ②는 답이 될 수 없다.

READING GUIDE learning/learned, (trial and many) errors, mistakes

UNDERSTAND
DEEPLY　1 (1) 주방 (2) 실수 (3) 요리 (4) 실수[시행착오] (5) 학습
　　　　2 cooking was a good learning tool

1 이 글은 필자가 어렸을 때 주방에서 많은 실수를 하면서 요리를 배운 경험을 예로 들어 실수[시행착오]를 통해서 학습할 수 있다는 요지를 전달하고 있다.
2 세 번째 문장에 필자의 엄마가 필자가 주방을 어지럽히도록 두었다는 내용과 그 이유가 제시되어 있다.
해석 Q: 필자의 엄마는 왜 자신의 아이가 주방을 어지럽히도록 두었는가? A: 그녀는 요리가 좋은 학습 도구라고 생각했다.

READ CLOSELY p. 23

❶ I began helping / in the kitchen / when I turned three years old.

나는 돕기 시작했다 / 주방에서 / 내가 세 살이 되었을 때

❷ Everyone told my mom / that I would be a hindrance / rather than a help.

모두가 엄마에게 말했다 / 내가 방해가 될 것이라고 / 도움보다는

❸ But my mom let me / make a mess / in the kitchen / because she thought / cooking was a good learning tool.

하지만 엄마는 내가 ~하도록 두셨다 / 어지르도록 / 주방에서 / 왜냐하면 그녀는 생각했기 때문에 / 요리가 좋은 학습도구라고

❹ Of course, / I didn't care about / any of that learning stuff.

물론 / 나는 ~에 대해 관심이 없었다 / 그 어떤 배울 것

❺ I just thought / it was fun, / and I still do.

나는 그저 생각했다 / 그것이 재미있다고 / 그리고 나는 여전히 그런다

❻ I learned to cook / through trial and many errors.

나는 요리하는 것을 배웠다 / 많은 시행착오를 통해서

❼ I can't remember / how many times / I have dropped eggs / on the floor.

나는 기억할 수 없다 / 몇 번이나 / 내가 달걀을 떨어뜨렸는지 / 바닥에

❽ I have often covered the kitchen / with flour / or boiled things over / on the stove.

나는 종종 주방을 뒤덮었다 / 밀가루로 / 또는 음식을 끓어 넘치게 했다 / 레인지 위에서

❾ The point is, / I have made many mistakes.

요점은 ~이다 / 내가 많은 실수를 해 왔다는 것

❿ But, / as my mom always says, / mistakes are the best teachers.

그러나 / 엄마가 항상 말씀하시는 것처럼 / 실수는 최고의 선생님이다

⓫ Through those mistakes / I have learned / what works and what doesn't.

그러한 실수를 통해서 / 나는 배워 왔다 / 무엇이 잘되는지 그리고 무엇이 잘되지 않는지

지문해석 내가 세 살이 되었을 때 나는 주방에서 돕기 시작했다. 모두가 엄마에게 내가 도움보다는 방해가 될 거라고 말했다. 하지만 엄마는 내가 주방을 어지럽히도록 두셨는데, 요리가 좋은 학습도구라고 생각하셨기 때문이었다. 물론, 나는 그 어떤 배울 것에 대해서도 관심이 없었다. 나는 그저 그것이 재미있다고 생각했고, 지금도 여전히 그렇게 생각한다. 나는 많은 시행착오를 통해서 요리하는 것을 배웠다. 나는 내가 몇 번이나 달걀을 바닥에 떨어뜨렸는지 기억할 수 없다. 나는 종종 주방을 밀가루로 뒤덮고, 레인지 위에서 음식을 끓어 넘치게 했다. 요점은, 내가 많은 실수를 해 왔다는 것이다. 그러나 엄마가 항상 말씀하시는 것처럼, 실수는 최고의 선생님이다. 그러한 실수를 통해서 나는 무엇이 잘되고, 무엇이 잘되지 않는지를 배워 왔다.

문장 돋보기

❷ Everyone told my mom [that I would be a hindrance
수여동사 간접목적어 직접목적어(that절)
rather than a help].
~보다는

⓫ Through those mistakes I have learned [what works]
~을 통하여   동사   목적어1
and [what doesn't (work)].
목적어2 (간접의문문: 의문사(주어) + 동사)

READING 06 정답 ⑤   p. 24

발표를 할 때 말하는 속도에 대하여 조언하는 글이다. faster, a normal speed, speed up, more slowly 등과 같이 속도와 관련된 표현들이 반복적으로 등장하고, 마지막 문장에서 훌륭한 발표자는 너 천천히 말한다고 했으므로 필자의 주장으로 ⑤가 가장 적절하다.

오답풀이 글의 중심 소재인 '말하는 속도'를 언급한 선택지라는 점에서 ①을 답으로 생각할 수 있으나, 이 글은 청중별로 발표 속도를 다르게 해야 한다는 내용은 아님에 유의한다.

READING GUIDE ❾

UNDERSTAND
DEEPLY 1 ③ 2 presentation, understood, slowly

1 필자는 긴장을 약간 풀도록 노력하라고 했다.

2 발표에서 발표자가 말하는 것의 수보다는 청중에게 이해되는 것의 수가 중요하며, 훌륭한 발표자들은 더 천천히 말한다고 했다.
해석 발표를 할 때, 여러분의 말은 청중에게 이해되어야 한다. 따라서 더 천천히 말하도록 노력해라.

READ CLOSELY   p. 25

❶ Do you often give presentations / in front of people?

여러분은 자주 발표를 하는가 / 사람들 앞에서

❷ When you are giving a presentation, / do you tend to speak / faster than usual?

여러분이 발표를 하고 있을 때 / 여러분은 말하는 경향이 있는가 / 평소보다 더 빠르게

❸ I have given a lot of presentations, / and what I have come to realize is / if I think / I am speaking / at a normal speed, / then I am speaking / too fast.

나는 많은 발표를 해 봤다 / 그리고 내가 깨닫게 된 것은 ~이다 / 만약 내가 생각한다면 / 내가 말하고 있다고 / 보통 속도로 / 그러면 나는 말하고 있는 것 / 너무 빨리

❹ It is unlikely / that we will ever speak too slowly / when we give presentations, / because our nerves automatically speed us up.

~할 것 같지 않다 / 우리가 너무 천천히 말할 / 우리가 발표를 할 때 / 왜냐하면 우리의 신경이 자동으로 우리의 속도를 높이기 때문에

❺ So, / focus on your words, / think carefully, / and try to relax a little.

그러므로 / 여러분의 말에 집중하고 / 신중하게 생각하고 / 긴장을 약간 풀도록 노력해라

❻ Also, / focus on / the stress and intonation of your words.

또한 / ~에 집중해라 / 여러분의 말의 강세와 억양

❼ Finally, / pause / before saying an important word, / because this will give it / more impact.

마지막으로 / 잠시 멈춰라 / 중요한 단어를 말하기 전에 / 왜냐하면 이것이 그것에 줄 것이기 때문에 / 더 많은 효과를

❽ A presentation is not / about the number of things / that we say, / but rather / it's about the number of things / that are understood.

발표는 ~이 아니다 / 것들의 수에 관한 / 우리가 말하는 / 그러나 오히려 / 그것은 것들의 수에 관한 것이다 / 이해되는

❾ Good presenters master / what is simple but powerful: / they speak / more slowly.

훌륭한 발표자들은 숙달한다 / 간단하지만 강력한 것을 / 그들은 말한다 / 더 천천히

지문해석 여러분은 자주 사람들 앞에서 발표를 하는가? 여러분은 발표를 할 때, 평소보다 더 빠르게 말하는 경향이 있는가? 나는 발표를 많이 해 봤으며, 내가 깨닫게 된 것은 내가 보통 속도로 말하고 있다고 생각한다면 내가 너무 빨리 말하고 있다는 것이다. 우리가 발표를 할 때 너무 천천히 말하는 경우는 없을 것 같은데, 우리의 신경이 자동으로 우리의 속도를 높이기 때문이다. 그러므로 여러분의 말에 집중하고, 신중하게 생각하고, 긴장을 약간 풀도록 노력해라. 또한 여러분의 말의 강세와 억양에 집중해라. 마지막으로, 중요한 단어를 말하기 전에 잠시 멈춰라. 왜냐하면 이렇게 하는 것이 그 단어에 더 많은

효과를 줄 것이기 때문이다. 발표는 우리가 말하는 것의 수에 관한 것이 아니라, (청중에게) 이해되는 것의 수에 관한 것이다. 훌륭한 발표자들은 간단하지만 강력한 것을 숙달하고 있는데, 그들은 더 천천히 말한다.

❹ It is unlikely [that we will ever speak too slowly
가주어   진주어(that절)
when we give presentations], because our nerves
시간의 부사절을 이끄는 접속사   이유의 부사절을 이끄는 접속사
automatically speed us up.
동사＋목적어(대명사)＋부사
❼ Finally, pause before saying an important word,

because this will give it more impact.
수여동사＋간접목적어＋직접목적어

07 정답 ④   p. 26

글의 도입부에서 '종착지 병'이라는 소재를 제시하고 많은 사람들이 고등학교 졸업 후에는 책을 전혀 읽지 않는다는 연구 결과를 덧붙인 후, 글의 마지막 부분에서 나이에 관계없이 배움과 성장을 지속해야 한다고 주장하고 있으므로 필자의 주장으로 ④가 가장 적절하다.

오답풀이 평생 학습의 필요성에 대해 주장하는 글이기 때문에 ⑤를 답으로 생각할 수 있지만, 프로그램 개발과 관련된 내용은 언급되지 않았음에 유의한다.

READING GUIDE ❿

UNDERSTAND
DEEPLY **1** Destination disease   **2** (1) half (2) age

1 많은 사람들이 '종착지 병'을 겪는데, 이는 삶의 일정 시점에 이르고 원하던 목표를 달성한 후에는 열심히 노력하기를 멈추는 것을 말한다고 했다.

해석 종착지 병은 어떤 목표를 달성하면 더 이상 배우거나 성장할 필요가 없다는 믿음이다.

2 (1) 50퍼센트의 사람들이 고등학교를 졸업한 후에는 책을 한 권도 채 읽지 않을 것이라는 연구 결과가 있다고 했으므로, 절반을 의미하는 **half**가 알맞다. (2) 승자는 평생 배움을 계속해 나간다고 했으므로, '어느 나이에도'를 의미하도록 **age**가 쓰여야 한다.

해석 (1) 연구에 따르면 절반의 사람들이 고등학교 졸업 후에 한 권의 책도 읽지 않을 것이다. (2) 성공한 사람들은 어느 나이에도 배움을 결코 멈추지 않는다.

READ CLOSELY   p. 27

❶ Too many people / suffer from destination disease.
너무나 많은 사람들이 / 종착지 병을 앓는다

❷ In other words, / once they reach / a certain point in life, / earn their degrees, / buy their dream homes, / and so on, / then they just stop working hard.

다시 말해서 / 일단 그들이 도달하고 / 삶의 어느 시점에 / 학위를 받고 / 그들이 꿈꾸던 집을 사고 / 기타 등등이면 / 그러면 그들은 그냥 열심히 노력하는 것을 멈춘다

❸ Studies tell us / that 50 percent of people, / after they graduate from high school, / will never read an entire book / for the rest of their life.

연구는 우리에게 말해 준다 / 50퍼센트의 사람들이 / 그들이 고등학교를 졸업한 후에 / 책 한 권 전체를 결코 읽지 않을 것이라고 / 그들의 남은 생애 동안

❹ One reason may be / that they see learning / as something you do only in school / instead of as a way of life.

한 가지 이유는 ～일 수도 있다 / 그들이 배움을 본다는 것 / 여러분이 학교에서만 하는 것으로 / 삶의 방식으로 대신에

❺ We all learned / when we were in school.
우리 모두는 배웠다 / 우리가 학교에 있었을 때

❻ Our teachers, coaches, and parents / taught us.
우리의 선생님들, 코치들, 그리고 부모님들이 / 우리를 가르쳤다

❼ We were expected / to learn / when we were of school age.

우리는 기대되었다 / 배울 것으로 / 우리가 학교에 다닐 나이였을 때

❽ But some tend to think, / "I'm out of school / forever. // I've got my job," / once they finish / a certain level of education.

하지만 일부 사람들은 생각하는 경향이 있다 / 나는 학교를 떠났어 / 영원히 // 나는 직장을 얻었어 / 그들이 일단 끝내면 / 일정 수준의 교육을

❾ Winners continue learning / throughout life.
승자는 배움을 계속한다 / 평생

❿ Whether you're nine or ninety years old, / you should constantly be learning, / improving your skills, / and getting better / at what you do.

여러분이 아홉 살이든 아흔 살이든 / 여러분은 끊임없이 배우고 있어야 하고 / 여러분의 기술을 향상시키고 있어야 하고 / 그리고 나아지고 있어야 한다 / 여러분이 하는 것에서

지문해석 너무나 많은 사람들이 종착지 병을 앓는다. 다시 말해서, 그들이 일단 삶의 어느 시점에 도달하고, 학위를 받고, 그들이 꿈꾸던 집을 사고 기타 등등을 하면, 열심히 노력하는 것을 그저 멈춘다. 연구는 50퍼센트의 사람들이 고등학교를 졸업한 후에 그들의 남은 생애 동안 책을 한 권도 채 읽지 않을 것이라고 우리에게 말해 준다. 한 가지 이유는 그들이 배움을 삶의 방식으로가 아니라 학교에서만 하는 것으로 여기기 때문일 수도 있다. 우리 모두는 학교에 다닐 때 배웠다. 우리의 선생님들, 코치들, 부모님들이 우리를 가르쳤다. 우리는 학교에 다닐 때 배울 것으로 기대되었다. 하지만 일부 사람들은 일단 그들이 일정 수준의 교육을 끝마치면 "나는 영원히 학교를 떠났어. 나는 직장을 얻었거든."이라고 생각하는 경향이 있다. 승자는 평생 배움을 계속해 나간

다. 여러분이 아홉 살이든 아흔 살이든 간에, 여러분은 끊임없이 배우고, 여러분의 기술을 향상시키고, 여러분이 하는 일에서 나아지고 있어야 한다.

❸ Studies tell us [that 50 percent of people, {after
　　　　수여동사+간접목적어+직접목적어(that절)　　 that절의 주어
they graduate from high school,} will never read
　　삽입 부사절　　　　　　　　　　　　that절의 동사
an entire book for the rest of their life].

❹ One reason may be [that they see learning as
　　　　　　　　동사　　 보어(that절)　　 see A as B: A를 B로 보다
something {(that) you do only in school} instead
　　　　　　　목적격 관계대명사절　　　　　　～ 대신에
of as a way of life].

REVIEW TIME

p. 28

1 (1) acquire　　　　　(2) intonation
　(3) point　　　　　　(4) continue
2 (1) ①　　(2) ④　　(3) ③　　(4) ②
3

M	A	S	T	E	R	B	U	N	F	W
B	I	Y	N	Q	X	Y	J	K	X	B
D	V	R	W	D	F	I	T	U	T	Z
H	R	E	P	I	U	R	B	O	Z	H
Z	U	C	N	E	B	P	S	H	O	C
X	B	E	H	T	H	M	D	T	H	L
M	U	N	E	A	O	A	V	Z	Y	J
L	C	T	T	R	C	O	B	X	J	M
T	J	O	N	Y	Y	W	L	I	O	F
E	M	L	I	S	D	V	K	S	T	K
S	T	U	F	F	K	O	E	G	S	Q
N	L	H	A	Y	W	C	T	Y	C	H

　(1) dietary　　(2) habit　　(3) master
　(4) recent　　(5) stuff　　(6) tool
4 (1) focus on　　　　　(2) rather than
　(3) suffer from　　　　(4) instead of
5 (1) make　(2) what　(3) what　(4) I have
6 (1) spent watching　　(2) Keep working
　(3) does it become　　(4) stop working

2 (1) entire, ① whole 전체의, 모든
　(2) improve 향상시키다, ④ develop 개발하다
　(3) focus, ③ concentrate 집중하다
　(4) impact, ② effect 효과, 영향

5 (1) 사역동사 let은 목적격 보어로 동사원형을 취하므로 make가 알맞다.
　해석 엄마는 내가 주방을 어지럽히도록 두셨다.

---

(2) 뒤에 주어가 없는 불완전한 절이 오므로 '～하는 것'의 의미를 나타내는 선행사를 포함하는 관계대명사 what이 알맞다.
　해석 훌륭한 발표자들은 간단하지만 강력한 것을 숙달한다.
(3) 전치사 at의 목적어 역할을 하는 명사절을 이끌면서 '～하는 것'의 의미를 나타내야 하므로 선행사를 포함하는 관계대명사 what이 알맞다.
　해석 여러분은 끊임없이 여러분이 하는 일에서 나아지고 있어야 한다.
(4) 간접의문문의 어순은 「의문사＋주어＋동사」이므로 I have가 알맞다.
　해석 나는 내가 몇 번이나 달걀을 바닥에 떨어뜨렸는지 기억할 수 없다.

6 (1) 시간을 '보낸' 것이므로 과거분사 spent를 쓰고, '～하는 데 (시간을) 보내다'는 「spend＋시간＋동명사」로 표현하므로 동명사 watching을 쓴다.
(2) '계속 ～하다'는 「keep＋동명사」 형태로 표현한다.
(3) 부정어 not only가 강조되어 문장 맨 앞으로 나왔으므로 「조동사＋주어＋동사원형」의 어순이 되어야 한다.
(4) '～하는 것을 멈추다'는 「stop＋동명사」 형태로 표현한다.

제목 추론하기

08　정답 ③

p. 30

컴퓨터 화면으로 읽을 때와 종이로 읽을 때의 수행 능력을 비교한 연구를 통해 화면으로 읽는 것이 독해를 어렵게 함을 설명하는 글이므로, 글의 제목으로 ③ '화면으로 읽는 것이 그다지 효과적이지 않은 이유'가 가장 적절하다.
　오답풀이 ① 독해 기술을 가르치는 것의 중요성 ② 독해 속도를 높이기 위한 전략 ④ 아이들의 독서 습관과 기술 이용 ⑤ 전자책: 종이책에 대한 훌륭한 대안

READING GUIDE the performance of readers using a computer screen

UNDERSTAND DEEPLY　1 ② 2 (1) paper, screen (2) Hypertext

1 컴퓨터 화면을 통한 읽기는 빠르게 읽기부터 단순한 단어 찾기까지 다양한 전략을 포함한다고 했다.
2 (1) 컴퓨터 화면을 통한 읽기가 종이를 이용한 읽기에 비해 다양한 독해 전략으로 독해력을 떨어뜨리고, 하이퍼텍스트 기능으로 독자가 집중하기 어렵게 할 수 있다고 했다. (2) 마지막 문장에서 하이퍼텍스트는 글을 이해하는 데 도움이 되지 않을 수 있고 집중하는 것을 어렵게 할 수 있다고 했다.
　해석 (1) 독자들은 화면에서보다 종이 위에서 더 나은 글 이해력을 보인다. (2) 하이퍼텍스트는 읽고 있는 것을 이해하기 어렵게 할 수 있다.

READ CLOSELY

p. 31

❶ Anne Mangen / at the University of Oslo /compared/

the performance of readers / using a computer screen
/ to that of readers / using paper.

Anne Mangen은 / Oslo 대학의 / 비교했다 / 독자들의 수행 능력을 /
컴퓨터 화면을 이용하는 / 독자들의 그것(수행 능력)과 / 종이를 이용하는

❷ Her study showed / that reading on a computer screen
/ includes various strategies / —from quick reading to
simple word finding.

그녀의 연구는 보여 주었다 / 컴퓨터 화면으로 읽는 것이 / 다양한 전략들
을 포함한다는 것을 / 빠르게 읽기부터 단순한 단어 찾기까지

❸ Applying those different strategies on screen / makes
reading comprehension / poorer / than when you are
reading the same texts on paper.

그러한 다양한 전략들을 화면상에 적용하는 것은 / 독해력을 만든다 / 더
떨어지게 / 여러분이 같은 글을 종이 위에서 읽을 때보다

❹ Also, / screens have an additional feature: / hypertext.

또한 / 화면들은 추가적인 특징을 가지고 있다 / 하이퍼텍스트라는

❺ Someone else makes hypertext, / and it may not
always be connected with the way / you think.

다른 누군가가 하이퍼텍스트를 만든다 / 그리고 그것은 방식과 항상 관계
가 있지는 않을 수 있다 / 여러분이 생각하는

❻ Therefore, / it may not help you / understand / what
you are reading, / and it may even make it / hard / to
focus.

그러므로 / 그것은 여러분을 돕지 않을 수도 있다 / 이해하도록 / 여러분이
읽고 있는 것을 / 그리고 그것은 심지어 만들 수도 있다 / 어렵게 / 집중하
는 것을

지문해석 Oslo 대학의 Anne Mangen은 컴퓨터 화면을 이용한 독자들의
수행 능력을 종이를 이용한 독자들의 수행 능력과 비교했다. 그녀의 연구는
컴퓨터 화면으로 읽는 것이 빠르게 읽기부터 단순한 단어 찾기까지 다양한 전
략을 포함한다는 것을 보여 주었다. 그러한 다양한 전략을 화면상에 적용하는
것은 여러분이 종이로 같은 글을 읽을 때보다 독해력이 떨어지게 만든다. 또
한 화면에는 하이퍼텍스트라는 추가적인 특징이 있다. 다른 어떤 사람이 하이
퍼텍스트를 만들며, 그것은 여러분이 생각하는 방식과 항상 관계가 있지는 않
을 수 있다. 그러므로 그것은 여러분이 읽고 있는 것을 이해하는 데 도움이 되
지 않을 수도 있고, 그것은 심지어 집중하는 것을 어렵게 만들 수도 있다.

❶ Anne Mangen at the University of Oslo compared
　　　　　　　　　　　　　　compare A to B: A를 B와 비교하다
[the performance of readers {using a computer
　　　　　　　　　　　　　　　　현재분사구
screen}] to [that of readers {using paper}].
　　　= the performance　　　현재분사구

❺ Someone else makes hypertext, and it may not
　　　　　　　　　　　　　= how (the way how (×))
always be connected with the way [you think].
　　　　　　　　　　　　　　　　관계부사절

❻ Therefore, it may not help you understand
　그러므로　　　　　help+목적어+목적격 보어(동사원형 또는 to부정사)
[what you are reading], and it may even make it
선행사를 포함하는 관계대명사 what이 이끄는 명사절(~하는 것)　가목적어
hard to focus.
진목적어(to부정사)

09 정답 ①　　　　　　　　　　　　　　　p. 32

역대 최고의 테니스 선수로 여겨지는 Roger Federer도 우승보다는 패배
를 훨씬 더 많이 했다는 예를 들면서 실패가 성공하기 위한 과정의 일부임을
이야기하는 글이다. 따라서 글의 제목으로 가장 적절한 것은 ① '성공은 실
패 없이 오지 않는다'이다.

오답풀이 ② 여러분이 여러분 자신의 기회를 만들어 낸다　③ 계획 없는 목
표는 소망일 뿐이다　④ 여러분 자신을 남과 비교하지 마라　⑤ 인생에서 가
장 슬픈 것은 낭비된 재능이다

READING GUIDE ❽

UNDERSTAND DEEPLY

1 (1) 우승　(2) 패배　(3) 실패자　(4) 챔피언　(5) 실패　(6) 성공
2 (1) F　(2) T

1 글의 도입부에서 이기는 것이 전부라는 말이 있지만 이기기만 하는 사람
은 없다고 했다. 이어서 예로 든 Roger Federer는 최고의 테니스 선수
이지만 출전한 그랜드 슬램 경기 중 3분의 2가 넘는 경기에서 졌다고 했
다. 마지막 문장에서는 실패가 성공하기 위한 과정의 일부라고 했다.

2 (1) 60개가 넘는 그랜드 슬램 경기에 출전하여 17회 우승했다고 했으므
로 일치하지 않는다. (2) 실패는 성공에 앞서 온다고 했으므로 일치한다.
　해석 (1) Roger Federer는 그가 출전한 모든 경기에서 우승했다.
(2) 실패는 성공을 위해 필요하다.

READ CLOSELY　　　　　　　　　　　　　　p. 33

❶ There is a saying / in sports culture: / "Winning is
everything."

속담이 있다 / 스포츠 문화에는 / '이기는 것이 전부이다'라는

❷ However, / I'm not aware of anyone / who ever won /
every game, / or every event, / or every championship
/ he or she competed in.

하지만 / 나는 그 누구도 알지 못한다 / 항상 이긴 / 모든 게임에서 / 또는
모든 경기에서 / 또는 모든 선수권 대회에서 / 그 또는 그녀가 출전한

❸ Roger Federer, / the tennis player / whom people refer
to as the greatest of all time, / has won / a record
seventeen Grand Slam titles.

Roger Federer는 / 테니스 선수인 / 사람들이 역대 최고라고 부르는 /
따냈다 / 기록적인 17회의 그랜드 슬램 타이틀을

❹ Yet, / he has competed in / more than sixty Grand
Slam events.

그러나 / 그는 ~에 출전했다 / 60회보다 많은 그랜드 슬램 경기

❺ This means / that even the greatest tennis player / has
failed / more than two-thirds of the time.

이것은 의미한다 / 최고의 테니스 선수조차 / 실패했다는 것을 / 3분의 2보
다 많은 시간

❻ Yet, / we don't think of him / as a failure, / but rather
as a champion.

그러나 / 우리는 그를 생각하지 않는다 / 실패자로 / 하지만 오히려 챔피언
으로 (생각한다)

❼ The fact is / that he failed much more / than he
succeeded, / and that's generally the way / things are
for everyone.

사실은 ~이다 / 그가 훨씬 더 많이 실패했다는 것 / 그가 성공한 것보다 /
그리고 그것은 일반적으로 방식이다 / 상황이 모두에게 작용하는

❽ Failure comes / before success.

실패는 온다 / 성공에 앞서

❾ Simply accept / that failure is part of the process / to
succeed.

그저 받아들여라 / 실패가 과정의 일부라는 것을 / 성공하기 위한

지문해석 스포츠 문화에는 "이기는 것이 전부이다"라는 속담이 있다. 하지만,
나는 출전한 모든 게임, 혹은 모든 경기, 혹은 모든 선수권 대회에서 항상 이
긴 어떤 누구도 알지 못한다. 사람들이 역대 최고라고 부르는 테니스 선수인
Roger Federer는 기록적인 17회의 그랜드 슬램 타이틀을 따냈다. 그러나
그는 60회가 넘는 그랜드 슬램 경기에 출전했다. 이것은 최고의 테니스 선수
조차 3분의 2가 넘는 시간은 실패했다는 것을 의미한다. 그러나 우리는 그를
실패자로 여기는 것이 아니라, 오히려 챔피언으로 여긴다. 사실은 그가 성공
한 것보다 훨씬 더 많이 실패했다는 것이고, 그것은 일반적으로 모두에게 상
황이 작용하는 방식이다. 성공에 앞서 실패가 온다. 실패가 성공하기 위한 과
정의 일부임을 그저 받아들여라.

❷ However, I'm not aware of anyone [who ever won
every game, or every event, or every championship
{(that) he or she competed in}].

❸ Roger Federer, the tennis player [whom people
refer to as the greatest of all time], has won a
record seventeen Grand Slam titles.

❻ Yet, we don't think of him as a failure, but rather
as a champion.

10 정답 ③   p. 34

특정 색들의 의미는 변해 왔지만 변하지 않은 사실도 있다고 하면서 여러 가
지 색이 의미하는 바를 차례로 설명하는 글이다. 따라서 글의 제목으로 가장
적절한 것은 ③ '색들이 무엇을 의미하는가?'이다.

오답풀이 잠을 더 잘 자거나 아기들이 더 많이 우는 등 특정 색이 사람들에
게 미치는 영향이 언급되어 ④를 답으로 생각할 수 있지만 글의 중심 내용은
여러 가지 색이 상징하는 의미이다.

① 색채 요법이란 무엇인가? ② 우리는 어떻게 색을 보는가? ④ 색은 우리
의 삶에 어떻게 영향을 미치는가? ⑤ 어느 색들이 서로 잘 어울리는가?

READING GUIDE The meanings of certain colors

UNDERSTAND
DEEPLY 1 (1) 파란색 (2) 노란색   2 rare in nature

1 (1) 잠을 더 잘 잘 수도 있으므로 침실에 파란색이 사용된다고 했다.
  (2) 아기들이 노란색으로 칠한 방에서 더 많이 우는 것은 증명된 사실이
라고 했다.
2 보라색은 자연에서 드물기 때문에 인공적인 것으로 여겨진다고 했다.
  해석 Q: 왜 보라색은 때때로 인공적이라고 여겨지는가? A: 그것이 자연
에서 드물기 때문이다.

READ CLOSELY   p. 35

❶ The meanings of certain colors / have changed /
throughout the course of history, / but some facts
remain true.

어떤 색들의 의미는 / 변해 왔다 / 역사의 흐름 내내 / 그러나 어떤 사실들
은 진실로 남아 있다

❷ Blue means / silence and peace.

파란색은 의미한다 / 고요와 평화를

❸ People use blue / in their bedrooms / because they

may be able to sleep better.

사람들은 파란색을 사용한다 / 그들의 침실에 / 왜냐하면 그들이 잠을 더
잘 잘 수 있을 수도 있기 때문에

❹ Blue also symbolizes increased productivity, / so
business meetings are often held / in blue rooms.

파란색은 또한 증대된 생산성을 상징한다 / 그래서 업무 회의가 자주 열린
다 / 파란색 방에서

❺ On the other hand, / blue can sometimes give / a cold
and depressing impression.

한편 / 파란색은 때때로 줄 수 있다 / 차갑고 우울한 인상을

❻ Yellow is / the color of freshness, happiness, and joy.

노란색은 ~이다 / 신선함, 행복, 그리고 기쁨의 색

❼ But this color can have side effects / if it is overused.

그러나 이 색은 부작용이 있을 수 있다 / 그것이 과도하게 사용되면

❽ For example, / it is a proven fact / that babies cry more
/ in rooms / painted yellow.

예를 들어 / 증명된 사실이다 / 아기들이 더 많이 운다는 것은 / 방에서 /
노란색으로 칠해진

❾ Orange, / the blend of red and yellow, / is / a mixture
of the energy from red and the happiness from yellow.

주황색은 / 빨간색과 노란색의 혼색인 / ~이다 / 빨간색의 에너지와 노란
색의 행복함의 혼합물

❿ Purple is often associated with / royalty, power, and
ambition.

보라색은 종종 ~와 연관된다 / 왕족, 권력, 그리고 야망

⓫ It also stands for / creativity, mystery, and magic.

그것은 또한 ~을 의미한다 / 창의성, 미스터리, 그리고 마법

⓬ However, / because it is rare in nature, / purple is
sometimes thought / to be artificial.

그러나 / 그것이 자연에서 드물기 때문에 / 보라색은 때때로 여겨진다 / 인
공적이라고

지문해석 어떤 색들의 의미는 역사가 흐르는 내내 변해 왔지만, 어떤 사실들
은 진실로 남아 있다. 파란색은 고요와 평화를 의미한다. 사람들은 잠을 더 잘
잘 수도 있으므로 자신의 침실에 파란색을 사용한다. 파란색은 또한 증대된
생산성을 상징해서 업무 회의가 파란색 방에서 자주 열린다. 한편, 파란색은
때때로 차갑고 우울한 인상을 줄 수 있다. 노란색은 신선함, 행복, 기쁨의 색이
다. 그러나 이 색은 과도하게 사용되면 부작용이 있을 수 있다. 예를 들어, 아
기들이 노란색으로 칠해진 방에서 더 많이 운다는 것은 증명된 사실이다. 빨
간색과 노란색의 혼색인 주황색은 빨간색의 에너지와 노란색의 행복함의 혼
합물이다. 보라색은 종종 왕족, 권력, 야망과 연관된다. 그것은 또한 창의성,
미스터리, 마법을 의미한다. 그러나 보라색은 자연에서는 드물기 때문에, 때때
로 인공적이라고 여겨진다.

REVIEW TIME

p. 36

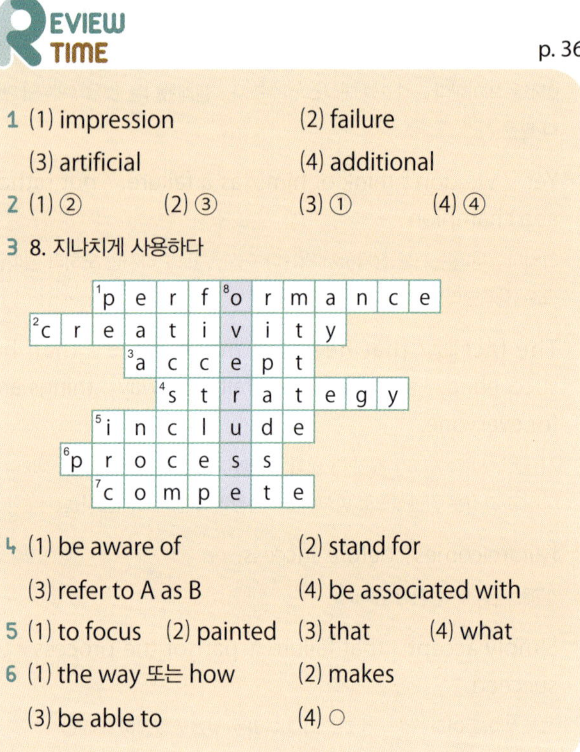

1 (1) impression   (2) failure
(3) artificial   (4) additional

2 (1) ②   (2) ③   (3) ①   (4) ④

3 8. 지나치게 사용하다

4 (1) be aware of   (2) stand for
(3) refer to A as B   (4) be associated with

5 (1) to focus   (2) painted   (3) that   (4) what

6 (1) the way 또는 how   (2) makes
(3) be able to   (4) ○

1 (1) 고요한 : 고요, 침묵 = 인상 깊은 : 인상 (형용사 : 명사 관계)
(2) 성공하다 : 성공 = 실패하다 : 실패 (동사 : 명사 관계)
(3) 드문 : 흔한, 일반적인 = 자연적인 : 인공의, 인위적인 (반의어 관계)
(4) 효과 : 효과적인 = 추가 : 추가적인 (명사 : 형용사 관계)

2 (1) blend, ② mixture 혼합(물)
(2) saying, ③ proverb 속담, 격언
(3) represent, ① symbolize 나타내다, 상징하다
(4) various, ④ different 다양한

5 (1) 앞에 가목적어 it이 쓰였으므로 진목적어로 to부정사 to focus가 알
맞다.
해석 하이퍼텍스트는 심지어 집중하는 것을 어렵게 만들 수도 있다.
(2) '칠해진'이라는 수동의 의미로 rooms를 수식해야 하므로 과거분사
painted가 알맞다.
해석 아기들은 노란색으로 칠해진 방에서 더 많이 운다.
(3) 뒤에 완전한 절이 오므로 명사절을 이끄는 접속사 that이 알맞다. 선

행사를 포함하는 관계대명사 what 뒤에는 불완전한 절이 온다.

해석 실패는 성공하기 위한 과정의 일부임을 받아들여라.

(4) 뒤에 목적어가 없는 불완전한 절이 오므로 '~하는 것'을 의미하는 선행사를 포함하는 관계대명사 what이 알맞다.

해석 하이퍼텍스트는 여러분이 읽고 있는 것을 이해하는 데 도움이 되지 않을 수도 있다.

6 (1) 선행사 the way와 관계부사 how는 함께 쓰지 않으며 둘 중 하나만 써야 한다.

해석 그것은 일반적으로 모든 사람에게 작용하는 방식이다.

(2) 동명사구 주어는 단수 취급하므로 동사를 단수형 makes로 써야 한다.

해석 그러한 전략들을 적용하는 것은 독해력이 떨어지게 만든다.

(3) 조동사는 두 개를 연달아 쓸 수 없으므로 can을 be able to로 바꿔 써야 한다.

해석 사람들은 잠을 더 잘 잘 수도 있으므로 자신의 침실에 파란색을 사용한다.

(4) 동사 showed의 목적어 역할을 하는 명사절을 이끄는 접속사로 that의 쓰임은 알맞다.

해석 그녀의 연구는 컴퓨터 화면으로 읽는 것이 다양한 전략을 포함한다는 것을 보여 주었다.

PART 1 　중심 내용 파악하기

UNIT 04

요약하기

정답 ①　　　　　　　　　　　　　　　　　p. 38

필자는 자신이 배우고 있는 것(경도와 위도)을 이미 알고 있는 것(north라는 단어)과 '연결함'으로써 시험 전에 학습 자료를 쉽게 '암기하고' 문제를 모두 맞힐 수 있었다. 따라서 빈칸 (A)와 (B)에 들어갈 말로 가장 적절한 것은 ①이다.

오답풀이 ② 연결하는 것 – 출판하다　③ 제시하는 것 – 출판하다　④ 대체하는 것 – 평가하다　⑤ 대체하는 것 – 암기하다

READING GUIDE　(A): ❺　(B): ❻

UNDERSTAND DEEPLY　**1** ⑤　**2** (1) 경도와 위도를 계속 혼동함 (2) 경도(longitude)의 n을 north와 연결시켜 기억함

1 글의 초반부에서 필자는 경도와 위도를 계속 혼동하여 울 뻔할 정도로 매우 좌절하고 창피해했다고 했으며, 이어서 이를 쉽게 암기할 방법을 알아내어 결국 시험에서 모든 문제를 맞혔다고 했다. 따라서 필자의 심경 변화로 가장 적절한 것은 ⑤이다.

해석 ① 혼란스러워하는 → 언짢은　② 놀란 → 슬픈　③ 만족한 → 긴장한　④ 외로운 → 무서워하는　⑤ 우울한 → 기쁜

2 필자는 경도와 위도의 개념을 계속 혼동하였으며, 이에 대한 해결책으로 경도(longitude)의 n을 north와 연결시켜 그 의미를 기억해 냈다.

---

❶ When I was in eighth grade, / we were studying / longitude and latitude / in geography class.

내가 8학년이었을 때 / 우리는 공부하고 있었다 / 경도와 위도를 / 지리 수업에서

❷ Every day for a week, / we had a quiz, / and I kept confusing / longitude and latitude.

일주일 동안 매일 / 우리는 쪽지 시험을 보았다 / 그리고 나는 계속 혼동했다 / 경도와 위도를

❸ I went home / and almost cried / because I got so frustrated and embarrassed / by the fact / that I couldn't properly understand them.

나는 집에 갔다 / 그리고 울 뻔했다 / 왜냐하면 내가 너무 좌절감을 느끼고 창피했기 때문에 / 그 사실에 의해 / 내가 그것들을 제대로 이해하지 못했다는

❹ I stared and stared at those words / until suddenly I figured out / what to do.

나는 그 단어들을 쳐다보고 또 쳐다보았다 / 갑자기 내가 알아냈을 때까지 / 무엇을 해야 할지

❺ I told myself, / 'When you see that *n* in longitude, / it will remind you of the word *north*. // So it will be easy / to remember / that longitude lines go / from north to south.'

나는 나 자신에게 말했다 / 네가 경도에서 그 n을 보면 / 그것은 너에게 north라는 단어를 생각나게 할 거야 // 그래서 쉬울 거야 / 기억하는 것이 / 경도선이 이어진다는 것을 / 북쪽에서 남쪽으로

❻ It worked; / I got them all right / on all the quizzes / and also on the final test.

그것은 효과가 있었다 / 나는 그것들을 모두 맞혔다 / 모든 쪽지 시험에서 / 그리고 또한 기말 시험에서

지문해석 내가 8학년이었을 때, 우리는 지리 수업에서 경도와 위도를 공부하고 있었다. 일주일간 매일, 우리는 쪽지 시험을 봤고 나는 경도와 위도를 계속 헷갈렸다. 나는 그것들을 제대로 이해하지 못한다는 사실에 너무 좌절감을 느끼고 창피했기 때문에 집에 가서 울 뻔했다. 나는 갑자기 내가 무엇을 해야 할지를 알아냈을 때까지 그 단어들을 쳐다보고 또 쳐다보았다. 나는 나 자신에게 '네가 경도(longitude)에서 그 'n'을 보면, 그것은 너에게 'north'라는 단어를 생각나게 할 거야. 그래서 경도선이 북쪽에서 남쪽으로 이어진다는 걸 기억하기가 쉬울 거야.'라고 말했다. 그것은 효과가 있었는데, 나는 모든 쪽지 시험과 기말 시험에서도 그것들을 모두 맞혔다.

→ 위의 이야기는 여러분이 배우고 있는 것을 여러분이 이미 아는 것과 연결하는 것이 여러분이 학습 자료를 암기하도록 도와준다는 것을 시사한다.

12 정답 ① p. 40

두 가지 소음을 이용한 실험에서 참가자들은 길이가 두 배로 길어도 뒷부분이 덜 불쾌한 소음을 다시 들을 소음으로 선택했다. 즉, 어느 소음을 다시 들어야 할지를 결정하는 데 영향을 주는 것은 소음의 길이(length)가 아니라, 참가자들이 마지막 순간(last moment)에 느낀 감정이었다. 따라서 빈칸 (A)와 (B)에 들어갈 말로 가장 적절한 것은 ①이다.

오답풀이 ② 길이 – 절정 ③ 소리의 세기 – 시작 ④ 소리의 세기 – 마지막 순간 ⑤ 유쾌함 – 절정

READING GUIDE (A): ❼ (B): ❾

UNDERSTAND
DEEPLY   1 (1) T (2) F   2 (1) longer (2) second

1 (1) 첫 번째 소음은 8초, 두 번째 소음은 16초라고 했으므로 일치한다.
  (2) 두 번째 소음의 뒷부분 8초는 앞부분 8초만큼 소리가 크지 않았다고 했으므로 일치하지 않는다.

2 (1) 첫 번째 소음은 8초, 두 번째 소음은 16초동안 지속되었다고 했으므로 두 번째 소음이 더 길었다. (2) 대부분의 사람들이 다시 들을 소음으로 두 번째 소음을 선택했다고 했다.

  해석 (1) 두 번째 소음은 첫 번째 것보다 더 길었다. (2) 더 많은 사람들이 이 두 번째 소음을 다시 듣기로 결정했다.

READ CLOSELY p. 41

❶ Participants in a laboratory study / were asked / to listen to / a pair of very loud, unpleasant noises / played through headphones.

한 실험실 연구의 참가자들은 / 요청을 받았다 / ~을 들으라는 / 두 개의 아주 크고 불쾌한 소음 / 헤드폰을 통해 재생되는

❷ One noise lasted / for eight seconds.

한 소음은 지속되었다 / 8초간

❸ The other lasted / for sixteen.

다른 하나는 지속되었다 / 16초간

❹ The first eight seconds of the second noise / were identical to the first noise.

두 번째 소음의 첫 8초는 / 첫 번째 소음과 동일했다

❺ The second eight seconds, / while still unpleasant, / were not as loud as / the first eight seconds.

두 번째 8초는 / 여전히 불쾌한 반면에 / ~만큼 소리가 크지 않았다 / 첫 번째 8초

❻ Later, / the participants were told / that they would have to listen to / one of the noises / again, / but that they could choose / which one to listen to.

나중에 / 참가자들은 들었다 / 그들이 ~을 들어야 할 것이라고 / 그 소음 중 하나 / 다시 / 그러나 그들이 선택할 수 있다고 / 어느 것을 들을지

❼ Clearly, / the second noise is worse / — the unpleasantness lasted / twice as long.

분명히 / 두 번째 소음이 더 안 좋다 / 불쾌함이 지속되었다 / 두 배나 오래

❽ Nevertheless, / most people chose the second noise. // Why?

그럼에도 불구하고 / 대부분의 사람들은 두 번째 소음을 선택했다 // 왜일까?

❾ Although both noises were unpleasant, / the second one had / a less unpleasant ending.

두 가지 소음이 모두 불쾌하기는 했지만 / 두 번째 것이 가지고 있었다 / 덜 불쾌한 끝부분을

❿ So, / people remembered the second one / as less annoying / than the first one.

그래서 / 사람들은 두 번째 것을 기억했다 / 덜 짜증 나게 하는 것으로 / 첫 번째 것보다

지문해석 한 실험실 연구의 참가자들은 헤드폰을 통해 재생되는 두 가지의 아주 크고 불쾌한 소음을 들으라는 요청을 받았다. 한 소음은 8초간 지속되었다. 다른 소음은 16초간 지속되었다. 두 번째 소음의 첫 8초는 첫 번째 소음과 동일했다. 두 번째 8초는 여전히 불쾌하지만 첫 번째 8초만큼 소리가 크지는 않았다. 나중에, 참가자들은 (두 가지) 소음 중 하나를 다시 들어야 하지만 그들이 어느 것을 들을지 선택할 수 있다고 들었다. 분명히 두 번째 소음이 더 안 좋은데, 불쾌함이 두 배로 오래 지속되었기 때문이다. 그럼에도 불구하고, 대부분의 사람들이 두 번째 소음을 선택했다. 왜일까? 두 가지 소음이 모두 불쾌했지만 두 번째 소음의 끝부분이 덜 불쾌했기 때문이다. 그래서 사람들은 두 번째 소음을 첫 번째 소음보다 덜 짜증 나게 하는 것으로 기억했다.
→ 한 실험에 따르면, 어느 소음을 다시 들어야 할지에 대한 결정에 영향을 주는 것은 소음의 길이가 아니라, 마지막 순간에 그들이 어떻게 느꼈는가이다.

❺ The second eight seconds, [while still unpleasant],
　　주어　　　　　　　　　　접속사(~한 반면에)
were not as loud as the first eight seconds.
　동사　　as+형용사/부사의 원급+as: ~만큼 …한/하게
❼ Clearly, the second noise is worse — the
　　　　　　　　　　　　　　　　　　(as the first noise)
unpleasantness lasted twice as long.
　　　　　　　배수사+as+형용사/부사의 원급+as: ~의 (몇) 배로 …한/하게
❿ So, people remembered the second one as less

annoying than the first one.
less+형용사/부사의 원급+than: ~보다 덜 …한/하게

13 정답 ④   p. 42

사람들에게 꽃 이미지를 보여 줬을 때보다 한 쌍의 눈 이미지를 보여 줌으로
써 자신의 행동이 '관찰되고' 있다고 느끼게 했을 때 상자에 지불된 금액이
'증가했다'. 따라서 빈칸 (A)와 (B)에 들어갈 말로 가장 적절한 것은 ④이다.

오답풀이 ① 감소했다 – 속은 ② 감소했다 – 관찰되는 ③ 변화했다 – 지
지되는 ⑤ 증가했다 – 지지되는

READING GUIDE (A): ❻ (B): ❽

UNDERSTAND DEEPLY
1 (1) 눈 (2) 꽃 (3) (한 쌍의) 눈 (4) 3 (5) 관찰되고 있을
2 cheating the system

1 한 쌍의 눈 이미지와 꽃 이미지를 번갈아 게시한 결과, 눈 이미지가 게시
되었을 때 거의 3배 더 많은 돈이 지불되었으며, 사람들이 자신이 관찰되
고 있다는 생각에 정직하게 행동했다는 결론이 도출되었다.

2 마지막 문장에서 알 수 있듯이 실험에 사용된 눈 이미지는 참가자들로 하
여금 자신이 시스템을 속이고 있는지를 다른 사람들이 지켜보고 있다고
느끼게 하는 역할을 했다.

READ CLOSELY   p. 43

❶ An experiment (proved) / the importance of reputation
/ in increasing cooperation.

한 실험이 증명했다 / 평판의 중요성을 / 협력을 증진시키는 데 있어서의

❷ Bateson and colleagues (analyzed) / the amounts of
money / put into an 'honesty box' / for drinks / in a
coffee room.

Bateson과 동료들은 분석했다 / 돈의 총액을 / '정직 상자' 안으로 들어간
/ 음료 값으로 / 커피 마시는 공간에서

❸ Images / (always posted / above the recommended
price list) / of a pair of eyes / (were swapped) / every
week / with images of flowers.

이미지들은 / (항상 게시되는 / 권장 가격 목록 위에) / 한 쌍의 눈의 / 바뀌
었다 / 매주 / 꽃 이미지들로

❹ Then / they (compared) / the amounts of money / in
the box.

그런 다음 / 그들은 비교했다 / 돈의 총액을 / 상자 안에 있는

❺ The amount of drinks / consumed each week / (was)
almost the same.

음료의 양은 / 매주 소비된 / 거의 똑같았다

❻ Surprisingly, / almost three times more money / (was
paid) / in weeks / when eyes were shown, / compared
to when flowers were shown.

놀랍게도 / 거의 세 배 더 많은 돈이 / 지불되었다 / 주에 / 눈이 보인 / 꽃
이 보인 때와 비교하여

❼ Of course / this experiment (was) only (conducted) / in
one location, / but the effect size (was) impressive.

물론 / 이 실험은 단지 실시되었다 / 한 장소에서 / 하지만 그 효과 크기는
인상적이었다

❽ It (seems) to show / that people don't want others / to
see them / cheating the system.

그것은 보여 주는 것 같다 / 사람들이 다른 사람들을 원하지 않는다는 것
을 / 그들을 보는 것을 / 시스템을 속이고 있는 것을

지문해석 한 실험이 협력을 증진시키는 데 있어서 평판의 중요성을 증명했
다. Bateson과 동료들은 커피 마시는 공간에서 음료 값으로 '정직 상자' 안
에 들어간 돈의 총액을 분석했다. (항상 권장 가격 목록 위에 게시되는) 한 쌍
의 눈의 이미지들은 매주 꽃 이미지들로 바뀌었다. 그런 다음 그들은 상자 안
에 있는 돈의 총액을 비교했다. 매주 소비된 음료의 양은 거의 똑같았다. 놀랍
게도 꽃이 보인 때에 비해 눈이 보인 주에 거의 세 배 더 많은 돈이 지불되었
다. 물론 이 실험은 한 장소에서 실시되었을 뿐이지만 그 효과 크기는 인상적
이었다. 그것은 사람들이 자신이 시스템을 속이고 있는 것을 다른 사람들이
보기를 원하지 않음을 보여 주는 것 같다.
→ 사람들이 '정직 상자' 안에 넣은 돈의 총액은 이미지가 그들이 관찰되고 있
다고 느끼게 만들었을 때 증가했다.

문장 돋보기

❸ Images [(always posted above the recommended
　　주어　　　　　　　　과거분사('게시되는'이라는 수동의 의미)
price list)] of a pair of eyes were swapped every
　　　　　　　　　　　　　　　　　　동사(수동태)
week with images of flowers.

❻ Surprisingly, almost three times more money was
　　　　　　　　┌시간을 나타내는 선행사
paid in weeks [when eyes were shown], compared
　　　　　　　　└관계부사절　　　　　　　　　　　~와 비교하여
to [when flowers were shown].
　　　명사절 접속사(~할 때)

❽ It seems to show [that people don't want others
　　　　　　　　　　　　　명사절 접속사
to see them cheating the system].
지각동사 see+목적어+목적격 보어(현재분사): ~이 …하고 있는 것을 보다

1 (1) conduct (2) experiment
(3) colleague (4) publish

2 (1) reputation (2) unpleasant
(3) memorize (4) decision

3

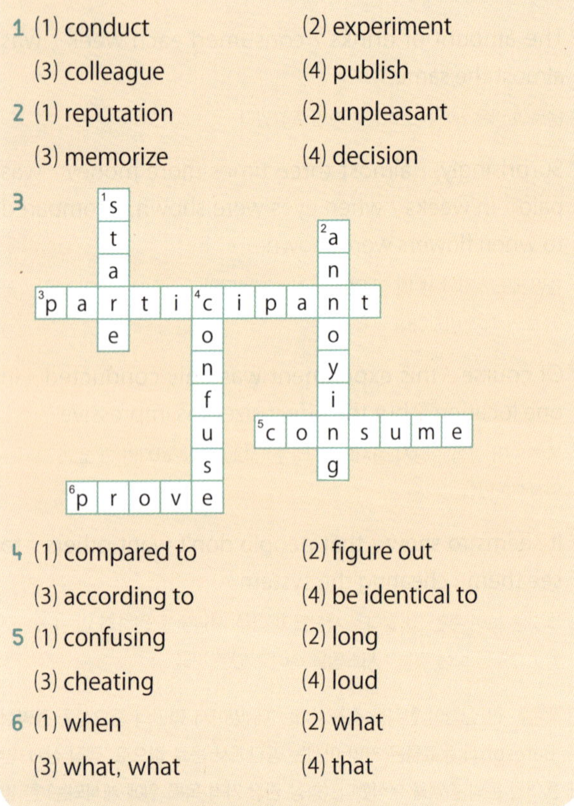

Across / Down 낱말 퍼즐:
- ¹state
- ²annoying
- ³participant
- ⁴confuse
- ⁵consume
- ⁶prove

4 (1) compared to (2) figure out
(3) according to (4) be identical to

5 (1) confusing (2) long
(3) cheating (4) loud

6 (1) when (2) what
(3) what, what (4) that

---

5 (1) 동사 keep은 목적어로 동명사를 취해 '계속 ～하다'의 의미를 나타내므로 동명사 confusing이 알맞다.

해석 나는 경도와 위도를 계속 헷갈렸다.

(2) '～의 (몇) 배로 …하게'를 의미하는 배수 비교 구문 「배수사+as+부사 원급+as」의 형태가 되어야 하므로 부사 long이 알맞다.

해석 두 번째 소음은 첫 번째 것의 두 배로 오래 지속되었다.

(3) 지각동사 see의 목적격 보어로 동사원형이나 현재분사가 쓰이므로 현재분사 cheating이 알맞다.

해석 사람들은 자신들이 시스템을 속이고 있는 것을 다른 사람들이 보기를 원하지 않는다.

(4) '～만큼 …한'을 의미하는 동등 비교 구문 「as+형용사 원급+as」의 형태가 되어야 하므로 형용사 loud가 알맞다.

해석 두 번째 8초는 첫 번째 8초만큼 소리가 크지 않았다.

6 (1) 시간을 나타내는 선행사 weeks를 수식해야 하므로 관계부사 when이 알맞다.

해석 눈이 보인 주에 더 많은 돈이 지불되었다.

(2) '무엇을 ～할지'의 의미는 「의문사 what+to부정사」로 표현하므로 의문사 what이 알맞다.

해석 나는 내가 무엇을 해야 할지 알아냈을 때까지 그 단어들을 쳐다보고 또 쳐다보았다.

(3) 두 빈칸 모두 '～하는 것'을 의미하는 절을 이끌어야 하므로 선행사를 포함하는 관계대명사 what이 알맞다.

해석 여러분이 배우고 있는 것을 여러분이 이미 알고 있는 것과 연결해라.

(4) the fact와 동격을 이루는 절을 이끌어야 하므로 접속사 that이 알맞다.

해석 나는 내가 그것들을 제대로 이해하지 못했다는 사실에 너무 좌절감을 느꼈다.

Play Time

▶ 각 종이 비행기의 윗면을 찾아보세요.

정답: 1 – 15, 2 – 12, 3 – 14, 4 – 11, 5 – 9, 6 – 16, 7 – 13, 8 – 10

내용 일치 파악하기

 14 정답 ⑤   p. 48

마지막 문장에서 새끼는 젖을 뗀 뒤에도 보호받기 위해 가끔씩 어미의 주머니로 돌아간다고(Even after the young no longer need the mother's milk, they return at times to the pouch for protection.) 했으므로 ⑤가 글의 내용과 일치하지 않는다.

READING GUIDE ①: , , ②: , ③: , ④: ❻, ⑤: ❾

UNDERSTAND DEEPLY

1 ①   **2** (1) that has a pouch to carry and raise its young (2) has no power to suck milk with its mouth

1 유대류(marsupial)가 태어난 후 어미의 주머니에서 성장하는 방식을 중점적으로 다루고 있으므로 글의 중심 소재로 ①이 가장 적절하다.

2 (1) 글의 앞부분에서 유대류를 처음 언급하면서 새끼를 데리고 다니며 키우는 주머니를 가지고 있는 동물이라고 했다. (2) 새끼가 처음에는 제 입으로 젖을 빨 힘이 전혀 없어서 어미의 젖이 새끼의 입으로 직접 들어간다고 했다.

해석 (1) Q: 유대류는 어떤 종류의 동물인가? A: 그것은 새끼를 데리고 다니며 키우는 주머니를 가지고 있는 동물이다. (2) Q: 왜 처음에 어미의 젖이 새끼의 입으로 직접 들어가는가? A: 새끼가 자기 입으로 젖을 빨아들일 힘이 전혀 없기 때문이다.

READ CLOSELY   p. 49

❶ In many species, / the young are carried / on their mother's back.

많은 종(種)에서 / 새끼들은 옮겨진다 / 그들의 어미의 등 위에서

❷ However, / this is not the case / for all animals.

그러나 / 이것이 경우는 아니다 / 모든 동물들에 대한

❸ A marsupial is an animal / that has a pouch / to carry and raise its young.

유대류는 동물이다 / 주머니를 가지고 있는 / 자신의 새끼들을 데리고 다니며 키우는

❹ Wallabies, kangaroos, and koalas / are all examples of marsupials.

왈라비, 캥거루, 그리고 코알라는 / 모두 유대류의 예이다

❺ Its baby is born / at a very early stage of development / when it is about the size of a jelly bean.

그것의 새끼는 태어난다 / 아주 이른 발달 단계에 / 그것이 젤리빈 크기 정도일 때인

❻ At birth, / it takes a long journey / to reach the pouch / by holding the mother's fur.

태어났을 때 / 그것은 긴 여행을 한다 / 주머니에 도달하기 위해 / 어미의 털을 잡음으로써

❼ There, / it continues to grow.

거기서 / 그것은 성장하기를 계속한다

❽ At first, / the baby has no power / to suck milk with its mouth, / so the mother's milk goes into the baby's mouth / directly.

처음에는 / 새끼는 아무런 힘이 없다 / 자신의 입으로 젖을 빨아들일 / 그래서 어미의 젖이 새끼의 입으로 들어간다 / 직접

❾ Even after the young no longer need the mother's milk, / they return / at times / to the pouch / for protection.

심지어 새끼들이 어미의 젖을 더 이상 필요로 하지 않는 후에도 / 그들은 돌아간다 / 가끔 / 주머니로 / 보호를 위해

지문해석 많은 종(種)에서, 새끼들은 제 어미 등에 업혀 옮겨진다. 그러나 이것은 모든 동물들에 해당하는 경우는 아니다. 유대류는 새끼를 데리고 다니며 키우는 주머니를 가지고 있는 동물이다. 왈라비, 캥거루, 코알라는 모두 유대류의 예이다. 유대류의 새끼는 그것이 젤리빈 정도의 크기일 때인 아주 이른 발달 단계에 태어난다. 태어나서 그것은 어미의 털을 잡고서 주머니에 도달하기 위해 긴 여행을 한다. 거기서(어미의 주머니에서) 그것은 계속 성장한다. 처음에는 새끼가 제 입으로 젖을 빨아들일 힘이 전혀 없어서, 어미젖이 새끼 입으로 직접 들어간다. 심지어 새끼에게 더 이상 어미젖이 필요하지 않은 후에도, 새끼는 보호받기 위해 종종 주머니로 돌아간다.

문장 돋보기

❶ In many species, the young are carried on their mother's back.
주어(the+형용사: 복수 명사)   동사(수동태)

❺ Its baby is born at a very early stage of development
be born: 태어나다
[when it is about the size of a jelly bean].
시간을 나타내는 선행사를 수식하는 관계부사

 15 정답 ③   p. 50

Dorothy West의 첫 소설은 평론가들로부터는 긍정적인 반응을 얻었다고 (Her first novel, ~ received positive responses from critics ~.) 했으므로 ③이 글의 내용과 일치하지 않는다.

READING GUIDE ①: ❶, ②: ❷, ③: ❸, ④: ❺, ⑤: ❼, ❽

UNDERSTAND DEEPLY

1 (1) *The Living Is Easy* (2) 1948 (3) *The Wedding* (4) 1995   **2** (1) F (2) F

1 첫 번째 소설의 제목과 출판 연도는 세 번째 문장에 나와 있으며, 두 번째 소설의 제목은 네 번째 문장에, 출판 연도는 일곱 번째 문장에 나와 있다.

2 (1) Dorothy West의 첫 소설은 많은 독자를 끄는 데 실패했다고 했다.
(2) Jacqueline Onassis는 West가 이미 지역 신문에 제출한 단편 소설들에 주목했다고 했다.

해석 (1) Dorothy West의 첫 번째 소설은 많은 독자를 끌었다.
(2) Jacqueline Onassis는 West가 그녀의 단편 소설들을 Martha's Vineyard의 지역 신문에 제출하도록 도왔다.

READ CLOSELY

p. 51

❶ Dorothy West, / born on June 2, 1907, / is remembered / as one of the Harlem Renaissance writers.

Dorothy West는 / 1907년 6월 2일에 태어난 / 기억된다 / 할렘 르네상스 작가들 중 한 명으로

❷ West mainly wrote about / the life of rich African Americans.

West는 주로 ~에 대해 썼다 / 부유한 아프리카계 미국인들의 삶

❸ Her first novel, *The Living Is Easy*, / published in 1948, / received positive responses / from critics, / but failed to draw many readers.

그녀의 첫 번째 소설 *The Living Is Easy*는 / 1948년에 출판된 / 긍정적인 반응을 얻었다 / 비평가들로부터 / 하지만 많은 독자를 끄는 데 실패했다

❹ She wrote / her second novel, *The Wedding*, / in 1950, / but did not complete it / because she was not able to find a publisher.

그녀는 썼다 / 그녀의 두 번째 소설 *The Wedding*을 / 1950년에 / 그러나 그것을 완성하지 않았다 / 왜냐하면 그녀가 출판업자를 찾을 수 없었기 때문에

❺ Jacqueline Onassis noticed the short stories / that West submitted / to the local newspaper / at Martha's Vineyard.

Jacqueline Onassis는 단편 소설들에 주목했다 / West가 제출한 / 지역 신문에 / Martha's Vineyard의

❻ Onassis encouraged West / to complete her novel / and later served as her editor.

Onassis는 West를 격려했다 / 그녀의 소설을 완성하도록 / 그리고 나중에 그녀의 편집자로 일했다

❼ Her second novel / was published / in 1995 / and was made into a television movie / produced by Oprah Winfrey.

그녀의 두 번째 소설은 / 출판되었다 / 1995년에 / 그리고 텔레비전 영화로 만들어졌다 / Oprah Winfrey에 의해 제작된

❽ It was aired / in 1998.

그것은 방송되었다 / 1998년에

❾ West died / on August 16, 1998.

West는 사망했다 / 1998년 8월 16일에

지문해석 1907년 6월 2일에 태어난 Dorothy West는 할렘 르네상스 작가들 중 한 명으로 기억된다. West는 주로 부유한 아프리카계 미국인들의 삶에 대해 썼다. 그녀의 첫 번째 소설 *The Living Is Easy*는 1948년에 출간되었는데, 비평가들로부터 긍정적인 반응을 얻었지만 많은 독자를 끄는 데는 실패했다. 그녀는 1950년에 그녀의 두 번째 소설인 *The Wedding*을 썼으나 출판업자를 찾을 수 없었기 때문에 그것을 완성하지 않았다. Jacqueline Onassis는 West가 Martha's Vineyard의 지역 신문에 제출한 단편 소설들에 주목했다. Onassis는 West가 그녀의 소설을 완성하도록 격려했고 나중에 그녀의 편집자로 일했다. 그녀의 두 번째 소설은 1995년에 출간되었고 Oprah Winfrey에 의해 제작된 텔레비전 영화로 만들어졌다. 그것은 1998년에 방송되었다. West는 1998년 8월 16일에 사망했다.

문장 돋보기

❶ Dorothy West, [born on June 2, 1907], is remembered
　　　주어　　　　　　　　과거분사구　　　　　　　동사(수동태)
as one of the Harlem Renaissance writers.
　　　　one of+복수 명사: ~ 중 하나
❸ Her first novel, *The Living Is Easy*, [published in
　　　주어　　　└ 동격　　　　　　　　　과거분사구
1948], received positive responses from critics,
　　　　동사1
but failed to draw many readers.
　동사2　동사 fail은 목적어로 to부정사를 취함
❺ Jacqueline Onassis noticed the short stories [that
West submitted to the local newspaper at Martha's
목적격 관계대명사절
Vineyard].

16 정답 ④

p. 52

1898년에는 Munich Academy에서 공부를 하며 미술 경력을 시작했고 (In 1898, he began his art career by studying at the Munich Academy.), 그 후 1921년부터 Bauhaus에서 회화를 가르쳤다고 (Afterwards, he taught painting at the Bauhaus from January 1921 to April 1931.) 했으므로 ④가 글의 내용과 일치하지 않는다.

READING GUIDE ①: , ②: , , ③: , ④: ❽, ⑤: ⑩

UNDERSTAND DEEPLY

1 (1) 1898 (2) Munich Academy (3) 1921
(4) Bauhaus (5) 1만 (6) 5천 **2** ④

1 (1), (2) In 1898, ~ by studying at the Munich Academy.
(3), (4) he taught painting at the Bauhaus from January 1921
(5), (6) over ten thousand drawings and nearly five thousand paintings

2 수많은 미술 서적과 소묘 및 회화 작품을 남겼다고 했지만 대표 작품의 제목은 글에 언급되지 않았다.

❶ Paul Klee (was born) / in Bern, Switzerland, / on December 18, 1879.

Paul Klee는 태어났다 / 스위스의 베른에서 / 1879년 12월 18일에

❷ His father (was) a music teacher / and his mother (was) / a singer and an amateur painter.

그의 아버지는 음악 선생님이었다 / 그리고 그의 어머니는 ～였다 / 가수이자 아마추어 화가

❸ As a child, / Paul (drew) / constantly.

아이였을 때 / Paul은 그림을 그렸다 / 끊임없이

❹ His favorite subject / was cats.

그가 가장 좋아하는 대상은 / 고양이였다

❺ Then / at the age of seven, / he (learned) / how to play the violin, / and he (continued) to play / as an adult, too.

그러고 나서 / 일곱 살 때 / 그는 배웠다 / 바이올린 연주하는 법을 / 그리고 그는 연주하는 것을 계속했다 / 어른이었을 때도

❻ In fact, / he even (played) / with the Berlin Municipal Orchestra / for a while.

사실 / 그는 심지어 연주했다 / 베를린 시립 오케스트라와 함께 / 한동안

❼ Although music was important / to Paul, / he (decided) to pursue visual art / and (became) an artist.

음악이 중요하기는 했지만 / Paul에게 / 그는 시각 예술을 추구하기로 결심했다 / 그리고 화가가 되었다

❽ In 1898, / he (began) / his art career / by studying / at the Munich Academy.

1898년에 / 그는 시작했다 / 그의 미술 경력을 / 공부함으로써 / Munich Academy에서

❾ Afterwards, / he (taught) painting / at the Bauhaus / from January 1921 to April 1931.

그 후에 / 그는 회화를 가르쳤다 / Bauhaus에서 / 1921년 1월부터 1931년 4월까지

❿ Paul also (kept) a notebook / filled with his artistic beliefs and ideas, / and (published) / a number of books / about art.

Paul은 또한 노트를 기록했다 / 그의 예술적 신념과 아이디어로 가득 찬 / 그리고 출판했다 / 많은 책을 / 미술에 관한

⓫ By his death in 1940, / he (had created) / an impressive amount of work: / over ten thousand drawings / and nearly five thousand paintings.

1940년 그의 사망까지 / 그는 만들어 냈다 / 인상적인 양의 작품을 / 1만 점이 넘는 소묘 / 그리고 거의 5천 점의 회화

지문해석 Paul Klee는 1879년 12월 18일에 스위스의 베른에서 태어났다. 그의 아버지는 음악 선생님이었고 그의 어머니는 가수이자 아마추어 화가였다. 어렸을 때 Paul은 끊임없이 그림을 그렸다. 그가 가장 좋아하는 (그림의) 대상은 고양이였다. 그리고 일곱 살 때 그는 바이올린 연주하는 법을 배웠고, 어른이 되어서도 계속 (바이올린을) 연주했다. 사실, 그는 한동안 베를린 시립 오케스트라와 함께 연주하기도 했다. 음악이 Paul에게 중요하긴 했지만, 그는 시각 예술을 추구하기로 결심하고 화가가 되었다. 1898년에 그는 Munich Academy에서 공부함으로써 그의 미술 경력을 시작했다. 그 이후, 그는 1921년 1월부터 1931년 4월까지 Bauhaus에서 회화를 가르쳤다. Paul은 또한 그의 예술적 신념과 아이디어로 가득 찬 노트를 기록했고, 미술에 관한 많은 책을 출판했다. 1940년에 사망하기까지 그는 인상적인 양의 작품을 만들어 냈는데, 1만 점이 넘는 소묘와 5천 점에 가까운 회화를 남겼다.

문장 돋보기

❿ Paul also kept a notebook [filled with his artistic beliefs and ideas], and published a number of books about art.
동사1 / 과거분사구 / 동사2 / 많은

REVIEW TIME

p. 54

1 (1) critic　(2) mainly
(3) growth　(4) amateur

2 (1) protection　(2) development
(3) complete　(4) encourage
(5) continue　(6) impressive

3

A	Q	B	X	V	N	B	L	B	F	P
K	R	W	J	I	T	O	B	C	Q	D
J	L	V	K	O	P	N	V	X	C	L
L	C	N	O	J	U	A	T	E	B	P
C	A	R	E	E	R	R	S	S	L	Z
K	U	Q	Z	P	S	T	N	X	P	S
V	T	Z	Y	B	U	I	Z	E	U	W
S	Y	G	Y	O	E	S	S	A	Y	R
C	E	P	G	L	K	T	I	A	B	L
O	W	S	P	E	C	I	E	S	D	C
K	T	G	E	Z	M	C	H	R	G	H

(1) species　(2) artistic　(3) pursue
(4) novel　(5) journey　(6) career

4 (1) filled with　(2) be made into
(3) for a while　(4) at times

5 (1) to play　(2) to complete
(3) are　(4) because

6 (1) to grow 또는 growing　(2) to suck
(3) filled　(4) published

1 (1) 편집하다 : 편집자 = 비평하다 : 비평가 (동사 : 직업 명사 관계)

(2) 가까운 : 거의 = 주된, 주요한 : 주로 (형용사 : 부사 관계)

(3) 반응하다 : 반응 = 성장하다, 자라다 : 성장 (동사 : 명사 관계)

(4) 쉬운 : 어려운 = 전문적인, 직업적인 : 비전문적인, 아마추어의 (반의어 관계)

5 (1) 동사 continue는 to부정사와 동명사를 목적어로 취하므로 to play가 알맞다.

해석 그는 어른이 되어서도 계속 바이올린을 연주했다.

(2) 동사 encourage는 목적격 보어로 to부정사를 취하므로 to complete가 알맞다.

해석 Onassis는 West가 그녀의 소설을 완성하도록 격려했다.

(3) 「the+형용사」는 복수 명사를 나타내므로 동사로 복수형 are가 알맞다.

해석 많은 종에서, 새끼들은 제 어미 등에 업혀 옮겨진다.

(4) 뒤에 주어와 동사를 포함하는 절이 오므로 접속사 because가 알맞다. because of는 전치사이다.

해석 그녀는 출판업자를 찾을 수 없었기 때문에 그녀의 소설을 완성하지 않았다.

6 (1) 동사 continue는 to부정사와 동명사를 모두 목적어로 취하므로 to grow 또는 growing이 알맞다.

(2) 앞에 있는 명사 power를 수식해야 하므로 형용사적 용법의 to부정사 to suck이 알맞다.

(3) '가득 찬'이라는 수동의 의미를 나타내야 하므로 과거분사 filled가 알맞다.

(4) 소설 *The Living Is Easy*가 '출간된' 것이므로 수동을 의미하는 과거분사 published가 알맞다.

PART 2   세부 내용 파악하기

UNIT 06

안내문·도표 파악하기

17   정답 ③   p. 56

독백 대본을 완전히 암기해야 한다고(You should memorize your monologue completely.) 했으므로 ③이 안내문의 내용과 일치한다.

오답풀이 ① 동영상 제출로 오디션에 참가할 수 없다고 했다.(It is not possible to audition by sending in a video clip of your presentation.) ② 독백은 2분보다 길지 않아야 한다고 했다.(Your monologue must be no longer than two minutes.) ④ 오디션 당일에 독백 대본 2부를 가져오라고 했다.(Bring two copies of your monologue with you on audition day.) ⑤ 영화, TV 드라마, 시에서는 대본을 선택하지 말라고 했다.(DO NOT select it from films, TV dramas, or poems.)

READING GUIDE ①: ❹, ②: ❺, ③: ❻, ④: ❼, ⑤: ❾

---

1 지원자들에게 연기 과정 오디션에 참가하는 방법을 안내하기 위해 쓰인 글이다.

해석 ① 연기력을 향상시키는 방법 ② 연기 학교를 선택하는 방법 ③ 오디션에 참가하는 방법 ④ 오디션용 동영상을 촬영하는 방법

2 (1) 오디션 날에는 독백 대본 2부를 가져오라고 했다. (2) 독백은 연극에서 선택하라고 했다.

해석 (1) 오디션 날, 지원자들은 자신의 독백 대본 2부를 가져와야 한다. (2) 지원자들은 자신의 독백을 연극에서 선택해야 한다.

READ CLOSELY   p. 57

❶ Hello, applicants!

안녕하세요, 지원자 여러분

❷ You will be given a chance / to demonstrate / your talent and potential.

여러분은 기회가 주어질 것입니다 / 보여 줄 / 여러분의 재능과 잠재력을

❸ You must attend the audition / in person.

여러분은 오디션에 참석해야 합니다 / 직접

❹ It is not possible / to audition / by sending in / a video clip of your presentation.

불가능합니다 / 오디션을 받는 것은 / ~을 제출함으로써 / 여러분의 발표 동영상

❺ Your monologue must be no longer / than two minutes.

여러분의 독백은 더 길지 않아야 합니다 / 2분보다

❻ You should memorize your monologue / completely.

여러분은 여러분의 독백을 암기해야 합니다 / 완전히

❼ Bring two copies of your monologue / with you / on audition day.

여러분의 독백 대본 2부를 가져오세요 / 여러분과 함께 / 오디션 날

❽ Choose your monologue / from plays.

여러분의 독백을 선택하세요 / 연극에서

❾ DO NOT select it / from films, TV dramas, or poems.

그것을 선택하지 마세요 / 영화, TV 드라마, 또는 시에서

지문해석   연기 과정 오디션

안녕하세요, 지원자 여러분!

여러분은 여러분의 재능과 잠재력을 보여 줄 기회가 주어질 것입니다. 여러분은 오디션에 직접 참석해야 합니다. 여러분의 발표가 담긴 동영상을 제출함으로써 오디션을 받는 것은 불가능합니다.

- 여러분의 독백은 2분보다 길지 않아야 합니다.
- 여러분은 여러분의 독백을 완전하게 암기해야 합니다.
- 독백 대본 2부를 오디션 보는 날 가져오세요.
- 여러분의 독백을 연극에서 선택하세요. 그것을 영화, TV 드라마, 또는 시(詩)에서 선택하지 마세요.

❷You will be given a chance [to demonstrate your talent and potential].
will be+과거분사: 미래시제 수동태 → to부정사의 형용사적 용법

18 정답 ④ p. 58

자전거 대여와 관련된 항목인 Bike Reservation에서 자전거를 사용하려면 반드시 행사 당일 전에 온라인으로 예약해야 함을 확인할 수 있다. 따라서 ④는 안내문의 내용과 일치하지 않는다.

READING GUIDE ①: ❶, ②: ❺, ③: ❻, ④: ❽, ⑤: ❾

UNDERSTAND DEEPLY 1 ⑤ 2 100

1 숙소를 제공한다고 했지만 구체적인 장소는 언급되지 않았다.

2 Event Fee 항목에서 행사 참가비는 50달러인데 12살 미만의 어린이는 무료라고 했으므로, 성인 두 명에 대한 요금인 100달러를 지불해야 한다.

해석 **Q:** 성인 두 명과 10살짜리 소년 한 명이 행사에 참가하고 싶어 한다. 그들은 얼마를 지불해야 하는가? **A:** 그들은 100달러를 지불해야 한다.

READ CLOSELY p. 59

❶The Great Green Bike Ride / is an annual two-wheeled weekend adventure event / to raise funds / for local environmental conservation.

The Great Green Bike Ride는 / 연례의 두 바퀴로 달리는 주말 모험 행사입니다 / 기금을 모으기 위한 / 지역 환경 보존을 위한

❷Join the event, / and you can help save the environment.

행사에 참가하세요 / 그러면 여러분은 환경을 구하는 것을 도울 수 있습니다

❸Date: Saturday 26 – Sunday 27, / September 2020

날짜: 26일 토요일 ~ 27일 일요일 / 2020년 9월

❹Route: Day 1 – City Hall to the Central Forest: / 85 miles

주행로: 첫째 날 – 시청에서 Central Forest까지: / 85마일

❺Day 2 – Explore the Central Forest: / 35 miles

둘째 날 – Central Forest를 탐험하세요: / 35마일

❻Event Fee: $50 / and FREE / for children under 12

행사 참가비: 50달러 / 그리고 무료 / 12세 미만 어린이에 대해서

❼Bike Reservation: Reserve / your free bikes / before the event day / at www.greatgreenbike.org.

자전거 예약: 예약하세요 / 여러분의 무료 자전거를 / 행사일 전에 / www.greatgreenbike.org에서

❽You have to make a reservation / if you want to use our bikes.

여러분은 예약을 해야만 합니다 / 여러분이 우리의 자전거를 사용하기를 원한다면

❾Overnight Stay: We offer / a delicious BBQ dinner / and a place / to stay.

숙박: 우리는 제공합니다 / 맛있는 바비큐 저녁 식사를 / 그리고 장소를 / 숙박할

지문해석 **The Great Green Bike Ride**

The Great Green Bike Ride는 지역 환경 보존 기금을 마련하기 위한, 두 바퀴로 달리는 주말 모험 연례행사입니다. 행사에 참가하세요, 그러면 여러분은 환경을 구하는 데 도움을 줄 수 있습니다.

■ 날짜: 2020년 9월 26일 토요일 ~ 27일 일요일
■ 주행로: 첫째 날 – 시청에서 Central Forest까지: 85마일
　　　　　둘째 날 – Central Forest를 탐험하세요: 35마일
■ 행사 참가비: 50달러, 12세 미만 어린이는 무료
■ 자전거 예약: 행사일 전에 www.greatgreenbike.org에서 무료 자전거를 예약하세요. 우리 자전거를 사용하기를 원하면 예약을 해야만 합니다.
■ 숙박: 맛있는 바비큐 저녁 식사와 숙박할 장소를 제공합니다.

❶The Great Green Bike Ride is an annual two-wheeled weekend adventure event [to raise funds for local environmental conservation].
→ to부정사의 형용사적 용법

❾Overnight Stay: We offer [a delicious BBQ dinner]
목적어1
and [a place to stay].
목적어2 → to부정사의 형용사적 용법

19 정답 ④ p. 60

휴대 전화(Mobile)와 현금 자동 입출금기(ATMs)의 선호도는 2013년에 비해 2014년에 각각 2퍼센트포인트와 3퍼센트포인트 증가했지만, 우편(Mail)은 1퍼센트포인트 감소했으므로, ④는 도표의 내용과 일치하지 않는다.

오답풀이 ②에서 the preference는 the preference of Internet Banking을 말한다. 인터넷 뱅킹 선호도는 2013년 39퍼센트에서 2014년 31퍼센트로 8퍼센트포인트 감소했으므로 ②는 도표와 일치한다.

READING GUIDE 제목: 2013년~2014년에 선호되는 은행 업무 방법 / 범례: 2013년, 2014년

UNDERSTAND DEEPLY 1 (1) F (2) T 2 (1) decreased (2) most

1 (1) 두 해 모두 인터넷 뱅킹(Internet Banking)(39%, 31%)이 지점(Branches)(18%, 21%)보다 더 많이 선호되었다. (2) 2014년에 전화와 우편을 선호한 사람들의 백분율 합계는 13%였다.

해석 (1) 두 해 모두 인터넷 뱅킹이 지점보다 덜 선호되었다. (2) 2014년에 전화와 우편을 선호하는 사람들의 백분율 합계는 13퍼센트였다.

2 (1) 우편(Mail)의 선호도는 2013년 7퍼센트에서 2014년 6퍼센트로 감소했다. (2) 인터넷 뱅킹(Internet Banking)의 선호도는 2013년(39%)과 2014년(31%) 모두 가장 높은 비율을 차지했다.

해석 (1) 우편의 선호도는 2013년에 비해 2014년에 감소했다. (2) 두 해 모두 인터넷 뱅킹이 가장 많이 선호되는 은행 업무 방법이었다.

READ CLOSELY
p. 61

❶ The charts above (show) / preferred banking methods / based on a survey of 1,000 Americans / in 2013 and 2014.

위의 도표들은 보여 준다 / 선호되는 은행 업무 방법들을 / 1,000명의 미국인들에 대한 설문 조사에 기초한 / 2013년과 2014년에

❷ The sum of the percentages of people / preferring Internet Banking and Branches / (was) over 50 percent / in both years.

사람들의 백분율의 합계는 / 인터넷 뱅킹과 지점을 선호하는 / 50퍼센트를 넘었다 / 두 해 모두

❸ In 2013, / 39 percent of people (said) / Internet Banking was their favorite way of banking, / while the preference dropped / 8 percentage points / in 2014.

2013년에는 / 39퍼센트의 사람들이 말했다 / 인터넷 뱅킹이 그들이 가장 좋아하는 은행 업무 방법이라고 / 그 선호도가 떨어진 반면에 / 8퍼센트포인트 / 2014년에

❹ The preference of Branches / (increased) 3 percentage points / in 2014 / compared to 2013.

지점의 선호도는 / 3퍼센트포인트 증가했다 / 2014년에 / 2013년과 비교해서

❺ Mail, Mobile, and ATMs / (increased) slightly / from 2013 to 2014.

우편, 휴대 전화 그리고 현금 자동 입출금기는 / 약간 증가했다 / 2013년부터 2014년까지

❻ Telephone (remained) the same / at 7 percent / in both years.

전화는 똑같이 유지되었다 / 7퍼센트로 / 두 해 모두

지문해석 위의 도표들은 2013년과 2014년에 미국인 1,000명을 대상으로 한 설문 조사에 기초하여 선호되는 은행 업무 방법들을 보여 준다. 인터넷 뱅킹과 은행 지점을 선호하는 사람들의 백분율 합계는 두 해 모두 50퍼센트를 넘어섰다. 2013년에 39퍼센트의 사람들이 인터넷 뱅킹이 그들이 가장 선호하는 은행 업무 방법이라고 말한 반면, 2014년에는 그 선호도가 8퍼센트포인트 떨어졌다. 은행 지점의 선호도는 2013년에 비해 2014년에 3퍼센트포인트 증가했다. 우편, 휴대 전화, 현금 자동 입출금기는 2013년부터 2014년까지 약간 증가했다. 전화는 두 해 모두 7퍼센트로 똑같이 유지되었다.

문장 돋보기

❷ The sum of the percentages of people [preferring ← 현재분사구
　　　　　　주어
Internet Banking and Branches] was over 50
　　　　　　　　　　단수 동사 (주어인 The sum에 수 일치)
percent in both years.

READING **20** 정답 ③
p. 62

2012년에 모바일 기기를 이용한 인터넷 사용 시간은 1.6시간이고, 데스크톱이나 노트북 컴퓨터를 이용한 인터넷 사용 시간은 2.5시간이므로 ③은 도표의 내용과 일치하지 않는다.

오답풀이 모바일 기기를 이용한 인터넷 사용 시간과 데스크톱이나 노트북 컴퓨터를 이용하여 인터넷을 사용한 시간이 동일한 해는 2013년이다.

READING GUIDE 제목: 기기별 평균 일일 인터넷 사용 / 범례: 2011년, 2012년, 2013년, 2014년, 2015년

UNDERSTAND DEEPLY
1 (1) T (2) F **2** (1) same (2) longer

1 (1) 2011년에 데스크톱이나 노트북 컴퓨터를 통한 인터넷 사용 시간은 2.6시간으로, 모바일 기기를 통한 인터넷 사용 시간인 0.8시간보다 더 길다. (2) 2012년 모바일 기기를 통한 일평균 인터넷 사용 시간은 1.6시간이다.

해석 (1) 2011년에 데스크톱이나 노트북 컴퓨터를 통한 인터넷 사용 시간은 모바일 기기를 통한 것보다 더 길었다. (2) 2012년에 모바일 기기를 통한 일평균 인터넷 사용 시간은 2.5시간이었다.

2 (1) 2013년의 일평균 인터넷 사용 시간은 모바일 기기를 통한 것과 데스크톱이나 노트북을 통한 것이 모두 2.3시간으로 동일하다. (2) 2014년 모바일 기기를 통한 인터넷 사용 시간은 2.6시간으로, 데스크톱이나 노트북 컴퓨터를 통한 인터넷 사용 시간인 2.4시간보다 더 길다.

해석 (1) 2013년에 미국인들은 그들이 모바일 기기에서 보냈던 것과 동일한 평균 시간을 데스크톱이나 노트북에서 보냈다. (2) 2014년에 모바일 기기를 통한 인터넷 사용 시간은 데스크톱이나 노트북 컴퓨터를 통한 것보다 더 길었다.

READ CLOSELY
p. 63

❶ The graph above (shows) / Americans' average daily Internet usage time / by device / from 2011 to 2015.

위 도표는 보여 준다 / 미국인들의 평균 일일 인터넷 사용 시간을 / 기기별로 / 2011년부터 2015년까지

❷ Overall, / the total Internet usage time / (increased) steadily / from 2011 to 2015.

전반적으로 / 총 인터넷 사용 시간은 / 꾸준히 증가했다 / 2011년부터 2015년까지

❸ In 2011, / Internet usage time via mobile / (was) shorter / than that via desktop or laptop.

2011년에 / 모바일 기기를 통한 인터넷 사용 시간은 / 더 짧았다 / 데스크톱이나 노트북 컴퓨터를 통한 그것(인터넷 사용 시간)보다

❹ In 2012, / however, / Americans spent the same hours / on mobile devices / as they did / on desktops or laptops.

2012년에 / 그러나 / 미국인들은 똑같은 시간을 보냈다 / 모바일 기기로 / 그들이 그랬던(보냈던) 것과 같은 / 데스크톱이나 노트북 컴퓨터로

❺ In 2014, / Internet usage time from mobile devices / was longer / than that from desktops or laptops.

2014년에 / 모바일 기기를 통한 인터넷 사용 시간은 / 더 길었다 / 데스크톱이나 노트북 컴퓨터를 통한 그것(인터넷 사용 시간)보다

❻ In 2015, / Americans spent / an average of 5.6 hours / a day / on the Internet.

2015년에 / 미국인들은 보냈다 / 평균 5.6시간을 / 하루에 / 인터넷에서

지문해석 위 도표는 2011년부터 2015년까지 기기별 미국인들의 평균 일일 인터넷 사용 시간을 보여 준다. 전반적으로 총 인터넷 사용 시간은 2011년부터 2015년까지 꾸준히 증가했다. 2011년에 모바일 기기를 통한 인터넷 사용 시간은 데스크톱이나 노트북 컴퓨터를 통한 인터넷 사용 시간보다 더 짧았다. 그러나 2012년에 미국인들은 그들이 데스크톱이나 노트북 컴퓨터로 보낸 것과 동일한 시간을 모바일 기기로 보냈다. 2014년에 모바일 기기를 통한 인터넷 사용 시간은 데스크톱이나 노트북 컴퓨터를 통한 인터넷 사용 시간보다 더 길었다. 2015년에 미국인들은 인터넷에서 하루 평균 5.6시간을 보냈다.

문장 돋보기

❸ In 2011, Internet usage time via mobile was
　　　　　　　주어　　　　　　　　　　　　　동사
shorter than that via desktop or laptop.
= Internet usage time (앞에 나온 명사구를 대신하는 대명사 that)

❹ In 2012, however, Americans spent the same
글의 흐름을 전환하는 연결어(그러나)
hours on mobile devices as they did on desktops
= spent (앞에 나온 동사를 대신하는 대동사 do)
or laptops.

1 (1) preference　　(2) applicant　　(3) monologue
　(4) steadily　　　(5) adventure　　(6) environment

2 (1) ③　　　(2) ④　　　(3) ①　　　(4) ②

3

		¹a			²s		
	³o	v	e	r	a	l	l
		r		v			
⁴u	s	a	g	e			
		g			⁵r		
⁶p	o	t	e	n	t	i	a	l
					i		
					s		
					e		

4 (1) compared to　　　(2) based on
　(3) in person　　　　(4) send in

5 (1) to demonstrate　　(2) preferred
　(3) to audition　　　(4) preferring

6 (1) and　　　(2) as　　　(3) while

2 (1) select, ③ choose 선택하다, 선정하다
　(2) reserve, ④ book 예약하다
　(3) drop, ① fall 떨어지다
　(4) demonstrate, ② show 보여주다

5 (1) 명사 a chance를 '~할'이라는 의미로 수식해야 하므로 형용사적 용법의 to부정사 to demonstrate가 알맞다.
　해석 여러분은 여러분의 재능을 보여 줄 기회가 주어질 것입니다.
　(2) '선호되는'이라는 수동의 의미로 banking methods를 수식해야 하므로 과거분사 preferred가 알맞다.
　해석 위의 도표들은 한 설문 조사에 기초한 선호되는 은행 업무 방법들을 보여 준다.
　(3) It이 가주어이므로 to부정사구 진주어가 되도록 to audition이 쓰여야 한다.
　해석 여러분의 발표가 담긴 동영상을 제출함으로써 오디션을 받는 것은 불가능합니다.
　(4) '지점을 선호하는'이라는 의미로 people을 수식해야 하므로 현재분사 preferring이 알맞다.
　해석 지점을 선호하는 사람들의 백분율 합계는 50퍼센트가 넘었다.

6 (1) '~해라, 그러면 …'은 「명령문, and ….」로 표현할 수 있으므로 접속사 and가 알맞다.
　(2) '~한 것과 같은 …'을 의미하는 「the same+명사+as+절」 구문이 되어야 하므로 접속사 as가 알맞다.
　(3) '~한 반면에'라는 의미로 두 가지 사실을 대조하는 접속사로 while이 알맞다.

1 삼각형이 생기지 않도록 성냥 한 개를 옮기세요.

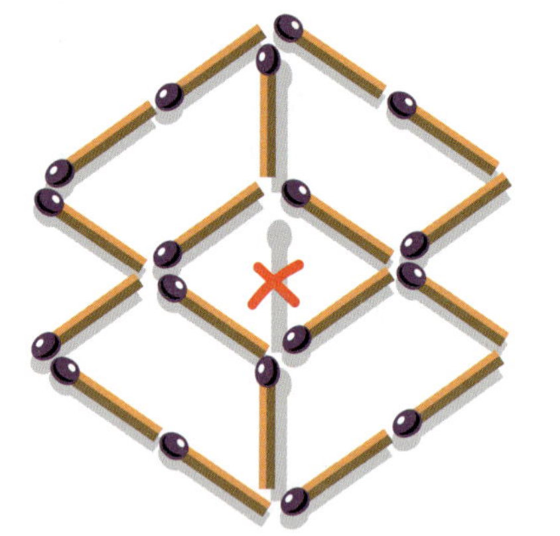

2 정사각형 7개가 생기도록 성냥 두 개를 옮기세요.

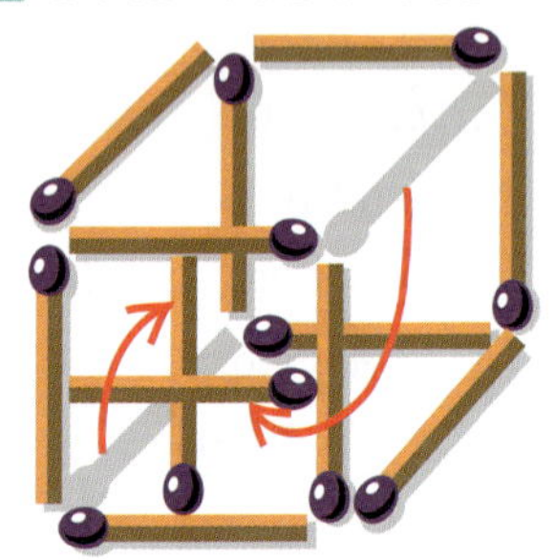 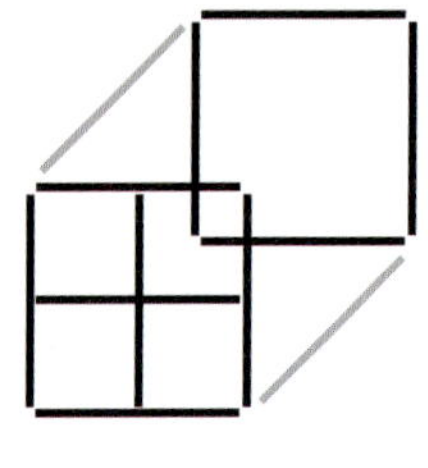

목적·심경·분위기 파악하기

21  정답 ⑤
p. 68

교사가 학부모의 문의에 답변하는 글로, 학부모의 수업 프로젝트 마감일 연장 요청에 대해 계획된 일정에 따라 작업이 진행되고 있기 때문에 마감일을 연장할 수 없다고 거절하고 있다. 따라서 글의 목적으로 가장 적절한 것은 ⑤이다.

오답풀이 일정대로 수업 프로젝트를 마치기 위해 열심히 노력해 왔으며, 수업 일정표를 보낸다는 말에서 ②를 답으로 생각할 수 있지만, 이는 자녀의 학교생활을 알려주기 위함이 아니라 마감일을 연장할 수 없음을 납득시키기 위함이다.

READING GUIDE 7

UNDERSTAND DEEPLY

1 a deadline extension   **2** (1) T (2) F (3) F

1 your request for a deadline extension에서 Ms. Jones가 마감일 연장을 요청했었음을 알 수 있다.

2 (1) I know it can be hard to ask these kinds of questions as a parent.에서 Ms. Jones가 학부모임을 알 수 있으므로 일치한다.
(2) I'm enclosing a copy of our class calendar에서 Bryan Roberts가 수업 일정표를 동봉한다고 했으므로 일치하지 않는다.
(3) I'm afraid I can't extend the deadline에서 마감일을 연장할 수 없다고 했으므로 일치하지 않는다.

해석 (1) Ms. Jones는 학부모이다. (2) Bryan Roberts는 수업 일정표 한 부를 동봉하는 것을 잊었다. (3) 수업 프로젝트 마감일은 연장될 것이다.

READ CLOSELY
p. 69

❶ Dear Ms. Jones,

친애하는 Jones님께

❷ Thank you / for raising your concerns.

감사합니다 / 당신의 우려를 제기해 주신 것에 대해

❸ I know / it can be hard / to ask these kinds of questions / as a parent.

저는 압니다 / 어려울 수 있다는 것을 / 이러한 종류의 질문을 하는 것이 / 부모로서

❹ I understand your concern / about the degree of work / involved in this class project, / as well as your request / for a deadline extension.

저는 당신의 우려를 이해합니다 / 작업의 정도에 대한 / 이 수업 프로젝트에 관련된 / 당신의 요청뿐만 아니라 / 마감일 연장에 대한

❺ We've been working hard / over the course of the last month / in order to finish the work / in time.

저희는 열심히 노력해 왔습니다 / 지난달 내내 / 작업을 끝내기 위해서 / 제시간에

⑥ In case you didn't see it, / **I'm enclosing** / a copy of our class calendar.

당신이 그것을 보지 않으셨을 경우에 대비해서 / 저는 동봉합니다 / 저희의 수업 일정표 한 부를

⑦ As we've been working hard / to keep this schedule, / **I'm afraid** / I can't extend the deadline.

저희가 열심히 노력해 왔기 때문에 / 이 일정에 따르기 위해 / 유감입니다 / 저는 마감일을 연장할 수 없습니다

⑧ **I'm sure** / that this is a fair timeline.

저는 확신합니다 / 이것이 타당한 일정이라고

⑨ I **believe** / we can understand each other.

저는 믿습니다 / 저희가 서로를 이해할 수 있다고

⑩ **Thank** you.

감사합니다

⑪ Sincerely, Bryan Roberts

Bryan Roberts 드림

〈지문해석〉 친애하는 Jones님께,

어머님의 우려를 제기해 주신 것에 대해 감사드립니다. 학부모로서 이러한 종류의 문의를 하는 것이 어려울 수 있다는 것을 알고 있습니다. 저는 마감일 연장에 대한 어머님의 요청뿐만 아니라 이 수업 프로젝트에 관련된 작업 정도에 대한 어머님의 우려를 이해합니다. 저희는 제시간에 작업을 끝내기 위해 지난달 내내 열심히 노력해왔습니다. 어머님께서 보지 못하셨을 경우를 생각하여 저희의 수업 일정표 한 부를 동봉합니다. 저희가 이 일정에 따르기 위해 열심히 노력해 왔기 때문에 유감입니다만 저는 마감일을 연장할 수 없습니다. 저는 이것이 타당한 일정이라고 확신합니다. 저는 저희가 서로 이해할 수 있다고 믿습니다. 감사합니다.

Bryan Roberts 드림

〈문장 돋보기〉

④ I understand [your concern about the degree of
        목적어1
work involved in this class project], as well as [your
        과거분사구(involved in: ~에 관련된)   B as well as A:
                                                      A뿐만 아니라 B도
request for a deadline extension].
        목적어2   (= not only A but also B)

⑦ As we've been working hard to keep this schedule,
        접속사(이유)   현재완료 진행형   to부정사의 부사적 용법(목적)
I'm afraid [(that) I can't extend the deadline].
              명사절 접속사 that이 생략됨

22 〈정답〉 ③   p. 70

글쓰기 센터에서 대학 내 유학생들을 대상으로 무료 글쓰기 개인 교습 프로

그램을 제공하고 있다고 하며 이를 활용할 것을 권하고 있다. 따라서 이 글의 목적으로 가장 적절한 것은 ③이다.

〈오답풀이〉 유학생과 글쓰기 센터가 언급된다는 점에서 ②를 답으로 생각할 수 있지만, 글쓰기 센터 설립을 건의하는 글이 아니라 프로그램을 홍보하는 글이다.

READING GUIDE  **④**

UNDERSTAND
DEEPLY **1** ②   **2** call → email

1 ① 유료가 아니라 무료 글쓰기 프로그램이라고(a free tutoring program) 했으므로 일치하지 않는다. ② 11월 28일부터 3일 동안만 등록할 수 있다고(Registration will be opened from November 28 for three days only.) 했으므로 일치한다. ③ 프로그램에 등록하면 글쓰기 센터에서 지도 강사를 연결해 준다고(we will match you with the perfect tutor) 했으므로 일치하지 않는다.

2 HRWC 사무국장에게 전화를 하는 것이 아니라 이메일을 보내라고 했다.

〈해석〉 더 많은 정보를 얻고 싶으면 HRWC 사무국장에게 전화하면 된다.

READ CLOSELY   p. 71

① **Want** to improve / your Korean writing?

향상시키기를 원하십니까 / 여러분의 한국어 글쓰기를

② Writing **is** an essential tool / that will help you / adjust to Korean university life.

글쓰기는 필수적인 도구입니다 / 여러분을 도와줄 / 한국 대학 생활에 적응하도록

③ The Ha-Rang Writing Center / **offers** a free tutoring program / to all international students / at our university.

하랑 글쓰기 센터는 / 무료 개인 교습 프로그램을 제공합니다 / 모든 유학생들에게 / 우리 대학교에 있는

④ We **encourage** you / to take advantage of this program.

우리는 여러분에게 권합니다 / 이 프로그램을 이용할 것을

⑤ The program **has** always **been** very popular / among international students.

이 프로그램은 늘 매우 인기 있어 왔습니다 / 유학생들 사이에서

⑥ Registration **will be opened** / from November 28 / for three days only.

등록은 열릴 것입니다 / 11월 28일부터 / 3일 동안만

⑦ Once you are registered, / we **will match** you / with the perfect tutor / and **contact** you / to arrange your schedule.

일단 여러분이 등록되면 / 우리는 여러분을 연결할 것입니다 / 완벽한 개인 지도 강사와 / 그리고 여러분에게 연락할 것입니다 / 여러분의 일정을 조정하기 위해

⑧ We **are sure** / that you will be satisfied with / our well-experienced tutors.

우리는 확신합니다 / 여러분이 ~에 만족할 거라고 / 우리의 경험 많은 개인 지도 강사들

❾ Don't miss / this great opportunity / to improve your Korean writing.

놓치지 마십시오 / 이 좋은 기회를 / 여러분의 한국어 글쓰기를 향상시킬

❿ For more information, / feel free to email / Jiyoung Yoon, HRWC Director, / at jyoon@hrwc.org.

더 많은 정보를 위해 / 자유롭게 이메일을 보내십시오 / HRWC 사무국장 윤지영에게 / jyoon@hrwc.org로

지문해석 한국어 글쓰기 능력을 향상시키고 싶으신가요? 글쓰기는 여러분이 한국 대학 생활에 적응하는 것을 도울 필수적인 도구입니다. '하랑 글쓰기 센터'는 우리 대학의 모든 유학생들에게 무료 개인 교습 프로그램을 제공합니다. 우리는 여러분에게 이 프로그램을 이용할 것을 권합니다. 이 프로그램은 늘 유학생들 사이에서 인기가 많았습니다. 등록은 11월 28일부터 3일 동안만 가능합니다. 일단 여러분이 등록되면, 우리는 여러분을 완벽한 개인 지도 강사와 연결하고, 여러분의 일정을 조정하기 위해 여러분에게 연락할 것입니다. 우리는 여러분이 우리의 경험 많은 강사들에 만족할 거라고 확신합니다. 한국어 글쓰기 능력을 향상시킬 이 좋은 기회를 놓치지 마세요. 더 많은 정보를 원하시면, HRWC 사무국장 윤지영에게 jyoon@hrwc.org로 자유롭게 이메일을 보내세요.

문장 돋보기

❷ Writing is an essential tool [that will help you
주격 관계대명사
adjust to Korean university life].
help+목적어+목적격 보어(동사원형 또는 to부정사)

❾ Don't miss this great opportunity [to improve
to부정사의
형용사적 용법
your Korean writing].

23 **정답** ① p. 72

felt really thrilled, satisfied, pleased 등의 표현에서 알 수 있듯이 졸업식에서 특별 우등상을 받은 Amy의 심경으로 가장 적절한 것은 ① '자랑스럽고 행복한'이다.

오답풀이 ② 침착하고 안도하는 ③ 짜증 나고 초조한 ④ 두렵고 필사적인 ⑤ 실망하고 분노한

READING GUIDE ❹, ❺

UNDERSTAND DEEPLY 1 (1) F (2) T 2 a passionate doctor
3 (1) 신이 남 (2) 만족(감) (3) 기쁨

1 (1) 두 번째 문장에서 5명에게 금메달이 수여되었다고 했으므로 일치하지 않는다. (2) 세 번째 문장에서 Wilkinson 박사가 Amy와 악수하고 그녀의 성과에 대해 축하해 주었다고 했으므로 일치한다.

해석 (1) 상위 10명의 의대 졸업생들이 금메달을 받았다.
(2) Wilkinson 박사가 Amy의 성과를 축하해 주었다.

2 마지막 문장의 her life-long dream of becoming a passionate doctor에서 Amy의 평생의 꿈이 열정적인 의사가 되는 것임을 알 수 있다.

해석 Q: Amy의 평생의 꿈은 무엇인가? A: 그것은 열정적인 의사가 되는 것이다.

3 (1) 글의 초반부에서 Amy는 단상 위에 올라가서 Wilkinson 박사에게 상을 받고 정말 신이 났다고(felt really thrilled) 했다. (2), (3) 글의 중반부에서 Amy는 자리에 돌아오면서 자신의 학업 성과에 만족하고(satisfied with her academic performance) 자신의 성공에 기뻐했다고(pleased with her success) 했다.

READ CLOSELY p. 73

❶ When Amy heard someone / call her name, / she stood up from her seat / and went up on the stage.

Amy가 누군가의 소리를 들었을 때 / 그녀의 이름을 부르는 / 그녀는 그녀의 자리에서 일어났다 / 그리고 단상 위로 올라갔다

❷ Dr. Wilkinson was giving a gold medal / to each of the top five medical graduates.

Wilkinson 박사가 금메달을 주고 있었다 / 상위 5명의 의대 졸업생들 각각에게

❸ He shook Amy's hand / and congratulated her on her performance.

그는 Amy와 악수를 했다 / 그리고 그녀의 성과를 축하했다

❹ Amy felt really thrilled / to be recognized / as one of the top five medical graduates of her school.

Amy는 정말로 신이 났다 / 인정받아서 / 그녀의 학교의 상위 5명의 의대 졸업생들 중 한 명으로

❺ Amy walked back to her seat, / satisfied with her academic performance / and pleased with her success.

Amy는 그녀의 자리로 걸어서 돌아갔다 / 그녀의 학업 성과에 만족하면서 / 그리고 그녀의 성공에 기뻐하면서

❻ She just received a special honor.

그녀는 방금 특별 우등상을 받았다

❼ This special recognition / would help her / to continue realizing / her life-long dream / of becoming a passionate doctor.

이 특별한 인정은 / 그녀를 도와줄 것이었다 / 계속해서 실현하도록 / 그녀의 평생의 꿈을 / 열정적인 의사가 되는

지문해석 Amy는 누군가가 자신의 이름을 부르는 것을 들었을 때, 자리에서 일어나 단상 위로 올라갔다. Wilkinson 박사가 상위 5명의 의대 졸업생들 각각에게 금메달을 수여하고 있었다. 그는 Amy와 악수를 했고 그녀의 성과를 축하해 주었다. Amy는 자신의 학교의 상위 5명의 의대 졸업생들 중 한 명

으로 인정받아서 정말로 신이 났다. Amy는 자신의 학업 성과에 만족하고 자신의 성공에 기뻐하면서 자리로 돌아갔다. 그녀는 방금 특별 우등상을 받았다. 이 특별한 인정은 그녀가 열정적인 의사가 되겠다는 평생의 꿈을 계속 실현해 나가도록 그녀를 도와줄 것이었다.

❺ Amy walked back to her seat, [satisfied with her
분사구문1(동시동작)
academic performance] and [pleased with her
분사구문2(동시동작)
success].

❼ This special recognition would help her to continue
help+목적어+목적격 보어(to부정사 또는 동사원형)
realizing her life-long dream of becoming a
동사 continue는 목적어로 동명사를 취함 ┌ 동격 ┐
passenger doctor.
(동격을 나타내는 of)

²⁴ 정답 ④ p. 74

매물된 광부들을 수색하는 과정에서 구조대원들이 목숨을 잃고, 광부들도 실종되고 사망한 것으로 여겨지면서 결국 수색을 포기하는 상황을 다룬 글이다. 따라서 글의 분위기로 가장 적절한 것은 ④ '비극적이고 낙담하게 하는'이다.

오답풀이 ① 기이하고 이상한 ② 평온하고 평화로운 ③ 무섭고 불가사의한 ⑤ 단조롭고 지루한

READING GUIDE dangerously, killed, exploded, missing, dead, stopped, switched off, unplugged

UNDERSTAND DEEPLY 1 (1) search for the six missing miners (2) missing and dead 2 (1) 6 (2) 6 (3) 3 (4) 0

1 (1) 두입부에서 6명의 실종된 광부들을 수색하기 위해 광산에 구멍을 뚫고 산소 감지기, 카메라, 마이크와 같은 장비를 내려 보냈다고 했다.
(2) 후반부에서 광부들의 어떠한 자취도 발견되지 않았기 때문에 그들이 모두 실종되고 사망한 것으로 여겨졌다고 했다.
해석 (1) 구조대원들은 6명의 실종된 광부들을 수색하기 위해 광산 안으로 다양한 장비를 보냈다. (2) 구조대원들은 모든 6명의 광부들이 실종되고 사망했다고 생각했다.

2 (1) 6개의 구멍이 뚫렸다.(Six holes were drilled into ~ the mine.)
(2) 6명의 광부들이 실종되었다.(the six missing miners) (3) 3명의 구조 팀원들이 수색 중 사망했다.(Three rescue team members ~ were killed) (4) 구조대원들이 광부들의 어떠한 자취도 보거나 듣지 못했다고 했다.(Rescuers never saw or heard any sign of the miners)
해석 (1) 광산으로 몇 개의 구멍이 드릴로 뚫렸는가? (2) 몇 명의 광부들이 광산에 매몰되었는가? (3) 몇 명의 구조 팀원들이 수색 중 사망했는가? (4) 실종한 광부들의 자취가 몇 개 발견되었는가?

❶ Six holes were drilled / into different areas of the mine.
6개의 구멍이 드릴로 뚫렸다 / 광산의 여러 지역으로

❷ They sent / oxygen sensors, cameras, and microphones / down through plastic pipes / to search for the six missing miners.
그들은 보냈다 / 산소 감지기, 카메라, 그리고 마이크를 / 플라스틱 파이프를 통해 아래로 / 6명의 실종된 광부들을 수색하기 위해서

❸ During the search, / the oxygen levels were misread / and determined / to be dangerously low.
수색 중에 / 산소 수치가 잘못 해석되었다 / 그리고 결정되었다 / 위험할 정도로 낮다고

❹ Three rescue team members, / trying to dig the trapped miners out, / were killed / when a wall of the mine exploded.
3명의 구조 팀원들이 / 갇힌 광부들을 구조하려고 하다가 / 사망했다 / 광산 벽이 폭발했을 때

❺ Rescuers never saw or heard / any sign of the miners, / and all six men / were considered / missing and dead.
구조대원들은 결코 보거나 듣지 못했다 / 광부들의 어떠한 자취도 / 그리고 6명 모두 / 여겨졌다 / 실종되고 사망한 것으로

❻ All rescue efforts / were eventually stopped.
모든 구조 노력은 / 결국 중단되었다

❼ They simply switched off the drills / and unplugged / all the other equipment.
그들은 그저 드릴의 스위치를 껐다 / 그리고 플러그를 뽑았다 / 모든 다른 장비의

지문해석 광산의 여러 지역으로 6개의 구멍이 드릴로 뚫렸다. 그들은 6명의 실종된 광부들을 수색하기 위해 산소 감지기, 카메라, 마이크를 플라스틱 파이프를 통해 내려 보냈다. 수색 중에 산소 수치가 잘못 해석되었고 위험할 정도로 낮은 것으로 결정되었다. 3명의 구조 팀원들이 갇힌 광부들을 구조하려 하다가 광산 벽이 폭발했을 때 사망했다. 구조대원들은 광부들의 어떠한 자취도 결코 보거나 듣지 못했고, 6명 모두 실종되고 사망한 것으로 여겨졌다. 모든 구조 노력은 결국 중단되었다. 그들은 그저 드릴 스위치를 꺼 버렸고 나머지 모든 장비의 플러그를 뽑았다.

❸ During the search, the oxygen levels were misread and determined to be dangerously low.
수동태 병렬 구조(과거분사 misread와 determined가 모두 were에 연결됨)

❹ Three rescue team members, [trying to dig the
주어 분사구문(동시동작: ~하다가)
trapped miners out], were killed [when a wall of
동사(수동태) 시간의 부사절
the mine exploded].

REVIEW TIME p. 76

1 (1) timeline　　　(2) pleased
　(3) drill　　　(4) academic

2 (1) extension　　　(2) discouraging
　(3) recognition　　　(4) register

3

G	I	S	Q	O	V	C	O	P	F	C	M
M	Y	V	A	H	R	I	W	E	L	D	I
F	P	A	S	S	I	O	N	A	T	E	N
T	K	Q	R	E	B	R	W	M	U	R	E
A	A	K	B	R	N	V	B	K	R	A	R
W	Y	F	W	T	A	C	G	U	Z	D	H
Z	K	Y	E	X	V	N	L	C	I	U	S
Y	L	D	T	Q	M	B	G	O	X	A	D
B	Z	N	R	D	I	L	I	E	S	T	R
I	F	T	D	E	A	D	L	I	N	E	P
C	W	H	B	O	P	D	B	C	P	D	H
A	Y	P	E	Q	U	I	P	M	E	N	T

　(1) arrange　　(2) deadline　　(3) equipment
　(4) miner　　(5) passionate　　(6) enclose

4 (1) B as well as A　　　(2) search for
　(3) adjust to　　　(4) in time

5 (1) ○　　　(2) giving
　(3) ○　　　(4) to improve

6 (1) call 또는 calling　　　(2) to ask
　(3) to take　　　(4) involved

---

1 (1) timeline 일정 / schedule 일정 / calendar 일정표 (일정 관련 단어)
　(2) proud 자랑스러운 / nervous 긴장한 / pleased 기뻐하는 (심경을 나타내는 단어)
　(3) microphone 마이크 / drill 드릴 / sensor 감지기, 센서 (장비, 기기 관련 단어)
　(4) academic 학업의, 학문의 / honor 우등(상) / graduate 졸업생 (학업 관련 단어)

2 (1) extend 연장하다 → extension 연장
　(2) encouraging 용기를 북돋우는 → discouraging 낙담하게 하는
　(3) recognize 인정하다, 표창하다 → recognition 인정, 표창
　(4) registration 등록 → register 등록하다

5 (1) consider는 수동태로 바꿔 쓸 때 뒤에 형용사 목적격 보어를 그대로 쓰므로 형용사(구) missing and dead의 쓰임은 알맞다.
　해석 여섯 명 모두 실종되고 사망한 것으로 여겨졌다.
　(2) Wilkinson 박사가 우리 각자에게 금메달을 수여하고 있었다고 해야 하므로 현재분사 giving이 알맞다.
　해석 Wilkinson 박사는 우리 각자에게 금메달을 수여하고 있었다.
　(3) 한 달 동안 계속 노력해 왔다는 의미이므로 현재완료 진행형이 쓰인

것은 알맞다.
　해석 우리는 이 일정에 따르기 위해 한 달 동안 열심히 노력해 왔다.
　(4) this great opportunity를 '향상시킬'이라는 의미로 수식하도록 형용사적 용법의 to부정사 to improve가 쓰여야 한다.
　해석 여러분의 글쓰기 능력을 향상시킬 이 좋은 기회를 놓치지 마세요.

6 (1) 지각동사 hear는 목적격 보어로 동사원형이나 현재분사를 취하므로 call 또는 calling이 알맞다.
　(2) 앞에 가주어 it이 쓰였으므로 진주어로 to부정사 to ask가 알맞다.
　(3) encourage는 목적격 보어로 to부정사를 취하므로 to take가 알맞다.
　(4) '관련된'이라는 수동의 의미가 되어야 하므로 과거분사 involved가 알맞다.

PART 3　추론하기
UNIT 08　지칭 대상 파악하기

**25**　정답 ①　　　p. 78

①은 살아 있는 소를 가리키고, 나머지는 모두 인공 배양한 쇠고기를 가리킨다.
오답풀이 ③과 ④의 it은 각각 앞 문장에 언급된 a patty와 meat을 가리키며, 이는 모두 인공 배양한 쇠고기를 의미한다.

READING GUIDE　meat, lab, cow, tissue

UNDERSTAND DEEPLY
　1 (1) 동물　(2) 기아 문제　(3) 시간, 에너지, 공간　(4) 환경
　2 (1) muscle tissue taken from a cow
　　(2) 325,000

1 So what does this mean for humans? 이후로 고기 배양의 기대 효과가 크게 세 가지 제시되어 있다. 고기를 배양하면 동물을 죽일 필요가 없을 것이고, 전 세계 기아 문제를 해결하는 데 도움을 줄 수 있으며, 시간, 에너지, 공간을 절약함으로써 환경에 도움이 될 수 있다고 했다.

2 (1) 두 번째 문장에서 소에서 추출된 근육 조직을 배양했다고 했다.
　(2) 네 번째 문장에서 고기를 만드는 데 비용이 325,000달러가 든다고 했다.
　해석 (1) Q: 과학자들이 햄버거 고기를 만들기 위해 무엇을 배양했는가? A: 그들은 소에서 추출된 근육 조직을 배양했다. (2) Q: 고기를 만드는 데 얼마의 비용이 드는가? A: 325,000달러의 비용이 든다.

READ CLOSELY　　　p. 79

❶ Some scientists succeeded in / growing hamburger meat / in their lab.
몇몇 과학자들이 ~에 성공했다 / 햄버거 고기를 배양하는 것 / 그들의 실험실에서

② They didn't grow a cow / in the lab / but just grew muscle tissue / taken from a cow.

그들은 소를 사육하지 않았다 / 실험실에서 / 하지만 단지 근육 조직을 배양했다 / 소에서 추출된

③ They raised the tissue / until there was enough / to make a patty.

그들은 그 조직을 배양했다 / 충분한 양이 있었을 때까지 / 패티를 만들

④ Costing $325,000 to make, / it won't be showing up / at a grocery store / around you / any time soon.

만드는 데 325,000달러가 들기 때문에 / 그것은 등장하지 않을 것이다 / 식료품점에 / 여러분 주위의 / 금방은

⑤ So what does this mean / for humans?

그래서 이것은 무엇을 의미하는가 / 인간들에게

⑥ If we grow meat / in a lab, / we won't have to kill animals / anymore.

만약 우리가 고기를 배양한다면 / 실험실에서 / 우리는 동물들을 죽일 필요가 없을 것이다 / 더 이상

⑦ In addition, / it could help us / solve hunger problems / around the world.

게다가 / 그것은 우리를 도울 수도 있다 / 기아 문제를 해결하도록 / 전 세계의

⑧ If we grow / as much meat as we want, / we will be able to feed / as many people as needed.

만약 우리가 배양한다면 / 우리가 원하는 만큼 많은 고기를 / 우리는 먹을 것을 줄 수 있을 것이다 / 필요한 만큼 많은 사람들에게

⑨ Raising cows requires / a lot of resources.

소를 사육하는 것은 필요로 한다 / 많은 자원을

⑩ Growing meat could help the environment / by saving time, energy, and space

고기를 배양하는 것은 환경을 도울 수도 있다 / 시간, 에너지, 그리고 공간을 절약함으로써

지문해석 몇몇 과학자들이 그들의 실험실에서 햄버거 고기를 배양하는 데 성공했다. 그들은 실험실에서 소를 사육한 것이 아니라 단지 소에서 추출된 근육 조직을 배양했다. 그들은 패티를 만들 만큼 충분한 양이 있을 때까지 그 조직을 배양했다. 만드는 데 325,000달러의 비용이 들기 때문에, 그것은 여러분 주위의 식료품점에 금방은 등장하지 않을 것이다. 그래서 이것은 인간에게 무엇을 의미하는가? 만약 우리가 실험실에서 고기를 배양한다면, 우리는 더 이상 동물을 죽일 필요가 없을 것이다. 게다가 그것은 우리가 전 세계의 기아 문제를 해결하는 데 도움이 될 수 있다. 만약 우리가 원하는 만큼 많은 고기를 배양한다면, 우리는 필요한 만큼 많은 사람들에게 먹을 것을 줄 수 있을 것이다. 소를 사육하는 것은 많은 자원을 필요로 한다. 고기를 배양하는 것은 시간, 에너지, 그리고 공간을 절약함으로써 환경에 도움이 될 수 있다.

② They didn't grow a cow in the lab but just grew
— not A but B: A가 아니라 B —
muscle tissue [taken from a cow].
— 과거분사구

⑧ If we grow as much meat as we want, we will be
접속사(조건)   as+형용사 원급+명사+as: ~만큼 …한 (무엇)
able to feed as many people as needed.
~할 수 있을 것이다   as+형용사 원급+명사+as: ~만큼 …한 (무엇)

26 정답 ⑤ p. 80

⑤의 He는 Conan이 보이지 않아 불안해진 대상이므로 Harry를 가리키고, 나머지는 모두 Conan을 가리킨다.

오답풀이 Conan을 데리고 갔다가 돌려준다는 의미이므로 ④는 Conan을 가리킨다.

READING GUIDE Conan: 해안가에서 발견된 바다표범 / Harry: Conan을 발견하고 기른 사람

UNDERSTAND DEEPLY 1 (C) – (D) – (A) – (B) 2 ③

1 (C) Harry가 새끼였던 Conan을 항구에서 기르다가 (D) Conan이 자라나면서 그의 장난이 위험해지자 (A) Harry는 겨울에 Conan을 수족관에 보내기로 했으며 (B) 봄이 되어 Conan이 해변으로 돌아왔다는 흐름이 알맞다.

해석 (A) Harry는 겨울에 그를 수족관으로 보내기로 했다. (B) 봄이 오자 Conan이 마침내 돌아왔다. (C) Harry는 새끼 바다표범인 Conan을 항구에서 길렀다. (D) Conan이 자라남에 따라 그의 장난들은 위험해졌다.

2 처음에 Harry는 Conan을 어디에서도 볼 수 없어 '불안해했지만' 이틀 후에 마침내 Conan이 돌아왔다고 했으므로 '안심했을' 것이다. 따라서 필자의 심경 변화로 ③이 가장 적절하다.

해석 ① 불안한 → 슬픈 ② 불안한 → 무서워하는 ③ 불안한 → 안심하는 ④ 불안한 → 실망한 ⑤ 불안한 → 당황한

READ CLOSELY p. 81

① Conan was just a baby seal / when Harry found him / along the coast of New England.

Conan은 그저 새끼 바다표범이었다 / Harry가 그를 발견했을 때 / 뉴잉글랜드의 해안가에서

② Harry raised him / in the harbor, / but Conan lived freely.

Harry는 그를 길렀다 / 항구에서 / 그러나 Conan은 살았다 / 자유롭게

③ He went up and down the coast, / and always came back / to Harry.

그는 해안가를 이리저리 다녔다 / 그리고 항상 돌아왔다 / Harry에게

^❹ Conan (liked) to play, / and (learned) / a lot of tricks.

Conan은 장난치는 것을 좋아했다 / 그리고 배웠다 / 많은 재주들을

^❺ But as he got bigger, / some of his jokes, / like jumping into fishermen's boats, / (became) dangerous!

그러나 그가 더 커짐에 따라 / 그의 몇몇 장난들은 / 어부들의 배 안으로 뛰어 들어오는 것과 같은 / 위험해졌다

^❻ Harry (didn't know) / what to do.

Harry는 몰랐다 / 무엇을 해야 할지

^❼ One day, / Harry (was made) an offer / by the New England Aquarium.

어느 날 / Harry는 제안을 받았다 / 뉴잉글랜드 수족관으로부터

^❽ They (offered) to take Conan / in the winter / and return him / in the spring.

그들은 Conan을 데리고 갈 것을 제안했다 / 겨울에 / 그리고 그를 돌려줄 것을 / 봄에

^❾ Harry (agreed). // Then / spring (came).

Harry는 동의했다 // 그러고 나서 / 봄이 왔다

^❿ The aquarium (took) the seal / to the beach / and (let) him / go.

수족관은 그 바다표범을 데리고 갔다 / 해변으로 / 그리고 그를 ~하게 해주었다 / 가게

^⓫ But Harry (couldn't see) Conan / anywhere. // He (got) uneasy.

하지만 Harry는 Conan을 볼 수 없었다 / 어디에서도 // 그는 불안해졌다

^⓬ Then two days later, / a fisherman (saw) a seal / on one side of his boat.

그러고 나서 이틀 뒤, / 한 어부가 한 바다표범을 보았다 / 그의 배 한쪽에서

^⓭ Conan (was back) home / again!

Conan이 집으로 돌아왔다 / 다시

지문해석 Harry가 그를 뉴잉글랜드 해안가에서 발견했을 때, Conan은 그저 새끼 바다표범이었다. Harry가 그를 항구에서 길렀지만 Conan은 자유롭게 살았다. 그는 해안가를 이리저리 다녔고, 항상 Harry에게 돌아왔다. Conan은 장난치는 것을 좋아했고, 많은 재주들을 배웠다. 그러나 그가 커짐에 따라 어부들의 배 안으로 뛰어 들어오는 것과 같은 그의 몇몇 장난들은 위험해졌다! Harry는 어떻게 해야 할지를 몰랐다. 어느 날, Harry는 뉴잉글랜드 수족관으로부터 어떤 제안을 받았다. 그들은 겨울에 Conan을 데려갔다가 봄에 그를 돌려보내겠다고 제안했다. Harry는 동의했다. 그러고 나서 봄이 왔다. 수족관은 그 바다표범을 해변으로 데려가 놓아주었다. 그러나 Harry는 Conan을 어디에서도 볼 수 없었다. 그는 불안해졌다. 그러고 나서 이틀 뒤, 한 어부가 그의 배 한쪽에서 바다표범 한 마리를 보았다. Conan이 다시 집에 돌아온 것이었다!

27 정답 ⑤   p. 82

①~④는 모두 양을 훔친 죄로 낙인찍힌 채 속죄하면서 사는 남자를 가리키고, ⑤는 같은 마을 사람을 가리킨다.

오답풀이 ④의 the man은 앞 문장에서 언급된 an old man, 즉 노인이 된 낙인찍힌 남자를 가리킨다.

READING GUIDE Two brothers, a traveler, (an old man,) one villager

UNDERSTAND DEEPLY

1 can be a saint by making an effort to change
→ 양 도둑도 변화하려는 노력을 함으로써 성인이 될 수 있다.

2 ③

1 양 도둑이라는 낙인이 찍혔지만 오랜 세월 동안 마을 사람들을 대가 없이 도와줌으로써 존경받는 노인이 되었다는 내용의 글이다.

2 낙인찍힌 것이 부끄러워 다른 마을로 도망친 사람은 an old man의 형제이다.

READ CLOSELY   p. 83

^❶ Two brothers (were punished) / for stealing sheep.

두 형제가 벌을 받았다 / 양을 훔친 것에 대해

^❷ They each (were branded) / on the forehead / with the letters ST / for "sheep thief."

그들 각각은 낙인찍혔다 / 이마에 / ST라는 글자들로 / '양 도둑'을 뜻하는

^❸ One brother (was) so (embarrassed) / by this branding / that he ran away; / he (was never heard from) / again.

한 형제는 너무 부끄러웠다 / 이 낙인찍는 것으로 인해 / 그래서 그는 도망쳤다 / 그에게서 결코 소식이 들리지 않았다 / 다시는

^❹ The other brother (chose) to stay / in the village / and (tried) to make up for his offenses.

다른 형제는 머무르는 것을 선택했다 / 그 마을에 / 그리고 그의 죄를 만회하려고 노력했다

^❺ Whenever there was any work / to be done, / the sheep thief (came) / to help.

어떤 일이 있을 때마다 / 되어야 할 / 그 양 도둑은 왔다 / 도우러

^❻ He never (accepted) pay / for his good deeds, / and he (lived) his life / for others.

그는 결코 대가를 받지 않았다 / 그의 선행에 대한 / 그리고 그는 그의 삶을 살았다 / 다른 사람들을 위해

❼ Many years later, / a traveler came through the village.

수년 후 / 한 여행자가 그 마을을 지나갔다

❽ Sitting at a sidewalk cafe, / the traveler saw an old man / with a strange brand on his forehead / seated nearby.

보도 노천 카페에 앉아서 / 그 여행자는 한 노인을 보았다 / 그의 이마에 이상한 낙인이 있는 / 근처에 앉아 있는

❾ He noticed / that all the villagers / who passed the man / stopped / to pay their respects.

그는 알아차렸다 / 모든 마을 사람들이 / 그 남자를 지나가던 / 멈추는 것을 / 존경을 표하기 위해

❿ The stranger asked one villager / what the letters stood for.

그 이방인은 한 마을 사람에게 물었다 / 그 글자들이 무엇을 의미하는지

⓫ The villager replied, / "I don't know. // It happened / so long ago... / but I think / it stands for 'saint.'"

그 마을 사람은 대답했다 / 나는 모르겠습니다 // 그 일은 일어났습니다 / 너무 오래전에 / 그러나 나는 생각합니다 / 그것이 '성인'을 의미한다고

지문해석 두 형제가 양을 훔친 죄로 벌을 받았다. 그들은 각각 '양 도둑'을 뜻하는 ST라는 글자들로 이마에 낙인이 찍혔다. 한 형제는 이렇게 낙인찍힌 것이 너무 부끄러워서 도망쳤고, 다시는 그의 소식이 들리지 않았다. 다른 형제는 그 마을에 머무르는 것을 택했고 자신의 죄를 만회하고자 노력했다. 해야 할 일이 있을 때마다 그 양 도둑은 도우러 갔다. 그는 결코 그의 선행에 대한 대가를 받지 않았으며, 평생을 남을 위해 살았다. 수년 후에, 한 여행자가 그 마을을 지나가게 되었다. 그 여행자는 보도 노천카페에 앉아, 이마에 이상한 낙인이 있는 한 노인이 근처에 앉아 있는 것을 보았다. 그는 그 남자 옆을 지나가던 모든 마을 사람들이 존경을 표하고자 가던 길을 멈추는 것을 알아차렸다. 그 이방인은 한 마을 사람에게 그 글자들이 무엇을 의미하는지 물었다. 그 마을 사람이 대답했다. "모르겠습니다. 그 일이 너무 오래전에 일어나서요… 하지만 제 생각에는 그 낙인이 '성인'을 의미하는 것 같습니다."

문장 돋보기

❸ One brother was so embarrassed by this branding
  so+형용사+that+절: 너무 ~해서 …하다
that he ran away; he was never heard from again.
  능동태: hear from(~에게서 소식을 듣다)

❺ Whenever there was any work to be done, the
  복합관계부사(~할 때마다)   to부정사의 형용사적 용법
sheep thief came to help.
  to부정사의 부사적 용법(목적)

❽ Sitting at a sidewalk cafe, the traveler saw an old
  분사구문(동시동작)
man [with a strange brand on his forehead] seated
  형용사 역할을 하는 전치사구
nearby.
  과거분사구(an old man 수식)

1 (1) uneasy, anxious   (2) raise, grow
  (3) deed, act   (4) suggest, offer

2 (1) grocery   (2) respect
  (3) resource   (4) sidewalk

3 7. 기아, 굶주림

¹f	i	s	⁷h	e	r	m	a	n	
		²m	u	s	c	l	e		
³e	n	v	i	r	o	n	m	e	n	t
		⁴s	t	r	a	n	g	e	r
			⁵o	f	f	e	n	s	e
		⁶f	o	r	e	h	e	a	d

4 (1) stand for   (2) make up for
  (3) succeed in   (4) show up

5 (1) to stay   (2) Sitting
  (3) (to) solve   (4) taken

6 (1) what to do   (2) was made an offer
  (3) stopped to pay   (4) by saving

1 (1) uneasy, anxious 불안한, 걱정되는 / nearby 근처에
  (2) raise, grow 기르다, 사육하다 / require ~을 필요로 하다
  (3) deed, act 행위, 행동 / accept 받다, 받아들이다
  (4) suggest, offer 제안하다 / notice 알아차리다

5 (1) choose는 목적어로 to부정사를 취하므로 to stay가 알맞다.
  해석 다른 형제는 마을에 머무르는 것을 선택했다.
  (2) 동시동작을 나타내는 분사구문이 되어야 하므로 현재분사 Sitting이 알맞다.
  해석 보도 노천카페에 앉아서, 그 여행자는 한 노인을 보았다.
  (3) help는 목적격 보어로 동사원형이나 to부정사를 취하므로 solve 또는 to solve가 알맞다.
  해석 고기를 배양하는 것은 우리가 기아 문제를 해결하는 데 도움을 줄 수 있다.
  (4) muscle tissue를 '추출된'이라는 수동의 의미로 수식해야 하므로 과거분사 taken이 알맞다.
  해석 몇몇 과학자들은 소에서 추출된 근육 조직을 배양했다.

6 (1) '무엇을 해야 할지'는 「what+to부정사」로 표현하므로 what to do가 알맞다.
  (2) '제안을 받다'는 make an offer(제안하다)의 수동태인 be made an offer로 표현한다.
  (3) '~하기 위해'라는 목적의 의미는 부사적 용법의 to부정사로 나타낼 수 있으므로 stopped to pay가 알맞다.
  (4) '~함으로써'는 「by+동명사」로 표현하므로 by saving이 알맞다.

빈칸 채우기

28 정답 ④ p. 86

이 글에서 빈칸이 주어진 문장은 글의 주제문이며, 기분이 긍정적일수록 성공적으로 성과를 내는 사례들이 뒤에 이어지면서 주제문의 내용을 강화하고 있다. 따라서 빈칸에 들어갈 말로 가장 적절한 것은 ④ '더 행복하고 더 긍정적이다'이다.

오답풀이 ① 특정 목표에 집중하다 ② 다른 사람들과 잘 지내다 ③ 우리가 하는 일을 가장 잘하다 ⑤ 더 영감을 받고 창의적으로 느끼다

READING GUIDE **❻**

UNDERSTAND

DEEPLY **1** doctors, salespeople, students **2** ③
3 positive[happy], successful, negative, neutral

1 예시의 연결어 For example 이후로 의사, 영업사원, 학생들이 긍정적인 기분 상태일 때 더 좋은 성과를 내는 사례가 제시되어 있다.

2 긍정적인 기분 상태인 의사들이 더 높은 지능을 보이고 정확한 진단을 더 빠르게 내린다고 했고, 뇌는 긍정적으로 느끼고 있을 때 가장 잘 수행하도록 프로그램화되어 있다고 했다.

3 글의 핵심 내용은 마지막 문장에 잘 드러나 있다.
해석 긍정적인[행복한] 기분인 사람들이 부정적이거나 중립적인 기분인 사람들보다 자신의 일에서 더 성공하는 경향이 있다.

READ CLOSELY p. 87

❶ We are more successful / when we are happier and more positive.

우리는 더 성공적이다 / 우리가 더 행복하고 더 긍정적일 때

❷ For example, / doctors / who make a diagnosis / while in a positive mood / show / almost three times more intelligence / than doctors / in a neutral state.

예를 들어 / 의사들은 / 진단을 내리는 / 긍정적인 기분인 동안에 / 보인다 / 거의 3배 더 높은 지능을 / 의사들보다 / 중립적인 상태에 있는

❸ Also, / they make correct diagnoses / that are 19 percent faster.

또한 / 그들은 정확한 진단을 내린다 / 19 퍼센트 더 빠른

❹ Salespeople / who are positive / sell more / than those / who are negative.

영업사원들은 / 긍정적인 / 더 많이 판매한다 / 사람들(영업사원들)보다 / 부정적인

❺ Students / who are made / to feel happy / before taking math exams / do much better / than their neutral peers.

학생들은 / 만들어진 / 행복감을 느끼도록 / 수학 시험을 보기 전에 / 훨씬

더 잘한다 / 그들의 중립적인 또래들보다

❻ It has been proven / that our brains are programmed / to perform best / not when we are feeling negative or neutral, / but when we are feeling positive.

증명되었다 / 우리의 뇌가 프로그램화되어 있다는 것이 / 가장 잘 수행하도록 / 우리가 부정적이거나 중립적으로 느끼고 있을 때가 아니라 / 우리가 긍정적으로 느끼고 있을 때

지문해석 우리는 우리가 더 행복하고 더 긍정적일 때 더 성공한다. 예를 들어, 긍정적인 기분인 동안에 진단을 내리는 의사들은 중립적인 상태에 있는 의사들보다 거의 3배 더 높은 지능을 보인다. 또한, 그들은 정확한 진단을 19 퍼센트 더 빠르게 내린다. 긍정적인 영업사원들은 부정적인 영업사원들보다 더 많이 판매한다. 수학 시험을 보기 전에 행복감을 느끼게 되는 학생들은 그들의 중립적인 또래들보다 훨씬 더 잘한다. 우리의 뇌는 우리가 부정적이거나 중립적으로 느끼고 있을 때가 아니라, 우리가 긍정적으로 느끼고 있을 때 가장 잘 수행하도록 프로그램화되어 있음이 증명되었다.

문장 돋보기

❹ Salespeople [who are positive] sell more than those [who are negative].
주어 주격 관계대명사절 동사
주격 관계대명사절

❺ Students [who are made to feel happy before taking math exams] do much better than their neutral peers.
주어 주격 관계대명사절 동사 비교급 강조(훨씬)

❻ It has been proven [that our brains are programmed to perform best not {when we are feeling negative or neutral}, but {when we are feeling positive}].
가주어 진주어(that절)
not A but B: A가 아니라 B (A와 B에 모두 when 부사절이 쓰임)

29 정답 ② p. 88

이 글에서 빈칸이 주어진 문장은 연결어 So에서도 알 수 있듯이 글의 결론에 해당한다. 글 전반에서 협상 당사자들이 서로 멀리 떨어져 있으면 협상이 더 쉽다는 연구 결과를 다루고 있으므로, 빈칸에 들어갈 말로 가장 적절한 것은 ② '멀리서 시작하다'이다.

오답풀이 ① 분명한 시간제한을 두다 ③ 서로 가까워지다 ④ 세부 사항에 주의를 기울이다 ⑤ 더 작은 문제들을 우선 처리하다

READING GUIDE 협상 상대방과의 거리가 협상 성사 가능성에 미치는 영향

UNDERSTAND

DEEPLY **1** 협상을 더 쉽게 만드는 방법 **2** (1) F (2) F
3 far(ther) apart

1 첫 번째 문장에서 협상을 더 쉽게 만드는 방법(a way to make negotiations easier)이 글의 소재로 제시되었다.

2 (1) 자신이 판매자로부터 멀리 떨어져 있다고 믿은 학생들이 더 흔쾌히 응했다고 했으므로 일치하지 않는 내용이다. (2) 사람들은 더 멀리 떨어져 있을 때 주요 이슈에 더 집중한다고 했으므로 일치하지 않는 내용이다.

[해석] (1) 자신이 판매자와 가까이 있다고 생각한 학생들이 더 흔쾌히 응했다. (2) 사람들은 더 멀리 떨어져 있을 때 협상하는 데 있어서의 주요 요인들에 주의를 덜 기울인다.

3 협상을 할 때 당사자들이 서로 멀리 떨어져 있으면 성사 가능성이 더 높다는 연구 결과에 관한 글이므로, far apart(멀리 떨어진) 또는 farther apart(더 멀리 떨어진)가 들어가는 것이 적절하다.

[해석] 여러분이 협상할 때, 여러분에게서 (더) 멀리 떨어져 있는 사람들과 거래를 더 쉽게 성사시킬 수 있다.

READ CLOSELY

p. 89

❶ A study suggests a way / to make negotiations easier.

한 연구는 방법을 시사한다 / 협상을 더 쉽게 만드는

❷ In this study, / students negotiated / the purchase of a motorcycle / over an online messenger.

이 연구에서 / 학생들은 협상했다 / 오토바이의 구매를 / 온라인 메신저를 통해

❸ It was shown / that negotiations went smoother / when students believed / they were far apart from the seller.

드러났다 / 협상이 더 원만하게 진행되었음이 / 학생들이 믿었을 때 / 그들이 판매자로부터 멀리 떨어져 있다고

❹ They were more agreeable / than those / who believed / they were only a few feet away.

그들은 더 흔쾌히 응했다 / 사람들(학생들)보다 / 믿었던 / 그들이 몇 피트만 떨어져 있다고

❺ The researchers explained / that when people are farther apart, / they consider factors / in a different way.

연구원들은 설명했다 / 사람들이 더 멀리 떨어져 있을 때 / 그들은 요인들을 고려한다고 / 다른 방식으로

❻ They focus / more on the main issues / rather than other less important points.

그들은 집중한다 / 주요 이슈들에 더 / 다른 덜 중요한 점들보다는

❼ So, / the researchers recommend / that next time you have to achieve a difficult deal, / it may be helpful / to begin from a distance.

따라서 / 연구원들은 권한다 / 다음에 여러분이 어려운 거래를 성사시켜야 할 때 / 도움이 될 수도 있다고 / 멀리서 시작하는 것이

[지문해석] 한 연구는 협상을 더 쉽게 만드는 방법을 시사한다. 이 연구에서 학생들은 온라인 메신저를 통해 오토바이 구매를 협상했다. 학생들이 자신이 판매자로부터 멀리 떨어져 있다고 믿었을 때 협상이 더 원만하게 진행되었음이

드러났다. 그들은 자신이 고작 몇 피트만 떨어져 있다고 믿은 사람들보다 더 흔쾌히 응했다. 연구원들은 사람들이 더 멀리 떨어져 있을 때 다른 방식으로 요인들을 고려한다고 설명했다. 그들은 다른 덜 중요한 점들보다는 주요 이슈들에 더 집중한다. 따라서, 연구원들은 다음에 여러분이 까다로운 거래를 성사시켜야 할 때 멀리서 시작하는 것이 도움이 될 수도 있다고 권한다.

[문장] 돋보기

❶ A study suggests a way [to make negotiations easier].
└ to부정사의 형용사적 용법

❹ They were more agreeable than those [who believed {(that) they were only a few feet away}].
= Students who believed they were far apart from the seller
주격 관계대명사절   believed의 목적어(명사절)

❼ So, the researchers recommend [that next time you have to achieve a difficult deal, it may be helpful to begin from a distance.]
┌ 다음에 ~할 때
동사   목적어(that절)
가주어
진주어(to부정사구)

30 [정답] ④

p. 90

빈칸이 주어진 문장이 이 글의 주제문이며, 이 내용을 강화하기 위해 '빨간색 – 딸기 맛', '초록색 – 라임이나 멜론 맛'과 같이 특정 색깔과 맛의 관련성을 보여 주는 예시들이 이어지고 있다. 또한, 색깔뿐만 아니라 색의 진한 정도와 질감 역시 맛에 대한 판단에 영향을 줄 수 있다고 했으므로 빈칸에 들어갈 말로 가장 적절한 것은 ④ '겉모습'이다.

[오답풀이] ① 기원 ② 요리법 ③ 재료 ⑤ 크기

[READING GUIDE] 맛을 판단하는 데 음식의 겉모습이 미치는 영향

[UNDERSTAND DEEPLY] **1** (1) For example (2) The degree (3) Texture can **2** looks, taste **3** ②, ④

1 맛에 대한 판단에 음식의 '겉모습'이 영향을 미친다는 주제문이 제시된 후, 그 세 가지 예로 색깔, 색의 정도, 질감이 제시되었다. 따라서 주제문 외에 색깔이 언급되는 부분(For example ~), 색의 정도가 언급되는 부분(The degree ~), 질감이 언급되는 부분(Texture can ~)으로 나눌 수 있다.

2 음식의 겉모습, 즉 어떻게 보이는가(The way food looks)가 사람들이 그 맛(taste)을 어떻게 판단하는지에 영향을 줄 수 있다는 내용의 글이다.

[해석] 음식이 보이는 방식이 사람들이 그 맛을 판단하는 방식에 영향을 미칠 수 있다.

3 음식의 맛에 대한 판단에 영향을 미치는 요소로 냄새와 가격은 언급되지 않았다.

[해석] ① 색깔 ② 냄새 ③ 질감 ④ 가격

① Judgments about flavor / are often affected / by predictions / based on the appearance of the food.

맛에 대한 판단은 / 종종 영향을 받는다 / 예측에 의해 / 음식의 겉모습에 기초한

② For example, / strawberry-flavored foods are expected / to be red.

예를 들어 / 딸기 맛인 음식은 예상된다 / 빨간색일 것으로

③ However, / if that food is colored green, / it would be difficult / to identify the flavor as strawberry.

하지만 / 만약 그 음식이 초록색으로 칠해진다면 / 어려울 것이다 / 그 맛을 딸기로 식별하는 것이

④ That's because green foods are usually related to flavors / such as lime or melon.

그것은 초록색 음식은 보통 맛과 관계가 있기 때문이다 / 라임이나 멜론 같은

⑤ The degree of the color / also affects the way / we identify flavor.

색의 정도가 / 또한 방식에 영향을 미친다 / 우리가 맛을 식별하는

⑥ A stronger color may give / an impression of a stronger flavor / in a product, / even if the stronger color results from / adding more food coloring.

더 진한 색은 줄 수 있다 / 더 강한 맛의 인상을 / 제품에 있는 / 그 더 진한 색이 ~에서 비롯된다 할지라도 / 더 많은 식용 색소를 첨가하는 것

⑦ Texture can also lead to misunderstandings.

질감 역시 오해로 이어질 수 있다

⑧ A thicker product may be considered / richer tasting or stronger / even though it was simply made thicker / with thickening substances.

더 걸쭉한 제품은 여겨질 수도 있다 / 맛이 더 진하거나 더 강하다고 / 그 것이 그저 더 걸쭉하게 만들어졌음에도 불구하고 / 걸쭉하게 하는 물질 들로

[지문해석] 맛에 대한 판단은 종종 음식의 겉모습에 기초한 예측에 영향을 받는다. 예를 들어, 딸기 맛 음식은 빨간색일 것으로 예상된다. 하지만 그 음식이 초록색으로 칠해진다면 그 맛을 딸기로 식별하기 어려울 것이다. 그것은 초록색 음식은 보통 라임이나 멜론 같은 맛과 관계가 있기 때문이다. 색의 정도 또한 우리가 맛을 식별하는 방식에 영향을 준다. 더 진한 색은 그것이 더 많은 식용 색소를 첨가하는 것에서 비롯된다고 할지라도 제품의 맛이 더 강하다는 인상을 줄 수 있다. 질감 역시 오해로 이어질 수 있다. 더 걸쭉한 제품은 그저 걸쭉하게 하는 물질들로 더 걸쭉하게 만들어졌음에도 불구하고 맛이 더 진하 거나 더 강한 것으로 여겨질 수도 있다.

④ That's because green foods are usually related to flavors such as lime or melon.

그것은 ~하기 때문이다 (*cf.* that's why: 그것이 ~한 이유이다)
be related to: ~와 관계 있다
~와 같은

⑤ The degree of the color also affects the way [we identify flavor].

주어 / 단수 동사
관계부사 how가 생략된 관계부사절(the way how로 쓸 수 없음)

1 (1) ② → prediction   (2) ④ → proof
   (3) ③ → judgment   (4) ① → negotiation

2 (1) ④   (2) ②   (3) ①   (4) ③

3

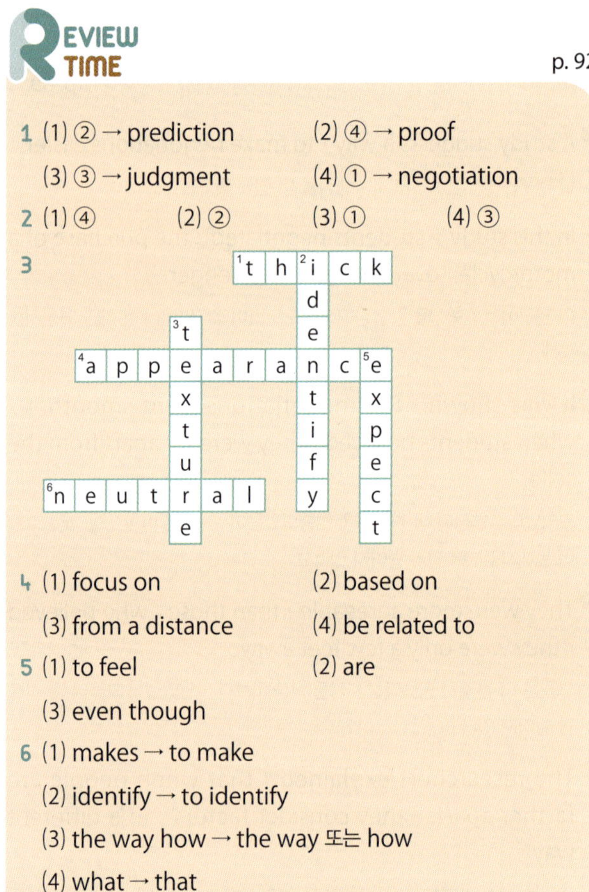

4 (1) focus on   (2) based on
   (3) from a distance   (4) be related to

5 (1) to feel   (2) are
   (3) even though

6 (1) makes → to make
   (2) identify → to identify
   (3) the way how → the way 또는 how
   (4) what → that

1 (1) prediction 예측   (2) proof 증거
   (3) judgment 판단   (4) negotiation 협상

2 (1) taste 맛; 맛이 나다, ④ flavor 맛; 맛을 내다
   (2) affect, ② influence 영향을 미치다
   (3) positive 긍정적인, ① optimistic 낙천적인
   (4) consider (~으로) 여기다, ③ believe (~이라고) 믿다

5 (1) 사역동사 make가 쓰인 문장이 수동태 문장으로 바뀔 때, 목적격 보어인 동사원형은 to부정사로 바뀌므로 to feel이 알맞다.
   [해석] 행복감을 느끼게 되는 학생들이 훨씬 더 잘한다.
   (2) 주어가 복수 명사 Judgments이므로 동사로 복수형인 are가 알맞다.
   [해석] 맛에 대한 판단은 종종 음식의 겉모습에 영향을 받는다.

(3) 뒤에 절이 오므로 접속사 even though가 알맞다. in spite of는 전치사이다.

해석 더 걸쭉한 제품은 그저 물질로 더 걸쭉하게 만들어졌음에도 불구하고 맛이 더 진하다고 여겨진다.

6 (1) 문장의 동사는 suggest이며, makes는 '만드는'이라는 의미로 a way를 수식하는 to부정사 to make로 고쳐야 한다.

해석 연구들은 협상을 더 쉽게 만드는 방법을 시사한다.

(2) 가주어 It이 쓰였으므로 identify가 진주어를 이끌도록 to부정사인 to identify로 고쳐야 한다.

해석 그 맛을 딸기로 식별하는 것은 어려울 것이다.

(3) '~하는 방식'을 의미하는 선행사 the way와 관계부사 how는 같이 쓸 수 없으며 둘 중 하나만 쓰는 것이 알맞다.

해석 색의 정도가 우리가 맛을 식별하는 방식에 영향을 미친다.

(4) 가주어 It이 쓰였으며, what 뒤에 오는 절이 완전한 절이므로 what을 접속사 that으로 고쳐야 한다.

해석 우리가 긍정적으로 느끼고 있을 때 우리의 뇌가 가장 잘 수행한다는 것이 증명되었다.

Play Time

▶ 5번 물체의 A, B, C 측면을 찾아보세요.

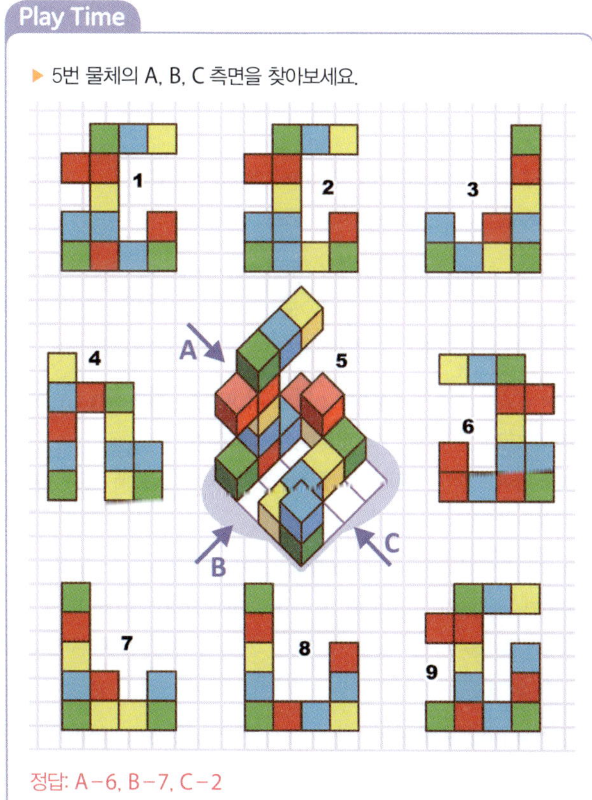

정답: A-6, B-7, C-2

연결어 넣기

31  정답 ②　　　　　　　　　p. 96

(A) 빈칸 앞은 아침 식사가 세 끼 중 가장 중요하므로 가장 든든하게 먹어야 한다고 뉴스 기사에 보도된다는 내용이고, 빈칸 뒤는 이러한 생각이 점심과 저녁 식사의 가치를 감소시킬 수 있다는 내용이므로, 빈칸에는 글의 흐름을 전환하는 However(그러나)가 가장 적절하다.

(B) 빈칸 앞은 점심과 저녁 식사도 양질의 에너지를 제공할 수 있다는 내용이고, 빈칸 뒤는 아침 식사의 양보다는 매 끼니에 어떤 음식을 먹는지가 건강 증진에 중요하다는 내용이므로, 빈칸에는 결론을 이끄는 Therefore(그러므로)가 가장 적절하다.

오답풀이 ① 그러나 – 마찬가지로 ③ 대조적으로 – 그럼에도 불구하고
④ 예를 들어 – 마찬가지로 ⑤ 예를 들어 – 그러므로

READING GUIDE 하루 세 끼 중 가장 중요하다고 보도되는 아침 식사

UNDERSTAND DEEPLY **1** (1) F (2) F **2** (1) the amount of food for breakfast (2) the kind of food people eat for each meal

1 (1) 뉴스 기사에 따르면 아침 식사를 가장 든든하게 하고 이후에는 덜 먹어야 한다고 했으므로 일치하지 않는다. (2) 아침 식사가 주된 에너지를 제공한다고 했으므로 일치하지 않는다.

해석 (1) 뉴스 기사들은 우리가 매 끼니로 같은 양의 음식을 먹어야 한다고 보도한다. (2) 점심과 저녁 식사가 하루 종일 우리 신체에 주된 에너지를 제공한다.

2 건강 증진을 위한 식사에 있어 뉴스 기사들은 아침 식사로 먹는 음식의 양이 중요하다고 보도하며, 필자는 그보다는 매 끼니에 먹는 음식의 종류가 중요하다고 주장하고 있다.

READ CLOSELY　　　　　　　　　p. 97

❶ Many news stories (report)/ that breakfast is the most important meal / of the day.

많은 뉴스 기사들이 보도한다 / 아침 식사가 가장 중요한 식사라고 / 하루 중

❷ According to those stories, / we (should have) the biggest meal / for breakfast / and (eat) less / as the day passes by.

그 기사들에 따르면 / 우리는 가장 든든한 식사를 해야 한다 / 아침 식사로 / 그리고 덜 먹어야 한다 / 하루가 흐름에 따라

❸ This (is) because breakfast provides the main energy / for both your body and brain / all day long.

이것은 아침 식사가 주된 에너지를 제공하기 때문이다 / 여러분의 신체와 두뇌 둘 다에 / 하루 종일

❹ However, / this idea (can reduce) / the worth of lunch and dinner.

그러나 / 이 생각은 감소시킬 수 있다 / 점심 식사와 저녁 식사의 가치를

⑤ Having a big breakfast / is not a good rule / for everyone.

든든한 아침 식사를 하는 것이 / 좋은 규칙은 아니다 / 모두에게

⑥ People's lifestyle and health condition / differ from one another.

사람들의 생활 방식과 건강 상태는 / 서로 다르다

⑦ Lunch and dinner / can also give quality energy / to people.

점심 식사와 저녁 식사는 / 또한 양질의 에너지를 줄 수 있다 / 사람들에게

⑧ Therefore, / it is the kind of food / people eat for each meal / —rather than just increasing / the amount of food for breakfast / — that plays an important role / in improving one's health.

그러므로 / 음식의 종류이다 / 사람들이 매 끼니로 먹는 / 그저 늘리는 것보다는 / 아침 식사를 위한 음식의 양을 / 중요한 역할을 하는 것은 / 건강을 증진시키는 데

지문해석 많은 뉴스 기사들은 아침 식사가 하루 중 가장 중요한 식사라고 보도한다. 그 기사들에 따르면 우리는 아침 식사로 가장 든든한 식사를 해야 하고 하루가 흐름에 따라 덜 먹어야 한다. 이것은 아침 식사가 하루 종일 여러분의 신체와 두뇌 둘 다에 주된 에너지를 제공하기 때문이다. 그러나 이러한 생각은 점심 식사와 저녁 식사의 가치를 감소시킬 수 있다. 든든한 아침 식사를 하는 것이 모두에게 좋은 규칙은 아니다. 사람들의 생활 방식과 건강 상태는 서로 다르다. 점심 식사와 저녁 식사도 사람들에게 양질의 에너지를 줄 수 있다. 그러므로 건강을 증진시키는 데 중요한 역할을 하는 것은 그저 아침 식사로 먹는 음식의 양을 늘리는 것보다는 사람들이 매 끼니로 먹는 음식의 종류이다.

문장 돋보기

「It is ~ that ...」 강조 구문: …한 것은 바로 ~이다

⑧ Therefore, it is [the kind of food (that[which])
그러므로   강조 대상(주어)   목적격 관계대명사절
people eat for each meal] — rather than just
                              ~보다는
increasing the amount of food for breakfast—that
plays an important role in improving one's health.
강조되는 대상이 주어 the kind이므로 단수 동사

32 정답 ⑤　　　　　　　　　　　　　　　　p. 98

(A) 빈칸 앞은 실내 식물이 실내 공기를 걸러내는 가장 좋은 방법이라는 내용이고, 빈칸 뒤는 실내 식물의 예로 자주달개비에 대해 서술하고 있으므로, 빈칸에는 예시를 나타내는 For example(예를 들어)이 가장 적절하다.
(B) 빈칸 앞은 실내 식물들이 공기 오염을 줄일 수 있다는 내용이고, 빈칸 뒤는 식물을 잘 돌보지 않으면 해로운 벌레들의 번식지가 될 수 있다는 내용이

므로, 빈칸에는 글의 흐름을 전환하는 However(그러나)가 가장 적절하다.
오답풀이 ① 마찬가지로 – 게다가　② 그 결과 – 그러나　③ 그 결과 – 게다가　④ 예를 들어 – 다시 말해서

READING GUIDE　실내 공기를 정화하는 실내 식물

UNDERSTAND DEEPLY
1 (1) 실내[집안] 공기　(2) 이산화 탄소　(3) 이산화 탄소　(4) 산소　(5) 공기 오염　(6) 해충[해로운 벌레들]
2 house plants, indoor air

1 이 글은 실내 공기를 정화하는 방법으로 실내 식물을 제시한 후 자주달개비를 예로 들어 이산화 탄소를 잘 흡수하고 기르기 쉬운 특징을 서술하고, 이산화 탄소를 산소로 바꿈으로써 공기 오염을 감소시킬 수 있음을 부연 설명하고 있다. 또한, 식물을 잘 돌보지 않으면 해충의 번식지가 될 수도 있다는 유의점을 덧붙이고 있다.

2 실내 공기를 정화하기 위해 실내 식물을 기를 것을 제안하는 글이다.
해석 실내 식물을 기르는 것은 실내 공기를 깨끗하게 유지하기 위한 가장 좋은 방법이다.

READ CLOSELY　　　　　　　　　　　　p. 99

① You can do / a number of things / to keep the air in your home / clean.

여러분은 할 수 있다 / 많은 것들을 / 여러분의 집안 공기를 유지하기 위해 / 깨끗하게

② Most of them / don't require much effort.

그것들 중 대다수는 / 많은 노력을 필요로 하지 않는다

③ House plants are / by far the best way / to filter indoor air.

실내 식물들은 ~이다 / 단연 가장 좋은 방법 / 실내 공기를 걸러내는

④ For example, / spider plants love to absorb carbon dioxide, / and they are easy / to grow.

예를 들어 / 자주달개비는 이산화 탄소를 흡수하는 것을 매우 좋아한다 / 그리고 그것들은 쉽다 / 기르기

⑤ In fact, / they grow so thick / that before long you'll have / a huge number of little baby spider plants.

사실 / 그것들은 너무 무성하게 자란다 / 그래서 머지않아 여러분은 가지게 될 것이다 / 대단히 많은 작고 어린 자주달개비를

⑥ Other house plants / also absorb / different kinds of air pollutants.

다른 실내 식물들은 / 또한 흡수한다 / 다양한 종류의 공기 오염 물질을

⑦ They can reduce air pollution / by changing carbon dioxide / back into oxygen.

그것들은 공기 오염을 줄일 수 있다 / 이산화 탄소를 바꿈으로써 / 다시 산소로

⑧ However, / remember that, / if you don't take good

care of the plants, / they can be excellent breeding grounds / for harmful bugs.

그러나 / ~임을 기억해라 / 만약 여러분이 그 식물들을 잘 돌보지 않는다면 / 그것들은 훌륭한 번식지가 될 수 있음을 / 해로운 벌레들에게

⑨ If you want plants / in your house, / you should be prepared / to take care of them.

만약 여러분이 식물들을 원한다면 / 여러분의 집안에 / 여러분은 준비가 되어 있어야 한다 / 그것들을 돌볼

지문해석 여러분은 집안 공기를 깨끗하게 유지하기 위해 많은 것들을 할 수 있다. 그것들 중 대다수는 많은 노력을 필요로 하지 않는다. 실내 식물들은 실내 공기를 걸러내는 단연코 가장 좋은 방법이다. 예를 들어, 자주달개비는 이산화 탄소를 흡수하는 것을 매우 좋아하며, 그것들은 기르기 쉽다. 사실, 그것들은 매우 무성하게 자라서 머지않아 여러분은 대단히 많은 작고 어린 자주달개비를 가지게 될 것이다. 다른 실내 식물들도 다양한 종류의 공기 오염 물질을 흡수한다. 그것들은 이산화 탄소를 다시 산소로 바꾸어 놓음으로써 공기 오염을 감소시킬 수 있다. 그러나 만약 여러분이 그 식물들을 잘 돌보지 않는다면 그것들은 해충들에게 훌륭한 번식지가 될 수 있음을 기억해라. 만약 여러분이 집안에 식물들을 들이기를 원한다면 여러분은 그것들을 돌볼 준비가 되어 있어야 한다.

문장 돋보기

❸ House plants are by far the best way [to filter indoor air].
최상급 강조(단연) / to부정사의 형용사적 용법

❹ For example, spider plants love to absorb carbon dioxide, and they are easy to grow.
to부정사의 명사적 용법(목적어) / to부정사의 부사적 용법(형용사 수식)

❺ In fact, they grow so thick that before long you'll have a huge number of little baby spider plants.
사실 / =spider plants / so+부사+that+절: 너무 ~해서 …하다 / a (huge) number of: (대단히) 많은

33 정답 ④   p. 100

(A) 빈칸 앞에서 언급된 '큰 프로젝트에 크게 실패했음에도 일자리를 잃지 않는 경우'가 빈칸 뒤에서 Virgin 항공사의 예로 제시되고 있으므로 빈칸에는 예시의 연결어 For instance(예를 들어)가 가장 적절하다.
(B) 빈칸 앞뒤로 Joe Ferry가 좌석 디자인 프로젝트를 이끌었지만, 테스트 결과 승객들이 그의 디자인을 좋아하지 않았다는 내용이 이어지므로, 빈칸에는 글의 흐름을 전환하는 연결어인 However(그러나)가 가장 적절하다.
오답풀이 ① 즉 – 그러므로 ② 즉 – 게다가 ③ 예를 들어 – 게다가 ⑤ 다시 말해서 – 그러나

READING GUIDE 큰 프로젝트에 크게 실패하면 일자리를 잃을 수 있다는 통념에 반하는 경우

1 another chance to people who failed and caused a loss → 실패해서 손해를 끼친 사람들에게 또 다른 기회를 주어라. **2** (1) F (2) T

1 이 글은 디자인 프로젝트에 실패했던 Joe Ferry가 몇 년 후 다른 디자인으로 회사의 매출을 상승시킨 사례를 들며 실패한 사람들에게 만회할 기회를 주는 것이 좋음을 이야기하고 있다.

2 (1) 평평하게 누울 수 있는 좌석은 British 항공사에서 개발한 것이므로 일치하지 않는다. (2) Virgin 항공사는 Joe Ferry가 디자인 프로젝트에 실패했지만 해고하지 않고 만회할 기회를 주었으므로 일치한다.
해석 (1) Joe Ferry는 실제로 평평하게 누울 수 있는 좌석을 디자인했다. (2) Virgin 항공사는 Joe가 프로젝트에 실패했음에도 불구하고 그를 해고하지 않았다.

READ CLOSELY   p. 101

❶ Most people would agree / that if you planned a big project / for your company / but failed in a big way, / you could lose your job.

대부분의 사람들은 동의할 것이다 / 만약 여러분이 큰 프로젝트를 기획한다면 / 회사를 위한 / 하지만 크게 실패한다면 / 여러분이 일자리를 잃을 수 있다는 데

❷ That's no longer always the case.

그것은 더 이상 항상 사실이 아니다

❸ For instance, / take Virgin Airlines.

예를 들어 / Virgin 항공사를 살펴보아라

❹ The airline wanted to design / a new kind of seat / for business class / that would allow passengers / to lean back / so that they could sleep comfortably.

그 항공사는 디자인하기를 원했다 / 새로운 종류의 좌석을 / 비즈니스 클래스를 위한 / 승객들에게 허락할 / 뒤로 젖히도록 / 그들이 편안하게 잠잘 수 있도록

❺ The man / who led the project / was Joe Ferry.

그 남자는 / 그 프로젝트를 이끌었던 / Joe Ferry였다

❻ However, / tests showed / that passengers didn't like his design.

그러나 / 테스트들이 보여주었다 / 승객들이 그의 디자인을 좋아하지 않았다는 것을

❼ To make matters worse, / British Airways developed / much better seats / that could actually lie flat, / and Virgin lost out.

설상가상으로 / British 항공사가 개발했다 / 훨씬 더 좋은 좌석들을 / 실제로 평평하게 누울 수 있는 / 그리고 Virgin은 손해를 보았다

❽ But Virgin Airlines was smart enough / to keep Joe Ferry.

그러나 Virgin 항공사는 충분히 현명했다 / Joe Ferry를 계속 데리고 있을 만큼

⑨ A few years later, / he came up with a great design / that worked nicely for the company, / and it increased Virgin's sales.

몇 년 후에 / 그는 훌륭한 디자인을 생각해 냈다 / 그 회사에 좋은 결과를 가져온 / 그리고 그것은 Virgin의 매출을 증가시켰다

⑩ If the company had fired him, / it would have resulted in a big loss.

만약 그 회사가 그를 해고했다면 / 그것은 큰 손실을 초래했을 것이다

지문해석 대부분의 사람들은 회사를 위한 큰 프로젝트를 기획했다가 크게 실패하면 일자리를 잃을 수도 있다는 데 동의할 것이다. 그것은 더 이상 사실인 것은 아니다. 예를 들어, Virgin 항공사를 살펴보자. 그 항공사는 승객들이 편안하게 잠잘 수 있도록 뒤로 젖힐 수 있게 할 비즈니스 클래스용의 새로운 종류의 좌석을 디자인하기를 원했다. 그 프로젝트를 이끌었던 남자는 Joe Ferry였다. 그러나 승객들이 그의 디자인을 좋아하지 않는다는 것을 테스트들이 보여주었다. 설상가상으로, British 항공사가 실제로 평평하게 누울 수 있는 훨씬 더 좋은 좌석을 개발했고, Virgin 항공사는 손해를 보았다. 그러나 Virgin 항공사는 Joe Ferry를 계속 데리고 있을 만큼 충분히 현명했다. 몇 년 후에, 그는 회사에 좋은 결과를 가져온 훌륭한 디자인을 생각해 냈고, 그것은 Virgin 항공사의 매출을 증가시켰다. 만약 회사가 그를 해고했다면 그것은 큰 손실을 초래했을 것이다.

문장 돋보기

⑦ To make matters worse, British Airways developed
— 설상가상으로
much better seats [that could actually lie flat], and
— 비교급 강조(훨씬)   — 주격 관계대명사절
Virgin lost out.

⑧ But Virgin Airlines was smart enough to keep Joe
— 형용사+enough+to부정사: ~할 만큼 충분히 …한
Ferry.

⑩ If the company had fired him, it would have
— 가정법 과거완료(if+주어+had+과거분사, 주어+조동사의 과거형+have+과거분사): 만약 ~했다면 …했을 텐데
resulted in a big loss.

1 (1) absorb　　　(2) require
　(3) passenger　　(4) oxygen

2 (1) ②　　(2) ④　　(3) ①　　(4) ③

3

Y	C	B	Z	P	D	U	B	C	E	O	L
E	S	O	J	T	A	O	N	W	O	L	Y
T	W	N	M	K	R	F	R	Y	X	M	H
S	O	G	P	F	P	S	T	O	I	N	O
B	R	T	N	O	O	I	I	H	P	Y	N
L	T	S	V	T	L	R	Q	R	D	K	D
S	H	X	K	A	L	L	T	U	P	F	H
F	U	Z	U	E	S	E	U	A	Q	R	Y
L	O	Q	D	B	N	V	C	T	B	H	N
A	E	T	Z	E	I	P	I	D	I	L	L
T	B	E	J	H	K	W	X	A	L	O	Y
X	A	G	L	U	H	R	G	B	U	G	N

　(1) comfortably　(2) flat
　(3) worth　　　(4) pollution
　(5) bug　　　　(6) quality

4 (1) result in　　(2) come up with
　(3) take care of　(4) differ from

5 (1) is　　　(2) the best
　(3) plays　　(4) a number of

6 (1) to keep　　(2) could
　(3) to learn　　(4) changing

2 (1) fire 해고하다 ↔ ② hire 고용하다
　(2) harmful 해로운 ↔ ④ harmless 무해한
　(3) indoor 실내의 ↔ ① outdoor 실외의
　(4) reduce 감소시키다 ↔ ③ increase 증가시키다

5 (1) 동명사구가 주어로 쓰이면 단수 취급하므로 단수 동사 is가 알맞다.
　해석 푸짐한 아침 식사를 하는 것이 모든 사람에게 좋은 규칙은 아니다.
　(2) by far는 '단연'이라는 의미로 최상급을 강조하는 부사이므로 the best가 알맞다.
　해석 실내 식물들은 실내 공기를 걸러내는 단연 가장 좋은 방법이다.
　(3) 「it is ~ that …」 강조 구문에서 강조된 주어가 the kind이므로 단수 동사 plays가 알맞다.
　해석 건강을 향상시키는 데 중요한 역할을 하는 것은 음식의 종류이다.
　(4) '많은 것들을 할 수 있다'라는 의미가 되어야 하므로 '많은'을 의미하는 a number of가 알맞다. the number of는 '~의 수'라는 의미이다.
　해석 여러분은 집안 공기를 깨끗하게 유지하기 위해서 많은 것들을 할 수 있다.

6 (1) '~할 만큼 충분히 …한'은 「형용사+enough+to부정사」 형태로 표현하므로 to keep이 알맞다.

(2) 가정법 과거의 주절에서 동사는 「조동사의 과거형+동사원형」의 형
태로 쓰므로 could가 알맞다.
(3) allow는 목적격 보어로 to부정사를 취하므로 to lean이 알맞다.
(4) '~함으로써는 「by+동명사」로 표현하므로 changing이 알맞다.

무관한 문장 찾기

34   정답 ④   p. 104

이 글은 우리의 뇌가 늘 수많은 다양한 자극에 대해 반응해야 하기 때문에
우리가 언제든 실수를 할 수 있다는 내용으로, 껍질 대신 껍질을 벗긴 감자
를 쓰레기통에 넣는 실수와 첨부한다고 한 파일을 첨부하지 않고 이메일을
보내는 실수를 예로 들고 있다. 따라서 알려지지 않은 출처의 파일을 여는 것
은 위험하다는 내용의 ④는 전체 글의 흐름과 관계 없는 문장이다.

READING GUIDE   Mistakes, brain(s)

UNDERSTAND DEEPLY   **1** ①   **2** mistakes, respond   **3** 껍질을 벗긴 감자를 쓰
레기통에 버리고 껍질을 냄비에 넣는 것 / (첨부한다고 한) 파
일을 첨부하지 않고 이메일을 보내는 것

1 이 글은 우리의 뇌가 끊임없이 수천 가지의 다양한 자극에 반응해야 하므
로 우리가 언제든 실수를 하기 쉬움을 이야기하고 있다.

2 이 글은 사람들이 한 순간 실수를 하는 예를 들며 자극에 대한 뇌의 반응
을 이유로 설명하고 있다.

해석   우리가 종종 실수를 하는 이유는 우리의 뇌가 매 순간 다양한 자극
에 반응해야 하기 때문이다.

3 첫 두 문장에 실수의 두 가지 예가 제시되어 있다.

READ CLOSELY   p. 105

❶ Have you ever thrown the peeled potato / into the bin
/ and the peelings / into the pot?

여러분은 껍질을 벗긴 감자를 던진 적이 있는가 / 쓰레기통에 / 그리고 껍
질을 / 냄비에

❷ How about sending an email / without attaching a
file?

이메일을 보내는 것은 어떤가 / 파일을 첨부하지 않고

❸ Mistakes like these / always happen.

이와 같은 실수들은 / 항상 일어난다

❹ That's because our brains have to respond / to
thousands of different stimuli / all the time / when
we're awake.

그것은 우리의 뇌가 반응해야 하기 때문이다 / 수천 개의 다양한 자극에 /

내내 / 우리가 깨어 있을 때

❺ Even though a second earlier we wrote / that we were
attaching a file / to the email, / the very next second /
our brain orders our fingers / to send the email /
without the file.

잠깐 전에 우리가 썼음에도 불구하고 / 우리가 파일을 첨부할 것이라고 /
이메일에 / 바로 다음 순간에 / 우리의 뇌는 우리의 손가락들에게 명령을
내린다 / 이메일을 보내라고 / 파일 없이

❻ It's dangerous / to open some files / from an unknown
source.

위험하다 / 어떤 파일들을 여는 것은 / 알려지지 않은 출처로부터의

❼ Sometimes / we don't even realize our mistake / until
we get an email / from the receiver / pointing it out.

때때로 / 우리는 심지어 우리의 실수를 깨닫지 못한다 / 우리가 이메일을
받을 때까지 / 수신자로부터 / 그것을 지적하는

지문해석   여러분은 껍질을 벗긴 감자는 쓰레기통에, 껍질은 냄비에 던져 넣
은 적이 있는가? 파일을 첨부하지 않고 이메일을 보내는 것은 어떤가? 이와
같은 실수들은 항상 일어난다. 그것은 우리의 뇌가 우리가 깨어 있을 때 내내
수천 개의 다양한 자극에 반응해야 하기 때문이다. 잠깐 전에 우리가 이메일
에 파일을 첨부할 것이라고 썼음에도 불구하고, 바로 다음 순간에 우리의 뇌
는 파일 없이 이메일을 보내라고 우리의 손가락들에게 명령을 내린다. (알려
지지 않은 출처로부터 온 어떤 파일들을 여는 것은 위험하다.) 때때로 우리는
심지어 수신자로부터 그것을 지적하는 이메일을 받고 나서야 비로소 우리의
실수를 깨닫는다.

문장 돋보기

❺ Even though a second earlier we wrote [that we
~에도 불구하고(= Although)
were attaching a file to the email], the very next
wrote의 목적어(that절)
second our brain orders our fingers to send the
order+목적어+목적격 보어(to부정사):
~에게 …하라고 명령하다
email without the file.

❼ Sometimes we don't even realize our mistake
not ~ until ...: …하고 나서야 비로소 ~하다
until we get an email from the receiver [pointing
현재분사구
it out].
= 파일을 첨부하지 않은 것

35   정답 ③   p. 106

이 글은 포유류에 비해 조류가 다양한 목적으로 소리를 사용하는 데 더 능숙
하다는 내용이다. 따라서 포유류는 사는 곳, 돌아다니는 방식, 먹는 것에 있
어서 서로 다르다는 내용의 ③은 전체 글의 흐름과 관계 없는 문장이다.

READING GUIDE   소리를 사용하는 포유류와 조류

1 sounds, birds, mammals **2** (1) F (2) T **3** (자신의 존재를 알리고 서로 의사소통을 하기 위해) 소리를 사용하는 것

1 조류와 포유류 모두 서로 의사소통하기 위해 흔히 소리를 사용하며, 포유류는 노래를 하는 조류와는 달리 일반적으로 음악적이지 않다고 했다.

해석 조류와 포유류 둘 다 소리를 사용함으로써 서로 의사소통하지만, 조류가 포유류보다 훨씬 더 음악적이다.

2 (1) 조류만큼 많은 다양한 종류의 소리를 낼 수 있는 포유류는 거의 없다고 했다. (2) 몇몇 포유류가 큰 소리를 내며, 인간과 고래 외에 노래를 하는 포유류는 거의 없다고 했다.

해석 (1) 많은 포유류가 조류만큼 많은 다양한 종류의 소리를 낼 수 있다. (2) 모든 포유류가 큰 소리를 내거나 노래를 부르는 것은 아니다.

3 세 번째 문장의 it은 바로 앞 문장에 제시된 내용을 가리킨다.

READ CLOSELY
p. 107

❶ Both mammals and birds / are noisy creatures.

포유류와 조류 둘 다 / 떠들썩한 동물들이다

❷ They commonly use sounds / for announcing their presence / and for communicating with each other.

그것들은 흔히 소리를 사용한다 / 자신들의 존재를 알리기 위해 / 그리고 서로 의사소통을 하기 위해

❸ But birds are far better at it.

하지만 조류가 그것에 훨씬 더 능숙하다

❹ Birds also make sounds / to warn other birds / that a predator is nearby.

조류는 또한 소리를 낸다 / 다른 새들에게 경고하기 위해 / 포식자가 근처에 있다는 것을

❺ Many mammals produce different sounds / for different reasons, / but few mammals can make / as many different kinds of sounds as birds.

많은 포유류가 다양한 소리를 낸다 / 다양한 이유로 / 하지만 낼 수 있는 포유류는 거의 없다 / 조류만큼 많은 다양한 종류의 소리를

❻ With the exception of human beings, / mammals in general / are not musical / and there is little evidence / that they try to be.

인간을 제외하고 / 포유류는 일반적으로 / 음악적이지 않다 / 그리고 증거가 거의 없다 / 그것들이 그러려고 한다는

❼ Mammals differ / depending on where they live, / how they move around, / and what they eat.

포유류는 다르다 / 그것들이 사는 곳에 따라 / 그것들이 돌아다니는 방식(에 따라) / 그리고 그것들이 먹는 것(에 따라)

❽ Some mammals make loud sounds, / but few mammals sing, / apart from human beings and perhaps whales.

일부 포유류가 큰 소리를 낸다 / 하지만 노래하는 포유류는 거의 없다 / 인간과 아마도 고래를 제외하고

❾ Yet many birds are famous for their songs, / and some of the most wonderful songsters / are the ones / we encounter most often.

하지만 많은 조류는 그것들의 노래로 유명하다 / 그리고 가장 멋진 명금(고운 소리로 우는 새) 중의 일부는 / 것들이다 / 우리가 가장 자주 마주치는

지문해석 포유류와 조류 둘 다 떠들썩한 동물들이다. 그것들은 흔히 자신들의 존재를 알리고 서로 의사소통을 하기 위해 소리를 사용한다. 하지만 조류가 그것에 훨씬 더 능숙하다. 조류는 또한 다른 새들에게 포식자가 근처에 있다는 것을 경고하기 위해 소리를 낸다. 많은 포유류가 다양한 이유로 다양한 소리를 내지만, 조류만큼 많은 다양한 종류의 소리를 낼 수 있는 포유류는 거의 없다. 인간을 제외하고 포유류는 일반적으로 음악적이지 못하며, 그것들이 음악적이려고 한다는 증거도 거의 없다. (포유류는 사는 곳, 돌아다니는 방식, 그리고 먹는 것에 따라 서로 다르다.) 일부 포유류가 큰 소리를 내기는 하지만, 인간과 아마도 고래 외에 노래하는 포유류는 거의 없다. 하지만 많은 조류는 그것들의 노래로 유명하며, 가장 멋진 명금(고운 소리로 우는 새) 중의 일부는 우리가 가장 자주 마주치는 것들이다.

문장 돋보기

❶ both A and B: A와 B 둘 다 (복수 취급)
[Both mammals and birds] are noisy creatures.
　　　　주어　　　　　　　　　동사

❻ With the exception of human beings, mammals
　　　~을 제외하고
in general are not musical and there is little
　일반적으로　　　　　　　　　　　　　　(양이) 거의 없는
evidence [that they try to be (musical)].
　　　　　└동격┘

36 정답 ④
p. 108

현대 도시에서 유리 건물이 하는 역할에 대해 설명한 글로, 유리는 적정한 가격의 건축 자재이지만 유리 공학은 많은 돈이 들어서 유리 건물 시장이 독점적이 되게 한다는 ④는 전체 글의 흐름과 관계 없는 문장이다.

READING GUIDE glass

1 How much natural light is there
2 (1) reasonable (2) brighter **3** Glass, protects, the[bad] weather, natural light

1 세 번째 문장에 사람들이 새 집이나 직장에 관해 처음으로 묻는 질문 중 하나가 제시되어 있다.

해석 Q: 사람들이 새 집을 원할 때 하는 첫 번째 질문들 중 하나는 무엇인가? A: 그것은 '자연광이 거기에 얼마나 들어오는가?'이다.

2 (1) 이 글은 유리가 현대 도시에서 건물을 건축하기에 좋은 자재임을 설명하고 있다.

(2) 유리는 주로 실내에서 보내는 우리의 삶을 훨씬 더 밝게 해 준다고 했다.

해석 (1) 집을 짓기 위해 유리를 사용하는 것은 합리적이다. (2) 현대 유리 건물들은 우리가 실내에서 훨씬 더 밝은 삶을 살게 한다.

3 유리는 현대 도시에서 중요한 건축 자재로, 바람, 추위, 비와 같은 궂은 날씨로부터 보호해 주고 도둑의 침입과 같은 범죄로부터 안전하게 해 줄 뿐 아니라 어둠 속에서 살지 않게 한다고 했다.

해석 유리는 현대 도시에서 중요한 건축 자재인데, (궂은) 날씨와 침입으로부터 우리를 보호할 뿐만 아니라 충분한 자연광을 제공하기 때문이다.

READ CLOSELY

p. 109

① It ⟨is⟩ impossible / to imagine a modern city without glass.

불가능하다 / 유리가 없는 현대 도시를 상상하는 것은

② We ⟨expect⟩ our buildings / to protect us from the weather; / this ⟨is⟩ / what they are for, / after all.

우리는 우리의 건물들에 기대한다 / 우리를 날씨로부터 보호하기를 / 이것은 ~이다 / 그것들이 존재하는 이유 / 결국

③ And yet, / when it comes to a new home or workplace, / one of the first questions / people ask ⟨is⟩, / "How much natural light ⟨is⟩ there?"

그럼에도 불구하고 / 새로운 집이나 직장에 관해서라면 / 첫 번째 질문들 중 하나는 / 사람들이 묻는 / ~이다 / 얼마나 많은 자연광이 / 있는가

④ Modern glass buildings / ⟨satisfy⟩ these different desires: / the desire / to be protected from bad weather, / such as the wind, the cold, and the rain; / the desire / to be secure from the invasion of the thieves; / and, at the same time, / the desire / not to live in darkness.

현대 유리 건물들은 / 이러한 서로 다른 욕구들을 충족시킨다 / 욕구 / 궂은 날씨로부터 보호 받고자 하는 / 바람, 추위 그리고 비와 같은 / 욕구 / 도둑의 침입으로부터 안전하고자 하는 / 그리고 동시에 / 욕구 / 어둠 속에서 살지 않고자 하는

⑤ Although glass is a reasonable building material, / glass engineering ⟨is⟩ expensive / and it ⟨causes⟩ / the glass building market / to be exclusive.

유리가 합리적인 건축 자재이기는 하지만 / 유리 공학은 비싸다 / 그리고 그것은 ~하게 한다 / 유리 건물 시장을 / 독점적이 되게

⑥ Glass ⟨makes⟩ our lives, / which are spent mostly indoors, / much brighter and more delightful.

유리는 우리의 삶을 만든다 / 주로 실내에서 보내지는 / 훨씬 더 밝고 더 유쾌하게

지문해석 유리가 없는 현대 도시를 상상하기란 불가능하다. 우리는 우리의 건물이 날씨로부터 우리를 보호해 주기를 기대하는데, 이것이 결국 건물이 존재하는 이유이다. 그럼에도 불구하고, 새로운 집이나 직장에 관해서라면 사람들이 처음으로 묻는 질문 중 하나는 '자연광이 거기에 얼마나 들어오는가?'이다. 현대 유리 건물들은 바람, 추위 그리고 비와 같은 궂은 날씨로부터 보호

받고자 하는 욕구, 도둑의 침입으로부터 안전하고자 하는 욕구, 그리고 동시에 어둠 속에서 살지 않고자 하는 욕구 등 이러한 서로 다른 욕구들을 충족시킨다. (유리가 적정한 가격의 건축 자재이기는 하지만, 유리 공학은 돈이 많이 들어서 유리 건물 시장이 독점적이 되게 한다.) 유리는 주로 실내에서 보내는 우리의 삶을 훨씬 더 밝고 더 유쾌하게 만들어 준다.

문장 돋보기

② expect + 목적어 + 목적격 보어(to부정사): ~이 …할 것을 기대하다
We expect our buildings to protect us from the
　　동사　　　　목적어　　　　　목적격 보어
weather; this is what they are for, after all.
　　　　　　보어(선행사를 포함하는 관계대명사 what이 이끄는 절)

⑥ make + 목적어 + 목적격 보어(형용사): ~을 …하게 만들다
Glass makes our lives, [which are spent mostly
　　　동사　　　목적어　　 주격 관계대명사절
indoors], much brighter and more delightful.
　　　　　　　목적격 보어(형용사구)

REVIEW TIME

p. 110

1 (1) invasion　　　　(2) respond
(3) present　　　　(4) attachment

2 (1) ③　　(2) ①　　(3) ④　　(4) ②

3

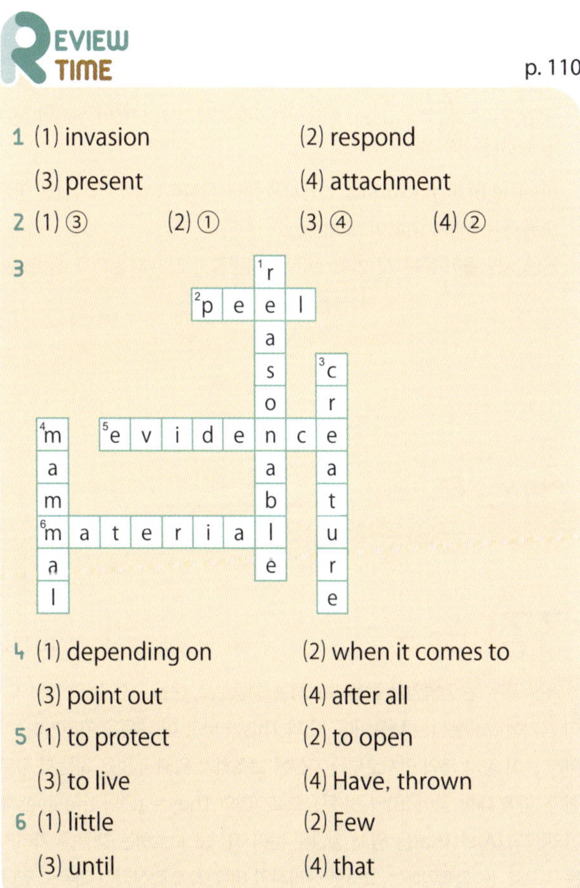

4 (1) depending on　　　(2) when it comes to
(3) point out　　　　　(4) after all

5 (1) to protect　　　　(2) to open
(3) to live　　　　　　(4) Have, thrown

6 (1) little　　　　　　(2) Few
(3) until　　　　　　　(4) that

1 (1) invade 침입하다, 침범하다 → invasion 침입, 침범
(2) response 반응 → respond 반응하다
(3) presence 존재 → present 존재하는, 참석한
(4) attach 첨부하다 → attachment 첨부물, 부속물

2 (1) darkness 어둠, 암흑 ↔ ③ brightness 밝음, 채광
(2) noisy 시끄러운, 떠들썩한 ↔ ① quiet 조용한

(3) indoors 실내에서 ↔ ④ ourdoors 실외에서

(4) unknown 알려지지 않은 ↔ ② well-known 잘 알려진, 유명한

5 (1) expect는 목적격 보어로 to부정사를 취해 '~이 …할 것을 기대하다'를 의미하므로, to protect가 알맞다.

(2) 가주어 It이 쓰였으므로 진주어 to부정사구가 되도록 to open이 쓰여야 한다.

(3) the desire를 '살지 않고자 하는'이라는 의미로 수식해야 하므로 형용사적 용법의 to부정사 to live가 알맞다.

(4) '~한 적이 있다'라고 경험을 이야기할 때는 현재완료시제 「have+과거분사」를 사용하므로 Have와 thrown이 알맞다.

6 (1) 셀 수 없는 명사인 evidence(증거)를 수식하는 것으로 양이 거의 없음을 나타내는 little이 알맞다.

해석 포유류가 음악적이려고 한다는 증거는 거의 없다.

(2) 셀 수 있는 명사인 mammals(포유류)를 수식하는 것으로 수가 거의 없음을 나타내는 few가 알맞다.

해석 조류만큼 많은 다양한 종류의 소리를 낼 수 있는 포유류는 거의 없다.

(3) '…하고 나서야 비로소 ~하다'라는 의미의 「not ~ until ....」 구문이 되도록 until이 쓰여야 한다.

해석 우리는 심지어 그것을 지적하는 이메일을 받고 나서야 우리의 실수를 깨닫는다.

(4) The first question을 선행사로 하는 목적격 관계대명사절을 이끌도록 관계대명사 that이 쓰여야 한다.

해석 사람들이 묻는 첫 번째 질문은 '자연광이 거기에 얼마나 들어오는가?'이다.

글의 순서 찾기

37 **정답** ⑤　　　　　　　　　　　　　　　　　　p. 112

주어진 글은 눈 깜빡임은 눈을 보호하는 행동으로, 눈을 뜨면 눈의 10분의 1이 공기에 노출된다는 내용이다. (C)의 This가 바로 이 내용을 가리키며, 이어서 눈이 공기 중의 먼지로부터 자신을 보호하기 위해 무엇을 하는지 질문한다. 이에 대한 답이 (B)의 첫 문장으로, (B)의 They는 (C)의 the eyes를 가리킨다. (A)의 That은 앞서 설명된 눈이 자신을 보호하는 행동을 가리키는 것으로, 눈 깜빡임에는 그러한 생리적인 이유 외에 정신적인 이유도 있다는 내용이 어이진다. 따라서 글의 순서로 가장 적절한 것은 ⑤이다.

READING GUIDE　(A) That　(B) They　(C) This

UNDERSTAND
DEEPLY　**1** protect, dust, worries, fear, stress, tension
　　　　　2 A layer of tears covers the eyes and washes away all the tiny bits of dust on them.

1 눈 깜빡임은 먼지로부터 눈을 보호하는 행동이며, 정신적 요인들도 눈을

깜빡이는 데 영향을 준다고 했다.

해석 우리가 눈을 깜빡이는 생리적인 이유는 공기 중에 있는 먼지로부터 눈을 보호하기 위함이다. 우리는 걱정, 두려움, 스트레스, 그리고 긴장과 같은 정신적인 이유들로도 눈을 깜빡인다.

2 (B)의 마지막 문장에서 눈을 깜빡일 때 어떤 작용이 일어나는지 구체적으로 설명하고 있다.

해석 Q: 우리가 눈을 깜빡일 때 어떤 일이 일어나는가? **A:** 눈물 막이 눈을 덮어서 눈 위에 있는 모든 작은 먼지를 씻어낸다.

READ CLOSELY　　　　　　　　　　　　　　　　　　p. 113

① Blinking is an action / that protects the eyes.

눈 깜빡임은 행동이다 / 눈을 보호하는

② When the eyes are open, / one-tenth of the total eye surface area / is exposed to the air.

눈이 뜨여 있을 때 / 전체 눈 표면적의 10분의 1이 / 공기에 노출된다

③ That is the physiological reason / behind blinking, / but we blink / for mental reasons as well.

그것은 생리적인 이유이다 / 눈 깜빡임의 이면에 있는 / 하지만 우리는 눈을 깜빡인다 / 정신적인 이유로도

④ For instance, / worries, fear, stress, and tension / have an effect on / the number of times / we blink.

예를 들어 / 걱정, 두려움, 스트레스, 그리고 긴장이 / ~에 영향을 미친다 / 횟수 / 우리가 눈을 깜빡이는

⑤ They blink.

그것들은 깜빡인다

⑥ Blinking makes the eyes / wet / and keeps / the front part of the eyes / clear / for good vision.

눈 깜빡임은 눈을 만든다 / 촉촉하게 / 그리고 유지해 준다 / 눈의 앞부분을 / 깨끗하게 / 좋은 시야를 위해

⑦ When we blink, / a layer of tears / covers the eyes / and washes away / all the tiny bits of dust / on them.

우리가 눈을 깜빡일 때 / 눈물 막이 / 눈을 덮는다 / 그리고 씻어낸다 / 모든 작은 먼지를 / 그것들 위에 있는

⑧ This means / the eye, / the weakest and most sensitive part of the body, / has to resist the dust / present in the air.

이것은 의미한다 / 눈이 / 신체에서 가장 약하고 가장 민감한 부위인 / 먼지에 저항해야 한다는 것을 / 공기 중에 존재하는

⑨ So, / what do the eyes do / to protect themselves?

그래서 / 눈은 무엇을 하는가 / 자신을 보호하기 위해

지문해석 눈 깜빡임은 눈을 보호하는 행동이다. 눈을 뜨면 전체 눈 표면적의 10분의 1이 공기에 노출된다. (C) 이것은 신체에서 가장 약하고 가장 민감한 부위인 눈이 공기 중에 존재하는 먼지에 저항해야 함을 의미한다. 그래서 눈

은 자신을 보호하기 위해 어떤 일을 하는가? (B) 눈은 깜빡인다. 눈 깜빡임은 눈을 적셔 주고 좋은 시야를 위해 눈의 앞부분을 깨끗하게 유지해 준다. 우리가 눈을 깜빡이면, 눈물 막이 눈을 덮어서 눈 위에 있는 모든 작은 먼지를 씻어낸다. (A) 그것은 눈 깜빡임의 이면에 있는 생리적인 이유이지만, 우리는 정신적인 이유로도 눈을 깜빡인다. 예를 들어, 걱정, 두려움, 스트레스, 그리고 긴장이 우리가 눈을 깜빡이는 횟수에 영향을 미친다.

문장 돋보기

⑥ Blinking makes the eyes wet and keeps the front
make + 목적어 + 목적격 보어(형용사): ~을 …하게 만들다
part of the eyes clear for good vision.
keep + 목적어 + 목적격 보어(형용사): ~을 …하게 유지하다

⑧ This means [(that) the eye, the weakest and most
명사절 접속사 that이 생략됨   that절의 주어   동격
sensitive part of the body, has to resist the dust
that절의 동사
{present in the air}].
형용사구

38 정답 ④ p. 114

주어진 글에 제시된 원숭이와 인간의 유사점에 대한 예로 원숭이 남매를 대상으로 한 실험을 소개하는 (B)가 이어지고, 바나나를 얻는 데 성공한 Kanzi를 관찰한 내용인 (C)가 먼저 온 후, Kanzi와 달리 칼을 만들지 못했으나 Kanzi의 도움으로 바나나를 얻은 Panbanisha에 대한 내용인 (A)가 이어지는 것이 자연스럽다. 따라서 글의 순서로 가장 적절한 것은 ④이다.

오답풀이 ①, ②, ③ (A)의 However는 주어진 글이 아니라 Kanzi가 칼을 만들어 바나나를 얻는 데 성공했다는 (C)에 대조되는 내용을 연결하는 연결어이므로 (C)의 뒤에 와야 한다. ⑤ Kanzi와 Panbanisha를 처음으로 소개한 (B)가 맨 앞에 와야 한다.

READING GUIDE (A) However, his sister Panbanisha (B) A team of researchers, a pair of bonobo monkeys named Kanzi and Panbanisha (C) The researchers

UNDERSTAND DEEPLY

1 (1) 칼 (2) 바나나 (3) 여자 형제 (4) 원숭이 (5) 가까움
2 (1) T (2) F

1 원숭이 남매 중 Kanzi는 칼을 잘 만들어 바나나를 얻었고, 그의 여자 형제인 Panbanisha가 이용할 수 있도록 자신의 칼을 몰래 놓아두었다고 했다. 이는 원숭이의 우애를 보여주는 것으로, 인간처럼 원숭이의 가족 간의 관계가 가까움을 알 수 있다.

2 (1) 보노보 원숭이 남매가 돌로 칼을 만드는 법을 배웠다고 했으므로 일치한다. (2) Kanzi의 도움으로 Panbanisha도 바나나를 얻었다고 했으므로 일치하지 않는다.

해석 (1) 두 보노보 원숭이가 모두 칼 만드는 법을 배웠다. (2) 두 보노보 원숭이 중 한 마리는 바나나를 얻지 못했다.

❶ Monkeys are similar to humans / in many ways.
원숭이들은 인간들과 유사하다 / 여러 면에서

❷ For example, / the relationships in a monkey family, / such as between brothers and sisters, / are often very close.
예를 들어 / 원숭이 가족에서의 관계들은 / 남매간 같은 / 종종 매우 가깝다

❸ However, / his sister Panbanisha / could not make a knife.
그러나 / 그의 여자 형제 Panbanisha는 / 칼을 만들 수 없었다

❹ The researchers did not let Kanzi / give his knife / to her.
연구원들은 Kanzi가 ~하지 못하게 했다 / 그의 칼을 주지 / 그녀에게

❺ So, / Kanzi secretly put his knife / where his sister could easily find it, / and she finally got her banana.
그래서 / Kanzi는 그의 칼을 몰래 두었다 / 그의 여자 형제가 그것을 쉽게 찾을 수 있는 곳에 / 그리고 그녀는 마침내 그녀의 바나나를 얻었다

❻ A team of researchers studied / a pair of bonobo monkeys / named Kanzi and Panbanisha.
한 연구팀은 연구했다 / 보노보 원숭이 한 쌍을 / Kanzi와 Panbanisha라고 이름 지어진

❼ The brother and sister learned / how to make knives / from stones.
그 남매는 배웠다 / 칼을 만드는 방법을 / 돌로

❽ The researchers decided to record / how good they were / at making knives.
연구원들은 녹화하기로 했다 / 그들이 얼마나 능숙한지를 / 칼을 만드는 것에

❾ The researchers got two boxes / and put a banana / in each box.
연구원들은 상자 두 개를 가져왔다 / 그리고 바나나 한 개를 두었다 / 각 상자 안에

❿ Then / they gave the bonobos / whatever they needed / to make a knife.
그러고 나서 / 그들은 보노보들에게 주었다 / 그들이 필요로 한 것은 무엇이든지 / 칼을 만들기 위해

⓫ Kanzi made / a very good knife.
Kanzi는 만들었다 / 매우 좋은 칼을

⓬ With the knife, / he cut open his box / and succeeded in / getting the banana.
그 칼을 가지고 / 그는 그의 상자를 잘라서 열었다 / 그리고 ~에 성공했다 / 그 바나나를 얻는 것

지문해석 원숭이는 여러 면에서 인간과 유사하다. 예를 들어, 원숭이가 가족에서 남매 사이 같은 관계들은 종종 매우 가깝다. (B) 한 연구팀은 Kanzi와 Panbanisha라는 이름의 보노보 원숭이 한 쌍을 연구했다. 그 남매는 돌로 칼을 만드는 방법을 배웠다. 연구원들은 그들이 얼마나 칼을 잘 만드는지를 녹화하기로 했다. (C) 연구원들은 상자 두 개를 가져와서 각 상자 안에 바나나 한 개씩을 두었다. 그리고 나서 그들은 보노보들에게 그들이 칼을 만들기 위해 필요로 한 것은 무엇이든지 주었다. Kanzi는 매우 좋은 칼을 만들었다. 그 칼로 그는 자신의 상자를 잘라서 열고 바나나를 얻는 데 성공했다. (A) 그러나 그의 여자 형제 Panbanisha는 칼을 만들지 못했다. 연구원들은 Kanzi가 그의 칼을 그녀에게 주지 못하게 했다. 그래서 Kanzi는 몰래 그의 칼을 그의 여자 형제가 쉽게 찾을 수 있는 곳에 두었고, 그녀는 마침내 바나나를 얻었다.

문장 돋보기

⑧ The researchers decided [to record how good
they were at making knives].

⑩ Then they gave the bonobos [whatever they
needed to make a knife].

39 정답 ②   p. 116

주어진 글은 인간은 습관의 동물이라는 내용으로, (B)에서 이를 부연 설명하고 있으며, (B)의 마지막 문장의 ninety-five를 (A)에서 that particular number로 받아 내용을 이어가고 있다. 또한, (A)의 마지막 문장에서 언급되기 시작한 습관 형성 과정이 (C)에서 이어지고 있다. 따라서 글의 순서로 가장 적절한 것은 ②이다.

오답풀이 ③, ⑤ (C)의 that thread는 (A)의 a kind of invisible thread를 가리키므로 답이 될 수 없다.

READING GUIDE (A) that particular number, a kind of invisible thread (B) In fact, we're even more the result of habit, ninety-five (C) But, that thread

UNDERSTAND DEEPLY 1 habit, habit 2 repetition

1 우리는 습관의 동물이며, 정확한 수치에는 이견이 있을 수 있지만 95% 정도의 행동이 습관을 통해 형성될 만큼 습관이 우리에게 큰 영향을 미친다고 했다.

해석 인간은 습관의 동물이며, 인간 행동의 많은 부분이 습관을 통해 형성된다.

2 (C)에서 우리는 어떤 행동을 반복함으로써 그것을 강화하고 습관을 만들어 나간다고 했다.

해석 Q: 우리는 어떻게 어떤 행동을 우리의 습관으로 만드는가? A: 우리는 그 행동의 반복을 통해서 그렇게 한다.

READ CLOSELY   p. 117

❶ We're creatures of habit, / and I've never seen anyone / argue against that old expression.

우리는 습관의 동물이다 / 그리고 나는 그 누구도 결코 본 적이 없다 / 그 오래된 표현에 대해 이의를 제기하는 것을

❷ It's probably because there's so much truth / to it.

그것은 아마도 그만큼 많은 진실이 있기 때문이다 / 그것에

❸ While someone might disagree with / that particular number, / it is clear / that our habits have a powerful effect on us.

누군가 ~에 동의하지 않을지도 모르지만 / 그 특정한 수치 / 분명하다 / 우리의 습관이 우리에게 강력한 영향을 미친다는 것은

❹ Most of them start / innocently and unintentionally.

그것들의 대부분은 시작된다 / 순수하게 무심코

❺ At the beginning, / they form / a kind of invisible thread.

처음에 / 그것들은 형성한다 / 일종의 보이지 않는 실을

❻ In fact, / we're even more the result of habit / than most people realize.

사실 / 우리는 훨씬 더 습관의 결과물이다 / 대부분의 사람들이 깨닫는 것보다

❼ Some psychologists believe / that up to ninety-five percent of our behavior / is formed / through habit.

어떤 심리학자들은 믿는다 / 우리 행동의 95퍼센트까지가 / 형성된다고 / 습관을 통해

❽ But through repetition, / that thread becomes twisted / into a cord / and later into a rope.

하지만 반복을 통해 / 그 실은 꼬이게 된다 / 끈으로 / 그리고 나중에는 밧줄로

❾ Each time we repeat an act, / we add to it / and strengthen it.

우리가 어떤 행동을 반복할 때마다 / 우리는 그것에 더한다 / 그리고 그것을 강화한다

❿ The rope becomes a chain / and then a cable.

그 밧줄은 사슬이 된다 / 그런 다음에는 굵은 철제 밧줄이

⓫ Eventually, / we become our habits.

결국 / 우리는 우리의 습관이 된다

⓬ As English poet John Dryden said, / we first make our habits, / and then our habits make us.

영국의 시인 John Dryden이 말했듯이 / 우리는 먼저 우리의 습관을 만든다 / 그리고 나서 우리의 습관이 우리를 만든다

우리는 습관의 동물이며, 나는 이 오래된 표현에 대해 그 누구도 이의를 제기하는 것을 본 적이 없다. 이는 아마도 그 말에는 그만큼 많은 진실이 있기 때문일 것이다. (B) 사실, 우리는 대부분의 사람들이 깨닫고 있는 것보다 훨씬 더 습관의 결과물이다. 어떤 심리학자들은 우리 행동의 95퍼센트까지가 습관을 통해 형성된다고 믿는다. (A) 누군가는 그 특정한 수치에 동의하지 않을지도 모르지만, 우리의 습관이 우리에게 강력한 영향을 미친다는 것은 분명하다. 그것들의 대부분은 순수하게 무심코 시작된다. 처음에 그것들은 일종의 보이지 않는 실을 형성한다. (C) 하지만 반복을 통해 그 실은 끈으로 꼬이게 되고 이후에는 밧줄로 꼬이게 된다. 우리가 어떤 행동을 반복할 때마다, 우리는 그것에 더하고 그것을 강화한다. 그 밧줄은 사슬이 되고, 그런 다음 굵은 철제 밧줄이 된다. 결국, 우리는 우리의 습관이 된다. 영국의 시인 John Dryden이 말했듯이 우리가 먼저 우리의 습관을 만들고 나면 우리의 습관이 우리를 만든다.

문장 돋보기

❶ We're creatures of habit, and I've never seen
현재완료 경험(본 적 없다)
anyone argue against that old expression.
지각동사 see + 목적어 + 목적격 보어(동사원형): ~이 …하는 것을 보다

❷ Some psychologists believe [that up to ninety-
주어   동사   목적어(that절)
five percent of our behavior is formed through
that절의 주어   that절의 동사(수동태)
habit].

REVIEW TIME

1 (1) protection   (2) success
    (3) repetition   (4) strength

2 (1) invisible   (2) eventually
    (3) innocently   (4) relationship
    (5) present   (6) sensitive

3

P	Q	B	Z	P	D	H	P	C	E	V	L
S	L	O	J	T	A	M	N	W	O	L	Y
J	P	N	M	B	E	H	A	V	I	O	R
S	A	G	P	L	P	S	T	O	Y	W	O
B	R	E	S	I	S	T	I	H	R	P	T
A	T	S	V	N	L	E	C	R	D	J	D
E	I	X	K	K	V	L	L	U	M	F	H
F	C	Z	U	C	S	I	O	A	Q	R	Y
L	U	Q	D	B	N	V	S	T	U	D	Y
H	L	T	X	E	I	P	E	I	I	B	L
C	A	E	J	Z	K	W	X	A	O	S	Y
X	R	G	L	U	H	R	G	B	U	N	N

  (1) particular   (2) vision   (3) study
  (4) resist   (5) behavior   (6) close

4 (1) be similar to   (2) have an effect on
    (3) be good at   (4) succeed in

5 (1) start   (2) even   (3) clear   (4) has

6 (1) wet   (2) give   (3) is   (4) ○

1 (1) protect 보호하다 → protection 보호
   (2) succeed 성공하다 → success 성공
   (3) repeat 반복하다 → repetition 반복
   (4) strengthen 강화하다 → strength 힘

5 (1) most of 다음에 복수 명사가 왔으므로 복수 동사 start가 알맞다.
해석 그 습관들의 대부분은 순수하게 무심코 시작된다.
   (2) 비교급 more를 강조하는 부사로 even이 알맞다. very는 원급이나 최상급을 수식할 때 쓰인다.
해석 우리는 대부분의 사람들이 깨닫고 있는 것보다 훨씬 더 습관의 결과물이다.
   (3) 동사 keep은 목적격 보어로 형용사를 써서 '~을 …하게 만들다'를 의미하므로 clear가 알맞다.
해석 눈 깜빡임은 좋은 시야를 위해 눈의 앞부분을 깨끗하게 유지해 준다.
   (4) 핵심 주어가 the eye이므로 단수 동사 has가 알맞다.
해석 이것은 신체에서 가장 약한 부위인 눈이 먼지에 저항해야 함을 의미한다.

6 (1) 동사 make는 목적격 보어로 형용사를 써서 '~을 …하게 만들다'를 의미하므로 wet이 알맞다.
해석 눈 깜빡임은 눈을 촉촉하게 만든다.

(2) 사역동사 let은 목적격 보어로 동사원형을 취하므로 give가 알맞다.

 연구원들은 Kanzi가 그의 칼을 그의 여자 형제에게 주지 못하게 했다.

(3) Ninety-five percent of 다음에 단수 명사가 왔으므로 동사로 단수형 is가 알맞다.

 우리 행동의 95퍼센트가 습관을 통해 형성된다.

(4) '그들이 칼을 만들기 위해 필요로 한 것은 무엇이든지'라는 의미의 명사절을 이끄는 복합관계대명사 whatever의 쓰임은 알맞다.

 연구원들은 보노보들에게 그들이 칼을 만들기 위해 필요로 한 것은 무엇이든지 주었다.

PART 4 흐름 파악하기

UNIT 13

주어진 문장 넣기

40 정답 ② p. 120

주어진 문장은 실제로 상어가 공격할 가능성은 매우 적다는 내용이고, However로 시작하므로 글의 흐름이 전환되는 곳에 들어가야 한다. 따라서 사람들이 상어 때문에 바다 수영이 위험하다고 믿게 되었다는 내용과, 실제로는 상어 공격의 위험보다 해변을 오가며 운전하는 동안의 위험이 더 크다는 내용의 사이인 ②에 주어진 문장이 들어가는 것이 가장 적절하다.

READING GUIDE However, a shark attack

UNDERSTAND DEEPLY

1 작은 해변 마을에서의 일련의 상어 공격의 영상들

2 (1) F (2) F (3) T

1 세 번째 문장의 These images는 앞 문장의 images of a series of shark attacks in a small beach town을 가리킨다.

2 (1) 영화 〈죠스〉는 상어의 공격에 대한 공포감을 자아내어 많은 사람들로 하여금 바다 수영을 시도하지 못하게 했다고 했으므로 일치하지 않는 내용이다. (2) 2007년에 71건의 상어 공격과 1건의 사망이 있었다고 했으므로 일치하지 않는 내용이다. (3) 2007년, 상어의 공격으로 인한 사망률이 벌과 뱀의 공격으로 인한 사망률보다 훨씬 더 낮았다고 했으므로 일치하는 내용이다.

 (1) 1975년 영화 〈죠스〉는 많은 사람들이 바다 수영을 시도하도록 용기를 북돋웠다. (2) 2007년에는 상어 공격에 의한 사망이 없었다. (3) 2007년, 벌에 쏘이고 뱀에 물리는 것으로 인한 사망률이 상어 공격으로 인한 것(사망률)보다 높았다.

READ CLOSELY p. 121

❶ However, / the actual chance of a shark attack / is very small.

하지만 / 상어 공격의 실제 가능성은 / 매우 적다

❷ Fear of sharks / has kept many pool swimmers / from testing the ocean water.

상어에 대한 두려움은 / 풀장에서 수영하는 많은 사람들을 못하게 해 왔다 / 바닷물을 시험하는 것을

❸ The 1975 movie *Jaws* provided / images of a series of shark attacks / in a small beach town.

1975년 영화 〈죠스〉는 제공했다 / 일련의 상어 공격의 영상들을 / 작은 해변 마을에서의

❹ These images made many people / believe / that ocean swimming is only for these big fish.

이 영상들은 많은 사람들을 만들었다 / 믿게 / 바다 수영이 이 큰 물고기들만을 위한 것이라고

❺ In reality, / you are at greater risk / while driving to and from the beach.

사실 / 여러분은 더 큰 위험에 처한다 / 해변을 오고 가며 운전하는 동안

❻ According to the International Shark Attack File, / there is a low number of shark attacks / and these big fish / do not feed on humans / by nature.

국제 상어 공격 파일에 따르면 / 적은 수의 상어 공격이 있다 / 그리고 이 큰 물고기들은 / 인간을 먹고 살지 않는다 / 본래

❼ Most shark attacks / simply happen / because of sharks / mistaking humans for fish.

대부분의 상어 공격은 / 단순히 발생한다 / 상어들 때문에 / 인간을 물고기로 착각하는

❽ In 2007, / there were 71 reported shark attacks / worldwide / and only one death.

2007년에 / 71건의 보고된 상어 공격이 있었다 / 전 세계적으로 / 그리고 단 한 건의 사망이

❾ It is much lower / than the 2007 death rate / for bee stings and snake bites.

그것은 훨씬 더 낮다 / 2007년 사망률보다 / 벌에 쏘이고 뱀에 물리는 것으로 인한

 상어에 대한 두려움은 풀장에서 수영하는 많은 사람들이 바닷물을 시험해 보지 못하게 해 왔다. 1975년 영화 〈죠스〉는 작은 해변 마을에서의 일련의 상어 공격의 영상들을 제공했다. 이 영상들은 많은 사람들이 바다 수영은 이 큰 물고기들만을 위한 것이라고 믿게 만들었다. 하지만 상어 공격의 실제 가능성은 매우 적다. 사실 여러분은 해변을 오고 가며 운전하는 동안 더 큰 위험에 처한다. 국제 상어 공격 파일에 따르면 상어 공격의 수는 적고, 이 큰 물고기들은 본래 인간을 먹고 살지 않는다. 대부분의 상어 공격은 단순히 인간을 물고기로 착각하는 상어들 때문에 발생한다. 2007년에 전 세계적으로 71건의 보고된 상어 공격과 단 한 건의 사망이 있었다. 그것은 벌에 쏘이고 뱀에 물리는 것으로 인한 2007년 사망률보다 훨씬 더 낮다.

❷ Fear of sharks has kept many pool swimmers from
keep+목적어+from+동명사: ~이 …하지 못하게 하다
testing the ocean water.

❹ These images made many people believe [that
사역동사 make+목적어+목적격 보어(동사원형): ~이 …하게 하다
ocean swimming is only for these big fish].
believe의 목적어(that절)

41 정답 ③ p. 122

주어진 문장은 길거리에 더 많은 경찰을 배치하는 대신에 클래식 음악을 재생하기로 했다는 내용이다. 이는 마을에 길거리 범죄가 늘어나자 지역 주민들이 거리에서 위험인물들을 없앨 방법을 생각해 냈다는 내용과, 클래식 음악으로 모차르트, 바흐, 베토벤의 음악을 재생했다는 내용 사이인 ③에 들어가는 것이 가장 적절하다.

READING GUIDE classical music / the music of Mozart, Bach, and Beethoven

UNDERSTAND DEEPLY 1 ② 2 (1) 길거리 범죄 (2) 클래식 음악 (3) 위험인물 (4) 기차역 (5) 클래식 음악

1 이 글은 클래식 음악을 재생하여 길거리 범죄를 감소시켰다는 내용으로, 마지막 문장에서 클래식 음악이 범죄 감소에 매우 효과적인 것으로 보인다는 결론이 제시되었다. 따라서 글의 주제로 가장 적절한 것은 ②이다.
해석 ① 길거리 범죄의 급격한 증가 이유 ② 범죄를 줄이는 것에 대한 클래식 음악의 효과 ③ 사회 문제를 해결하는 데 있어서의 수학의 중요성 ④ 호주에서의 클래식 음악 인기 감소

2 (1) 길거리 범죄 수가 2년 전보다 훨씬 더 많았다. (2), (3) 어두워진 후 주요 거리에서 위험인물들을 없애기 위한 방법으로 클래식 음악을 재생하기로 했다. (4) 덴마크 코펜하겐에 있는 주요 기차역이 농일한 해결책을 채택했다. (5) 마지막 문장에서 클래식 음악이 범죄 감소에 매우 효과적인 것으로 보인다고 했다.

READ CLOSELY p. 123

❶ Instead of putting more police / on the street, / they chose to play classical music.
더 많은 경찰을 배치하는 대신에 / 길거리에 / 그들은 클래식 음악을 재생하기를 택했다

❷ A very interesting experiment / took place / in a small Australian village.
매우 흥미로운 실험이 / 실시되었다 / 어느 작은 호주 마을에서

❸ At that time, / the number of street crimes in the village / was much higher / than two years earlier, / and it was still rapidly increasing.

그 당시 / 그 마을에서의 길거리 범죄 수는 / 훨씬 더 많았다 / 2년 전보다 / 그리고 그것은 여전히 빠르게 증가하고 있었다

❹ Local people, / scared by the increase in street crime, / got together / and decided on the best way / to deal with the problem.
지역 사람들은 / 길거리 범죄 증가에 겁을 먹은 / 한데 모였다 / 그리고 최선의 방법을 결정했다 / 그 문제를 처리할

❺ The idea was / to remove the dangerous characters / from the main street / after dark.
그 아이디어는 ~이었다 / 위험인물들을 없애는 것 / 주요 거리에서 / 어두워진 후에

❻ Loud speakers began playing / the music of Mozart, Bach, and Beethoven.
소리가 큰 스피커들이 재생하기 시작했다 / 모차르트, 바흐 그리고 베토벤의 음악을

❼ In less than a week, / the village reported / a rapid decrease in crime.
일주일도 안 되어 / 그 마을은 보고했다 / 범죄의 빠른 감소를

❽ The experiment was so successful / that the main train station in Copenhagen, Denmark / adopted the same solution / —with similar results, too.
그 실험은 매우 성공적이었다 / 그래서 덴마크 코펜하겐에 있는 주요 기차역이 / 동일한 해결책을 채택했다 / 역시 비슷한 결과와 함께

❾ It seems / that classical music is very effective / for reducing crime.
~인 것 같다 / 클래식 음악이 매우 효과적인 / 범죄를 줄이는 데

지문해석 매우 흥미로운 실험이 어느 작은 호주 마을에서 실시되었다. 그 당시 그 마을에서의 길거리 범죄 수는 2년 전보다 훨씬 더 많았고 그것은 여전히 빠르게 승가하고 있었다. 지역 사람들은 길거리 범죄 증가에 겁을 먹어 한데 모여서 그 문제를 처리하기 위한 최선의 방법을 결정했다. 그 아이디어는 어두워진 후에 주요 거리에서 위험인물들을 제거하는 것이었다. 길거리에 더 많은 경찰을 배치하는 대신에, 그들은 클래식 음악을 재생하는 것을 택했다. 소리가 큰 스피커가 모차르트, 바흐 그리고 베토벤의 음악을 재생하기 시작했다. 일주일도 안 되어 그 마을은 범죄의 급격한 감소를 보고했다. 그 실험이 매우 성공적이어서 덴마크 코펜하겐에 있는 주요 기차역이 동일한 해결책을 채택했는데, 역시 비슷한 결과를 얻었다. 클래식 음악이 범죄를 줄이는 데 매우 효과적인 것으로 보인다.

④ Local people, [scared by the increase in street
　　　　　주어　　　　과거분사구
crime], got together and decided on the best way
　　　　　　동사1　　　　　　동사2
[to deal with the problem].
　　to부정사의 형용사적 용법

⑧ The experiment was so successful [that the main
　　　　　　　　　so+형용사+that+절: 너무 ~해서 …하다
train station {in Copenhagen, Denmark} adopted
that절의 주어　　　수식어구　　　　　　　　that절의 동사
the same solution — with similar results, too].

⑨ It seems [that classical music is very effective for
가주어　　　　　　　진주어(that절)
reducing crime].

42　정답 ⑤　　　　　　　　　　　　　p. 124

글의 흐름을 전환하는 연결어 however를 포함하는 주어진 문장은 시간이
지나면서 사람들은 자신이 가지고 있는 좋은 것들에 익숙해져서 그것들을
의식하지 못하게 된다는 내용이다. 이는 사람들이 가지고 있는 행복한 것들
의 예를 언급하는 문장 다음이자 관련 속담으로 내용을 정리하는 문장 앞인
⑤에 들어가는 것이 가장 적절하다.

READING GUIDE however

UNDERSTAND DEEPLY

1 옛말에서 그러하듯이, 여러분은 그것이 사라질 때까지 여
러분이 무엇을 가지고 있는지 알지 못한다(여러분은 그것이
사라지고 나서야 비로소 여러분이 무엇을 가지고 있는지 알
게 된다). **2** disappears, pleasant, forget
3 Exactly the same

1 이 글은 사람들은 자신이 이미 가지고 있는 것에 익숙해져 그것이 사라지
기 전까지는 그 소중함을 의식하지 못한다는 내용으로, 마지막 문장에 제
시된 옛말에 이러한 글의 요지가 잘 드러나 있다.

2 시간이 지남에 따라 갓 구운 빵 냄새를 의식하지 못하게 되는 것처럼, 가
지고 있는 것들에 익숙해져서 그것들을 기억하지 못하게 된다고 했다.
해석 갓 구운 빵 냄새가 우리의 의식에서 사라지는 것처럼, 우리는 우리
가 가지고 있는 기분 좋은 것들에 익숙해져서 그것들을 잊게 된다.

3 이 글은 갓 구운 빵 냄새가 의식에서 사라지는 것과 관련된 비유 부분
(When ~ again.)과, 이 개념을 삶에 적용한 본론 부분(Exactly ~
gone.)으로 나눌 수 있다.

READ CLOSELY　　　　　　　　　　　p. 125

❶ As time passes, / however, / people get used to / what
they have / and, just like the smell of bread, / these
wonderful things / disappear from their consciousness.

시간이 지남에 따라 / 그러나 / 사람들은 ~에 익숙해진다 / 그들이 가진

것 / 그리고 빵 냄새와 마찬가지로 / 이러한 멋진 것들은 / 그들의 의식에
서 사라진다

❷ When walking into a room / that smells of freshly
baked bread, / you quickly sense the pleasant aroma.

방으로 걸어 들어갈 때 / 갓 구운 빵 냄새가 나는 / 여러분은 그 기분 좋은
향기를 재빨리 감지한다

❸ However, / if you stay there / for a few minutes, / the
smell will seem to disappear.

그러나 / 여러분이 그곳에 머무르면 / 몇 분 동안 / 그 냄새는 사라지는 것
같을 것이다

❹ You won't even be able to remember / the good
feeling / you got / when you stepped into the room.

여러분은 심지어 기억할 수 없을 것이다 / 그 좋은 감정을 / 여러분이 가졌
던 / 여러분이 그 방으로 걸어 들어갔을 때

❺ In fact, / the only way / to feel it again / is to walk out
of the room / and come back in again.

사실 / 유일한 방법은 / 그것을 다시 느끼는 / 그 방에서 걸어 나가는 것이
다 / 그리고 다시 들어오는 것

❻ Exactly the same concept / applies to many areas of
our lives, / including happiness.

정확히 같은 개념이 / 우리 삶의 많은 영역에 적용된다 / 행복을 포함하여

❼ Everyone has something / to be happy about: / a
lovely spouse, / good health, / or a satisfying job.

모든 사람들은 어떤 것을 가지고 있다 / 행복해할 만한 / 사랑스러운 배우
자 / 좋은 건강 / 또는 만족스러운 직업

❽ As the old saying goes, / you don't know / what you've
got / till it's gone.

옛말에서 그러하듯이 / 여러분은 모른다 / 여러분이 무엇을 가지고 있는지
/ 그것이 사라질 때까지

지문해석 갓 구운 빵 냄새가 나는 방으로 걸어 들어갈 때 여러분은 그 기분
좋은 향기를 재빨리 감지하게 된다. 그러나 여러분이 그곳에 몇 분 동안 머무
르면 그 냄새는 사라지는 것 같을 것이다. 여러분은 심지어 여러분이 그 방으
로 걸어 들어갈 때 가졌던 그 좋은 감정을 기억할 수 없을 것이다. 사실 그것
을 다시 느끼는 유일한 방법은 그 방에서 걸어 나갔다가 다시 들어오는 것이
다. 정확히 같은 개념이 행복을 포함하여 우리 삶의 많은 영역에 적용된다. 모
든 사람들은 사랑스러운 배우자, 좋은 건강, 또는 만족스러운 직업과 같이 행
복할 만한 어떤 것을 가지고 있다. 하지만 시간이 지나면서 사람들은 그들
이 가진 것에 익숙해지고, 빵 냄새와 마찬가지로 이러한 멋진 것들은 그들의
의식에서 사라진다. 옛말에서 그러하듯이 여러분은 그것이 사라지고 나서야
비로소 여러분이 무엇을 가지고 있었는지 깨닫게 된다.

❹ You won't even be able to remember the good
~할 수 없을 것이다 (won't can (×))

feeling [(which[that]) you got when you stepped
목적격 관계대명사절

into the room].

❺ In fact, the only way [to feel it again] is to walk out
사실　　주어　　to부정사의 형용사적 용법　　동사

of the room and come back in again.

REVIEW TIME

p. 126

1 (1) chance, possibility　(2) give, provide
　(3) smell, aroma　(4) rapidly, quickly
2 (1) solution　(2) effective
　(3) satisfying　(4) appear
3 8. 개념

4 (1) deal with　(2) feed on
　(3) get used to　(4) take place
5 (1) interesting　(2) believe
　(3) mistaking　(4) scared
6 (1) As, what　(2) As, what　(3) so, that

1 (1) chance, possibility 가능성 / result 결과
　(2) give, provide 주다, 제공하다 / choose 선택하다
　(3) smell 냄새, aroma 향기, (좋은) 냄새 / area 영역, 분야
　(4) rapidly, quickly 빠르게, 빨리 / actually 실제로, 사실은

2 (1) solve 해결하다 → solution 해결책
　(2) effect 효과 → effective 효과적인
　(3) satisfy 만족시키다 → satisfying 만족스러운
　(4) disappear 사라지다 → appear 나타나다

5 (1) 명사 experiment를 능동의 의미('흥미로운')로 수식해야 하므로 현재분사 interesting이 알맞다.
　해석 어느 작은 마을에서 매우 흥미로운 실험이 실시되었다.
　(2) 사역동사 make는 목적격 보어로 동사원형을 취하므로 believe가 알맞다.

해석 이러한 영상들은 사람들로 하여금 바다 수영이 위험하다고 믿게 했다.
　(3) 명사 sharks를 능동의 의미('착각하는')로 수식해야 하므로 현재분사 mistaking이 알맞다.
　해석 대부분의 상어 공격은 인간을 물고기로 착각하는 상어들 때문에 일어난다.
　(4) 주어인 Local people이 '겁을 먹은' 것이므로 수동을 의미하는 과거분사 scared가 알맞다.
　해석 지역 사람들은 길거리 범죄 증가에 겁을 먹어 그 문제를 처리하기 위한 방법을 결정했다.

6 (1) '~함에 따라'는 접속사 as로 표현하며, '자신이 가지고 있는 것'이라는 명사절을 이끄는 것으로 선행사를 포함하는 관계대명사 what이 알맞다.
　(2) '~하듯이'는 접속사 as로 표현하며, '여러분이 무엇을 가지고 있는지'는 의문사 what이 이끄는 간접의문문으로 표현할 수 있다.
　(3) '너무[매우] ~해서 …하다'는 「so+형용사+that+절」로 표현하므로 so와 that이 알맞다.

Play Time

▶ 올바른 등식이 되도록 성냥을 한 개씩 옮기세요.

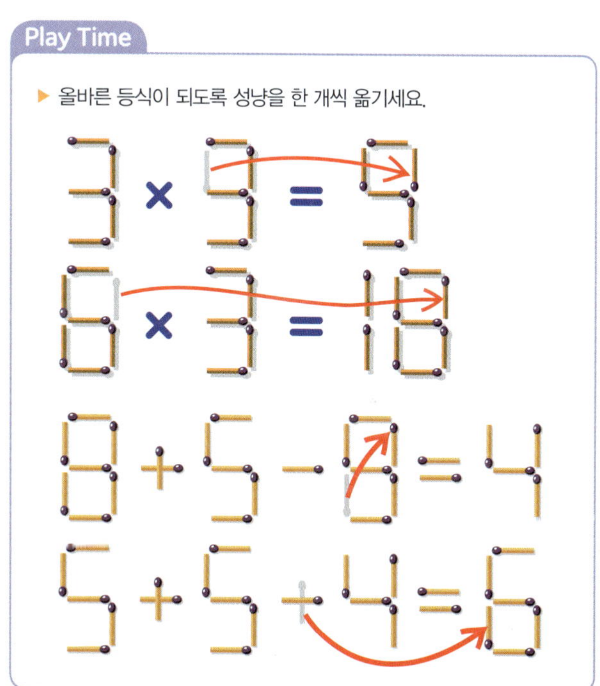

UNIT 14 장문 이해하기

43 정답 1 ④ 2 ③   p. 130

1 도입부에서 엄마들이 임신 중에 먹는 것과 아기들이 출생 후에 즐기는 음식이 연관되어 있다고 한 후 관련 연구 사례에 대한 내용이 이어지고 있다. 따라서 글의 제목으로 가장 적절한 것은 ④ '엄마가 먹는 것이 아기의 입맛에 영향을 미친다'이다.

오답풀이 ① 건강을 위해서 식단을 바꿔라 ② 당근을 사용하는 요리법에 대해 배워라 ③ 아기의 성장에 중요한 시기 ⑤ 건강에 좋은 음식을 먹는 것을 권하는 다양한 방법들

2 엄마 뱃속에서 당근 주스의 맛을 경험한 아기들과 경험하지 않은 아기들을 비교한 연구에서 당근 주스에 거부 반응을 보이고 불만스러운 표정을 지은 아기들은 출생 전에 엄마 뱃속에서 당근 주스를 맛본 경험이 없었던 아기들이므로, 빈칸에 들어갈 말로 가장 적절한 것은 ③ '없었던'이다.

오답풀이 ① 사용했던 ② 잊었던 ④ 기억해 냈던 ⑤ 극복했던

READING GUIDE **1** interesting connections between what moms eat while pregnant and what foods their babies enjoy after birth **2 ④**

UNDERSTAND DEEPLY **1** healthy foods, pregnant
2 (1) 당근 주스 (2) 물 (3) 3주 (4) 당근 주스 (5) 시리얼 (6) 당근 주스 (7) 물 **3** preferences, experience

1 아기들이 태어나기도 전에 엄마가 임신 중 먹는 것을 맛보고 기억하고 그것에 대한 선호를 형성한다고 했으므로, 임신 중 건강한 음식을 먹음으로써 아기들이 건강한 음식을 좋아하도록 도울 수 있다고 할 수 있다.

해석 Q: 엄마들은 어떻게 자신의 아기들이 건강에 좋은 음식을 좋아하도록 도울 수 있는가? A: 그들은 임신 중에 건강에 좋은 음식을 먹음으로써 도울 수 있다.

2 Consider an interesting study about carrot juice. 이후로 당근 주스 또는 물을 섭취한 여성들과 그들의 아기들을 대상으로 한 구체적인 연구 내용이 전개되고 있다.

3 태어나기 전에 엄마 뱃속에서 특정 음식을 맛본 경험이 아기의 음식에 대한 선호에 영향을 준다고 했다.

해석 아기들의 음식에 대한 선호는 태어나기 전 그들이 그것을 맛본 경험과 관계가 있다.

READ CLOSELY   p. 132

❶ We can help our babies / learn to love healthy foods / even before they're born.

우리는 우리의 아기들을 도울 수 있다 / 건강에 좋은 음식들을 좋아하는 법을 배우도록 / 심지어 그들이 태어나기도 전에

❷ The latest science shows / interesting connections / between what moms eat while pregnant and what foods their babies enjoy after birth.

최신 과학은 보여 준다 / 흥미로운 연관성을 / 엄마들이 임신 중에 무엇을 먹는지와 그들의 아기들이 출생 후에 무슨 음식을 즐기는지 사이의

❸ Hard to believe, / but it's true.

믿기 어렵다 / 하지만 그것은 사실이다

❹ Babies taste, / remember, / and form preferences for / what Mom has eaten.

아기들은 맛본다 / 기억한다 / 그리고 ~에 대한 선호를 형성한다 / 엄마가 먹은 것

❺ Consider an interesting study / about carrot juice.

한 흥미로운 연구를 생각해 보아라 / 당근 주스에 대한

❻ As part of the study, / one group of pregnant women / drank carrot juice / four times a week / for three weeks.

그 연구의 일환으로 / 한 집단의 임신한 여성들은 / 당근 주스를 마셨다 / 주 4회 / 3주 동안

❼ Another group of women in the study / drank water.

그 연구에서의 또 다른 집단의 여성들은 / 물을 마셨다

❽ When their babies were old enough / to start eating cereal, / it was time to look for a difference / between the groups.

그들의 아기들이 충분히 나이를 먹었을 때 / 시리얼을 먹기 시작할 만큼 / 차이점을 찾아볼 때였다 / 그 집단들 간의

❾ A researcher / who didn't know / which group each baby belonged to / studied the babies / as they ate cereal / mixed with carrot juice.

한 연구원이 / 몰랐던 / 각 아기가 어느 집단에 속했는지 / 아기들을 연구했다 / 그들이 시리얼을 먹었을 때 / 당근 주스와 섞인

❿ The babies / who lacked the earlier experience of tasting carrot juice / refused / and made unhappy faces / about the taste.

아기들은 / 당근 주스를 맛본 이전의 경험이 없었던 / 거부했다 / 그리고 불만스러운 표정을 지었다 / 그 맛에 대해

⓫ On the other hand, / the other group of babies / easily accepted and enjoyed / the carrot juice in the cereal.

반면에 / 다른 집단의 아기들은 / 쉽게 받아들였고 즐겼다 / 시리얼에 있는 당근 주스를

⓬ There was a big difference / between babies who experienced carrot juice before they were born and babies who didn't.

큰 차이가 있었다 / 태어나기 전에 당근 주스를 경험한 아기들과 그러지(경험하지) 않은 아기들 사이에

지문해석 우리는 아기들이 태어나기도 전에 그들이 건강에 좋은 음식들을 좋아하는 법을 배우도록 도울 수 있다. 최신 과학은 엄마들이 임신 중에 무엇을

먹는지와 그들의 아기들이 출생 후 무슨 음식을 즐기는지 간의 흥미로운 연관성을 보여 준다. 믿기 어렵지만 그것은 사실이다. 아기들은 엄마가 먹은 것을 맛보고, 기억하고, 선호하게 된다. 당근 주스에 대한 한 흥미로운 연구를 생각해 보아라. 그 연구의 일환으로 한 임신한 여성 집단은 3주 동안 주 4회 당근 주스를 마셨다. 그 연구에서의 또 다른 여성 집단은 물을 마셨다. 그들의 아기들이 시리얼을 먹기 시작할 만큼 충분한 개월 수가 되었을 때, 이제 그 집단들 간의 차이점을 살펴볼 시간이었다. 각 아기가 어느 집단에 속하는지 모르는 한 연구원이 아기들을 당근 주스와 섞인 시리얼을 먹을 때 연구했다. 당근 주스를 맛본 사전 경험이 없었던 아기들은 거부했고 그 맛에 불만스러운 표정을 지었다. 반면에, 다른 아기 집단은 시리얼에 있는 당근 주스를 쉽게 받아들이고 즐겼다. 태어나기 전에 당근 주스를 경험했던 아기들과 그렇지 않았던 아기들 사이에는 큰 차이가 있었다.

❷ The latest science shows interesting connections
주어 / 동사 / 목적어
between [what moms eat while pregnant] and
between A and B: A와 B 사이의 (A, B 모두 간접의문문)
[what foods their babies enjoy after birth].

❽ When their babies were old enough to start
형용사+enough+to부정사: ~할 만큼 충분히 …한
eating cereal, it was time to look for a difference
it is time+to부정사: ~할 때이다
between the groups.

❾ A researcher [who didn't know {which group each
주어 / 주격 관계대명사절 / 간접의문문(didn't know의 목적어)
baby belonged to}] studied the babies as they ate
동사 / 접속사(~할 때)
cereal [mixed with carrot juice].
과거분사구

⓬ There was a big difference between [babies {who
between A and B: A와 B 사이에 (A, B 모두 명사구)
experienced carrot juice before they were born}]
주격 관계대명사절
and [babies {who didn't (experience carrot juice
주격 관계대명사절
before they were born)}].

44 정답 1 ④ 2 ② p. 134

1 이 글은 〈해리 포터〉 책의 예를 들어 오늘날에는 문화 상품에 있어서 다른 사람들이 좋아하는 것, 즉 인기가 개인의 선호에 큰 영향을 미칠 수 있으며, 문화 상품의 인기는 '눈덩이 효과'를 통해 큰 상업적 성공으로 이어질 수 있음을 이야기하고 있다. 따라서 글의 제목으로 가장 적절한 것은 ④ '인기가 상품 성공에 크게 영향을 미친다'이다.
[오답풀이] ① 책 대 영화: 끝없는 논쟁 ② 여러분이 읽는 것은 여러분이 누구인지 보여 준다 ③ 창의력: 작가의 기본 자질 ⑤ 인기 영화가 어린이들에게 영향을 미치는 방식

2 이것이 과거보다 널리 공유되어 문화 상품의 인기가 '눈덩이 효과'를 누리는 것이므로, 빈칸에 들어갈 말로 가장 적절한 것은 다른 사람들이 좋

아하는 것에 대한 정보, 즉 ② '사회적 정보'이다.
[오답풀이] ① 전통적 지식 ③ 도덕 철학 ④ 신체적 유사성 ⑤ 예술적 자유

READING GUIDE 1 ❻ 2 what they believe others like, lots of people bought it

UNDERSTAND DEEPLY 1 ②, ③ 2 snowball effect 3 Success, quality, popularity

1 ② 여덟 출판업자에게서 출판 거절되었다고 한 책은 〈해리 포터〉 시리즈의 첫 번째 책이다. ③ 오늘날에는 문화 상품의 성공이 작품성이나 완성도와 같은 품질 외에도 다른 사람들이 좋아하는 것에 의해 아주 많이 결정된다고 했다.

2 글 후반부에 언급된 '눈덩이 효과'에 대한 설명으로, 눈덩이가 커지는 것처럼 문화적 가공품(문화 상품)은 이미 인기가 있는 것이 더 크고 더 빠르게 인기를 얻게 되어 승자가 시장을 독식하게 된다고 했다.
[해석] 눈덩이 효과는 어떤 것이 크기나 중요성에 있어서 점점 더 빠르게 증가하는 현상을 말한다.

3 문화 상품의 성공은 적어도 부분적으로는 품질에 의해 결정되지만, 오늘날에는 다른 사람들이 좋아한다고 믿는 것, 즉 인기에 의해서도 아주 많이 결정될 수 있다고 했다.
[해석] 문화 상품의 성공은 그것의 품질뿐만 아니라 인기에 의해서도 아주 많이 영향을 받을 수 있다.

READ CLOSELY p. 136

❶ *Harry Potter and the Deathly Hallows*, / the seventh and final book of J. K. Rowling's fantasy series, / (was released) / in the United States / in 2007.
〈해리 포터와 죽음의 성물〉이 / J. K. Rowling의 판타지 시리즈 중 일곱 번째이자 마지막 책인 / 출간되었다 / 미국에서 / 2007년에

❷ It (sold) 8.3 million copies / in its first 24 hours / on sale.
그것은 830만 부가 팔렸다 / 그것의 첫 24시간 안에 / 판매되는

❸ (Is) the last *Harry Potter* book / that good?
마지막 〈해리 포터〉 책이 ~인가 / 그렇게 훌륭한

❹ Perhaps / it and the earlier six books of the series / (are) truly excellent, / although eight publishers refused to publish the first one.
어쩌면 / 그것과 그 시리즈의 이전 여섯 책들이 / 정말로 훌륭하다 / 여덟 출판업자들이 첫 번째 것(책)을 출판하는 것을 거절했기는 하지만

❺ Success (is) at least partly (decided) / by quality.
성공은 적어도 부분적으로 결정된다 / 품질에 의해

❻ In today's world, / however, / it (is) also possible / that what people come to like / depends very much on / what they believe others like.
오늘날 세상에서는 / 그러나 / 또한 가능하다 / 사람들이 좋아하게 되는 것이 / ~에 아주 많이 달려 있는 것이 / 다른 사람들이 좋아한다고 그들이 믿는 것

❼ The explanation / for why a particular book becomes a hit / may be as simple as this publisher's opinion: / "It sold well / because lots of people bought it."

설명은 / 왜 특정 책이 인기작이 되는지에 대한 / 이 출판업자의 의견만큼 단순할 수도 있다 / 그것은 잘 팔렸어요 / 많은 사람들이 그것을 샀기 때문에

❽ Social information is now shared / much more widely / than in the past.

사회적 정보는 이제 공유된다 / 훨씬 더 널리 / 과거에서보다

❾ Cultural artifacts / such as books and movies / can have 'a snowball effect' / in popularity / in ways / they could not a century ago.

문화적 가공품은 / 책과 영화 같은 / '눈덩이 효과'를 누릴 수 있다 / 인기에 있어서 / 방식들로 / 그것들이 한 세기 전에는 그럴 수 없었던

❿ It turns the cultural industries / into difficult-to-predict, winner-take-all markets.

그것은 문화 산업을 바꿔 놓는다 / 예측하기 어렵고 승자가 독식하는 시장으로

⓫ Tiny differences in performance / can make great differences / in making money.

성과에 있어서의 작은 차이들이 / 큰 차이들을 만들 수 있다 / 돈을 버는 데 있어서

[지문해석] J. K. Rowling의 판타지 시리즈 중 일곱 번째이자 마지막 책인 〈해리 포터와 죽음의 성물〉이 미국에서 2007년에 출간되었다. 그것은 판매된 첫 24시간 안에 830만 부가 팔렸다. 마지막 〈해리 포터〉 책이 그렇게 훌륭한가? 첫 번째 책을 출판하는 것을 여덟 출판업자들이 거절했기는 하지만, 어쩌면 그것(마지막 책)과 그 시리즈의 이전 여섯 책들이 정말로 훌륭할 수도 있다. 성공은 적어도 부분적으로는 품질에 의해 결정된다. 하지만 오늘날 세상에는 사람들이 좋아하게 되는 것이 그들이 다른 사람들이 좋아한다고 믿는 것에 의해 아주 많이 결정되는 것 또한 가능하다. 특정 책이 인기작이 되는 이유에 대한 설명은 "그것은 많은 사람들이 그것을 샀기 때문에 잘 팔렸어요."라는 이 출판업자의 의견만큼 단순할지도 모른다. 사회적 정보는 이제 과거보다 훨씬 더 널리 공유된다. 책과 영화 같은 문화적 가공품은 인기에 있어 그것들이 한 세기 전에는 그럴 수 없었던 방식들로 '눈덩이 효과'를 누릴 수 있다. 그것은 문화 산업을 예측하기 어렵고 승자가 독식하는 시장으로 바꿔 놓는다. 성과에서의 아주 작은 차이들이 돈을 버는 데 있어서 커다란 차이들을 만들 수 있다.

❹ Perhaps it and the earlier six books of the series
      주어
are truly excellent, although eight publishers
동사   접속사(~에도 불구하고, ~이기는 하지만)
refused to publish the first one.
refuse는 목적어로 to부정사를 취함

❻ In today's world, however, it is also possible [that
      가주어   진주어(that절)
{what people come to like} depends very much
that절의 주어(관계대명사 what이 이끄는 명사절)   that절의 동사
on {what they believe others like}].
on의 목적어(관계대명사 what이 이끄는 명사절)

❾ Cultural artifacts [such as books and movies] can
      주어   ~와 같은 (= like)   동사
have 'a snowball effect' in popularity in ways [they
could not a century ago].
관계부사 how가 생략된 관계부사절

READING 45 [정답] 1 ② 2 ①　　　　p. 138

1 인간은 삶에서 균형과 조화를 추구하지만 영화와 같은 이야기는 조화가 지나치고 갈등이 충분하지 못하면 지루해진다는 내용의 글이다. 따라서 글의 제목으로 가장 적절한 것은 ② '갈등: 좋은 이야기의 핵심'이다.

[오답풀이] ① 좋은 배우가 되는 방법 ③ 무엇이 사람들 사이에서 갈등을 일으키는가? ④ 모두가 누군가의 슈퍼히어로가 될 수 있다 ⑤ 여러분 자신을 변화시킴으로써 차이를 만들어라

2 지루하지 않은 좋은 이야기를 만들려면 지나친 조화로움을 깨는 충분한 갈등 요소가 있어야 한다고 했으므로 빈칸에는 ① '방해하는'이 들어가는 것이 가장 적절하다.

[오답풀이] ② 단순화시키는 ③ 회복시키는 ④ 촉진하는 ⑤ 나타내는

READING GUIDE 1 ❻ 2 conflict

UNDERSTAND
DEEPLY 1 ② 2 (1) a hungry white shark (2) Kryptonite (3) a scary wolf 3 Conflict, lively and energetic

1 갈등이 없이 평화롭기만 하면 관객의 흥미를 끄는 대신 이야기를 지루하게 만든다고 했다.

2 첫 문장에서 without 뒤에 오는 어구에 각 작품 속 갈등 요소가 언급되어 있다.

3 마지막 문장의 결론에서 이야기는 조화의 감각을 방해하는 변화, 즉 갈등으로부터 더 생동감 있고 활기 넘치게 된다고 했다.

[해석] 갈등은 이야기를 더 생동감 있고 활기 넘치게 만들기 때문에 좋은 이야기의 중요한 원천이다.

READ CLOSELY　　　　p. 140

❶ Imagine / *Jaws* without a hungry white shark, / *Superman* without Kryptonite, / or the tale of *Little*

Red Riding Hood without a scary wolf.

상상해 보아라 / 배고픈 백상어가 없는 〈죠스〉를 / 크립토나이트가 없는 〈슈퍼맨〉을 / 또는 무서운 늑대가 없는 〈빨간 모자를 쓴 아이〉 이야기를

2 The teenagers in *Jaws* / would have had a great summer / at the beach, / Superman would not have had a worry / in the world, / and Little Red Riding Hood would visit her grandmother / and then go home.

〈죠스〉에 나오는 십 대들은 / 멋진 여름을 보냈을 것이다 / 해변에서 / 슈퍼맨은 걱정거리가 없었을 것이다 / 세상에 / 그리고 빨간 모자를 쓴 아이는 그녀의 할머니를 방문할 것이다 / 그러고 나서 집에 갈 것이다

3 Words / like "boring" and "predictable" / have just come across your mind. // Right?

단어들이 / '지루한' 그리고 '예측할 수 있는'과 같은 / 지금 막 여러분의 뇌리에 떠올랐다 // 맞는가?

4 Movie director Nils Malmros / once said, / "Paradise on a Sunday afternoon / sounds great, / but it would be a boring scene / in film."

영화 감독 Nils Malmros는 / 이전에 말했다 / 일요일 오후의 낙원은 / 멋지게 들린다 / 하지만 그것은 지루한 장면일 것이다 / 영화에서

5 In other words, / too much harmony and not enough conflict in movies / doesn't appeal to audiences.

다시 말해서 / 영화에서의 지나친 조화와 충분하지 않은 갈등은 / 관객들에게 흥미를 일으키지 않는다

6 Conflict is / one of the great sources of making a good story.

갈등은 ~이다 / 좋은 이야기를 만드는 훌륭한 원천 중 하나

7 No conflict, / no story.

갈등이 없으면 / 이야기도 없다

8 But why is this the case?

하지만 왜 이것이 사실일까

9 The answer lies in human nature.

답은 인간의 본성에 있다

10 As humans, / we naturally look for / balance and harmony / in our lives.

인간으로서 / 우리는 자연스럽게 ~을 찾는다 / 균형과 조화 / 우리의 삶에서

11 We simply don't like to break the balance / between our surroundings and ourselves.

우리는 균형을 깨는 것을 단순히 좋아하지 않는다 / 우리의 환경과 우리 자신 간의

12 So, / as soon as harmony is interrupted, / we do / whatever we can / to restore it.

그래서 / 조화가 방해받자마자 / 우리는 한다 / 우리가 할 수 있는 것은 무엇이든지 / 그것을 회복하기 위해

13 We avoid / unpleasant situations, / feelings of stress, / or anxiety.

우리는 피한다 / 불쾌한 상황들을 / 스트레스의 감정들을 / 또는 불안을

14 If we have an unresolved problem / with our friends, family, or our colleagues, / it bothers us / until we take care of it / and return to a peaceful state.

만약 우리가 해결되지 않은 문제를 가지고 있다면 / 우리의 친구들, 가족, 또는 우리의 동료들과 / 그것은 우리를 괴롭힌다 / 우리가 그것을 처리할 때까지 / 그리고 평화로운 상태로 돌아갈 때까지

15 When faced with a problem — a conflict — / we automatically start to look for a solution.

문제, 즉 갈등에 직면했을 때 / 우리는 자동적으로 해결책을 찾기 시작한다

16 Conflict forces us / to act.

갈등은 우리에게 강요한다 / 행동하도록

17 Thus, / a story becomes / more lively and energetic / from changes / that disturb this sense of harmony.

그러므로 / 이야기는 ~하게 된다 / 더 생동감 있고 활기 넘치게 / 변화들로부터 / 이러한 조화의 감각을 방해하는

지문해석 배고픈 백상어가 없는 〈죠스〉, 크립토나이트가 없는 〈슈퍼맨〉, 또는 무서운 늑대가 없는 〈빨간 모자를 쓴 아이〉 이야기를 상상해 보아라. 〈죠스〉에 나오는 십 대들은 해변에서 멋진 여름을 보냈을 것이고, 슈퍼맨은 세상에 걱정거리가 없었을 것이며, 빨간 모자를 쓴 아이는 할머니를 방문하고 나서 집에 갈 것이다. '지루한' 그리고 '예측 가능한'과 같은 단어들이 지금 막 여러분의 뇌리에 떠올랐다. 맞는가? 영화감독 Nils Malmros는 "일요일 오후의 낙원은 멋지게 들리지만, 영화에서는 지루한 장면일 것이다."라고 언젠가 말한 적이 있다. 다시 말해, 영화에서 지나친 조화와 충분하지 않은 갈등은 관객들의 흥미를 끌지 못한다. 갈등은 좋은 이야기를 만드는 훌륭한 원천 중 하나이다. 갈등이 없으면 이야기도 없다. 그런데 왜 이런 것일까? 해답은 인간의 본성에 있다. 인간으로서, 우리는 자연스럽게 우리의 삶 속에서 균형과 조화를 찾는다. 우리는 단순히 우리의 환경과 우리 자신 간의 균형을 깨는 것을 좋아하지 않는다. 그래서 조화가 방해받자마자 우리는 그것을 회복하기 위해 우리가 할 수 있는 것은 무엇이든지 한다. 우리는 불쾌한 상황들이나 스트레스의 감정 또는 불안을 피한다. 만약 우리가 우리의 친구들, 가족, 또는 동료들과의 해결되지 않은 문제를 가지고 있다면, 우리가 그것을 처리하고 평화로운 상태로 돌아갈 때까지 그것은 우리를 괴롭힌다. 문제, 즉 갈등에 직면했을 때, 우리는 자동적으로 해결책을 찾기 시작한다. 갈등은 우리에게 행동하도록 강요한다. 그러므로, 이야기는 이러한 조화로움을 방해하는 변화들로부터 더 생동감 있고 활기 넘치게 된다.

❷ ┌ 앞 문장에서 가정한 상황
(Without a hungry white shark,) The teenagers in
= If there had not been a hungry white shark

Jaws would have had a great summer at the
가정법 과거완료 주절의 동사: 조동사의 과거형＋have＋과거분사

beach, (without Kryptonite,) Superman would
= if there had not been Kryptonite

not have had a worry in the world, and Little Red
가정법 과거완료 주절의 동사

Riding Hood would visit her grandmother and

then go home.

❺ In other words, [too much harmony and not
주어(하나의 개념으로 보아 단수 취급)

enough conflict in movies] doesn't appeal to
단수 동사

audiences.

❶❷ ┌ 접속사(~하자마자)
So, as soon as harmony is interrupted, we do
동사

┌ 복합관계대명사(~하는 것은 무엇이든지)
[whatever we can] to restore it.
목적어   to부정사의 부사적 용법(목적)

❶❻ Conflict forces us to act.
force＋목적어＋목적격 보어(to부정사): ~에게 …하도록 강요하다

1 (1) disturb, interrupt   (2) publish, release

(3) anxiety, worry   (4) reject, refuse

2 (1) ④   (2) ③   (3) ①   (4) ②

3

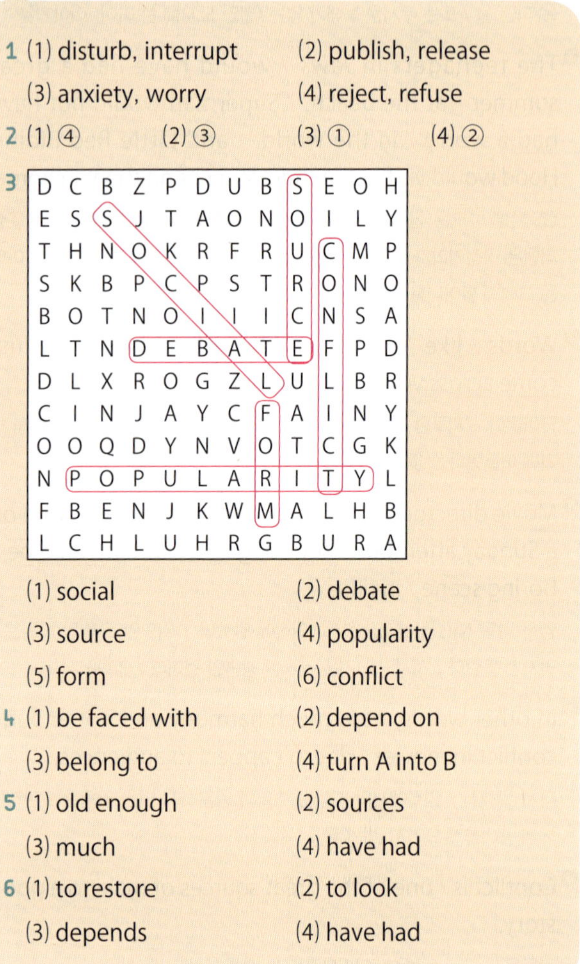

D	C	B	Z	P	D	U	B	S	E	O	H
E	S	S	J	T	A	O	N	O	I	L	Y
T	H	N	O	K	R	F	R	U	C	M	P
S	K	B	P	C	P	S	T	R	O	N	O
B	O	T	N	O	I	I	I	C	N	S	A
L	T	N	D	E	B	A	T	E	F	P	D
D	L	X	R	O	G	Z	L	U	L	B	R
C	I	N	J	A	Y	C	F	A	I	N	Y
O	O	Q	D	Y	N	V	O	T	C	G	K
N	P	O	P	U	L	A	R	I	T	Y	L
F	B	E	N	J	K	W	M	A	L	H	B
L	C	H	L	U	H	R	G	B	U	R	A

(1) social   (2) debate

(3) source   (4) popularity

(5) form   (6) conflict

4 (1) be faced with   (2) depend on

(3) belong to   (4) turn A into B

5 (1) old enough   (2) sources

(3) much   (4) have had

6 (1) to restore   (2) to look

(3) depends   (4) have had

1 (1) disturb, interrupt 방해하다 / promote 촉진하다

(2) publish, release 출판하다, 출간하다 / appeal 흥미를 일으키다

(3) anxiety, worry 불안, 걱정 / quality 품질, 자질

(4) reject, refuse 거부하다, 거절하다 / accept 받아들이다

5 (1) '~할 만큼 충분히 …한'은 「형용사＋enough＋to부정사」의 어순으로 표현하므로 old enough가 알맞다.
해석 그들의 아기들은 시리얼을 먹기 시작할 만큼 충분히 나이를 먹었다.

(2) '~ 중 하나'는 「one of the＋복수 명사」의 형태로 표현하므로 복수 명사 sources가 알맞다.
해석 갈등은 좋은 이야기를 만드는 훌륭한 원천 중 하나이다.

(3) 비교급 more widely를 강조하는 부사로 much가 알맞다.
해석 사회적 정보는 이제 과거보다 훨씬 더 널리 공유된다.

(4) '~했다면 …했을 텐데'를 의미하는 가정법 과거완료는 「if＋주어＋had＋과거분사, 주어＋조동사의 과거형＋have＋과거분사」로 표현하므로 have had가 알맞다.
해석 〈죠스〉에서 배고픈 백상어가 없었더라면 그 십 대들은 해변에서 멋진 여름을 보냈을 것이다.

6 (1) '~하기 위해'라는 목적의 의미는 부사적 용법의 to부정사로 표현할

수 있으므로 to restore가 알맞다.

(2) '~할 때이다'는 「It is time+to부정사」로 표현하므로 to look이 알맞다.

(3) what이 이끄는 명사절이 주어이고 명사절은 단수 취급하므로, 단수 동사 depends가 알맞다.

(4) 과거 사실과 반대되는 가정을 나타내는 가정법 과거완료의 주절은 「주어+조동사의 과거형+have+과거분사」 형태로 표현하므로 have had가 알맞다.

복합문단 이해하기

정답 1 ③ 2 ③ 3 ⑤   p. 144

1 (A)는 해군 제트기 조종사였던 Plumb 대령이 임무 중 그의 전투기가 격추된 후 베트남에서의 시련을 견뎌 내고 고향으로 돌아와 전쟁에서 배운 교훈에 대해 강연했다는 내용으로, 다음에는 강연하러 이동하던 중에 그의 낙하산을 포장했던 선원을 만났다는 내용의 (C)가 오고, 이를 계기로 그가 자신을 위해 일한 사람들에 대해서 생각하는 모습이 묘사되는 (D)가 이어지며, 마지막으로 강연에서 이러한 내용을 설명함으로써 많은 사람들에게 영감을 주었다는 내용의 (B)가 이어지는 것이 자연스럽다. 따라서 글의 순서로 가장 적절한 것은 ③이다.

2 (c)는 Plumb의 낙하산을 포장했던 선원을 가리키고, 나머지는 모두 Plumb을 가리킨다.

3 (D)에서 Plumb은 자신을 알아본 선원의 이름을 기억하지 못해서 미안함을 느꼈다고 했으므로, ⑤는 글의 내용과 일치하지 않는다.

오답풀이 ① (A) However, on his 75th mission, his fighter plane was shot down.

② (A) He ~ and in 1973 returned to his hometown. He was awarded the Silver Star Medal.

③ (B) He ~ was even selected as one of the top ten speakers in a survey of U.S. meeting planners.

④ (C) One day, ~ he went into a restaurant to eat. A man came up to his table and said, "You're Plumb! ~ You were shot down."

READING GUIDE **1** Plumb은 (A) 전투 임무 수행 중 격투기가 격추되어 베트남에서 투옥되었다가 고향으로 돌아와 전쟁 경험에서 배운 교훈에 대해 강연함 / (B) '그 경험' 이후, 강연에서 우리 모두에게는 우리를 위해 일해 온 누군가가 있음을 설명하면서 사람들에게 영감을 주고 명연설가가 됨 / (C) 강연하러 가던 중 어느 식당에서 자신의 낙하산을 포장하던 선원이었던 남자를 만남 / (D) 자신을 위해 낙하산을 포장해 준 남자를 알아보지도 못하고 이름도 몰랐던 것에 대해 미안함을 느낌 **2** Captain Charlie Plumb: 해군 제트기 조종사였던 명연설가 / A man[The sailor]: Plumb을 위해 낙하산을 포장한 Kitty Hawk 호의 선원이었던 남자 **3** ①: ❸, ②: ❻~❼, ③: ⓫, ④: ⓬~⓭, ⑤: ⓲

  1 (1) 1973 (2) a sailor
    2 그들은 세심하게 낙하산을 접고 포장했다.

1 (1) (A)에서 Plumb은 1973년에 고향으로 돌아왔다고 했다. (2) (C)에서 Plumb이 식당에서 만난 남자는 Kitty Hawk 호의 선원이었다고 했다.

해석 (1) Q: Plumb은 언제 그의 고향으로 돌아왔는가? A: 그는 1973년에 그의 고향으로 돌아왔다. (2) Q: 식당에 있던 남자는 어떻게 Plumb에 대해서 알고 있었는가? A: 그는 Kitty Hawk 호의 선원이었다.

2 (D)의 마지막 문장에서 Plumb이 만난 남자와 다른 선원들이 Plumb의 안전을 위해 세심하게 낙하산을 접고 포장했었다고(carefully folding and packing parachutes) 했다.

READ CLOSELY   p. 146

❶ Captain Charlie Plumb [was] / a U.S. Navy jet pilot.
Charlie Plumb 대령은 ~였다 / 미 해군 제트기 조종사

❷ He [flew] / many successful fighting missions.
그는 비행했다 / 많은 성공적인 전투 임무를

❸ However, / on his 75th mission, / his fighter plane / [was shot down].
그러나 / 그의 75번째 임무에서 / 그의 전투기가 / 격추되었다

❹ He [escaped] / and [reached] the ground / safely / using a parachute.
그는 탈출했다 / 그리고 땅에 도달했다 / 안전하게 / 낙하산을 이용하여

❺ Unfortunately, / he [was captured] / and [spent] six years / in a Vietnamese prison.
불행하게도 / 그는 붙잡혔다 / 그리고 6년을 보냈다 / 베트남 감옥에서

❻ He [survived] the terrible situation / and in 1973 / [returned] to his hometown.
그는 그 끔찍한 상황에서 살아남았다 / 그리고 1973년에 / 그의 고향으로 돌아왔다

❼ He [was awarded] / the Silver Star Medal.
그에게 수여되었다 / 은성훈장이

❽ After that, / he [gave] lectures / about the lessons / he learned from his war experiences.
그 후 / 그는 강연했다 / 교훈에 대해 / 그가 그의 전쟁 경험으로부터 배운

❾ After that experience, / Plumb [would ask] the audiences / in his lectures, / "Who's packing your parachute?"
그 경험 후 / Plumb은 청중들에게 질문하곤 했다 / 그의 강연에서 / 누가 여러분의 낙하산을 포장하고 있나요

❿ He [would continue] to explain / that we all have someone / who has performed services for us.
그는 계속해서 설명하곤 했다 / 우리 모두 누군가를 가지고 있다는 것을 /

우리를 위해 일해 온

⑪ He [inspired] / thousands of people / through his lectures / and [was] even [selected] / as one of the top ten speakers / in a survey of U.S. meeting planners.

그는 영감을 주었다 / 수천 명의 사람들에게 / 그의 강연을 통해 / 그리고 심지어 선정되었다 / 명연설가 10인 중 한 명으로 / 미국의 회의 기획자들을 대상으로 한 조사에서

⑫ One day, / while he was traveling to a lecture, / he [went into] a restaurant / to eat.

어느 날 / 그가 강연으로 이동하는 동안 / 그는 어느 식당에 들어갔다 / 식사를 하기 위해

⑬ A man [came up to] his table / and [said], / "You're Plumb! // You [flew] jet fighters / in Vietnam / from the aircraft carrier Kitty Hawk. // You [were shot down]."

한 남자가 그의 테이블로 다가왔다 / 그리고 말했다 / 당신은 Plumb이군요 // 당신은 제트 전투기들을 조종했지요 // 베트남에서 / 항공모함 Kitty Hawk 호의 // 당신은 격추되었지요

⑭ Plumb [looked at] the man / and [asked], / "How [did] you [know] that?"

Plumb은 그 남자를 쳐다봤다 / 그리고 물었다 / 당신은 어떻게 그것을 알았나요

⑮ He [replied], / "I [was] a sailor / on the Kitty Hawk. // I [packed] your parachute / that day."

그는 대답했다 / 저는 선원이었어요 / Kitty Hawk 호의 // 제가 당신의 낙하산을 포장했어요 / 그날

⑯ Plumb [shook hands with] the man / and [thanked] him.

Plumb은 그 남자와 악수했다 / 그리고 그에게 고마워했다

⑰ Plumb [couldn't sleep] / that night, / thinking about the sailor.

Plumb은 잠을 잘 수 없었다 / 그날 밤에 / 그 선원에 대해 생각하면서

⑱ He [felt] sorry / because he neither recognized him nor remembered his name.

그는 미안함을 느꼈다 / 왜냐하면 그는 그를 알아보지도 그의 이름을 기억해 내지도 못했기 때문에

⑲ When he was a fighter pilot, / he never [thought about] / who packed his parachute / before every mission.

그가 전투기 조종사였을 때 / 그는 ~에 대해 결코 생각하지 않았다 / 누가 그의 낙하산을 포장하는지 / 모든 임무 전에

⑳ The sailor and others / [used to spend] long hours / carefully folding and packing parachutes / for his personal safety / during his service in the Navy.

그 선원과 다른 사람들은 / 긴 시간을 보내곤 했다 / 세심하게 낙하산을 접고 포장하는 데 / 그의 개인적인 안전을 위해 / 해군에서의 그의 복무 동안

문장 돋보기

⑱ He felt sorry [because he neither {recognized him}
이유의 부사절   neither A nor B: A도 B도 아닌
nor {remembered his name}].
(A, B 모두 과거동사구)

⑳ = would
The sailor and others used to spend long hours
과거의 습관(~하곤 했다)
carefully folding and packing parachutes for his
spend+시간+동명사: ~하는 데 (시간)을 보내다
personal safety during his service in the Navy.

47 정답 1 ③   2 ⑤   3 ③   p. 148

1 주택 페인트공인 Henry의 아버지에 대해 소개하는 (A) 다음에는 Henry가 아버지를 도우러 간 일화가 시작되는 (C)가 이어지고, Henry의 아버지가 Henry가 페인트를 칠하는 모습을 지켜본 (D)가 이어진 후, Henry에게 페인트칠에 대해 조언하는 내용인 (B)가 마지막에 오는 것이 자연스럽다. 따라서 글의 순서로 ③이 가장 적절하다.

2 (e)는 일을 망치거나 아버지를 곤혹스럽게 하지 않기 위해 페인트칠에 집중하는 Henry이고, 나머지는 모두 Henry의 아버지를 가리킨다.

3 (B)의 마지막 문장 중 His father did spill a few drops에서 Henry의 아버지가 몇 방울을 흘리면서 페인트칠을 했음을 알 수 있으므로 ③은 글의 내용과 일치하지 않는다.

 ① (A) He was a happy, outgoing man who made friends easily.

② (B) Finally, his father offered Henry some advice. / Always put enough paint on the brush.

④ (B) Then, he turned around and applied a thick coat of paint to the wall, and continued his conversation with the homeowner. / (C) He was actually laughing and talking with the homeowner while applying a good amount of paint to the wall.

⑤ (D) At one point, Henry's father stopped working and watched him.

READING GUIDE **1** Henry의 아버지의 훌륭한 페인트 작업과 관련된 내용 **2** Henry, Henry의 아버지 **3** ①: ❸, ②: ⓫, ③: ⓭, ④: ⓬, ⓱, ⑤: ⓳

UNDERSTAND
DEEPLY **1** 흘리거나 망치는 것을 두려워하지 마라. / 사람을 대하는 방식으로 관대하고 즐겁게 벽을 다루어라. / 항상 붓에 충분한 페인트를 묻혀라. **2** make a mess and embarrass his father

1 (B)의 두 번째 문장에 Henry의 아버지의 조언이 구체적으로 언급되어 있는데, 흘리거나 망칠 것을 걱정하지 말고, 관대하고 즐겁게 벽에 페인트칠을 하되, 늘 붓에 페인트를 충분히 적시라고 했다.

2 (D)의 마지막 문장에서 Henry는 자신이 일을 망쳐서 아버지를 난처하게 할까 봐 두려웠기 때문에 페인트칠을 하면서 웃거나 농담을 하지 않았다.
해석 Q: 왜 Henry는 페인트칠을 하면서 웃거나 농담을 하지 않았는가?
A: 그는 망쳐서 아버지를 난처하게 하는 것을 원치 않았다.

READ CLOSELY
p. 150

❶ Henry's father was a house painter.
Henry의 아버지는 주택 페인트공이었다

❷ In his lifetime, / he must have painted / hundreds of houses, / inside and out.
그의 일생 동안 / 그는 칠했음에 틀림없다 / 수백 채의 집들을 / 안과 밖으로

❸ He was / a happy, outgoing man / who made friends easily.
그는 ~이었다 / 행복하고 외향적인 사람 / 친구들을 쉽게 사귀는

❹ It wasn't hard / to tell / that he loved his work as well as his life.
어렵지 않았다 / 아는 것은 / 그가 그의 삶뿐만 아니라 그의 일도 사랑한다는 것을

❺ He was also an excellent painter.
그는 또한 훌륭한 페인트공이었다

❻ No one could paint a wall / like him, / which is / why his service was always popular with people.
누구도 벽을 칠할 수 없었다 / 그처럼 / 그것이 ~이다 / 그의 일이 늘 사람들에게 인기 있었던 이유

❼ Finally, / his father offered Henry / some advice.
마침내 / 그의 아버지는 Henry에게 제공했다 / 몇 가지 조언을

❽ "Don't worry about / spills and messes.
~에 대해 걱정하지 마라 / 흘리는 것과 망치는 것

❾ They can always be cleaned up.
그것들은 항상 깨끗하게 될 수 있다

❿ Treat a wall / the way you treat people / — be generous and have fun.
벽을 다루어라 / 네가 사람들을 대하는 방식으로 / 관대하고 즐겨라

⓫ Always put enough paint / on the brush."
항상 충분한 페인트를 묻혀라 / 붓에

⓬ Then, / he turned around / and applied / a thick coat of paint / to the wall, / and continued his conversation / with the homeowner.
그리고 나서 / 그는 돌아섰다 / 그리고 칠했다 / 두툼한 페인트를 / 벽에 / 그리고 그의 대화를 계속했다 / 집주인과

⓭ Henry's father did spill a few drops, / but he made a better-looking wall / while having fun.
Henry의 아버지는 몇 방울을 흘렸다 / 그러나 그는 더 보기 좋은 벽을 만들었다 / 즐기면서

⓮ Once, / while in college, / Henry went to help his father / paint a house.
언젠가 / 대학에 있는 동안 / Henry는 그의 아버지를 도우러 갔다 / 집을 칠하는 것을

⓯ Henry was working inside / and noticed / how skilled his father was.
Henry는 안에서 일하고 있었다 / 그리고 알아차렸다 / 그의 아버지가 얼마나 능숙한지를

⓰ He was quickly applying / a quality coat of paint / to a wall.
그는 빠르게 칠하고 있었다 / 양질의 페인트칠을 / 벽에

⓱ He was actually laughing and talking / with the homeowner / while applying / a good amount of paint / to the wall.
그는 사실 웃고 이야기하고 있었다 / 집주인과 / 칠하면서 / 많은 양의 페인트를 / 벽에

⓲ He painted three walls / compared to Henry's one.
그는 세 개의 벽을 칠했다 / Henry의 한 개에 비교하여

⓳ At one point, / Henry's father stopped working / and watched him.

어느 순간에 / Henry의 아버지는 일하는 것을 멈추었다 / 그리고 그를 지켜보았다

㉠ He (noticed) / how Henry took his time / dipping the brush in the paint bucket / and how carefully he wiped off / both sides of the brush / when he pulled it out / trying not to waste any paint.

그는 알아차렸다 / Henry가 얼마나 시간을 들이는지 / 페인트 통에 붓을 적시는 데 / 그리고 얼마나 세심하게 그가 닦아 내는지 / 붓의 양면을 / 그가 그것을 꺼낼 때 / 조금의 페인트도 낭비하지 않도록 노력하면서

㉑ Henry then (spread) / a thin coat of paint / on the wall / without spilling a drop.

Henry는 그러고 나서 펴 발랐다 / 얇은 페인트칠을 / 벽 위에 / 한 방울도 흘리지 않고

㉒ It (was) / a slow, boring process.

그것은 ~이었다 / 느리고 지루한 과정

㉓ He (didn't laugh) or "(joke around)" / because he was afraid / that he might make a mess and embarrass his father.

그는 웃거나 '농담을 하지' 않았다 / 왜냐하면 그는 두려웠기 때문에 / 그가 망치고 그의 아버지를 난처하게 할지도 모른다는 것이

지문해석 (A) Henry의 아버지는 주택 페인트공이었다. 일생동안 그는 집 수백 채의 안과 밖을 칠했음에 틀림없다. 그는 친구들을 쉽게 사귀는 행복하고 외향적인 사람이었다. 그가 자신의 삶뿐만 아니라 자신의 일을 사랑한다는 것을 아는 것은 어렵지 않았다. 그는 또한 훌륭한 페인트공이었다. 누구도 그처럼 벽을 칠하지 못했고, 그것이 그의 일이 사람들에게 늘 인기가 있었던 이유이다. (C) 대학 시절 언젠가 Henry는 그의 아버지가 집을 칠하는 것을 도우러 갔다. Henry는 집 안에서 일하고 있었고 그의 아버지가 얼마나 능숙한지를 알게 되었다. 그는 벽에 양질의 페인트를 빠르게 칠하고 있었다. 그는 사실 벽에 많은 양의 페인트를 칠하면서 집주인과 웃으며 대화를 하고 있었다. Henry가 벽 하나를 칠한 것에 비해서 그는 세 개의 벽을 칠했다. (D) 어느 순간에, Henry의 아버지는 일하던 것을 멈추고 그를 지켜보았다. 그는 Henry가 페인트 통에 붓을 적시는 데 얼마나 시간을 들이는지, 그리고 그가 조금의 페인트도 낭비하지 않으려고 노력하면서 붓을 꺼낼 때 얼마나 조심스럽게 붓의 양면을 닦는지 알게 되었다. Henry는 그러고 나서 한 방울도 흘리지 않고 벽 위에 페인트를 얇게 펴 발랐다. 그것은 느리고 지루한 과정이었다. 그는 망쳐서 그의 아버지를 난처하게 할 수도 있다는 것이 두려웠기 때문에 웃거나 '농담도 하지' 않았다. (B) 마침내, 그의 아버지는 Henry에게 몇 가지 조언을 했다. "흘리거나 망칠 것에 대해 걱정하지 마라. 그것들은 항상 깨끗하게 될 수 있단다. 네가 사람들을 대하는 방식으로, 즉 관대하고, 즐기면서 벽을 다루거라. 항상 붓에 충분한 페인트를 묻히거라." 그러고 나서, 그는 돌아서서 벽에 두툼한 페인트를 칠하며 집주인과 대화를 계속했다. Henry의 아버지는 몇 방울을 흘렸지만, 즐기면서도 더 보기 좋은 벽을 만들었다.

문장 돋보기

❹ It wasn't hard [to tell {that he loved his work as well as his life}].
가주어 / 진주어(to부정사구) / 명사절(tell의 목적어)
B as well as A: A뿐만 아니라 B도 (= not only A but also B)

❻ [No one could paint a wall like him], which is [why his service was always popular with people].
누구도 ~ 아닌 / ~와 같이 / 계속적 용법의 관계대명사 (선행사: 앞 문장) / 간접의문문

㉠ He noticed [how Henry took his time dipping the brush in the paint bucket] and [how carefully he wiped off both sides of the brush when he pulled it out trying not to waste any paint].
동사 / 목적어1(간접의문문) / take+시간+동명사: ~하는 데 (시간)을 들이다 / 목적어2(간접의문문) / 시간의 부사절을 이끄는 접속사 / 분사구문(동시동작)

48

정답 1 ④ 2 ④ 3 ③

p. 152

1 (A)는 필자가 피치 못할 일로 약속에 늦어 아내에게 사과하고 늦을 의도가 아니었다고 이해를 구했지만 상황이 오히려 악화되었다는 내용으로, 이 경험을 가족 치료 교수인 친구에게 설명하여 친구가 그에 대해 조언해 주는 (D)가 이어서 나오고, 친구의 말을 필자가 다시 설명하는 (B)가 이어진 후, 마지막으로 자신과 다툰 상대방과의 소통에서 자신의 의도보다는 자신의 행동이 상대방에게 어떤 영향을 미쳤는가가 중요하다고 결론을 내리는 (C)가 오는 것이 자연스럽다. 따라서 글의 순서로 ④가 가장 적절하다.

2 (d)는 필자에게 상담해 주고 있는 가족 치료 교수인 친구를 가리키고, 나머지는 모두 필자를 가리킨다.

3 (B)의 I was focused on my intention, while Eleanor was focused on the outcome에서 필자는 자신의 행동의 결과가 아니라 의도에만 집중했기 때문에 다툼이 일어난 것이라고 했으므로 ③은 글의 내용과 일치하지 않는다.

오답풀이 ① (A) I told her about the client meeting.

② (A) My explanation seemed to make things worse. And that started to make me angry.

④ (C) From this battle, I came to realize that ~ the other person.

⑤ (D) I described the situation to my friend who is a professor of family therapy

READING GUIDE 1 (A) 필자가 불가피하게 아내와의 약속에 늦은 후 자신의 의도가 아니었음을 설명했으나 이해받지 못함 / (B) 필자는 필자의 의도에, 아내는 결과에 집중한 것이라는 '그'의 말을 듣고 필자는 오해로 인해 다툼이 생긴 것임을 인지함 / (C) 결국, 자신의 의도보다는 자신의 행동이 상대방에게 어떤 영향을 미쳤는가가 중요함을 깨달음 / (D) 가족 치료 교수인 친구에게 '그 상황'을 설명하자 친구가 조언해 줌 2 (A) You: 필자, (D) You: 필자, I: 필자의 친구, yourself: 필자, your: 필자 3 ①: ❽, ②: ❾~❿, ③: ⓫, ④: ⓰, ⓲, ⑤: ⑳

1 필자의 교수 친구가 어디에서 학생들을 가르치는지는 글에 언급되지 않았으므로 ③은 대답할 수 없다.

[해석] ① 필자와 그의 아내는 어디서 만났는가? ② 필자는 왜 화가 났는가? ③ 필자의 친구는 어디에서 학생들을 가르치는가? ④ 무엇이 필자와 그의 아내 사이에 다툼을 일으켰는가? ⑤ 다툼에서 필자는 무엇을 깨달았는가?

2 약속에 늦은 것을 이해해 주지 않는 아내에게 화가 났지만, 친구의 말을 듣고 아내를 이해하게 되었으므로 필자의 심경 변화로 가장 적절한 것은 ⑤이다.

[해석] ① 언짢은 → 이해 받지 못한 ② 불안해하는 → 질투하는 ③ 기쁜 → 긴장하는 ④ 불편한 → 무관심한 ⑤ 화가 난 → 이해하는

READ CLOSELY

p. 154

❶ I was running late.

나는 늦어지고 있었다

❷ My wife, Eleanor, and I / had agreed to meet / at the restaurant / at seven o'clock, / and it was already half past.

나의 아내 Eleanor와 나는 / 만나기로 했었다 / 레스토랑에서 / 7시에 / 그리고 이미 30분이 지난 상태였다

❸ I had a good excuse: / a client meeting lasted / longer than expected, / and I'd wasted no time / getting to the dinner / as quickly as possible.

나는 타당한 이유가 있었다 / 고객 만남이 계속됐다 / 예상보다 더 오래 / 그리고 나는 어떤 시간도 낭비하지 않았었다 / 저녁 식사에 도착하는 데 / 가능한 한 빨리

❹ When I arrived at the restaurant, / I apologized / and told my wife / I didn't mean to be late.

내가 레스토랑에 도착했을 때 / 나는 사과했다 / 그리고 나의 아내에게 말했다 / 내가 늦으려고 의도하지 않았다고

❺ She answered, / "You never mean to be late."

그녀는 대답했다 / 당신은 절대 늦으려고 의도하지 않죠

❻ Uh oh, / she was mad.

이런 / 그녀는 화가 나 있었다

❼ "Sorry," / I replied. // "It was unavoidable."

미안해요 / 나는 대답했다 // 그것은 피할 수 없었어요

❽ I told her / about the client meeting.

나는 그녀에게 말했다 / 고객 만남에 대해

❾ My explanation seemed to make things / worse.

나의 설명이 상황을 만드는 것 같았다 / 더 안 좋게

❿ And that started to make me / angry.

그리고 그것이 나를 만들기 시작했다 / 화나게

⓫ In other words, / he meant, / I was focused on my intention, / while Eleanor was focused on the outcome.

다시 말해서 / 그는 의미했다 / 나는 나의 의도에 집중했다고 / Eleanor는 결과에 집중한 반면

⓬ She and I / were having two different conversations.

그녀와 나는 / 두 개의 다른 대화를 나누고 있었다

⓭ In the end, / we both felt / misunderstood and angry.

결국 / 우리는 둘 다 느꼈다 / 이해 받지 못하고 화가 난다고

⓮ The more I thought about / what my friend had said, / the more I recognized / that this battle was about / the misunderstanding between us.

내가 ～에 대해 생각하면 생각할수록 / 나의 친구가 말했던 것 / 나는 더 인지하게 되었다 / 이 다툼이 ～에 대한 것이었다는 것을 / 우리 사이의 오해

⓯ As it turns out, / the important thing is / neither the thought nor the action.

밝혀지듯이 / 중요한 것은 ～이다 / 생각도 행동도 아닌

⓰ That's because Eleanor doesn't experience / my thoughts or actions.

그것은 Eleanor가 경험하지 않기 때문이다 / 나의 생각이나 행동을

⓱ She experiences / the outcome of my actions.

그녀는 경험한다 / 나의 행동의 결과를

⓲ From this battle, / I came to realize / that when I upset her or someone else / —no matter who's right— / I should always start the conversation / by noticing / how my actions have affected the other person.

이 다툼으로부터 / 나는 깨닫게 되었다 / 내가 그녀나 다른 누군가를 언짢게 할 때 / 누가 옳든지 간에 / 나는 항상 대화를 시작해야 한다는 것을 / 알아차림으로써 / 나의 행동이 상대방에게 어떻게 영향을 미쳤는지

⓳ After all, / my intentions don't matter / much.

결국 / 나의 의도는 중요하지 않다 / 크게

⓴ Several weeks later, / when I described the situation / to my friend / who is a professor of family therapy, / he smiled.

몇 주 후에 / 내가 그 상황을 설명했을 때 / 나의 친구에게 / 가족 치료 교수인 / 그는 웃었다

㉑ "You made a classic mistake, / as I have done before," / he told me.

너는 전형적인 실수를 했다 / 내가 이전에 했듯이 / 그는 나에게 말했다

㉒ "You only think about yourself," / he said.

너는 오직 네 자신에 대해서 생각한다 / 그가 말했다

㉓ "You didn't mean to be late / but that's not the point.

너는 늦으려고 의도하지 않았다 / 하지만 그것이 중요한 게 아니다

24 What's important / in your communication /  / how your lateness affected Eleanor."

중요한 것은 / 너의 의사소통에서 / ～이다 / 너의 늦음이 Eleanor에게 어떻게 영향을 미쳤는가

지문해석 (A) 나는 늦어지고 있었다. 나의 아내 Eleanor와 나는 7시에 레스토랑에서 만나기로 했었는데, 이미 30분이 지난 상태였다. 나에게는 타당한 이유가 있었다. 고객과의 만남이 예상보다 더 오래 계속됐고, 나는 가능한 한 빨리 저녁 식사에 도착하는 데 어떤 시간도 낭비하지 않았었다. 내가 레스토랑에 도착했을 때, 나는 사과하면서 아내에게 늦을 의도는 없었다고 말했다. 그녀는 "당신은 절대 늦을 의도가 없겠죠."라고 대답했다. 이런, 그녀는 화가 나 있었다. 나는 "미안해요, 어쩔 수 없었어요."라고 대답했다. 나는 그녀에게 고객과의 만남에 대해 말했다. 나의 설명이 상황을 악화시키는 것 같았다. 그리고 그것이 나를 화나게 만들기 시작했다.

(D) 몇 주 후에, 내가 그 상황을 가족 치료 교수인 나의 친구에게 설명했을 때 그는 웃었다. "너는 내가 전에 그랬던 것처럼 전형적인 실수를 했구나."라고 그가 나에게 말했다. "너는 오직 네 자신에 대해서만 생각하는 거야."라고 그가 말했다. "너는 늦을 의도가 없었지만 그것이 중요한 게 아냐. 너의 의사소통에서 중요한 것은 네가 늦은 것이 Eleanor에게 어떻게 영향을 미쳤느냐는 거야."

(B) 다시 말해서, 그의 말은 나는 나의 의도에 집중한 반면, Eleanor는 결과에 집중했다는 것이었다. 그녀와 나는 서로 다른 두 개의 대화를 하고 있었다. 결국, 우리는 둘 다 이해받지 못했다고 느꼈고 화가 나 있었다. 나는 나의 친구가 말했던 것에 대해 생각하면 생각할수록, 이 다툼이 우리 둘 사이의 오해에 대한 것이었다는 것을 더 인지하게 되었다.

(C) 여기서 밝혀지듯이, 중요한 것은 생각도 아니고 행동도 아니다. 왜냐하면 Eleanor는 나의 생각이나 행동을 경험하지 않기 때문이다. 그녀는 나의 행동의 결과만을 경험한다. 이 다툼으로부터, 나는 내가 아내나 다른 누군가를 언짢게 할 때, 누가 옳든지 간에 항상 나의 행동이 상대방에게 어떤 영향을 미쳤는지를 인지함으로써 대화를 시작해야 한다는 것을 깨닫게 되었다. 결국, 나의 의도는 그다지 중요하지 않은 것이다.

문장 돋보기

18 From this battle, I came to realize [that when I
(목적어(that절))
upset her or someone else — no matter who's
(누가 ～하더라도 (= whoever))
right — I should always start the conversation by
noticing {how my actions have affected the other
(by+동명사: ～함으로써)   (noticing의 목적어(간접의문문))
person}].

24 What's important in your communication is how
(주어(관계대명사 what이 이끄는 명사절))   (동사)
your lateness affected Eleanor.
(보어(간접의문문))

REVIEW TIME

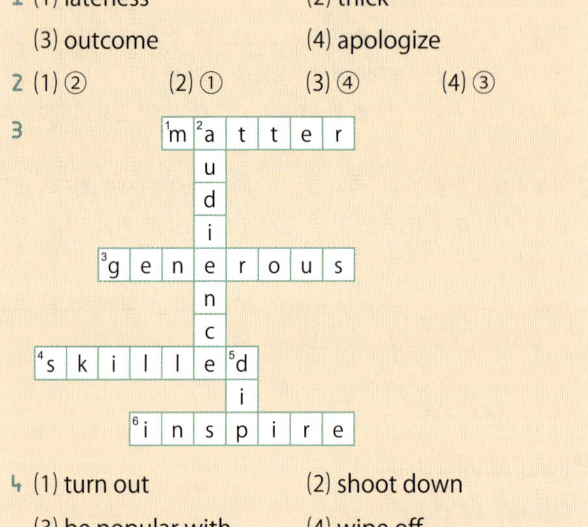

1 (1) lateness　　　　(2) thick
　(3) outcome　　　　(4) apologize
2 (1) ②　　(2) ①　　(3) ④　　(4) ③
3

¹m	²a	t	t	e	r		
	u						
	d						
	i						
	³g	e	n	e	r	o	u s
	n						
	c						
⁴s k i l l e	⁵d						
	i						
	⁶i n s p i r e						

4 (1) turn out　　　　(2) shoot down
　(3) be popular with　(4) wipe off
5 (1) nor　　　　　(2) packing
　(3) What　　　　(4) more, more
6 (1) thinking　　　(2) to tell
　(3) must have painted

1 (1) 안전한 : 안전 = 늦은 : 늦음 (형용사 : 명사 관계)
　(2) 거부하다, 거절하다 : 받아들이다 = 얇은 : 두꺼운 (반의어 관계)
　(3) 설명하다 : 설명하다, 묘사하다 = 결과 : 결과 (유의어 관계)
　(4) 수행, 성취 : 수행하다 = 사과 : 사과하다 (명사 : 동사 관계)

2 (1) mean, ② intend 의도하다
　(2) capture, ① catch 붙잡다
　(3) battle, ④ fight 다툼, 싸움
　(4) offer, ③ give 제공하다, 주다

5 (1) 'A도 B도 아닌'이라는 의미의 neither A nor B가 되어야 하므로 nor가 알맞다.
　해석 Plumb은 그를 알아보지도 그의 이름을 기억하지도 못했다.
　(2) '～하는 데 (시간을) 보내다'라는 의미의 「spend＋시간＋동명사」 형태가 되어야 하므로 packing이 알맞다.
　해석 그 선원은 Plumb을 위해 낙하산을 포장하는 데 오랜 시간을 보내곤 했다.
　(3) '～하는 것'이라는 의미의 절을 이끌며 문장의 주어 역할을 하는 것으로 선행사를 포함하는 관계대명사 What이 알맞다.
　해석 당신의 의사소통에서 중요한 것은 당신의 늦음이 Eleanor에게 어떻게 영향을 미쳤는지이다.
　(4) '～할수록 더 …하다'라는 의미의 「the＋비교급 ～, the＋비교급 …」 구문이 되어야 하므로 more가 알맞다.
　해석 그의 말에 대해 생각하면 생각할수록 나는 그 다툼이 오해에 대한 것임을 더 인지했다.

6 (1) '~하면서'라는 동시동작을 나타내는 분사구문이 되어야 하므로 현재
분사 thinking이 알맞다.
(2) 앞에 나온 It이 가주어에 해당하므로 진주어를 이끄는 to부정사 to
tell이 알맞다.
(3) '~했음에 틀림없다'라는 과거에 대한 강한 추측은 「must have＋
과거분사」로 표현하므로 mush have painted가 알맞다.

▶ 모든 주사위와 일치하도록 빈 면에 점을 그려보세요.

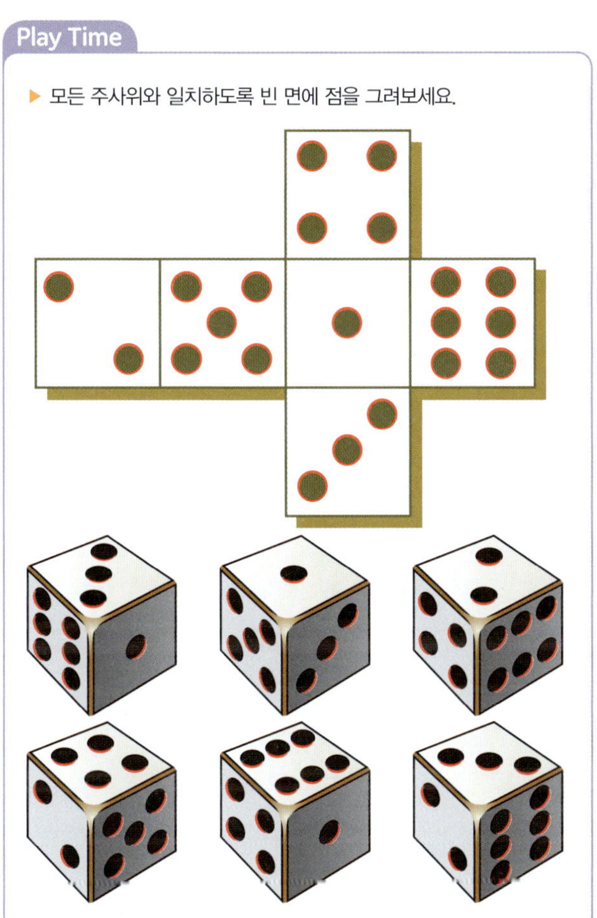

Memo

Memo

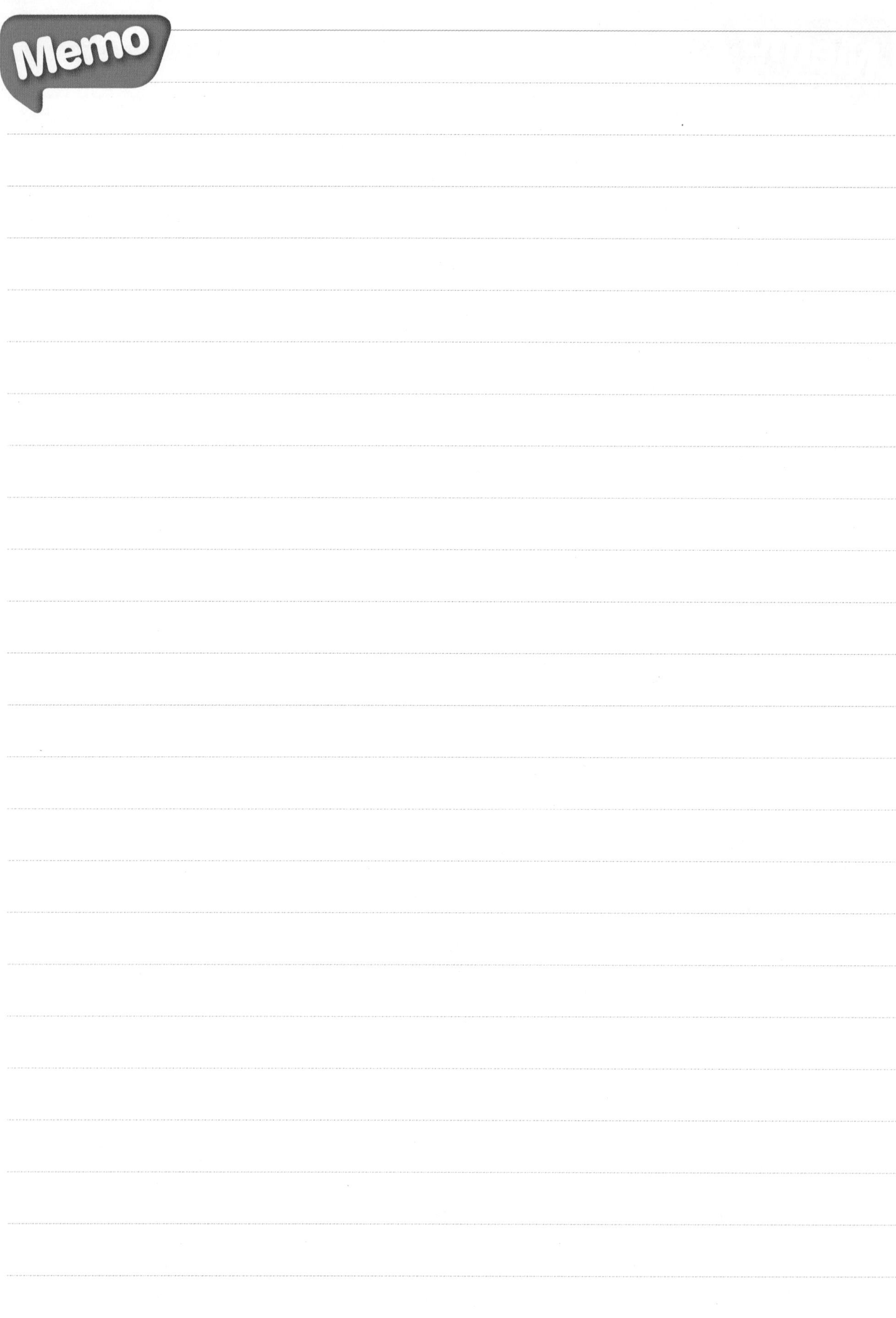
Memo